Comic Venus

Contemporary Approaches to Film and Media Series

A complete listing of the books in this series can be found online at wsupress.wayne.edu.

General Editor
Barry Keith Grant
Brock University

Advisory Editors
Robert J. Burgoyne
University of St. Andrews

Caren J. Deming
University of Arizona

Patricia B. Erens
School of the Art Institute of Chicago

Peter X. Feng
University of Delaware

Lucy Fischer
University of Pittsburgh

Frances Gateward
California State University, Northridge

Tom Gunning
University of Chicago

Thomas Leitch
University of Delaware

Walter Metz
Southern Illinois University

Comic Venus

Women and Comedy in American Silent Film

KRISTEN ANDERSON WAGNER

Wayne State University Press
Detroit

© 2018 by Wayne State University Press, Detroit, Michigan 48201. All rights reserved. No part of this book may be reproduced without formal permission.

Library of Cataloging Control Number: 2017956167
ISBN 978-0-8143-4102-5 (paperback) | ISBN 978-0-8143-4103-2 (ebook)
ISBN 978-0-8143-4529-0 (cloth)

Wayne State University Press
Leonard N. Simons Building
4809 Woodward Avenue
Detroit, Michigan 48201–1309

Visit us online at wsupress.wayne.edu

*For my mom, who loved to laugh with me,
and my daughter, the greatest comedienne I've ever known*

Contents

Acknowledgments ix

Introduction 1

1. "Have Women a Sense of Humor?" 25

2. "An Inferiority Complex in a One-Piece Bathing Suit": Beauty, Femininity, and Comedy 73

3. "Cupid Lips and an Ungodly Appetite": Sensuality, Sexuality, and Desire 133

4. "Ever on the Move": Modernity and the New Woman 183

Conclusion 233

Abbreviations 241

Appendix: Selected Filmographies 243

Notes 259

Bibliography 281

Index 291

Acknowledgments

"Dying is easy," the old saying goes. "Comedy is hard." As it turns out, writing about comedy is pretty hard too. This book would not have been possible without the support and encouragement of a great many people over a great many years, and I would like to take a moment to thank some of them.

This project first took shape at the University of Southern California, and I am endlessly grateful to Tara McPherson, Rick Jewell, and Alice Gambrell, each of whom helped shape this book with their insightful comments, suggestions, and guidance. Tara, especially, deserves a tremendous amount of credit for keeping this project on track with a mixture of patience, persistence, exasperation, and encouragement. I'm not sure how many times I heard the question, "So, what do we need to do to get you to finish?" but I'm glad she never stopped asking. Jan Olsson's enthusiasm for silent film is both infectious and inspiring, and I've been so lucky to have him as a mentor. Dana Polan, Marsha Kinder, Lynn Spigel, Jeffrey Sconce, and David James offered suggestions and feedback at various points that were greatly appreciated. Running things behind the scenes was Linda Overholt, without whom I'm pretty sure the entire department would have crumbled.

I have the good fortune to be surrounded by a community of very smart people who are also very generous with their time and feedback. I can't adequately express how grateful I am to Shelley Stamp and Maggie Hennefeld for their comments on various iterations of this book and their willingness to talk women, comedy, and silent film with me. My good friend Michele Leigh pestered me mercilessly to keep writing and talked me off of more ledges than I can count, for which I'm eternally thankful. Michele and Lora Mjolsness offered such amazing feedback and encouragement in our little writing group that they almost made this process fun. Almost.

Much of this research was presented at Society for Cinema and Media Studies and Women and the Silent Screen conferences, and conversations with friends and colleagues at these gatherings have inspired me and informed my research and writing. Vicki Callahan, Kristine Karnick, Linda Mizejewski, Joanna Rapf, Victoria Sturtevant, Mark Lynn Anderson, Jennifer Bean, Laura Horak, Denise McKenna, April Miller, Nina Cartier, Heather Osborne-Thompson,

Sofia Bull, Anke Brouwers, Shelleen Greene, Yiman Wang, Susan Potter, and Diana Anselmo-Sequeira have all been instrumental in various ways in shaping this project, and I thank them all.

My research for this project required logging a lot of hours in libraries and archives, including the Margaret Herrick Library at the Academy of Motion Picture Arts and Sciences, the Billy Rose Theatre Division of the New York Public Library, the New York Museum of Modern Art, the UCLA Film and Television Archive, and the Cinematic Arts Library at USC. I am grateful to the staffs at these institutions for sharing their knowledge and for their assistance in helping me find needles in haystacks. There are a number of online resources that have proved incredibly valuable as well, especially the Media History Digital Library, the Internet Archive, the Women Film Pioneers Project, and Marilyn Slater's Looking for Mabel Normand website. Many thanks to everyone who runs these sites, for ensuring that archival materials are accessible to researchers around the world. Thank you to Jim Kerkhoff, who provided the cover image for this book. Gale Henry never looked better! And a huge thank you to Paige and Stephane Conte for giving me a couch to sleep on while doing my research in New York.

I feel so fortunate to have found a home for this project at Wayne State University Press. My editor, Annie Martin, was so generous, patient, and enthusiastic that I feel even worse for blowing past all those deadlines. My copyeditor, Jennifer Backer, made wonderful suggestions and improved the text immeasurably. Everyone at the Press has been so kind and helpful that I almost want to jump right in and write another book. Almost.

This book is dedicated to my mother, Donna Anderson, who was the most supportive, loving, and caring parent a person could ever hope to have. Every day I strive to live up to the example she set for me. My father, Martin Anderson, filled my childhood with laughter and a love of learning and has kept me grounded while writing this book by reminding me what it was like to write his dissertation in the days before computers. My parents' love and encouragement have motivated me for many years, and I am so grateful for that.

This book is also dedicated to my daughter, Amelia, who makes me laugh every single day. Her curiosity, intelligence, silliness, and fierceness give me hope for the future. And finally, I'd like to thank my husband, Jeff Wagner. This book would not have been possible without his patience and support. Jeff's (mostly) gentle encouragement kept me on track, his love of silent film helped me stay passionate about my topic, and his sense of humor reminded me not to take any of this too seriously.

Introduction

> When you know how to play comedy, you know how to play anything.
> —*Bebe Daniels*

When I tell people that I'm writing about female comedians in silent film, the first question I'm asked is invariably, "Were there any?" After a few moments of thought, most people can remember Mabel Normand, and a few can recall Clara Bow or Marie Dressler, but the popular knowledge of silent-era comediennes ends there. At the same time, even those who have never seen a silent film immediately recognize Charlie Chaplin and Buster Keaton. Of course, silent performers in general have fallen victim to this cultural amnesia, but in no other genre is the gender disparity between who is remembered and who has been forgotten so pronounced, with the result that silent comediennes have been virtually erased from the public memory.

This same pattern is evident in academia but with an important difference. While silent comediennes have been forgotten by the general public, they have generally been ignored by the film community, including film scholars and historians. Beginning with James Agee's influential 1949 essay "Comedy's Greatest Era," the pantheon of Chaplin, Keaton, Harry Langdon, and Harold Lloyd was established as the "Big Four" of silent comedy.[1] Later scholars have added other comedians to the mix, including Roscoe "Fatty" Arbuckle and John Bunny, but the contributions of female comics have been consistently overlooked, a fact that says more about the biases of those who have written film history than it does about the relative abilities of silent comediennes. In Walter Kerr's *The Silent Clowns*, for example, only two paragraphs in the more than 350-page book are dedicated to female comedians, and these paragraphs occur in a chapter titled "The Demiclowns," which describes comedians of lesser ability than the big four of Chaplin, Keaton, Langdon, and Lloyd.[2] This approach has continued in more recent critical works that glorify the canonical comedians to the exclusion of all others, although work by film historians, archivists, and feminist scholars such as Maggie Hennefeld, Linda Mizejewski, Rob King, Victoria Sturtevant, Joanna Rapf, Anke Brouwers, Steve Massa, Kristine Brunovska Karnick, Bambi Haggins, and Rebecca Krefting has turned more attention in recent years to women's contributions to comedy, in both historic and contemporary contexts. Despite the efforts of these researchers to, as Hennefeld puts it, "put these missing archival links back into circulation," silent comediennes remain largely forgotten.[3]

None of this is surprising, given the fact that women's humor in all forms has historically been overlooked and neglected. Whether in literature, theater, art, motion pictures, or everyday communication, comic women have traditionally been, for all intents and purposes, invisible; as Gail Finney argues, "thinkers as earnest as Schopenhauer, Bergson, and Freud have disqualified women from the comic arena; when they and other men have written about humor, laughter, and jokes, they have meant male humor, laughter and jokes."[4] Just as history is written by the winners, comic history has overwhelmingly been written by and about those in power, resulting in the virtual exclusion of women. Of course, this all begs the question, so what? Does it really matter if people remember Louise Fazenda's spit curls and blank deadpan, or if academics ponder the cultural and historical significance of Colleen Moore's Cinderella-as-flapper characters? After all, we're talking about jokes and pratfalls, rubber chickens, seltzer bottles, and custard pies. Why is this important?

The answer has to do with issues of cultural power and the ability to enact social change. A custard pie may not seem like much of a weapon, but humor has, in fact, historically been understood as an effective means of social control, as well as a way of commenting on and changing perceived flaws in society. Many theorists, especially those who write about women's humor, have noted this link between humor and cultural power.[5] For Henri Bergson laughter is a social corrective, and the "function of laughter" is to ensure that all members of a society adhere to mainstream values and behaviors, lest they be subjected to the derisive and controlling laughter of those around them.[6] While this conception of laughter as social control is somewhat limiting, it does highlight the important notion of humor as a means of exerting control, especially over those who are in subordinate positions.

A comparable dynamic is at work in sexuality, which, as Michel Foucault and many others have argued, is similarly tied up in issues of power and social control.⁷ "Like sexuality," Frances Gray writes,

> laughter has been sometimes highly valued, sometimes denigrated; but like sexuality—indeed *with* sexuality—laughter has been closely bound up with power.... Just as cultures in which sex was perceived as evil recognized women as having sexual desires, and cultures which saw sex as a normal healthy sport for chaps developed the concept of female frigidity, just so cultures which did not exalt humor to its current overblown status could attribute it to women.... Only when laughter is the sign of the civilized man ... do women appear to suffer from a mysterious frigidity of the funny bone.⁸

The pervasive denial and suppression of women's humor by both popular culture and academia is essentially a denial and suppression of women's social and cultural power. And if women are powerless objects rather than empowered subjects, it follows that they would be the butt of men's jokes rather than the joke makers. When women's humor is dismissed or ignored women are effectively being kept in a subordinate position; as Gray points out, "to define a joke, to be the class that decides *what is funny*, is to make a massive assumption of power."⁹ At the same time, to be excluded from humor is to be denied access to that power. These issues of power were especially resonant in the late nineteenth and early twentieth centuries, as women were making increasingly vocal demands for social and political equality with men.

Women's persistent lack of access to social, economic, and political power has led to cultural biases against women performing comedy. Rebecca Krefting argues that we are all socially conditioned to identify with those in power, and that "based on existing social inequalities there is simply no reward for engaging with or learning to identify with women whose power is already determined as secondary to men in this society."¹⁰ This certainly contributes to the pervasive stereotype, discussed more fully in chapter 1, that women aren't funny, as those who occupy positions of power in our society have no incentive to identify with those who hold no social or political capital: "Their logic: why would I need to or want to understand and identify with women's and/or minorities' lives and experiences when society continually reinforces that they are of little value."¹¹ Krefting argues that these power differentials affect women's comic expression as well as how female comics are received by audiences:

You can be a woman telling jokes, just do not call attention to your womanness or any other category of difference that might force listeners out of their comfort zone, because that forces them to learn from another perspective or identify with someone unlike them. Male humor is humor genera, and humor arising from any other position becomes "Other" humor, topical, or special interest. When men fail at comedy, failure is not seen as a product of their maleness or endemic to men as a whole; however, when women bomb, the default explanation is her being a woman.[12]

One response, according to Krefting, is for women and people of color to perform what she calls "charged humor," or humor that directly confronts "social inequality and cultural exclusion."[13] This type of comedy can undermine power structures and create commonality among marginalized groups. Those who occupy positions of power have long been the ones to proclaim what is and isn't funny, often to the exclusion of people of color and almost always to the exclusion of women. Charged humor, and the potential bond it creates between performers and audiences, can give voice to marginalized communities and encourage them to question who gets to determine what and who is funny.

In many ways, then, comedy is an ideal genre for women to push boundaries and challenge traditional gender roles, as the genre has long been used as a means of masking transgression and of rendering acceptable a wide range of behaviors. Along with being an expression of cultural power, humor can be an effective means of criticizing social structures and attempting to bring about change, a useful weapon for women and other repressed or oppressed groups because, as Nancy Walker argues, "an essential purpose of humor is to call the norm into question.... The humor of those on the 'threshold' is apt to reveal a perception of incongruity, that not only questions the rules of the culture, but also suggests a different order."[14] Kathleen Rowe points out that "all narrative forms contain the potential to represent transformation and change, but it is the genres of laughter that most fully employ the motifs of liminality,"[15] and Henry Jenkins stresses the importance of the comic performer's "freedom that comes from straddling cultural categories."[16] Comediennes can use this freedom—their liminal position between insider and outsider, masculine and feminine, empowered and subjugated—to draw attention to social and gender inequities.

But despite its links to power and social control, humor is often seen as nonthreatening because comedy is literally not taken seriously. As a result, controversial or unsettling topics are more readily accepted by audiences when presented in the form of a joke rather than as more serious rhetoric. As Bonnie J. Dow argues, "Comedy offers space for representing social controversy and social change that might be too threatening when encoded as realist drama."[17] Comedy's usefulness in critiquing social systems is important for female comics who have used humor to question gender boundaries, what Rowe describes as "the power of female grotesques and female laughter to challenge the social and symbolic systems that would keep women in their place."[18] This power was just as important to comediennes in the silent era as it is now, as women entered the workforce and political arena in greater numbers and the concepts of "femininity" and "womanhood" were increasingly open to question and debate.

Early twentieth-century comediennes addressed these issues in their comic routines with both overt and subtle comments on women's experiences. Stage comediennes during this time, especially those who appeared in vaudeville, often openly criticized sexism, supported suffrage, and critiqued the institution of marriage for women in acts that celebrated female independence and activity while depicting the traditional feminine roles of wife and mother as dreary and oppressive. Many stage comediennes challenged the Victorian ideal of women as pure and passive through their aggressive and sexually suggestive songs and routines. Motion picture performers faced certain constraints not found in vaudeville, including stricter censorship and, of course, the lack of synchronous sound and the actors' resultant inability to use their voices as an element of their performance. Also, whereas vaudeville performers used the liveness of their acts—the direct interaction with the audience and the ability to slip in subversive moments unnoticed by theater managers—film actors were necessarily removed from their audiences and therefore from the transgressive potential of live performance. On the other hand, motion pictures afforded comediennes a number of advantages over the stage. Films reached far larger audiences than stage performances, allowing screen actors to become national and often international celebrities. Close-ups made facial expressions legible to audiences, and location shooting, elaborate sets, editing, and special effects allowed for complex gags and stunts. The unique properties of film meant that the transgressive potential of Clara Bow's lustful glances at her leading men, Gale Henry's fearless stunts, and Marie Dressler's exuberant excessiveness could be relayed to audiences with a greater impact than would be possible from the stage.

In their comic performances, comediennes were helping to redefine what it meant to be a woman. Much of women's humor concerned their inability or unwillingness to play the role of the ideal woman and showed the joys of living outside of the narrow and restrictive boundaries of traditional femininity. In watching these performers, women in the audience were able to glimpse alternate femininities available to them. Of course, many of these performances can be read as somewhat regressive, as comediennes often engaged in self-deprecating humor that in many ways reinforced negative stereotypes about women; as Regina Barreca claims, "When you make self-deprecating jokes, you are solidifying your own lowly position in the power structure by seeming to agree that you deserve to be the victim or target of such humor."[19] And yet even comic performances that apparently confirm sexist images of women are more complex than they might seem. When Marie Dressler's Tillie character runs amok at Coney Island in *Tillie Wakes Up* (1917), she is certainly using her age, weight, and admitted homeliness as the source of much of her humor in a way that could be interpreted as self-deprecating. However, when Tillie escapes her depressing married life and runs off for the day with her neighbor's husband and then has, as a title tells us, "the *time* of her *Young Life*," she is making a case for the excitement of single life and illicit romance over the drudgery of a loveless marriage. And when Dressler uses her ample body to get laughs in the film, she is demanding visibility as a middle-aged woman who is not conventionally attractive. Rather than remaining demurely out of sight, Dressler places herself and her excessive body unapologetically front and center. Finally, any derisive laughter at Tillie's plight would be mitigated by appreciative laughter at Dressler's exceptional comic talents. So while comedy can be used to demean or belittle women, it can also be a site of resistance for women who were unwilling or unable to perform dominant notions of femininity, a space where excessive, unruly, and otherwise "unfeminine" women could command attention and respect, and in so doing question the ideology of idealized gender roles.

Discussing the role of gags in comic films, Tom Gunning has argued that gags' "explosive action, their interruption of the normal course of things" create disruptive moments.[20] Gunning likens gags to disruptive and destructive "crazy machines":

> Crazy machines are complex devices that appear rationally designed to achieve a purpose, but suddenly and comically assert a counter-will of their own, thwarting the purpose of the protagonist. . . . A structural analysis of gags and jokes . . . might best describe them as an unexpected undermining of an apparent purpose, a detouring, if not derailing, of a

rational system of discourse or action. The gag suddenly interrupts, or radically redefines, the apparent predictability of an action or system, leaving its original goals shattered and in tatters.[21]

This description can apply to comediennes themselves. Female comics in the late nineteenth and early twentieth centuries were transgressive, certainly, but they also disrupted traditional ideas about femininity and women's place in American society in a way that's analogous to Gunning's concept of the crazy machine. The clearly defined gender roles of the Victorian era, which traditionalists hoped and assumed would continue unchallenged and unabated, constituted the "rational system of discourse" that funny women derailed by "assert[ing] a counter-will of their own." Funny women were disruptive and destructive crazy machines that undermined patriarchal expectations for women, leaving those expectations "shattered and in tatters."

The importance of reclaiming women's comedy, then, has to do with humor's position as a site of cultural power and social criticism. When women engage in comic performances they are assuming this power and challenging the social structures that would keep them subordinate. As Rob King argues, "Laughter . . . clusters around points of tension within a given social order, where established patterns and relations are beginning to give way to new patterns, new relations; humor translates those conflicts into jokes and provides an articulation of social contradiction at moments of historic change."[22] In the early twentieth century there were numerous points of tension, including mechanization, urbanization, immigration, racial discord, and women's rights. Silent-era comediennes addressed these tensions through their performances, both by overtly questioning sexist structures and by their disruptive presence on-screen. This was not an empty exercise, as women (and men) in the audience could vicariously experience the freedoms and expanded roles played out by these actresses. As Susan Glenn points out, "Female performers explored, exaggerated, and exploited modern fears and fantasies about women's roles and identities. In doing so they inspired other women to dream and experiment."[23] The custard pies thrown by silent comediennes were more than just comic props; they represented a weapon that could be used to break boundaries.

Furthermore, the impact of silent-era comediennes continues to be felt today. Later comediennes from Lucille Ball and Carol Burnett to Margaret Cho and Amy Poehler owe a tremendous debt to Eva Tanguay, Louise Fazenda, Gale

Henry, and Clara Bow. The early twentieth-century debates about whether women have a sense of humor, and what types of comedy are appropriate for women to perform, continue to this day. Female comedians still push gender boundaries and are still punished for it. The comediennes discussed here were important not only because of their impact on future generations of female performers but because in many ways they forced those around them to rethink the traditional narrow definitions of gender. This is the legacy of these performers, one that continues to have an impact on how we understand gender.

Breaking Boundaries

A major impetus for this project was my desire to begin to recuperate an area of women's history that has been largely forgotten. Surprisingly little work has been done on the careers and significance of female comedians in silent film, an area that is quite rich and reveals a great deal about women's experience in the early twentieth century. This book strives to provide a cultural historical examination of the complex and often contradictory meanings created by and assigned to silent-era comediennes. I argue that silent comediennes played an important role in a societal reconceptualization of femininity and gender roles in the first decades of the twentieth century, providing audiences with an alternative to other, more restrictive models of femininity circulating in American society. At a time when popular conceptions of femininity were rapidly changing, silent comediennes were both reflections of and central figures in the creation of new, modern femininities, as they used comedy's inherent liminality and transgressiveness to disrupt patriarchal expectations and reinterpret and redefine femininity on their own terms. This project of redefinition and reconceptualization was both complex and problematic. Much of women's humor at this time was self-deprecating and could reinforce existing misogynistic stereotypes. Also, many screen comediennes resisted comedy, and comedy itself was frequently posited as a sort of generic ghetto that women must leave as soon as they could in favor of drama. Still, at a time when women's very ability to understand and appreciate humor was widely questioned, and women's presence in the public sphere was frequently criticized, the existence of funny women in the highly public forum of motion pictures is significant and worthy of study.

Silent comediennes contradicted and challenged conceptions of ideal femininity in four distinct areas: the idea that a proper woman of the early twentieth century should be refined, beautiful, chaste, and domestic. These are closely aligned to the four "cardinal virtues" of "piety, purity, submissiveness and domesticity" that Barbara Welter describes as essential to the Victoria-era True Woman, although drawing from the work of Lois Banner and Kathy Peiss detailing the increasing importance of female beauty at this time, and the supposed link between physical beauty and moral rectitude, I argue that beauty, more than piety, is an imperative for the ideal woman of the early twentieth century.[24] Comediennes frequently provided examples of women who actively rejected this model of ideal femininity and, significantly, were not penalized for their transgressions. Unlike lustful screen vamps who were usually punished in their films with death or adventurous heroines whose attempts at independence were met by white slavery or prostitution rings, comic characters could indulge in unladylike behavior and still make it to the end of their films unscathed.

Chapter 1 addresses the ways that silent-era comediennes contradicted the notion that refinement, passivity, and respectability are essential feminine traits. In the early twentieth century, many people assumed that women were incapable of understanding or appreciating humor because of their delicate sensibilities, their close alignment to nature, and their emotional, rather than intellectual, disposition. Comediennes showed that not only could women be funny but they could succeed, both artistically and financially, using the same type of knockabout slapstick as male comics. While pratfalls, chases, and pie throwing were clearly not ladylike behaviors, comediennes enthusiastically engaged in these activities on-screen. However, many comediennes expressed ambivalence toward this type of lowbrow comedy, an indication that cultural proscriptions against unruliness were deeply felt and difficult to overcome. These tensions are evident in parallel discursive threads that situate women as incapable of creating or even appreciating comedy but also celebrate comediennes as naturally funny and skilled craftswomen. Especially intriguing is the image of the "tragic comedienne," who longs to leave comedy and "graduate" to more highbrow fare, such as dramas and tragedies. This concept shows up in several films, including *The Extra Girl* (1923, starring Mabel Normand), *Ella Cinders* (1926, starring Colleen Moore), and *Show People* (1928, starring Marion Davies), and this chapter includes close readings of these films to examine how the comediennes both support and undermine these ideas.

Chapter 2 examines the complex ways the ideas of beauty and femininity were used in popular discourses surrounding silent comediennes and the ways comediennes challenged the assumption that beauty was an essential component of femininity. Beauty has long been seen as antithetical to a sense of humor, and for many actresses, appearing in comedies was presented in almost tragic terms. Fan magazines and studio publicity frequently described the sacrifices comediennes made to be funny, from covering their natural beauty with dowdy costumes to abandoning their dreams of success in dramatic films. Publicity surrounding many slapstick comediennes described the actresses' first painful discoveries that they were plain or clumsy or lacking in feminine wiles and therefore unsuited to dramatic roles. These accounts make these comediennes appear sympathetic, even pitiable. In fact, I argue that the press promoted a tension between "pretty" comediennes, such as Constance Talmadge and Colleen Moore, who appeared in romantic and light comedies, and "homely" comediennes such as Gale Henry and Marie Dressler, who were relegated to slapstick because they were, presumably, not attractive enough for more highbrow pursuits. While these discourses would seem to reinforce Hollywood's obsession with female beauty, this tension led to a wider range of physical types appearing in comedy, many of which fell outside the standards of screen beauty established by other genres. Furthermore, when comediennes such as Henry, Dressler, Alice Howell, Louise Fazenda, and others willfully embraced their image as "homely" characters, and, in fact, wore costumes and makeup that made them look especially unattractive, they were sending a message to female spectators that beauty was less important than personality and humor. This is further emphasized by the numerous magazine articles that feature photographs of comediennes in their full character makeup alongside glamorous studio portraits, a practice that implicitly created space for an alternate view of femininity in which "ideal" traits are shown to be artificial rather than natural qualities that all women possess. These juxtapositions serve to reassure audiences that their favorite comediennes are not as grotesque (and therefore threatening) as they appear on-screen, while at the same time proving that "beauty," "grace," and even "femininity" are not fixed or natural categories.

For many silent comediennes, desire and sexuality formed an important part of their on- and offscreen personae. The tension between these performances and the concept of women as chaste is discussed in chapter 3. Because comedy has traditionally been considered a "safe" genre, where audiences could laugh at, rather than feel threatened by, transgressive behavior, silent comediennes were able to engage in sexually aggressive or illicit behavior that would not have been tolerated in other genres. Flappers and light comediennes created comedy around sexually charged situations. Flappers in particular flaunted the mores of traditional Victorian culture and enacted aggressive sexuality. Even slapstick comediennes sometimes incorporated sexuality and desire into their performances, while in their performance of gags they made a case for female sensuality as they reveled in the pleasures of physical activity. By representing sexuality as fun and playful, suggesting that personal relationships could be fluid rather than stable, and crossing gender boundaries through inversion and cross-dressing, comediennes helped to symbolically broaden the notion of acceptable female sexual desire.

Chapter 4 explores comediennes' connection to the modern world and the ways that silent comediennes were exemplars of New Womanhood and symbols of modernity in the 1910s and 1920s. Not only did comediennes epitomize the spirit of modernity with their energy and activity, they also stood as visible symbols of the changing gender roles of the early twentieth century. By engaging in knockabout physical comedy, considered by many to be the rightful province of male comedians, and by moving freely in the public sphere, comediennes were both transgressing traditional gender roles and providing examples for their female fans of ways to successfully negotiate the changing social landscape. As working women who were shown to embrace modern technology, activities, and styles, comediennes were, in many ways, the embodiment of New Womanhood and the modern world. This chapter also examines the conservative anxiety that modern life was robbing women of their femininity—a fear that found its locus in the bobbed hairstyle sported by the majority of flapper stars—and argues that comediennes often confronted this fear head-on in their films.

This book engages with and builds on the work of a number of scholars who have written about comedy, early film history, women's history, or a combination of the three. The work of Jennifer Bean and Ben Singer on silent action heroines and serial-queen melodrama has provided a starting point from which to imagine active, assertive actresses and their relationship to broader societal issues, although genre differences, including comedy's increased potential for subversion and disruption, are significant. Singer claims that "at its most assertive, [serial-queen melodrama's] fantasy of female prowess gravitates toward a reversal of gender positions."[25] I argue that at its most assertive, slapstick comedy moves toward an *erasure* of gender positions, an obliteration of traditional gender roles, as the chaos and anarchy evident in the slapstick universe, including pervasive and persistent gender confusion, goes cheerfully unresolved at the end of the film. Action series and serials ultimately work toward maintaining order, including gender binaries (regardless of which gender is "on top"). Slapstick comedies, however, in their most anarchic form, reject the notion that there is a universal order that can be maintained. In a world where the laws of society, physiology, and even gravity are abandoned, the project of maintaining traditional gender positions comes across as an exercise in futility. Of course, not all comedy leans toward an erasure of gender positions in the same way that slapstick does; in fact, most feature-length comedies end with a traditional romantic union where gender roles are, to some degree, restored. And yet even in these films lies the possibility of gender disruption, as women played against the boundaries of appropriate femininity.

Work on silent comedy and silent comediennes by Maggie Hennefeld, Rob King, Victoria Sturtevant, Hilde d'Haeyere, Joanna Rapf, and Steve Massa offers invaluable context for the women discussed in this book. Hennefeld's work on comic women in early silent film provides an essential theoretical and historical foundation for my work and offers an important reminder of the astonishing variety of silent-era comediennes. Work on individual performers such as Marie Dressler, Fay Tincher, Alice Howell, and Gale Henry, as well as Mack Sennett's Bathing Beauties, provides further evidence that this is a rich area that warrants historical excavation. Research on contemporary funny women, by Linda Mizejewski, Bambi Haggins, Rebecca Krefting, and others, helps situate this work in its historical context, while also showing that some of the discourses and prejudices surrounding women's comedy that were evident in the early twentieth century are still circulating today.

The extensive work on gender inversion and unruliness in relation to women and comedy is tremendously useful when thinking through these possibilities for gender fluidity in silent comedy.[26] Certainly, many silent-era comediennes were unruly women, reveling in excessiveness, disruptiveness and unapologetic spectacle, challenging and upsetting gender positions and positing an alternative, transgressive model of femininity. The research of scholars such as Kathleen Rowe, Mary Russo, Natalie Zemon Davis, and M. Alison Kibler provides a social and historical context for silent comediennes, proving that they were not an aberration but, rather, were part of a larger constellation of women that ranges from the carnivalesque "woman on top" of the sixteenth century to the stand-up comediennes playing comedy clubs today. Much of the writing on unruly women points to their ability to use their disruptiveness and liminality to challenge traditional gender binaries while simultaneously aligning themselves with excessive women in the audience, and this potential certainly exists in the work of silent-era comediennes. Unruly women revel in their bodily excesses and pleasures, and ultimately present a vivid alternative to the passive object of the male gaze described by feminist film theorists.[27] Rowe argues that feminist film theory's focus on psychoanalysis, which "takes as its given women's identification with loss," has meant that the potentially radical subjectivity inherent in comic performances has been overlooked: "texts which might suggest an alternative view of female subjectivity have not received the scrutiny they might. I am referring in particular to those which position women as subjects of a laughter that expresses anger, resistance, solidarity, and joy—or those which show women using in disruptive, challenging ways the spectacle already invested in them as objects of a masculine gaze."[28] It is particularly intriguing to consider the ways in which comediennes might use "the spectacle already invested in them" to actively create meaning through their bodies and their image rather than passively having meaning assigned to them by (male) spectators. Comediennes embraced their physicality and used it in powerful ways, to demonstrate sensual enjoyment in physical activity, and to experience the sensual present, posited by Martin Heidegger as a way around modern alienation, rather than being passive objects.

Any research on silent film faces a unique set of challenges and obstacles. An alarmingly high percentage of films from the silent era have been lost; the Library of Congress estimates that only 20 percent of American feature films from the 1920s and 10 percent from the 1910s still exist, and the survival rate is much lower for shorts, newsreels, documentaries, independents, and avant-garde films.[29] The cellulose nitrate film stock used in most films until 1951 was highly unstable, and vast numbers of films made in that period have been lost to fire or decay. Many films were intentionally destroyed by the studios as a preventative measure against fire because of the volatility of the film stock, or to recover silver from the nitrate, or to simply make room in crowded storage vaults. Many of the films that survive are in varying states of decay and unavailable for viewing, and an unknown number of existing films are tucked away in the attics or closets of collectors or remain unidentified in archives. The occasional success story—for example, the recent discovery of a nitrate print of the presumed-lost Colleen Moore vehicle, *Her Wild Oat* (1927), in the Czech National Film Archive—is overshadowed by the knowledge that every day an unknown number of films decay beyond repair and are lost.

A major reason for silent comediennes' current obscurity, then, is that so few silent films exist. Because so many silent films have been lost, it follows that the stars of those films would also be "lost." A number of figures from the silent era, including Mack Sennett, made an effort to preserve their films, but many were unable to prevent their loss or were content to let their old films disappear. In fact, some were complicit in the destruction of their films: Mary Pickford argued in 1931 that the rapid technological innovations of the motion picture medium meant that older films would be rendered obsolete and "ridiculous" to future audiences, and as a result for several years she had been locating and destroying her old films. Pickford even put a clause in her will stipulating that her films were to be destroyed upon her death, although she ultimately rethought her stance on her old films and worked to preserve them.[30] It's unlikely that other comediennes actively sought to destroy their films, but at the same time there is no evidence of widespread efforts to safeguard them. The survival rates for the films of silent comediennes vary, but they are universally low. While over half of Louise Fazenda's sound features still exist, only about 20 percent of her silent films survive, mostly shorts made for Keystone. The survival rate of Fazenda's films is actually fairly high—while the films of some silent comediennes, including Mabel Normand, Clara Bow, and, despite her stated intentions, Mary Pickford, still exist in higher numbers, for other once-popular comediennes, including Gale Henry, Alice Howell, Polly Moran, and Constance Talmadge, an alarmingly small number of their films survive.

The deep-rooted notion that women aren't as funny as men has undoubtedly also played a role in film archiving and preservation. The films that were spared by the studios, and those that have been saved over the years by archives, are generally the ones considered "important" for various reasons—usually because of their director, star, writer, or studio. For this reason, the films of canonized male comedians such as Chaplin, Keaton, Lloyd, Arbuckle, and Laurel & Hardy survive in vastly greater numbers than films by other, lesser-known filmmakers and performers, including women. Because the established canon influences what films are seen on television, in video and DVD releases, and in film revivals and festivals, the public has been fed a steady diet of Chaplin and Keaton and is entirely unfamiliar with Howell and Fazenda.

The problems of accessibility and availability of film prints, however, don't present an insurmountable obstacle in conducting research. In fact, the films themselves are only one of many texts that can be analyzed to understand film culture. As Eric Smoodin points out in *Looking Past the Screen*, film scholarship has historically privileged the film text over other non-filmic materials such as newspapers, magazines, trade journals, production documents, and personal papers, despite the fact that all of these texts work together to create meaning.[31] Smoodin calls for "a conceptual model of history and of understanding films that lessens the priority of the film text itself," one that understands and acknowledges that "film audiences occupy competing and contradictory positions; positions that are themselves influenced by different forms of exposure to film culture."[32] The difficulties in finding extant and viewable silent films, then, are mitigated by the wide availability of other resources from the era. While a complete print of Colleen Moore's 1923 breakthrough film *Flaming Youth* no longer exists, contemporaneous articles and reviews, production photos, and Moore's discussion of the film in her 1968 autobiography all serve to form a more complete understanding of the film and its impact.

With this in mind this book makes extensive use of press resources, particularly fan magazines, trade journals, and newspapers, to inform its analysis of the cultural impact of silent-era comediennes. Richard deCordova has shown that newspaper and magazine articles about actors, both on-screen and off, were an essential element in the creation of that star's identity.[33] These sources provide an important point of entry for conceptualizing how audiences understood and interpreted movies and stars; through them we can trace a variety of discourses and begin to answer a number of questions, including:

1. What information about stars did studios feel was important to impart to fans?
2. What information actually got through to fans?
3. Which discourses/themes/myths resonated with fans, based on evidence including volume of articles, repetition of themes, and reader polls, and which did not?
4. What did fans' interaction with the press—through letters, poems, and contests—say about how they saw the stars?
5. What non-filmic information did studios and publishers think would interest fans, including beauty tips and social/etiquette advice?

Newspaper and magazine discourses were able to uniquely shape the audience's understanding of comediennes and their performances because, in many ways, they were more lasting than the one-reel comedy shorts that would pass through town in a week or less. Press articles could be collected, saved, read, and reread, and as such had the potential to create an equal or greater impact on fans than the films, as evidenced by the many fans who used press clippings to create scrapbooks and other tributes to their favorite stars.

Press discourses are not without their own set of problems, of course. Gaylyn Studlar has shown that stars' press agents were known to write newspaper and fan magazine articles, and celebrity interviews and articles purportedly written by stars were often written without the actors' involvement.[34] Newspaper columns about movies and stars were often syndicated and widely distributed, making it difficult to discern regional interests and tastes. And fan magazines' close relationship to the film industry, and the fact that their economic fortunes were aligned with those of the studios, meant that it was in their self-interest to project a positive image of stars, their films, and the movie industry. Still, even though press discourses must be read as biased and as doing their own cultural work, they remain a part of the overall public understanding of actors and films. Whether the stars actually wrote the articles or uttered the quotes attributed to them, or whether they were as domestic, delightful, spontaneous, or charming as the articles would have readers believe, is almost irrelevant. If the press accounts of stars are pure fabrication then we have less insight into that actor as a person, but it doesn't interfere with our understanding of that actor's public persona. Of course, it's impossible to know all of the different ways fans interpreted films or what exactly stars meant to their audiences. There is some indication of audience reaction in fan mail (some of which exists in archives), box office figures, theater manager reports, and sources such as Herbert Blumer's 1933 study *Movies and Conduct*. Press discourses, although problematic in the ways described, provide another useful source for theorizing fans' relationship to actors and their films.

Audiences, then, are an important element in the meaning-making process of the Hollywood star system. DeCordova talks about how the star's identity

> does not exist within the individual star (the way we might, however naively, believe our identities exist within us), but rather in the connections between and associations among a wide variety of texts—films, interviews, publicity photos, etc. The star's identity is intertextual, and the star system is made up in part of those ongoing practices that produce the intertextual field within which that identity may be seized by curious fans.[35]

I would argue that along with these other texts "fans" are one of the discursive fields that create the star's identity and the star system. Fans didn't just consume films and film-related texts (such as fan magazines, clothing, etc.)—they actively engaged with them, writing letters to actors, studios, and fan magazines, entering "Fame and Fortune" contests, creating scrapbooks, driving the types of films and merchandise produced through their consumption habits, and, most important, adopting styles, manners, and personality traits that they saw performed by actors in films and in "private" moments showcased in newspaper and magazine articles. Certainly fan magazines and studios exploited fans' enthusiasm as a means to sell all manner of goods, from beauty products to clothing to the films themselves. But the description of fans as complicit in the development and maintenance of the star's identity is important because it positions them as active rather than passive, producers rather than simply consumers. Furthermore, if fans participated in creating the stars' identities, and even adopted parts of those identities for themselves, then this suggests the possibility that the boundary pushing performed by comediennes in their films and as a part of their movie personae would be repeated by everyday women in their own lives.

Road Map

This project examines the work of comediennes in American silent films from the early 1910s to the late 1920s, a period that begins with the rise of the star system and the advent of motion picture fan magazines and ends with the introduction of talking pictures. There were comediennes appearing in films well before this time period; in fact, the star of one of the earliest films, Thomas Edison's *The Kiss* (1896), was the popular stage comedienne May Irwin. Comedies were a mainstay of film programs in the early silent era, and women were featured in many of these films. Shorts such as *How Bridget Made the Fire* (1900), *The Kitchen Maid's Dream* (1907), and *A Tin-Type Romance* (1910) feature comic performances by women, and a number of comediennes, including Flora Finch, Florence Turner, Kate Price, and Lucille McVey, were popular with audiences in these years. Many of these early film comediennes challenged gender norms in much the same way as those who followed them. But central to this study is discussion and analysis of comediennes' discursive construction in the press and in publicity materials, in addition to their performances on-screen. Early film actors were generally unidentified and therefore largely absent from the press. By 1910 studios and exhibitors were beginning to publicize actors' names, which led to the rise of what deCordova has termed "picture personalities," performers for whom "the site of interest was the personality of the player as represented on film. There was thus a kind of restriction of knowledge about the players to the textuality of the films they were in."[36] DeCordova notes that "extrafilmic discourse did talk about the players' personalities outside of films but only to claim that they were the same as those represented in films."[37] Audiences knew little about picture personalities beyond the characterizations they saw on-screen, which were reinforced by press and publicity materials. By the mid-1910s, according to deCordova, the star emerged as a distinct category:

> In 1913 and 1914 one can begin to see a significant transformation in the regulation of knowledge concerning the player, one that brought into existence the star. The star emerged out of a marked expansion of the type of knowledge that could be produced about the player. The picture personality was defined . . . by a discourse that restricted knowledge to the professional existence of the actor. With the emergence of the star, the question of the player's existence outside his or her work in film became the primary focus of discourse. The private lives of the players were constituted as a site of knowledge and truth.[38]

In this interplay between the comedienne/star's on-screen image and the supposed truth of her personal life one can find traces of cultural anxieties about funny women and about changing gender roles. Various magazine and newspaper articles described comediennes who, in "real life," loved comedy, hated comedy, longed to be beautiful, embraced their unconventional looks, enjoyed modern life, or espoused traditional values. These stories don't necessarily reveal much about the actual actresses, whose "personal lives" were often carefully crafted by studio publicists. They do, however, suggest a cultural fascination with and ambivalence toward women performing comedy. Were they clowns with aching hearts? Did their comedic skills come naturally, or did they have to cultivate them? How could a woman possibly be content to appear in public wearing grotesque makeup and unflattering costumes? The films contain the comediennes' performances; press discourses give us insight into how audiences might have interpreted those performances.

Much of my analysis, then, of the impact and influence of the comediennes discussed in this study is dependent on the discourses circulating in fan magazines and studio publicity, as well as audiences' familiarity with these discourses. This interest in and knowledge of the personal details of actors' lives was prompted by as well as contributed to the rise of fan magazines. The earliest fan magazines, *Motion Picture Story Magazine* and *Photoplay*, were first published in 1911, and by 1915 there were at least fifteen fan magazines in wide circulation.[39] These magazines, along with studio publicity, mainstream newspaper features and articles, merchandising, and the films themselves, formed the public image of actors that went beyond their work on the screen. Audiences' understanding of comediennes and their subversive potential was shaped by these sources, which form an integral part of this study.

Although there are those who don't believe silent comediennes ever existed, there were actually vast numbers of women performing comedy in the silent era, and it would be impossible to include every one of them in a single volume. With this in mind, I've limited my discussion to those who made a significant impact on their fans or had the greatest potential for breaking boundaries. I've used the term "comedienne" somewhat broadly, including performers such as Louise Fazenda, Mabel Normand, and Alice Howell, who made knockabout slapstick films and performed almost exclusively in comedies, as well as performers such as Mary Pickford, Dorothy Gish, and Marion Davies, who made "comedy-dramas" and were considered accomplished dramatic actresses. While it may seem that "comic actress" or "comic performer" would be a more appropriate term to use for such a wide range of actresses and performance styles, all of the women I discuss were described at the time as comediennes, by the press and in studio publicity, and audiences at the time would have understood them as comediennes, with all that that term implies.

Although there were women of color performing comedy onstage at this time, including Bessie White and the Whitman Sisters, they were largely absent from mainstream motion pictures. Because of this, all of the comediennes discussed here are white. There are a few tantalizing appearances by women of color in film comedies, including a delightful turn in *Laughing Gas* (1907) by African American actress Bertha Regustus as Mandy, a woman who leaves the dentist's office high on nitrous oxide and laughing uncontrollably. As Mandy passes through town she spreads her laughter to everyone she meets, leaving in her wake scores of people convulsed with laughter. Sadly, it doesn't appear that Regustus or any other non-white women achieved prominence in mainstream comedies. It's entirely possible that some of these women appeared in race films or films produced by small independent companies, but I have not been able to track their performances. It is certain that women of color made contributions to the field of film comedy during this period, and I hope that their history will one day be recovered.

The comediennes discussed in this book represent a wide variety of performance styles. The most popular mode of comedic performance in the early silent era was undoubtedly knockabout physical comedy. Slapstick shorts dominated film programs before 1908, accounting for as much as 70 percent of fiction films, but the film industry's desire to imbue itself with an aura of respectability in order to attract middle-class audiences led to a drop in slapstick comedies, which were seen as lowbrow.[40] Still, physical comedy remained popular; as Rob King has shown, Mack Sennett's Keystone continued making slapstick comedies despite their working-class connotations. Indeed, slapstick films were part of a larger constellation of sensationalistic entertainments that appealed to working-class audiences:

> From the belly laugh of variety entertainment to the "blood & thunder" scenes of cheap melodrama, from the thrills of the amusement park ride to the physical contact of the dance hall, popular forms thus reflected a hunger for intense bodily stimulation that, to genteel tastes, was the very definition of vulgarity.... The slapstick humor of vaudeville's "nut acts," "bone crunchers," and "facial" and "knockabout" clowns was a part of this culture of sensationalism; and, if its pleasures contradicted genteel emphasis on transcendence, they nonetheless crystallized the embodied orientation of working-class culture and experience.[41]

Despite the very physical and ostensibly "vulgar" nature of slapstick, numerous comediennes excelled in this type of comedy. Mabel Normand starred in and directed comedies for Keystone and was known for her energetic physical comedy, her expressive acting, and her beauty (a former artist's model, she was one of the few slapstick comediennes who didn't wear outlandish costumes or makeup). Normand frequently played what I call slapstick-ingénues, characters who appear sweet and wholesome, and are often positioned as a male character's love interest but who readily engage in physical comedy. It's said, perhaps apocryphally, that Normand was the first person to throw a pie on-screen. Louise Fazenda, Gale Henry, Alice Howell, and Polly Moran were also popular slapstick comediennes, performing knockabout physical comedy involving pratfalls and elaborate gags. Fazenda's on-screen persona varied throughout her career, but she was often gawky and gangly in her films, playing naive farm girls or clumsy servants. She wore a guileless deadpan when presented with difficult situations, and her response to romantic entanglements was generally either giddy flirtation or clocking the unlucky suitor with a blunt object. Henry made the most of her tall and angular frame in her comedies, throwing her long arms and legs in all directions while playing earnest, resilient characters. Howell's signature character was an unflappable slavey type, often a waitress, maid, or scrub woman, with mismatched clothes, bee-stung lips, and a mass of frizzy blonde hair piled high on her head. Howell gave her characters precise, often delicate gestures coupled with a flat-footed penguin-like waddle, and she was well-known for her daring stunts. Moran started at Keystone as a slapstick-ingénue but soon settled on an aggressive, rough-hewn persona. She was known for her demanding and dangerous stunts, especially in her series of one-reel comedies from the late 1910s and early 1920s playing the boisterous Sheriff Nell.

One- and two-reel comedy shorts continued to be made even after other genres turned to the longer feature-length format after 1915. But physical comedy continued to have lowbrow connotations, and by the late 1910s light comedy became increasingly popular as an alternative to slapstick. As Richard Koszarski notes, "Audiences now began to see two distinct types of comedy. The more 'high-class' comedy descended from Broadway adaptations and portrayed recognizable characters in believable situations. It was generally to be seen only in features. Short films were the province of 'low comedy,' a continuation of the slapstick tradition of nickelodeon days."[42] Gags continued to appear in light comedies as explosive, disruptive moments,[43] but by the 1920s there was a clear distinction between light comedy and slapstick. The humor in light comedies largely came from the plots, situations, and even the intertitles, a far cry from the anarchic and sensationalistic gag-driven comedy of the slapstick shorts. Because light comedy was seen as more respectable, comediennes who began their careers in slapstick were often said to aspire to light comedy. Dorothy Devore incorporated elaborate gags into her films but was best known for her light comedies. She was lively and energetic on-screen, often playing spunky girl-next-door types. Constance Talmadge appeared in light comedy features, often as a playfully flirtatious but utterly innocent "virtuous vamp." She enjoyed a long collaboration with writer Anita Loos, and Loos's witty intertitles and the films' comic situations drew laughs as much as Talmadge's vivacious personality. Marion Davies often incorporated bits of physical comedy into her light comedy features, but the comedy in her films, like that of Talmadge's films, was largely derived from the situations and clever intertitles. A skilled mimic, Davies included impersonations of other celebrities in some of her films. Mary Pickford was, without doubt, one of the most popular and successful actresses in silent film. Her feature films blended comedy and pathos as her characters struggled to overcome adversity. She very often played children, which allowed her to engage in some physical comedy in her films.

A subset of light comedies that appeared in the 1920s were the flapper films. The comediennes who appeared in these films were more sexually charged than the light comediennes, although the films made clear that the heroines were good girls at heart. Flapper films contained very little slapstick, instead drawing laughs from the situations and the actresses' sparkling personalities. Colleen Moore played one of the first screen flappers in *Flaming Youth* (1923) and appeared in a string of flapper films and romantic comedies.[44] Moore's characters were fun-loving and energetic, flirtatious but completely innocent. Clara Bow was the quintessential flapper, exuding sex and barely contained desire in her films. Bow's on-screen vitality was palpable; unable to contain her limitless energy, she would rarely stand still, instead darting around or dancing with abandon.

The Goddess of Beauty and Pratfalls

The title of this book, *Comic Venus*, is taken from the title of a 1918 *Photoplay* profile of Louise Fazenda. I like the inherent tension in the phrase, which would seem to be a contradiction in terms. Venus, the Roman goddess of love, is a symbol of beauty and fertility. Her representation in painting and sculpture generally has her lounging or standing but never moving. She is invariably beautiful, nude, passive, distant, and unsmiling—if she does smile, as in Titian's *Venus of Urbino*, her smile is faint and gentle. The thought of the goddess of love and beauty taking a pratfall, cracking a joke, laughing broadly, or hurling dishes at her partner while wiping custard pie from her face is irresistible. Marie Dressler as Tillie, tripping drunkenly around Coney Island, Louise Fazenda as a scorned wife ready to crown her husband with a baseball bat, or Clara Bow as a sexually charged shopgirl devouring hot dogs and wrapping her handsome boss's arms around her would seem to be everything that Venus is not. Comediennes counter the passive and enigmatic beauty of Venus with their activity, energy, assertiveness, and sensuality. And yet, just as Venus is a personification of a specific type of femininity, so do comediennes embody their own version of femininity. Their femininity may be just as fictional as the idealized version found in representations of Venus, but its existence and pervasiveness onstage and in the new popular art form of motion pictures provided a powerful reminder to audiences of the early twentieth century that there was more than one way to be a woman. Women who didn't see themselves reflected in the beautiful and retiring nude on the half shell might find it easier to relate to the laughing and vibrant demi-anarchists on-screen. Comediennes represented the possibility of multiple, equally acceptable conceptions of womanhood and argued for the complexity of femininity in society at large and in individual women who were not easily placed in extreme or idealized categories. Ultimately, comediennes proved that comedy and femininity could coexist—that Venus could throw a pie with the best of them.

1

"Have Women a Sense of Humor?"

In 1901 *Harper's Bazaar* asked, "Have women a sense of humor?" More than a hundred years later *Vanity Fair* published an article explaining "why women aren't funny."[1] These articles are part of a larger debate about women's capacity to engage in and appreciate humor that has existed for many years and clearly continues to this day: whether women are capable of engaging in and appreciating humor. Countless writers and critics have argued that femininity and a sense of humor are mutually exclusive and that women's "natural" inclination toward emotion and sensitivity has left them incapable of possessing a quality—humor—that many feel is dependent on "masculine" traits such as intellect and aggressiveness. Women, the argument goes, are far too refined and delicate to be funny. The True Woman, a feminine ideal that circulated widely for much of the late nineteenth century, was known for her morality, passivity, and spirituality, not for her ability to tell a joke. But just as women in the early twentieth century challenged assumptions about femininity established with the True Woman, female comedians during this time challenged the notion that women were inherently unfunny.

Comediennes in early twentieth-century entertainments such as vaudeville and silent film were performing at a time when these debates about women and comedy were at their most heated and when the very concepts of "woman" and "femininity" were undergoing massive transformation. Because of the pervasive belief that comedy was inappropriate for women, female comics were much more liable than other performers to be seen as engaging in unacceptable behavior and were subject to criticism for performing certain types of comedy thought to be unladylike. As a result of these concerns and criticisms, comediennes—along with fans and the popular press—were often highly ambivalent regarding the relationship between comedy and femininity. Rather than avoiding the genre altogether, early twentieth-century comediennes negotiated a comic space for themselves in myriad ways. Some, including Fay Tincher, Constance Talmadge, and Dorothy Devore, advocated a more refined, "feminine" comedy as an alternative to the rough-and-tumble slapstick that many felt was unsuitable for women, and some, acquiescing to prejudices against funny women, spoke of their desire to leave comedy for more respectable dramas. Other comediennes, like Alice Howell, Gale Henry, and Polly Moran, unapologetically embraced comedy, even lowbrow slapstick, to the delight of their fans and the consternation of their critics. Although these critics generally felt that physical comedy was antithetical to delicate femininity, many comediennes built highly successful careers on movies "of the 'custard pie' variety."[2]

"As Comical as a Crutch"

In February 2000, the U.S. Comedy Arts Festival in Aspen, Colorado, honored Jerry Lewis with a retrospective of his work and a discussion with comedian Martin Short, followed by a question-and-answer session with the audience. During the Q&A session, an audience member noted that Lewis had only mentioned male comics as influences and asked who his favorite female comics were. Lewis responded, "I don't like any female comedians." Short reminded Lewis of Lucille Ball, saying, "You must have loved her." But Lewis would not be swayed, replying simply, "No." He then explained: "A woman doing comedy doesn't offend me, but sets me back a bit. I, as a viewer, have trouble with it. I think of her as a producing machine that brings babies in the world."[3] Lewis's remarks drew a fair amount of negative attention, and several days later he apologized while simultaneously chastising the press for quoting him out of context. In a statement issued to the press, Lewis named several female comedians he does find funny, including Whoopi Goldberg, Elayne Boosler, Diane Ford, and Phyllis Diller. However, Lewis continued, "when women, doing comedy, do routines written for them by drill sergeants, I take objection. Their filth makes me and many ashamed to be in our business, and to me women doing anything, especially comedy, are looked upon by me as one of God's great miracles—they can make a baby."[4] Several months later, on CNN's *Larry King Live*, Lewis presented further clarification of his remarks: "a man comedian can do anything he wants and I'm not offended by it. But we're talking about a God-given miracle who produces a child. I have a difficult time seeing her do this on stage."[5]

King offered that Lewis was "only criticizing women when they do unwomanly things," and Lewis agreed, explaining that his discomfort stems from the fact that he's "mid-Victorian, old-fashioned."[6] Lewis seemed genuinely annoyed by the uproar surrounding his comments in Aspen, and he urged the press to "please accept my humble apology and let's go back to where we were."[7]

Jerry Lewis's plea to "go back to where we were" is both ironic and yet somehow fitting under the circumstances, as his comments are a perfect example of "where we were." While his attitudes toward female comedians are certainly a reflection of his "mid-Victorian" values, they also represent traces of a larger, longstanding prejudice in American culture against women performing comedy, a prejudice that has affected women's comic expression in every form and forum. Debates about whether women have a sense of humor and the nature of women's humor date to at least the seventeenth century and, as Lewis's comments illustrate, are still circulating. As early as 1695, playwright William Congreve wrote, "I must confess I have never made any observation of what I Apprehend to be true Humour in Women. . . . For if ever any thing does appear Comical or Ridiculous in a Woman, I think it is little more than an acquir'd Folly, or an Affectation."[8] And as recently as 2007 *Vanity Fair* ran an article titled "Why Women Aren't Funny" in which contributing editor Christopher Hitchens asked, "Why are women, who have the whole male world at their mercy, not funny? Please do not pretend not to know what I am talking about."[9]

The very vocal public insistence, usually by male writers, that women aren't funny is a clear example of the dominant culture attempting to control a marginalized group. As women made social and political gains around the turn of the twentieth century, they could be perceived as a threat to traditional culture. As Henry Jenkins argues, "This denial of female jocularity was probably tied to the dominant comic tradition's function as a release of male anxieties and fears; a laughing and joking woman posed a potential new threat to male authority and masculine dignity, intensifying the tensions masculine-centered comedy sought to resolve."[10] The threat posed by funny women was contained by the insistence that humor was incompatible with femininity itself, albeit an idealized and regressive version of femininity. By loudly proclaiming that women who cracked jokes or even laughed too heartily were essentially failed women, critics were attempting to curtail women's desire to engage in comic expression. Furthermore, those who argued against women's humor were denying comediennes and other funny women the capacity to engage in a mode of expression that has always been an especially effective way of critiquing and disrupting power structures. If women couldn't create—or even appreciate—comedy, then they would obviously be incapable of using comedy to question and poke fun at social and cultural forces that kept them subordinate to men.

The remarkable resilience of this stereotype means that the truly inane question of whether half the population is capable of humor continues to be rehashed, debated, rejected, and corroborated ad infinitum. Articles with titles such as "Why Do People Believe Women Aren't Funny?" and "Plight of the Funny Female" are continually circulating online and in newspapers and magazines.[11] Comedian Bonnie McFarlane's 2014 documentary *Women Aren't Funny* explores the topic in detail, and another documentary, *History of the Joke* (2008), devotes a segment to investigating whether women are funny, with host Lewis Black asking a variety of comics to give their opinions on the topic. Comedian Kathy Griffin's comments make it clear that the stereotype is alive and well:

> Unfortunately in this business, the line "chicks aren't funny" comes up a lot, and I'm pleasantly surprised when after my shows guys come up to me and say, "you know, normally I don't think chicks are that funny, but, you're really funny." To which I say, "Really? Would you go up to a black person and say 'normally I think you're lazy and shiftless but you seem to work hard?'" It's a conversation stopper.[12]

In her book *Bossypants* Tina Fey recounts an incident in the *Saturday Night Live* writers' room when star Jimmy Fallon jokingly told Amy Poehler that a bit she was working on wasn't "cute" and that he didn't like it. Poehler's response to Fallon—"I don't fucking care if you like it"—serves as a rallying cry for Fey:

> I think of this whenever someone says to me, "Jerry Lewis says women aren't funny," or "Christopher Hitchens says women aren't funny," or "Rick Fenderman says women aren't funny. . . . Do you have anything to say to that?"
> Yes. We don't fucking care if you like it.
> I don't say it out loud, of course, because Jerry Lewis is a great philanthropist, Hitchens is very sick, and the third guy I made up.
> Unless one of these men is my boss, which none of them is, it's irrelevant. My hat goes off to them. It is an impressively arrogant move to conclude that just because *you* don't like something, it is empirically not

good. I don't like Chinese food, but I don't write articles trying to prove it doesn't exist.[13]

Summing up the endless debates in 2005, a *New Yorker* columnist stated, "Comedy is probably the last remaining branch of the arts whose suitability for women is still openly discussed."[14] Rather than embarking on the familiar and ultimately futile endeavor of trying to disprove this stereotype, it's more productive to interrogate this line of thinking, to uncover what, specifically, about femininity is thought to be antithetical to comedy and how silent comediennes managed to make careers for themselves in comedy despite the misogynistic fears of women's power that are at the root of the "women aren't funny" stereotype.

Women's supposed reliance on emotion rather than logic or reason is frequently given as proof that women can't be funny. Throughout the nineteenth century, the "cult of domesticity," as defined by Barbara Welter, reinforced the image of women as emotional rather than intellectual beings, and as a result "womanly wit had difficulty maneuvering around the image of ideal womanhood—an image that denigrated woman's intellect in favor of her emotional and intuitive nature."[15] Writers who have debated the issue of female humor have often used her perceived capacity for emotion, rather than intellect, as justification to deny her the aptitude for either creating or appreciating comedy. Writing in 1842, a contributor to *Graham's Magazine* claimed that "there is a body and substance to true wit, with a reflectiveness rarely found apart from a masculine intellect. . . . The female character does not admit of it."[16] A 1909 newspaper article claimed that "a woman was made to be loved and fondled . . . she certainly was not made to be laughed at" and that "you do not find much in [women] to arouse your sense of humor. . . . Measured by the ordinary standards of humor she is about as comical as a crutch."[17] French philosopher Henri Bergson, in his 1900 essay on comedy, declared that those who are overly sensitive and emotional are unable to appreciate humor: "laughter has no greater foe than emotion. . . . Highly emotional souls, in tune and unison with life, in whom every event would be sentimentally prolonged and re-echoed, would neither know nor understand laughter."[18] Given the popular conception at the time of women as "highly emotional souls," it would follow that in Bergson's view women are excluded from laughter. Hitchens picked up this line of reasoning without missing a beat in his 2007 article, claiming that "male humor prefers the laugh to be at someone's expense, and understands that life is quite possibly a joke to begin with.... Whereas women, bless their tender hearts, would prefer that life be fair, and even sweet, rather than the sordid mess it actually is."[19] Whether humor is, in fact, dependent on intellect to the exclusion of emotion is open to debate (one can certainly question the intelligence necessary to enjoy The Three Stooges), and yet this belief has become conventional wisdom in writings and discussions on comedy, from well before Bergson's time to the present. Ultimately, whether comedy requires intellect, emotion, or some combination of the two to be successful is beside the point; what matters is that those who write about comedy have generally accepted it as truth, and this belief informs the understanding of those who declare that women's nature is incompatible with comedy.

Like Lewis, Hitchens argued that childbearing in some way contributed to women's lack of humor because "reproduction is, if not the only thing, certainly the main thing," and therefore "for women the question of funniness is essentially a secondary one. They are innately aware of a higher calling that is no laughing matter."[20] It's telling that both Lewis and Hitchens point to women's ability to create life as a reason for their inability to create comedy. This line of reasoning is presented by these men as a glorification of women—they're a "God-given miracle" with a "higher calling"—but ultimately denies women humanity, reducing them to their biological functions. This type of reductionist thinking can be found in a 1959 text titled *Humour in English Literature*, which is surprisingly virulent in its description of women's lack of humor:

> The truth is ... that women have not only no humor in themselves but are the cause of the extinction of it in others. This is almost too cruel to be true, but in every way women correspond to and are representative of nature. Is there any humor in nature? A glance at the zoo will answer this question.... Women are the undifferentiated mass of nature from which the contradictions of real and ideal arose and they are the unlaughing at which men laugh.[21]

Lewis, Hitchens, and numerous others espouse the essentialist viewpoint that women are so closely aligned with nature that they lack the (specifically human) traits widely accepted as necessary to appreciate and engage in humor, such as intellect, logic, and the ability for analytical thought. This line of reasoning holds that men, as intelligent, rational, logical beings, can appreciate humor, while women, whose biological imperative and close link to nature limit their intellectual capacity, are destined to be humorless killjoys. If humor is based on intelligence, observation, and understanding then women, who are mired in their own biological functions, must certainly be excluded from the comic realm.

Circulating alongside these arguments about women's biological functions was the idea that comedy and laughter were too physical for women. This thinking is in line with Victorian conceptions of idealized femininity as spiritual or emotional rather than physical. As Rob King argues, "The dominant female ideal of Victorian culture had emphasized feminine spirituality and transcendence, bracketing off the body as a locus of woman's self-expression: female comic performance upset such distinctions, proposing instead a species of bodily excess, a grotesque negation of the nurturing qualities that informed sentimental ideals of womanhood."[22] Laughter itself, with its spontaneous bodily convulsions, was deemed by many to be unfeminine at this time. Stories about women laughing themselves to death circulated in the press, with the explicit warning that "excessive, embodied, and involuntary laughter was simply not meant for women's bodies, because it might kill them (and often did). Death from laughter thereby represented a warning to women, a gendered deterrent from laughing in either the public or private sphere (for the home was no less hazardous to female laughers than the circus)."[23] Because of the potential for bodily harm that could result from overly enthusiastic laughter, Maggie Hennefeld points out that "women were instructed to efface all signs of bodily movement, acoustic volume, or visceral enjoyment from their laughter."[24] As spiritual beings, women were thought to be immune to bodily functions ranging from sexual desire to laughter.

The inherently aggressive nature of comedy is also diametrically opposed to the cultural ideal of femininity, especially as it was defined at the turn of the twentieth century, with its emphasis on submissiveness, deference, and passivity. For many critics and writers, humor was at odds with perceived notions of how proper middle- and upper-class women should behave. Comedians deliver *punch* lines and *kill* their audiences. They call attention to society's idiosyncrasies and failings rather than quietly accepting the world as it is, and in so doing they often expose truths that would otherwise go unspoken. In vaudeville, the aggressive nature of comedy was apparent in the fact that comedians frequently addressed the audience directly, actively engaging and confronting spectators, while singers, dancers, and other performers were more submissive, positioning themselves as recipients rather than bearers of the gaze. This dynamic can also be seen in Keystone comedies of the 1910s, as the comic actors (both male and female) engaged in violent knockabout routines and gags, while the Bathing

Beauties (always female) stood quietly on the sidelines and observed, but seldom participated in, the chaos. As Mack Sennett said, a pie in the face is funny, but "Shetland ponies and pretty girls are immune."[25] The bias against well-behaved women performing comedy was linked to a similar cultural proscription against female competitiveness. Women should passively support men, not actively compete with them; as Nancy Walker put it, "The lady laughs at men's jokes; she does not invent her own."[26]

In the nineteenth century, women were seen as guardians of morality, a trait that was considered antithetical to humorous expression. Men were not saddled with the responsibility of maintaining civility and gentility in society and so were allowed the freedom to revel in the comic, whereas women, as society's de facto moral compass, were left with the responsibility of curtailing men's fun, a dynamic that led to the pervasive stereotype of the female nag.[27] Empathy and compassion, stereotypically feminine traits that guided women's morality, were also to blame for women's supposed failure to find humor in many situations. Bergson wrote about humor as "corrective" with "an avowed intention to humiliate"; as a means by which "society avenges itself for the liberties taken with it. It would fail in its object if it bore the stamp of sympathy or kindness."[28] Sigmund Freud similarly described humor's potential for aggression, arguing that the tendentious (as opposed to innocent) joke could be "either a *hostile* joke (serving the purpose of aggressiveness, satire, or defense) or an *obscene* joke (serving the purpose of exposure)"; these jokes require someone to be "the object of the hostile or sexual aggressiveness."[29] And in a 1902 article in *Harper's Bazaar* titled "Have Women a Sense of Humor?"[30] the author claimed that "the tears from the woman's sympathetic heart fill her eyes before the laughter can ripple across her lips."[31] The idea of women as champions of morality, like many other stereotypes that exclude women from comedy, continues to this day: a 2000 book on film comedy makes the point that "women are commonly associated with civilization because, with their physical and sexual vulnerability to men, they stand to lose much more than men by civilization's breakdown. Socially they have to represent the superego to counteract the male id."[32] If women's responsibility is to make sure that men don't have too much fun, it's not surprising that women are seen as incapable of having fun themselves.

These discursive strands form the foundation of the pervasive "women aren't funny" stereotype. According to these arguments, women can't possibly be funny because the traits that comprise femininity—emotionality, submissiveness, passivity, empathy, morality—are antithetical to comedy. Jenkins points out that "again and again, these articles treat female comic performance as a problem to be analyzed, as a manifestation to be dreaded and pitied, as a detraction from the possibilities of feminine charm and beauty."[33] It's not surprising, then, that when women in the nineteenth and early twentieth centuries engaged in comic performances they sometimes downplayed stereotypically feminine traits and attributes. Writing in 1902, a theater critic commented on how female comedians "do not hesitate to sacrifice all of the vanities of their sex—looks and grace—to evoke laughter from their audience."[34] This description brings into focus the perceived incompatibility of femininity and humor, the fact that women were viewed as either feminine or funny but seldom both. In order to engage in comic performances, women had to "sacrifice" their feminine qualities, defined here as "looks and grace." The thinking was that a traditionally feminine woman performing comedy had the potential to create dissonance in the minds of audience members, as they might struggle to reconcile the femininity of the performer with the supposed masculinity of the performance; however, a "mannish" woman performing the same routine could seem less transgressive because she is already removed from the trappings of femininity. In "sacrificing" their femininity, then, the potential threat posed by women who engaged in the unruly and aggressive arena of comedy could be defused for audiences worried about changing gender roles.

When comediennes downplayed traditionally feminine attributes such as passivity and submissiveness in their acts, the femininity that they performed onstage and sometimes even offstage could be understood by spectators as somehow deviant, qualitatively different from and ultimately inferior to the femininity found in widely circulated images of ideal womanhood. When overweight vaudeville comediennes such as May Irwin and Trixie Friganza made jokes about their size, unruly comediennes such as Eva Tanguay and Marie Dressler ran amok on stage and screen, or slapstick film comediennes such as Louise Fazenda and Mabel Normand threw punches and pies they were deliberately choosing excessiveness, visibility, and aggression over modesty, deference, and submissiveness. This choice helped smooth the incongruity inherent in women performing comedy but ultimately excluded comediennes from the popular conception of what constituted normative femininity as defined by artists, writers, and popular (non-comedic) actresses of the late nineteenth and early twentieth centuries. While other performing women, including ingénues, chorines, and bathing beauties, projected the image of normative femininity, comediennes chose to relinquish stereotypically feminine traits in order to get a laugh.

And yet even a woman "sacrificing" femininity by deliberately presenting herself as more masculine in order to perform comedy could be unsettling to some. As gender roles continued to be in flux in the early decades of twentieth century, the idea that women were capable of appropriating and discarding feminine attributes such as grace, delicacy, and refinement would call into question the authenticity of those attributes. As Susan Glenn argues, "To sacrifice femininity, even in the name of artistic devotion, was really to emphasize it by calling attention to the difference between sanctioned and unsanctioned female behavior and looks."[35] When comediennes created characters who were loud, brash, ungraceful, and unrefined, they were exposing the artificial and constructed nature of femininity. In his review of comedienne Beatrice Lillie's 1952 stage act, George Jean Nathan expressed his discomfort with female comics and suggested a way to alleviate it: "I wouldn't get in the least mad if her acts were interrupted and supplemented by, say, a line of pretty dancing girls, maybe 30 or 40."[36] Nathan's solution—incorporating "pretty dancing girls" into Lillie's act—would certainly strike a balance between two types of femininity that many (including Nathan, apparently) saw as opposing: the intelligent and biting wit of Lillie, and the passive beauty of the chorus line.

Feminine Humor

Despite the depth of popular sentiment that femininity and comedy were incompatible, the increasing numbers of women making a living as comediennes onstage and in films prompted some to allow that they could, perhaps, have a sense of humor. However, even the writers and critics who conceded women's humor argued that women's sensitive and emotional, rather than intellectual, nature meant that they were capable of understanding and appreciating only the most subtle, delicate humor. In the 1901 *Harper's Bazaar* article titled "Have Women a Sense of Humor?" the writer, Constant Coquelin, is effusive in his praise of women's sense of humor—"Wit, humor, sparkle, they are gifts that the gods have liberally bestowed upon the feminine mind"—and yet makes it clear that "women's sense of humor is more sensitive than that of men, but not so broad. It encourages more often than it creates. It is more a hidden power than an active force." For women, the article claims, humor is a matter of instinct rather than reason, and a woman "knows the real [humor] because she feels it, and a woman's feelings are a true touchstone." Furthermore, the traditionally female quality of modesty is given as the reason why many men felt women didn't enjoy humor: "It is her appreciation of humor that makes her so companionable. Her delicacy and exquisite tact that keep her from thrusting it before your face. But just because she conceals it, men make the mistake of thinking it is not there."[37] In the opinion of Coquelin and many others, women are capable of understanding, enjoying, and sometimes even creating humor, but their humor is qualitatively different from that enjoyed by men, and these differences are rooted in fundamental differences between the genders. Women's humor in this viewpoint is inextricably tied to their inherently emotional nature, whereas men's humor runs the gamut of comedic expression, from slapstick to satire to sophisticated comedy. This reflects the longstanding correlation between women and nature but represents a shift from the viewpoint that claimed that women did not have the capacity for humor. In this revised view, women's emotional and sensitive nature doesn't exclude them from humor; instead it informs the types of humor they appreciate and enjoy. Rather than seeing comedy as incompatible with femininity, this viewpoint asserts that there is a type of comedy that is intrinsically feminine.

What, then, is "feminine" comedy? Like traditional femininity, feminine comedy was thought to be sensitive and emotional, gentle rather than aggressive, and passive rather than active.[38] Coquelin describes women's "delicacy and exquisite tact that keep her from thrusting [her sense of humor] before your face": her feminine propriety prevents her from the decidedly masculine and somewhat hostile act of "thrusting" anything in anyone's face. A 1926 description of Colleen Moore similarly celebrates this type of feminine humor: "Colleen's most charming quality is her sympathetic sense of humor—sympathetic, because it never carries a barb."[39] Along with being gentle and nonthreatening, feminine humor was often seen as effortless, the result of unconscious facility rather than active labor. Women's humor, then, "is no attempt at being funny, but just a natural flow of gentle wit, and the art of seeing the ludicrous."[40] Ultimately, this view allows women a space to enjoy and inspire but little space to create humor. Coquelin sees this as an admirable aspect of women's humor:

> It is only another example of woman's unselfishness that she has been willing to let us think that we men have a monopoly, as you say in this country, on humor. She did not dispute it. She did not claim any of our laurels. For woman does not try to be funny. She leaves that to man.

> When we ask, "What have you written that was true humor?" "Very little," she acknowledges. She can smile and be magnanimous in this, for she knows that she has inspired and enjoyed the humor of the world. She can well afford to rest content.[41]

Women can appreciate comedy and they can inspire male humorists, but actually creating comedy is too assertive, too competitive, to be ladylike behavior. Men produce humor; women inspire and appreciate their efforts.

If women were more inclined toward gentle, subtle, and emotional comedy, it follows that "low" types of physical comedy, such as slapstick, would be too coarse for women's sensibilities. Coquelin claimed that when women are confronted with wit and humor "in the form of what is boisterous and broad and rough, [they do] not recognize them," and writing in 1902, Robert Burdette explained that women's humor "is delicate, sympathetic, refined to the highest culture. True humor delights her, while buffoonery, if it be brutal, shocks her."[42] Twenty-five years later, *Moving Picture World* echoed this sentiment, saying that "slapstick comedy with man-made laughs, and broad masculine humor seldom please the woman patron.... The reason that Our Gang comedies are such a great success is because here is humor that is gentle and that the feminine heart can interpret and enjoy."[43] These writers allow for women's appreciation of humor, as long as the humor is suitably ladylike. Even Mack Sennett, who regularly cast women in knockabout comedies, felt that there were certain gags that shouldn't be performed by women: "movie fans do not like to see pretty girls smeared up with pastry.... You can put a pretty girl in a comedy shower bath. You can have her fall into mud puddles. They will laugh at that. But the spectacle of a girl dripping with pie is displeasing."[44] Even though Sennett seems to forget that comediennes took plenty of pies to the face while working in his films, his theory is revealing on a number of levels. First, it's telling that his admonition against throwing pies in women's faces only applies to *pretty* women; as I will discuss in chapter 2, for film comediennes there was a definite division of labor based on their appearance, with conventionally attractive women playing in "high-class" light or romantic comedies and less attractive comediennes appearing in slapstick. It's also interesting that in Sennett's view audiences would approve of a pretty woman being doused with water or covered in mud, but they wouldn't stand for her face being sullied by a pie. Physical comedy that accentuates the "pretty girl's" form or heightens her sexuality is apparently acceptable, but a gag that obscures her pretty face or represents an overt act of violence toward her—as a pie thrown in her face would be—is not allowed.

The idea that slapstick and "low" comedy were inherently unfeminine was especially problematic for female comedians in the late nineteenth and early twentieth centuries as this type of comedy was becoming increasingly prominent on the stage and later on the screen. A new type of comedy that reflected the energetic and chaotic modern world began gaining in popularity in the 1890s. This "New Humor" was violent, anarchic, and fast-paced and served as the basis for slapstick and unruly performances. Based in inversion and disorder, New Humor was a popular and decidedly lowbrow break from earlier forms of comedy that tended to be slower paced and more thoughtful. As vaudeville historian Albert McLean puts it, "Although the term was loosely applied and seldom defined, [New Humor] generally indicated a humor that was more excited, more aggressive, and less sympathetic than that to which the middle classes of the nineteenth century had been accustomed."[45] New Humor had strong ties to ribald and boisterous working-class and immigrant cultures, and its appearance on the vaudeville stage was seen as a counter to the legitimate theater, which had only recently positioned itself as respectable entertainment. According to theater historian Rick DesRochers,

> Whereas the legitimate theater was perceived to promote a quiet and thoughtful response to a play of literary merit, the comic vaudeville stage conversely encouraged audience response and participation. The rowdiness in a vaudeville house should have been discouraged, according to reformers and critics, because it incited spectators to shun polite and disciplined appreciation for the performing arts. It also stimulated the violent outbursts and crude behaviors that had characterized nineteenth-century popular entertainments. The new humor in particular was found to offend so-called sophisticated artistic sensibilities. These comic stage acts came under attack by social reformers and cultural critics to promote a standard for Anglo-American, middle-class cultural identity in the United States during the Progressive era.[46]

Despite the best efforts of vaudeville impresario Tony Pastor, among others, to refashion vaudeville as a refined, family-friendly entertainment, New Humor proliferated on its stages, and largely due to the high numbers of performers who worked in both vaudeville and silent film, this style of humor found its way into silent comedies of the 1910s and 1920s.

Traditionally defined femininity did not allow for enjoyment of New Humor and low comedy. Women were supposed to be too sensitive, too refined, too "ladylike" to enjoy comedy based on visceral humor and laughter based on shocks. Furthermore, it was assumed that women would not fully understand or appreciate the irony and satire of New Humor.[47] Still, many female comedians made use of New Humor and low comedy in their performances, onstage as well as on-screen. Marie Dressler made extensive use of pratfalls in her stage and film appearances in the 1900s and 1910s, violently hurtling her large body around and mugging broadly, and Sophie Tucker, known as the Last of the Red Hot Mamas, performed aggressive sexuality with songs such as "Nobody Knows What a Red-Headed Mamma Can Do" and "You've Got to See Mamma Every Night." When they incorporated low comedy into their acts, female comedians risked being labeled disreputable and unfeminine, and yet they served to contradict the popular notion that women were either uninterested in low comedy or incapable of performing it.

The burgeoning popularity of this type of low comedy was alarming to some theater owners and managers, who saw it as a threat to the theater's hard-fought and newfound respectability, and some tried to replace slapstick on their stages and in their movie theaters with more refined, genteel forms of comedy.[48] In the early twentieth century vaudeville and movie theater owners courted middle-class women to supplant unruly and boisterous audiences, in the hopes that their presence would add an air of respectability and refinement to entertainment forms that were increasingly associated with the lower classes.[49] According to Rob King,

> As observers at the time realized, the groundswell of laughter came, not from the drawing rooms of the genteel elite, but from an audience of laborers, recent immigrants, working-class families, and lower-middle-class salaried workers.... In such a climate, discourse on laughter soon became a vehicle for genteel anxieties about social change. For the self-appointed guardians of American culture, the new humor was nothing less than a symptom of civilization's decline.[50]

The industry's desire for respectability could be problematic for comedians, as comedy—and especially New Comedy—was considered distinctly lowbrow.

Mabel Normand confirmed this in a 1920 article, in which she told her readers, "I am not a highbrow. If I were, I wouldn't be earning my living by being funny—or trying to be."[51] In this assessment, being funny and being highbrow are mutually exclusive qualities—the fact that Normand is a comedienne automatically means that she can't be a highbrow. A review of Charlotte Greenwood's 1916 Broadway production of *So Long Letty* sets up a similar dialectic: "Nobody is pretending *So Long Letty* is high class. It does not want to be high class—it wants to be human and trolley-car-colony class."[52] While comediennes such as Normand and Greenwood were comfortable performing lowbrow comedy despite the broader desire for respectability within the theater and cinema industries, other comediennes made it clear that they were able to find some refinement in an otherwise unrefined genre. Fay Tincher, for example, was adamant that neither she nor her films were lowbrow:

> The truth is, that up to the last year or so comedy has never been handled seriously by either the producer or the public, and that is just the reason there has been so much cheap, vulgar, dime-novel comedy—slapstick, the managers call it.
>
> I could have done that sort of thing when I first began, and got big pay for it, too, but I won't do it. I hate it. There's no art in that sort of thing, and there's nothing funny in it, either, for people with any brains.[53]

While Normand cheerfully accepted comedy's lowbrow status, Tincher's rejection of "cheap, vulgar, dime-novel comedy" and her allusions to art and intellect echo the language of those who hoped to reform the theater and cinema. The opposition between these two points of view reflects the different challenges faced by comediennes in light of these reforms. Normand, who specialized in physical comedy, shrewdly embraced her style of comedy, despite its lowbrow connotations, while Tincher, who aspired to more refined light comedy and "comedy-drama," felt the need to distance herself from "vulgar" slapstick.

The theater and film industries saw attracting more female audiences as a linchpin of their parallel drives to respectability. Women were thought to be "morally superior patrons"[54] who would, by their very presence, calm the unruly (and largely male) audiences that had defined nineteenth-century theater.[55] Indeed, as Richard Butsch points out, "respectability was at its core a gendered concept. Middle-class women, particularly as wives and mothers, carried designations of respectability. . . . Drawing women into theaters at mid-century endowed these establishments with respectability."[56] In practice, however, female audiences were not necessarily as refined or respectable as theater owners hoped. M. Alison Kibler describes the "contrasts between the vaudeville industry's construction of a polite female spectator and the actual female patrons (often loose and raucous)."[57] Shelley Stamp notes similar discrepancies between idealized and actual female spectators in early film:

> Even though women's films and filmgoing were so often associated with cinema's growing cultural legitimacy in the transitional era, these examples suggest that women's patronage was also built with subject matter like sexuality, action-adventure stories, and feminist agitation not normally associated with a ladylike gentility. And women evidently sought visual pleasures, like erotic voyeurism in the case of white slave films and ongoing, intertextual engagement in the case of serials, that were at odds with refined, highbrow entertainments.[58]

While women were positioned as a civilizing force in late nineteenth and early twentieth-century theater and cinema, their actual role in legitimizing these industries was complex and contested.

Despite this, the desire of the theater and film industries to feminize their audiences ultimately led to a cultural privileging of "feminine" humor. This type of gentle and emotional humor was seen as relatively highbrow when compared to the anarchic roughhousing found in slapstick. A clear tension between advocates of slapstick humor and supporters of more refined comedy can be found in press discourses in the 1910s. A 1915 *Variety* review of the Marie Dressler film *Tillie's Tomato Surprise* complained that there was nothing for the cast to do "excepting 'funny' falls" and that there was "absolutely no 'class' to the picture."[59] That same year Charlotte Greenwood's *Jane* garnered praise for being "a good grouch chaser *without* slap stick" and "a model film comedy at which advocates of the non-slapstick photoplay may point with pride."[60] Two years later, however, *Motion Picture News* praised the physical comedy in Dressler's *Tillie Wakes Up*, saying that "the last three reels are in fact so slapstickedly good that one forgets the dragging of the first two," while *Wid's Daily* dismissed the film as "rough-and-tumble hokum comedy constructed around the skeleton of a story."[61] Reviewers, and presumably audiences, were clearly ambivalent about the use of physical comedy in motion pictures. Although physical comedy was still popular, the violence and chaos of this type of comedy were at odds with the motion picture industry's attempt to establish itself as a refined and respectable entertainment. Mabel Normand noted this conflict as early as 1915:

> The comedy of four or five years ago was a very different affair from those made today, but I think there is still plenty of room for improvement, and the next few years will witness as great a development.
>
> Of course there will always be the slap-stick work. That brand of humor is still popular on the stage, with some people, and there will always be more or less of a demand for this kind of fun.[62]

Although popular, the humor in slapstick comedy—full of bodies and machines running amok—didn't fit the image of respectability that the industry was aiming for. "Feminine" comedy, however, with its gentle, sensitive, and sympathetic humor, was the ideal generic counterpart to a more refined cinema.

By 1919 *Wid's* declared that "exhibitors everywhere are looking for good comedies of a type superior to the slapstick variety,"[63] and that same year screenwriter Anita Loos explained that she was "working [gradually] toward the production of high comedy."

> We began with farce; that was strong on plot, of course, but the satirical element in it saved the picture from being too much like the old "chase" pictures. Then we produced comedy-dramas that gradually resolved themselves into comedies with a strong dramatic interest. From them we want to develop a true high comedy, a comedy of ideas.[64]

Loos's "comedy of ideas" was based in situation rather than slapstick, as exemplified by the light comedies she wrote for Constance Talmadge. The reliance on situations and dialogue rather than gags and physical shtick meant that by the late 1910s and throughout the 1920s title cards became increasingly important. Loos herself was instrumental in this shift, as she was known for her innovative and clever titles that furthered the plot while often commenting wryly on the action. While D. W. Griffith complained that "most of the laughs are in the dialogue which can't be photographed," Douglas Fairbanks commented that "time and time again . . . I have sat through plays with Miss Loos and have heard the audience applaud her subtitles as heartily as the lively scenes."[65] The popularity of Loos's titles meant that they "instigated the recognizable shift to witty and prolix titles in films of the late 1910s."[66] Indeed, the *Christian Science*

Monitor in 1919 claimed that "it is perhaps for her reform of caption writing that Miss Loos has been most valuable to motion pictures. She brought to her work an alert sense of humor, which demanded that the captions for comedies should be as light as the comedy itself."[67]

As the captions became more important in the production of comedy, gags became less important, especially for female comedians. *Her Wild Oat* (1927), for example, features a fine light comedic performance by Colleen Moore as well as very funny titles, including a mention of "Girls in their short skirts getting tanned as far up as the Canadian border" (Figure 1.1). Reviewers noted the importance of the intertitles in the creation of the comedy, saying that the film "is free from the old type 'gag' comedy idea and is a radical departure in many respects because of the telling of the story pictorially, while the titles were the heavy artillery."[68] Moore's *Ella Cinders* (1926) similarly used titles to create a great deal of the film's comedy—as one reviewer noted, "except for one scene, almost all the humor in 'Ella Cinders' is contributed by the subtitles."[69] This growing reliance on titles as the "heavy artillery" in silent comedies was evident in the films of both male and female comedians. However, whereas male comedians such as Buster Keaton and Charlie Chaplin continued to use elaborate gags and stunts, female comedians increasingly based their comedy on situations, with titles becoming increasingly important for generating laughs. Physical comedy was still used by women in this era but far less frequently than in the 1910s.

"Women Are Sometimes Funny"

When female comedians eschewed physical gags in favor of situation- and personality-based comedy, it added fuel to the old idea that women simply weren't funny, that they had to rely on situations and intertitles rather than generating the comedy themselves. Instead of arguing that women were incapable of humor, however, some writers of the 1920s lamented that funny women were a possibility but there were few, if any, such women in Hollywood. A typical rant is found in *Film Daily* in 1924:

> A Need
>
> A comedienne. And needed muchly. True there are a few cavorting about. But they aren't getting so far—or so fast—that there isn't a lot of room for a new one. Where is the successor to Fazenda? Who is she? And what producer is developing her?

Figure 1.1. Intertitles, like the ones included here from *Her Wild Oat* (1927), were increasingly used to create comedy.

> Connie Talmadge had the field of her own to herself until she failed to find material. Mabel Normand once had a tremendous vogue. Where is it today?
>
> Colleen Moore looks a comer. But she has her own type of work—and is doing it very well indeed. Little Pauline Garon—if she was handled the right way—should find a place somewhere in that line. Mae Busch could do it—but then she can do almost anything. Why don't [*sic*] Metro give Viola Dana a chance in this direction?
>
> The world wants to laugh. If you disagree look at Chaplin and Lloyd—and their records—and quit arguing. The world will laugh as much with a woman star if she is given the right material. Will someone please start something?[70]

This writer certainly allows that women can be funny, and gives credit to a few women who have the potential to be strong comediennes, but at the same time diminishes the impact of the many popular comediennes who were then making films. Furthermore, the writer seems to be looking for a physical comedienne, a successor to Louise Fazenda and Mabel Normand, both of whom made their names in slapstick, rather than one who engages in "feminine" comedy. A similar plea for funny women appeared two years later in a *New York World* article written by Palmer Smith:

> In all but a few scenes *Ella Cinders* was stupid and boresome, and to me served only to emphasize that the screen has failed to develop any co-medienne to compare with Chaplin, Lloyd, Maclean, Griffith, Langdon or Hines. Mabel Normand, Bebe Daniels and Gloria Swanson approach nearest, but Paramount seems to favor dilution of the Daniels and Swanson comedy by wardrobe contrasts. Louise Fazenda has at times shown real promise of clowning ability if given opportunity. For the others the "leading ladies" of slapstick graduate and go to straight parts, while the male comedians are promoted from two reels to six. One of the real needs of the screen to-day will be met only by development of two or three first rate comediennes.[71]

As in the earlier example, in Smith's view a "first rate comedienne" would engage in slapstick comedy, not the sort of light comedy that Colleen Moore performed in *Ella Cinders*. Although he does mention, accurately, that for many comediennes slapstick was thought to be a starting point, something to "graduate" from (which will be discussed in more detail), he dismisses the fact that rather than going into "straight parts," many slapstick comediennes went into other types of comedy, including romantic comedy and farce. Smith also shares with the *Film Daily* writer an inclination to blame the studios for mishandling promising comediennes by not developing them or giving them the proper material to work with. This is likely a valid point, as the project of shaping the careers and public images of actors working under the studio system was often left to producers, publicists, and other studio personnel rather than to the actors themselves. Actors under contract often did not have a great deal of control over the trajectory of their careers and would not necessarily have been able to choose film projects for themselves that they felt best suited their talents or personae. However, blaming the studios does take some agency away from comediennes, several of whom were heads of their own production companies and had at least some control over their projects.[72] While *Film Daily* wants to know "what producer is developing" the next great comedienne and speculates on Pauline Garon's prospects "if she was handled the right way," these articles never question whether these women would fare better if they had the creative control that Charlie Chaplin, Harold Lloyd, and many other male comedians enjoyed. Furthermore, blaming studios for this perceived lack of female comedians shifts focus away from the pervasive prejudice against women performing comedy that ultimately led women away from slapstick and into the "straight parts" that Smith decries. If the studios' strategy to feature women in "feminine" comedies that were heavy on character and situation and light on stunts and gags was fueled by the industry's overall drive toward respectability, it was because of societal perceptions that women performing slapstick were vulgar and unladylike that made "feminine" comedy a respectable alternative in the first place.

In 1927 a similar viewpoint to Smith's was expressed by yet another writer. Under the heading "Women Are Sometimes Funny," "Celluloid" discusses why women aren't as funny as men:

> Women are sometimes comedians, too. Some of them are funny. Others just make-believe. There are half a dozen funny women on the screen. Go over them all and name those who could actually exude fun without doing stunts.
>
> I suppose Colleen Moore is one of the best, but she has to be made into characters. Bebe Daniels is the fastest comedian of all the women,

but she is seldom funny except in action—the faster the better. Clara Bow is comic mainly by character and invention. She is a type. Sally O'Neil is similar. The fact is we don't expect antics from the average actress, let alone the average woman. The girl in a company who sets out to be funny has to be careful not to overdo it. We don't enjoy laughing at women very often. When some of them are funny they are screams, especially fat women who become caricatures and imitate [*sic*] geniuses like Elsie Janis.[73]

Like Smith, Celluloid dismisses the type of character-based comedy performed by Moore and Clara Bow but also seems to dismiss comediennes who derive their humor through stunts. The only comediennes he seems to enjoy are "fat women" such as vaudeville stars Trixie Friganza and May Irwin, who made their large figures a central part of their acts, and Elsie Janis, who was famous for her imitations of celebrities and other public figures. Celluloid doesn't leave much room for women to be funny, other than performing self-deprecating caricatures of themselves or appropriating others' manners and personalities.[74] Laments such as these indicate a convergence of earlier opinions about women's humor, or lack thereof. The longstanding belief that women aren't funny is coupled with the concept of a subtle and refined "feminine" humor, with the resultant conclusion that women *can* be funny, but the feminized comedy favored by the industry beginning in the late 1910s and, by extension, its practitioners were simply not as funny as male comedy and comedians. Implicit in these discourses are a criticism of the desire for respectability in the theater and film industries and, more broadly, a criticism of the overall feminization of culture occurring during this time period. Despite the best efforts of the motion picture industry to move away from slapstick and promote "respectable" comedy, there were still those who longed for "clowning" and "antics"—"the faster the better"—over "character and invention."

In the midst of ongoing debates and changing definitions of respectability and femininity, female comediennes were trying to make a living being funny. Although women's comic abilities were widely questioned throughout the 1910s and 1920s, women found a great deal of success during this time performing comedy on the stage and screen. Fan magazines and trade journals generally acknowledged, and even promoted, women's humor, although traces of pervasive stereotypes about the incompatibility of comedy and femininity are evident in these discourses. Most often, however, the stereotypes appear in these publications only to be disproved and dismissed, a shrewd strategy for trade journals trying to market their stars and fan magazines whose largely female readership would likely be interested in stories of women's successes. And so *Moving Picture World* declared in 1917 that "women have demonstrated on the stage that they can be just as funny as the comedians of musical comedy, burlesque, vaudeville or farce,"[75] and the popular press was continually comparing film comediennes favorably to acknowledged male comic geniuses such as Charlie Chaplin, Harold Lloyd, and Harry Langdon.

Despite the longstanding and widely held biases against women and physical comedy, throughout the 1910s and 1920s slapstick comediennes performed the very types of "low" physical comedy that women weren't supposed to appreciate. The comedy that these women were performing was not the light "feminine" comedy advocated by many in the motion picture industry and by some critics; instead, they were engaging in a style of performance similar to that of many male comedians in theater and films. This style is marked by an emphasis on physicality, with knockabout slapstick, tussles, and pratfalls, and frequent use of sight gags and props. By succeeding in these performances, both artistically and professionally, comediennes were making a strong argument that the definition of "feminine" comedy should be expanded to include physical humor.

In 1918 *Photoplay* summed up Louise Fazenda's on-screen antics in this way:

> Custard pies, a chase, a fall, mud, a fire hose, soup, a leak in the plumbing, innumerable lost garments, broken dishes, a slide on a cake of soap, mud in the hair, pie in the eyes, soup down the back, a fall into a lake, policemen, a cleaning up, a bucket of suds and a mop, a slavey with a round-eyed, utterly blank expression, a Mack Sennett comedy, Louise Fazenda.[76]

The laundry list of gags mentioned here is a far cry from the sensitive and emotional comedy thought to be the province of women. As described here, Fazenda engages in physical activities such as chases, falls, and slides, and finds herself covered in mud, pies, and soup. A newspaper illustration that appeared the same year cements her persona as a knockabout comedienne, with Fazenda throwing pots and pans at her hapless partner and generally wreaking havoc in the kitchen (Figure 1.2). As the illustration suggests, the gags and behaviors performed by slapstick comediennes such as Fazenda often played with the iconography of traditional femininity, turning it on its ear in the service of comedy. And so

Figure 1.2. Louise Fazenda and "Kitchen Komedy," unsourced, 20 March 1918, Louise Fazenda clipping file, Robinson Locke scrapbook, NYPL.

Fazenda was the "comic of the kitchen," turning the center of women's domestic life into a chaotic whirl of "masculine" slapstick comedy, as "Mishaps with broken plumbing, cook stoves, mops and pails, pots and pans, are the subjects of most of her comic scenes."[77] This is illustrated in the 1917 Keystone short *Her Torpedoed Love,* as Fazenda's character leaves a soapy scrub brush in the middle of the kitchen floor, causing her husband to slip and break the enormous stack of plates he's carrying. Alice Howell creates similar chaos in the kitchen as a short-order cook in *Cinderella Cinders* (1920) when she cuts off a diner's long beard after it gets in his soup and assaults her boss with a pancake when he fires her. These comedies transform the kitchen from a peaceful space where women carry out their domestic duties to an anarchic setting featuring women run amok. In these films women's domestic sphere has been infiltrated by the unruly and decidedly "unfeminine" world of slapstick comedy. The very symbol of slapstick—the custard pie—sums up this conflict between feminine space and masculine comedy, as a traditional baked good is used as a comic projectile.

There is certainly nothing dignified or refined in any of the gags attributed to Fazenda—in fact, they are precisely the type of comedy that women were said to find shocking and offensive. And yet numerous comediennes were building careers based on pie throwing and anarchic chases. Polly Moran was described as "stopping stove lids, runaway flivvers, rabid motorcycles and fire engines with various parts of her anatomy,"[78] and Mabel Normand "was forever being chased by some one": "With a wee bit of plot the pictures consisted mainly of a series of chases. Mabel ran miles, pursued by Ford Sterling, who played opposite her then. Sometimes Mabel ran after Sterling and sometimes she was chased by the whole company."[79] Certainly these performances ran counter to the passive and dignified humor and appropriate behavior ascribed to women. Rather than keeping herself demurely out of harm's way, Moran is figured as using her body for gags that sound particularly painful, and Normand is equally at home whether she's chasing, or being chased by, men.

Despite their unladylike pursuits, however, the press often made the seemingly contradictory claim that slapstick comediennes were, in fact, ladies. *Photoplay*, for example, describes an Alice Howell film as "containing the conventional slapstick femininely applied,"[80] which would seem to be a contradiction in terms, and in describing Mabel Normand the same journal in 1919 declared, "Whether she is falling down a well, leaping through an upper window in a ball gown or visiting New York . . . she is startling, vivacious, girlish, and always funny."[81] The idea of knockabout comedy "femininely applied," or a woman "leaping through an upper window" and remaining "girlish" indicates the desire of fan magazines and trade journals to assimilate seemingly disparate notions of femininity, as well as the willingness of fans to accept that women could be both feminine and funny. Descriptions such as these were undoubtedly meant to confirm for readers that participating in slapstick didn't rob comediennes of their femininity. But by ascribing to physical comediennes an uneasy integration of traditionally feminine and masculine traits, accounts such as these highlighted tensions that resulted from rapidly shifting gender norms. A 1938 article about Louise Fazenda shows how her persona embodied this tension between conventional masculinity and femininity:

> Ever since she started out in Mack Sennett comedies away back when a custard pie in the face was a mere love tap, she has been building up a reputation as a quality bruiser—with just enough mild character roles in between to hold her franchise as a lady. The movie public has come to regard her as an unpredictable cross between Mother Hubbard and Strangler Lewis—the sort of full-rigged female who, if she happened to stand up all of a sudden in a crowd, you couldn't be altogether sure whether she was going to start a community sing or offer to wrastle any guy in the place for $5.[82]

Fazenda is a walking contradiction in this description—a "bruiser" who is also a lady, an unlikely cross between a lovable nursery rhyme matron and a champion wrestler. These roles and comic personae are playful representations of changing gender roles in the early twentieth century. As "comics of the kitchen," these comediennes demonstrated that "sacrificing" their femininity and instead blending traditionally feminine and masculine attributes and spaces could result in entertaining and successful comedy.

"She Was *Born* Funny"

In many cases comediennes were described, by the press or by their own accounts, as "naturally" funny, a concept that directly contradicts the essentialist notion that women's supposed lack of humor was linked to their biology. Readers were told that Polly Moran was "a born comedienne," Constance Talmadge "was born for comedy," Alice Howell has "a most delightful natural humor," Louise Fazenda was "a born comedienne" and "a true comedienne," and Charlotte Greenwood was "a possessor of abundant natural wit" and that "nature never intended this fair Charlotte for anything but comedy."[83] If Moran, Greenwood, and the rest of these comediennes were born funny, then they dispute the notion that women are biologically incapable of creating or appreciating comedy, an idea that's reinforced by the fact that all of the comediennes mentioned above were highly successful and, with the exception of Talmadge, performed rough-and-tumble slapstick as well as light comedy.

Describing Polly Moran, *Motion Picture Classic* claimed that she was not only born funny but indulged her humorous impulses even if that got her in trouble:

> Polly doesn't mean to be funny. God knows she doesn't *try* to be funny. She doesn't have to. She *is* funny. She was *born* funny. She says so herself. . . .
>
> She was frequently fired from the chorus because she could never resist the temptation of making faces at the principals. Especially when they were very serious, singing teary ballads about moonlight and roses and yoooou.[84]

This article implies that Moran's comedic nature excluded her from more traditionally feminine pursuits, such as "singing teary ballads" about sentimental and romantic topics. Not only did Moran opt out of such performances herself, but according to this account she actively injected her disruptive and unruly sense of humor into more "respectable" entertainment forms. A similar story was told about Louise Fazenda: "At the age of fifteen she left school and joined a dramatic stock company to play ingénue parts, but her sense of humor and her love of grimacing behind the backs of other players soon proved that she was not intended for serious drama."[85] Although these accounts are likely apocryphal, the fact that publicists would create backgrounds such as these for Moran and Fazenda is telling. In both cases, the women are presented as unwilling or unable to suppress their inherently comic natures when confronted with the type of refined performances that women were supposed to prefer. This discourse may be rooted in the idea of women as being emotional and instinctual rather than intellectual, as their comic origin stories have to do with spontaneous expressions of humor rather than careful thought and planning (although, as I'll discuss in what follows, comediennes' hard work was often recognized). At the same time, if Moran and Fazenda chose to make faces rather than sing sentimental ballads or play the ingénue, then they were tacitly rejecting the idea that women were naturally drawn to certain, serious genres or modes of performance and instead confirming that women could enjoy and appreciate humor. This was reinforced by the fact that these women were said to be "born comediennes." Mocking traditionally feminine performance styles, then, was an expression of a natural inclination rather than evidence of deviation from women's biologically determined sensitivity and refinement.

The concept of comediennes as "naturally funny" shows up, to varying degrees, in several films. Mabel Normand in *The Extra Girl* (1923), Colleen Moore in *Ella Cinders* (1926), and Marion Davies in *Show People* (1928) each plays an aspiring actress hoping to make a name for herself in dramatic roles. In each case, the character is clearly better suited to comedy, and this fact gets in the way of her dramatic ambitions. The inherent irony of these films lies in the fact that while the characters long to play dramatic roles but stumble upon comedy inadvertently, the actresses themselves were celebrated comediennes who worked hard to develop their comic technique. And so the trait—humor—that stands in the way of the characters realizing their goals is the same trait on which the actresses built their careers. The characters' failure is the actresses' triumph: while the characters' comic inclination thwarts their attempts at drama, the actresses' comic ability makes them a resounding success in their chosen genre.

The Extra Girl, *Ella Cinders*, and *Show People* each tell the stories of naïve young women who travel to Hollywood with the goal of gaining fame as dramatic actresses. In *The Extra Girl*, Sue Graham (Normand) sees Hollywood as an exciting escape from a small-town existence and a prearranged marriage to a man she doesn't love. She enters her picture in a magazine beauty contest and wins, but only because her rival for the man she truly loves has replaced her picture with that of a flawlessly beautiful Gibson Girl–type model. Sue's predilection for drama is evidenced early in the film, when she acts out melodramatic scenes involving sheiks and exaggerated swoons, but Normand's, and by extension Sue's, talent for comedy overshadows her attempts at drama. Once she arrives in Hollywood the studio head refuses to sign Sue to a contract and instead offers her a job in the costume department, but eventually she is able to make a screen test. Although she is testing for a drama, Sue is consistently, albeit unintentionally, funny. After stepping in gum she gets a brick stuck to her shoe, and then she sits on a workman's dirty glove, leaving a black handprint on her white bloomers. Entering the scene for another take she bends over, causing her hoop skirt to fly up and flashing her bloomers—complete with the handprint on her rear—to the assembled cast and crew, who howl with laughter (Figure 1.3). Unaware of the source of the comedy, Sue is nevertheless encouraged by the reaction to her screen test, gushing to her beau (Ralph Graves) that "the director said I was just naturally funny." Sue's unintentionally comic performance is reminiscent of the press accounts of Polly Moran and Louise Fazenda as uneasy chorines; like Sue, their attempts to join the ranks of serious actors are thwarted by their irrepressibly comic personalities. And while it may seem that Sue is the unwitting object of the crew's laughter—in

Figure 1.3. Sue Graham (Mabel Normand) displays her comic side in *The Extra Girl* (1923).

other words that the crew is laughing *at* her rather than *with* her—it is not apparent from the film that this is entirely the case. The director's comment that Sue is "naturally funny" is complimentary and indicates that he sees her as a comedienne, and therefore his (and, presumably, the rest of the crew's) laughter can be seen as appreciative rather than derisive. Also, the audience's extradiegetic knowledge of Mabel Normand as a successful and highly praised comedienne could potentially mitigate their response to this scene, as their laughter at Normand's performance would be echoed by the fictional crew's laughter at Sue's screen test. If the audience was laughing at Normand's skillful comic performance, then it's certainly possible that they would interpret the on-screen crew as appreciating Sue's antics on a similar level.

Like *The Extra Girl*, *Show People* centers on an aspiring dramatic actress—Peggy Pepper (Davies)—who is better suited for comedy. Arriving at a studio casting office with her father, Peggy puts on an impromptu audition, showcasing "the various moods"—meditation, passion, anger, sorrow, joy—by holding a handkerchief in front of her face and then lowering it to show her changed expressions. Although Peggy is quite earnest in her attempt at drama, the casting director laughs and tells her she's "very funny," the first indication within the narrative that she is a natural comedienne. Peggy's first experience before the camera resembles Sue's, in that the comedy she creates is inadvertent. Although Peggy's first film is a slapstick comedy, she believes she's appearing in a drama, and even recites some lines from a stage melodrama for the director before he begins shooting. When she enters the scene, however, she's sprayed in the face with seltzer water; outraged, she responds by throwing anything within reach at the other actors. As everyone laughs at her bravura performance she begins to cry and runs off the set, and when her friend Billy (William Haines) follows her she sobs, "I came here to do drama. Why didn't you tell me it was this?" Billy gently helps Peggy reapply her makeup as he comforts her, reminding her that "all the stars have had to take it on the chin—Swanson, Daniels, Lloyd—all of them." Peggy's sense of shame is palpable, and Billy's attempts to console her and prepare her for the next take are both tender and unsettling, as he paints her face while reassuring her that "it'll be easy from now on" and urging her to engage in a bodily activity that she finds both distasteful and humiliating. Despite her reservations, Peggy decides to "take it on the chin" and continue in comedy, eventually making a name for herself as a comedienne. However, when the chance comes to leave comedy and move to drama she jumps at the opportunity. Her dramatic screen test is the polar opposite of her work in comedy—instead of the physical abandon of slapstick, she is asked to sit in a chair and react as the director feeds her situations. The restricted mobility on-screen finds its parallel in Peggy's offscreen life, as she constrains her true (comedic) personality and instead becomes the pretentiously elegant Patricia Pepoire.

Although Peggy Pepper is uncertain about comedy, *Show People* is not. From the film's beginning it's clear to viewers that Peggy was meant for comedy, and, as with Sue Graham, even when she's engaged in "serious" drama she's funny. Furthermore, the film can be seen as a comment on Davies's own career, as she alternated comedies with historical dramas despite the fact that many critics thought she was a natural and very talented comedienne; the year *Show People* was released *Photoplay* called Davies "a superb comedienne," and *Variety* said that she "does some really great comedy work."[86] The film's happy ending doesn't just involve the romantic union between Peggy and Billy; it also involves Peggy abandoning her highbrow dramas and embracing her comic nature—"the *real*

Peggy Pepper" that the studio head lamented was lost in her high-class pictures. The film finds a generic middle ground for Peggy in a World War I film directed by King Vidor (who also directed *Show People*). An unmistakable reference to Vidor's blockbuster *The Big Parade* (1925), this fictional war film would be a far cry from the knockabout slapstick that started Peggy's career. However, *The Big Parade* (as well as Vidor's *The Crowd* [1928], released a few months before *Show People*) made liberal use of comedy scenes and moments, setting it apart from the humorless melodramas favored by Peggy. And so by turning to Vidor-style drama-with-comedy, Peggy can live out her dramatic aspirations while still indulging her natural flair for comedy.

Ella Cinders features another take on the trope of a woman whose natural humor stands in the way of her dramatic ambitions. In a retelling of the Cinderella tale based on a comic strip, Ella (Moore) is abused by her stepmother and stepsisters and lives a life of drudgery. Ella enters her photo in a beauty contest hoping to escape her life by winning a trip to Hollywood and a movie contract, but unbeknownst to her the picture submitted by the photographer was taken at the moment a fly landed on her nose (Figure 1.4). Instead of the glamorous portrait Ella had hoped to submit, her contest photo instead features her scrunching up her face and looking cross-eyed at the fly. Despite this, she wins the contest—as the fire chief/judge tells her, "Beauty means nothin'. We firemen see the best-lookin' wimmin at their worst. The movies needs newer and funnier faces." She is initially hurt by the thought that people are laughing at her but is reassured when her beau reminds her, "Not everyone can make people laugh, Ella. It's a great thing—making people happy." Although Ella worries that her outdated clothing and plain appearance would handicap her in the beauty contest, her natural humor—demonstrated earlier in the film when she's seen clowning around to entertain children that she's babysitting—is what sets her apart from the more conventionally attractive but humorless contestants and sends her to Hollywood. And while Ella eventually finds success in dramatic pictures, not comedies, Colleen Moore turns in an exceptional comedic performance in this and many other films, a fact that complicates the message of the film. Ella's natural flair for comedy—whether intentional or not—leads to her success as a dramatic actress, a plot point that would seem to privilege drama over comedy within the diegesis. However, Colleen Moore's extradiegetic commercial and artistic success as a comic actress provided a clear example of a funny woman who preferred to make a career in comedies.

Magazine and newspaper articles frequently emphasized the willingness of

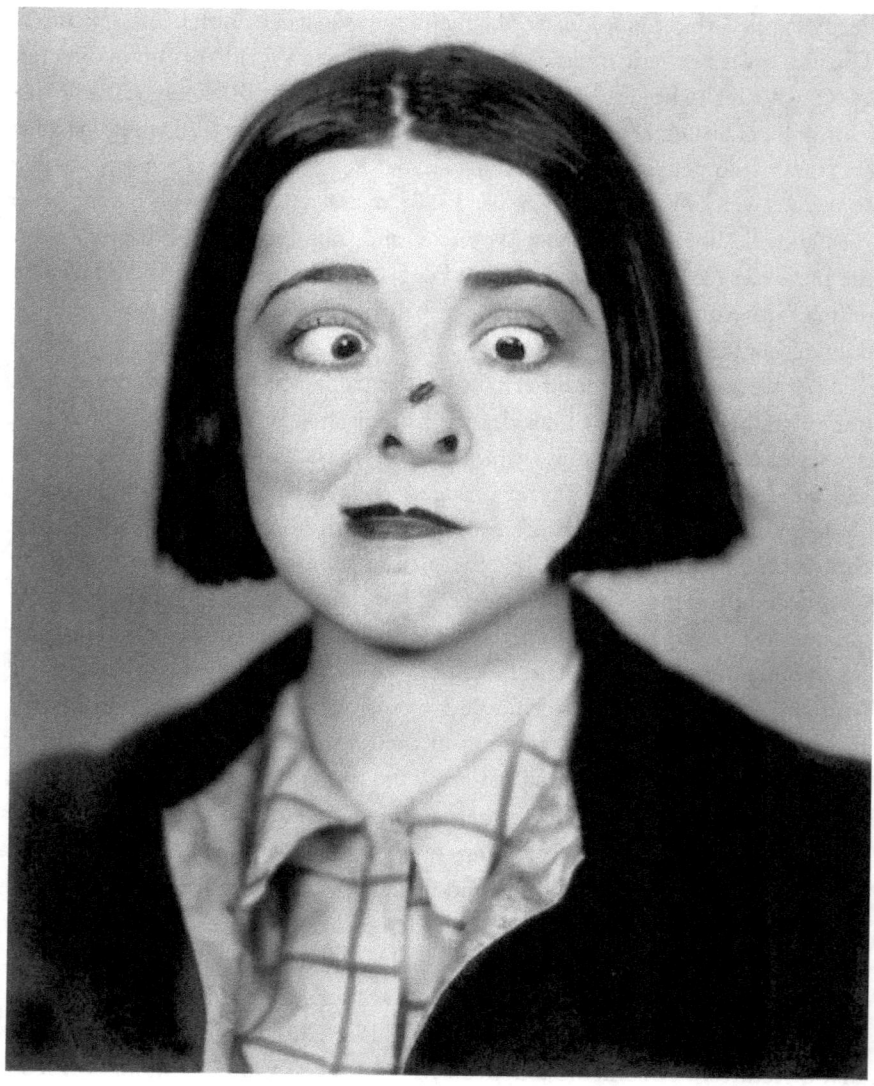

Figure 1.4. Colleen Moore in *Ella Cinders* (1926).

comediennes to embrace their comedic talents and in fact oftentimes claimed that their senses of humor left them better prepared to deal with the world around them. Being a funny woman wasn't always seen as entirely positive by either the comediennes themselves or the press; as I'll discuss later in this chapter and in chapter 2 comediennes were, for a variety of reasons, often ambivalent about performing comedy. But for many of these women performing comedy was presented as a logical and welcome career given their supposed natural inclination toward humor. In an article titled "Don't Fight against Nature," Charlotte Greenwood's advice to aspiring comic actresses is to embrace and develop their funny side: "it's a great mistake for a comedienne to pay any attention to Shaw or Shakespeare. She must just make up her mind to be funny and let it go at that, no matter what her family or Sunday school teacher may think."[87] For Greenwood, women shouldn't fight against their true selves and waste their time with drama if their proclivity is for comedy. Greenwood's advice can be applied to the career of stage comedienne Beatrice Lillie, who, according to *Motion Picture Magazine*, was a born comedienne but tried to suppress her natural good humor in order to find work as a serious actress. After a string of rejections, Lillie decided to change her tactic before visiting theater impresario Andre Charlot:

> All right, she would see Charlot—but not as she had seen the others. She would be herself for once. She threw away her solemnity as one discards a mask—what an ill-fitting mask it was that Beatrice had worn so long. Faith in herself swung gaily back into her heart. Thus Charlot was the first theatrical manager to see, and hear, the real Beatrice Lillie. She mocked, and ridiculed. She sang "with gestures." She walked out onto that stage as *herself*, and left the theater with a contract.[88]

According to this account, Lillie wasn't "herself" until she dropped the mock solemnity and embraced comedy. As was the case with Greenwood, Fazenda, Moore, and numerous other comediennes, Lillie's success comes only after she decides to drop any pretense of becoming a "serious" actress and accepts her natural comic talent. These discourses, then, contradict the essentialist argument that women were biologically excluded from humor. Instead, they argue that women could, in fact, be naturally predisposed toward comedy and even encourage women to find and embrace their comedic voice.

At the same time, although comediennes' performances came across as spontaneous and effortless on-screen, and were sometimes attributed to natural inclination, fan and trade magazines were often quick to point out that their comedy was actually the result of a great deal of work and deliberation on the part of the actresses. Comedy was frequently presented as skilled work, and comedians, both male and female, were depicted as honing their techniques through years of practice and study. When discussing female comedians, these discourses demonstrate an appreciation for women's labor and argue that women were actively involved in crafting their comic personae and developing their talents to achieve maximum financial and artistic success. Comediennes, according to these stories, excelled at comedy as a result of their own hard work.[89] Combined with stories about women being "naturally funny," these discourses provide an overall picture of comediennes as craftswomen who honed their natural talents to rise to the top of their chosen profession. They also provided an air of legitimacy and professionalism to women who were engaged in this supposedly unfeminine pursuit.

Numerous articles and interviews discussed, in detail, the nuts and bolts process of creating comedy. Articles described how comediennes thought up gags and comic situations, designed their costumes and makeup, and invented characters. These articles emphasize the craft and labor involved in film comedy and simultaneously express respect for comediennes while giving advice and information to readers who might aspire to be comic performers themselves. Many comediennes gave long and detailed talks about their views of comedy and what it took to incite laughter from the audience. Quoted in *Moving Picture Weekly*, Alice Howell expresses a thorough understanding of the mechanics of film comedy:

> Your whole body must work with you. The idea is to exaggerate just in the right place. You know how just one comic touch in the middle of a serious situation will upset everybody's gravity, like a very feeble joke in church, which makes everybody helpless with laughter. Well, that is the principle in a comic make up, indeed of all good comedy. Otherwise it is just senseless slapstick stuff, with all the absurdity dragged in by the hair. That sort of thing never makes people laugh really hard. An inch is a very small thing, except on the end of your nose. That is the principle in a nutshell.[90]

Howell's detailed description of how screen comedy works positions her as a knowledgeable artist, someone who thought through her character and routines. While Howell was described in the press as being a "natural" comedienne, her hard work was also recognized as contributing to her talent, as in this 1916 review: "Alice is not only a true artist, but a funny one as well, about as funny as a highly perfected technic [*sic*] and a most delightful natural humor can make her."[91] The idea of comediennes actively intellectualizing and crafting their innate talents and honing their comic technique is a far cry from the passive and instinctual humor that many attributed to women. The press emphasized the work of comediennes in perfecting their comedy and praised them for their successes. One writer insisted of Charlotte Greenwood, "She makes you laugh because she is a finished comedienne and she knows what she is about every moment. . . . She is funny because she has studied and perfected herself in the art of being funny."[92] Mabel Normand revealed that when she visited New York, she would go to the Lower East Side to get ideas for her characters: "Perhaps I see a character that strikes me as funny, either in deportment or way of dressing. Perhaps I can copy her costume or some of her odd gestures at a later date, when I'm working in a picture."[93] And Constance Talmadge declared, "The comedienne's head is not so empty as it seems. It is packed with gags, funny scenes, situations and bits of nonsense that life, the greatest moving picture of all, unreels for us."[94] Talmadge, Normand, Greenwood, and Howell are depicted as actively striving to enhance their natural talents and improve their comic techniques through study, practice, and observation and as having a thorough understanding of what they need to do to get a laugh. Overwhelmingly the popular press presented comediennes' labor as commendable and the comediennes themselves as hardworking artists and career women rather than gender transgressors trying to participate in a genre and performance type that they were socially or biologically unsuited for. This is exemplified in a quote from *Motion Picture Magazine* describing how Louise Fazenda was rewarded for her talent and hard work: "So active is her brain in conceiving grotesque and whimsical comedy effects, Mack Sennett has offered to let her direct her own company, the highest tribute that can be paid a film actress."[95] Indeed, Kristine Brunovska Karnick has found that "the labor involved in creating successful comedy was a prevalent and deliberate motif in profiles of Fazenda. Such approaches often began with nods to her intelligence."[96] Moreover, in articles such as "How to Be a Comedienne," "How to Be Funny," and "Have YOU Got the Makings of a COMEDIAN?"[97] fan magazines encouraged readers, the majority of whom were female, to dream of trying comedy for themselves and potentially achieving the kind of success enjoyed by Fazenda, Talmadge, Normand, and other screen comediennes.

When writers praised comediennes for their hard work, talent, and skill, they often insisted that comedy is more difficult to perform than drama. Numerous articles maintained that comic work was more strenuous than dramatic and less certain to succeed with audiences. In a typical quote, *Motion Picture Magazine* told its readers, "To be a good screen comedienne is harder, they say, than to be a tragedienne. If so, Miss Dorothy [Gish] has bridged the difficulty with ease," while another article insisted that Charlotte Greenwood "could, if she wished, be the Queen in *Hamlet* or Lady Macbeth, but that is not nearly as difficult as being the sort of comedienne Miss Greenwood is." Colleen Moore recalled director Mervyn LeRoy expressing a similar sentiment, declaring that "an onion can make any actress cry, but the vegetable has yet to be grown that can make her funny."[98] Part of the reason for the supposed difficulty was said to be the physical toll of performing comedy. Louise Fazenda described the difference when she returned to slapstick in 1924 after appearing in light comedies and dramas for a year:

> Physically and mentally it is so much harder than drama that there is no comparison. . . . Before I had appeared playing it "straight" I had heard actors talking about a difficult dramatic scene they had done. Especially some of the girls, as they told of spending an hour or so shedding tears for the camera. But that is only for one scene. Comedy is one steady grind from first to last. We fun-makers have to hold up the business for laughs. There is no story, only the slightest scaffolding to which the "gags" are attached and we must be responsible for those "gags" for the most part, and furnish hilarity as we go along.[99]

Comic actors also could never be sure of the audience's reaction to a gag. As Constance Talmadge wrote, "Certain dramatic situations—big love scenes, exciting rescues, moments of poignant suffering—are almost sure-fire, but there is nothing absolutely sure about comedy." Louise Fazenda similarly stated that "you have to go a lot farther for a laugh than you do a weep. They weep from their eyes but they laugh from their hearts, and the farther you go the harder it is."[100] Articles such as these that highlighted the difficulties in playing comedy and the uncertainties in audience response implicitly praised comediennes for being able to rise above the issues intrinsic to the genre.

Articles that discussed the comparative difficulties of comedy versus drama sometimes referenced the stereotype that women are inherently emotional to illustrate the challenge that comediennes faced. If women were, in fact, more emotional than men, it would follow that actresses would be better suited to drama than comedy. Comediennes, then, were depicted as facing hardships beyond the standard difficulties of gags, tone, and audience reaction. An article from the mid-1910s sums up this line of thinking:

> Comedy, as a rule, is the hardest sort of work of the theatrical profession. There is an old saying that any woman can be a great emotional actress because she is naturally emotional to start with, but that it requires a great many brains and a world of hard work to become a good comedienne.[101]

While women's "natural" tendency toward emotion apparently makes them ideal dramatic actresses, the implication here is that women don't naturally possess the brains or the fortitude to excel at comedy. This would certainly make an already difficult genre even harder although, as noted earlier, the press was quick to praise comediennes for their skillful comic technique. What could have been a reiteration of the sexist stereotype about women's inability to appreciate humor becomes in these discourses an acknowledgment of comediennes' ability to use their intellect, determination, and natural comedic talents to succeed in a "masculine" genre.

The popular press, then, recognized comediennes as skilled artists who were able to succeed in a difficult genre. Very often, writers expressed their praise by comparing comediennes to popular male comics. Alice Howell, Polly Moran, Mabel Normand, Marion Davies, Colleen Moore, Beatrice Lillie, and Marie Dressler were among the many comediennes who were described as feminine versions of Charlie Chaplin. Harold Lloyd, Harry Langdon, and Douglas Fairbanks were also frequently mentioned in these same terms. And so Davies "combines Charlie Chaplin's pathos with Harry Langdon's drollery and adds the breeziness of Harold Lloyd for good measure," Howell was apparently "aspiring to be the feminine edition of Charlie Chaplin," Normand "proves herself the feminine and artistically concentrated essence of a Chaplin-Fairbanks combination of humor and agility," Lillie's "technique at times closely resembles her compatriot, Charlie Chaplin," and Moore "is positively Chaplinesque in her quite brilliant portrayal of . . . 'Ella Cinders.'"[102] While these comparisons were meant to be complimentary, they also reinforced the notion that male comedians were the standard by which female comics should be measured and implied that women's achievements could only be recognized in terms of how they compared to those of men. Furthermore, the fact that male comedians are used as the standard of comic virtuosity supports the stereotype that there are no good female comedians. Although the point of these comparisons was, no doubt, to praise comediennes in the highest terms possible, those terms ultimately position them as lesser comics, aspiring to join the ranks of Chaplin, Lloyd, or Langdon. Not all comediennes were pleased with these comparisons; as Alice

Howell said, "I don't want any bestowed glory. . . . I am just as much a star in my own way as the well-known male funmakers."[103]

"Clowns with Aching Hearts"

In 1934 Louise Fazenda, one of the most popular and acclaimed comediennes of the silent era, was asked by *Movie Classic* to explain what it takes to become a comedian. Her response revealed a profound uneasiness toward comedy:

> The making of a comedian—a woman comedian, at least—comes from hurt feelings. No woman on earth wants to be funny. No woman on earth wants to be laughed at. In fact, the last thing on earth any woman wants is to be considered funny. I believe that every comedienne is the child of an inner tragedy. I don't know if all of the funny men are "clowns with aching hearts," but I do know that all funny women are, if they'll be honest about it—[104]

Fazenda's feelings of pain and disappointment about performing comedy were well-documented throughout her career, and her image as a reluctant comedienne became an important part of her offscreen persona.[105] But Fazenda was not the only comedienne who was said to be ambivalent about her profession. Articles in fan magazines with titles such as "Is It Tragic to Be Comic?" and "The Tragedy of Being Funny"[106] situated comediennes as victims—of their circumstances, their talents, and their looks—and films such as *Show People* and *Ella Cinders* to some degree supported the idea that being a funny woman was cause for pity as well as praise. This dynamic is perfectly illustrated in a *Motion Picture Classic* profile of Polly Moran:

> Is it tragic to be comic? Would *you* like to be laughed at everywhere, all the time? No matter what you might say or do? No matter how you might feel?
>
> Mustn't there be moments when a comic would like to be taken seriously?
>
> And especially if the comic in question is a woman. Like—well, like Polly Moran.
>
> What do you suppose it *does* feel like to have the whole world know you as a ridiculous individual who can make it split its sides, but never break its heart?[107]

These discourses indicate the uneasy marriage of two disparate lines of thought—that femininity and comedy were incompatible, and that comediennes were skilled artists with a natural talent for comedy. This tension shows up in interviews and articles in which comediennes describe their uneasiness with comedy, relate their initial dismay at discovering their comic tendencies, and discuss their desire to "graduate" to drama or move away from "vulgar" slapstick. However, despite the "tragic" nature of comedy, a great many comediennes were ultimately depicted as happy with the opportunity to perform comedy, indicating a tacit approval of funny women by the press and the comediennes themselves.

If comediennes were born funny, they weren't always said to be pleased with their "natural" gifts. Reflecting the popular debates over femininity and comedy, comediennes were sometimes described as feeling shock and anguish when they first discovered that they were funny, as if admitting the presence of a sense of humor was tantamount to admitting the absence of femininity. As one writer phrased it, "It took Charlotte Greenwood six years to learn that she was funny. It took another year to reconcile herself to the idea."[108] The thought that Greenwood would have to "reconcile herself" to a trait that was the key to her fame and fortune indicates the extent to which women could have internalized negative stereotypes about being funny. Rather than seeing a sense of humor as a positive trait, it's presented as something that a woman must reluctantly come to terms with. As such, certain press discourses argue that women turn to comedy only as a last resort, like Greenwood, who "didn't start out in life to become a comedienne. Few comediennes do."[109] Similarly, Louise Fazenda describes her early attempts at drama and their disastrously comedic results:

> When I started into pictures I had the idea I could act; you know what I mean, highbrow stuff and dramatic things, and romantic pictures. The director gave me several bits in straight dramas but I always managed to ball things up. I was so awkward I was always falling over my feet or somebody else's feet, and once I ruined a whole scene by falling down a flight of stairs.
>
> Things like that happened right along, until it got to be a joke that I'd mess up any "bit" that was given me and turn it into comedy—unconsciously. At last I was kindly but firmly told that I had missed my vocation, which might be comedy, but which assuredly was not drama.[110]

These stories about Greenwood and Fazenda share a common narrative of the comedienne's dismay over the discovery of her humor and eventual reluctant acceptance. As such, they encapsulate both sides of the debates of women's humor—the idea that women could not (and should not) be funny and the notion that some women are born comediennes. That Greenwood and Fazenda were both slapstick comediennes is important to note, as their aptitude for physical comedy would have positioned them, in the press and in the public's imagination, further from popular conceptions of ideal femininity than light comediennes. Their reported consternation when faced with their comic tendencies could be explained by this gap between ideal femininity and the apparently degraded femininity that these comediennes saw themselves as possessing.[111]

Not surprisingly, given the cultural prejudices against women performing comedy, many actresses who began their careers as comediennes were only too glad to "graduate" to drama, what *Photoplay* in 1920 described as comediennes' "usual stunt of forsaking comedy for drama."[112] Like the main characters in *Ella Cinders*, *Show People*, and *The Extra Girl*, comedy was frequently depicted as a sort of generic ghetto for women, a starting point that must be abandoned as soon as possible if one had any hopes of becoming a legitimate actress. The fact that this general predisposition against comedy existed alongside descriptions of comedy as more difficult and requiring more skill than drama, and stories of comic actresses who cheerfully rejected drama in favor of comedy, indicates the depth of the ambivalence felt by the press, the film industry, audiences, and the actresses themselves toward the genre. A quote by Fay Tincher sums up these feelings:

> I hoped to again play "heavies" or even ingénue leads, but my reputation as a comedienne always caught up with me and finally forced me to play in two-reel funnicisms.
>
> Now at last I am to appear in roles I really care for. Screen farce has never appealed to me. Comedy is, at best, a transitory entertainment that seldom lingers in a person's mind after it is over. Drama is a different matter. Drama affects—for drama is life. That is why I want to play in dramas again—I want to portray life.[113]

Tincher's expressed feelings toward comedy approach contempt, as she describes being "forced" to appear in comedy shorts and dismisses comedy as "transitory entertainment." This disdain certainly wasn't limited to female comics, as comedy in general was often thought to be a less desirable genre, whether it featured the work of men or women. But when understood alongside the existing notion that most women were naturally suited to drama, and that drama was a more fitting genre for properly feminine women, one can see that the stakes for women performing comedy were higher than for men. The supposed incompatibility of femininity and humor, coupled with the general perception of comedy as lowbrow, led to the uncomfortable possibility of comediennes being regarded as lacking in both femininity and class. It's not surprising, then, that many comediennes echoed Tincher in expressing their eagerness to abandon the slums of comedy for the lofty perches of refined drama. Dorothy Devore told *Motion Picture Magazine*, "Of course, I do not want to remain in comedies always. . . . So many comedy girls have stepped right into dramatic work and that is where you'll see me some day," and the *Morning Telegraph* let readers know that Bebe Daniels "accepted less money than she was getting with [Pathé] in order to get away from comedies and get into the serious side of picture making."[114] A 1924 article on Devore spelled out the strategy of many actresses who started in comedy, describing her as "another of the young women film stars who is going to use her training in the comedy school as a stepping stone to the heavier dramatic roles in the silent drama."[115] Along with reporting on comediennes' desires to leave comedy, the press often implicitly passed judgment on the genre through the language it used, referring to Constance Talmadge's pictures as "mere refined comedy" and Gale Henry as "just a comedienne," and describing dramatic films as "important pictures" and "more ambitious things" and a dramatic performer as "a real actress."[116]

Some comediennes expressed an awareness of the unique difficulties that female comics faced as they tried to reconcile their gender with their genre and blamed this for the fact that male comedians were both more numerous and more successful in Hollywood. Bebe Daniels told a reporter, "I don't believe a girl can ever attain the success that a man can as a comedian. That is one of the reasons why I wanted to play the serious roles."[117] Constance Talmadge apparently agreed with Daniels's somewhat pessimistic assessment:

> People often wonder why so few actresses in Hollywood take up comedy as their métier. While there are fully a dozen well-known comedians, the screen comediennes who have reached stardom are few indeed. It is probably this very necessity for being a little ridiculous to get good comic scenes that results in there being so many more comedians than comediennes. Women are afraid of being laughed at—no matter how good-natured the merriment—and look forward to graduating as soon as possible from the comedy class.[118]

The reason Talmadge gives for women's lack of interest in performing comedy goes back to the idea that the genre is inherently unfeminine. "Being laughed at"—as the instigator, rather than the butt, of the joke—requires a willingness to put oneself on display and demand attention, to be "a little ridiculous." But unlike the passive and sexually objectified "to-be-looked-at" mode of display that Laura Mulvey describes as the inescapable position for women in classical Hollywood cinema, comic display is aggressive and assertive.[119] The necessity of—and anxieties about—stepping outside the bounds of traditional femininity to participate in what many considered a lowbrow genre could certainly have been a reason why so many comediennes left comedy for drama and is a demonstration of the pervasiveness of concerns about comedy's supposed incompatibility with femininity.

The ambivalence that many comediennes felt toward performing comedy was not only evidenced by their high rate of defection to dramatic films. In fact, many comediennes built their entire careers around comedy films, making few, if any, dramas. However, just as some saw comedy as a whole as a sort of generic ghetto, others perceived a hierarchy among different types of comedy, with light comedy viewed as far more respectable than slapstick. As I discussed earlier, women had a complicated relationship to slapstick; although physical comedy was considered lowbrow and at odds with proper feminine behavior, slapstick comediennes such as Louise Fazenda and Polly Moran were popular with audiences. Until the early 1910s slapstick was by far the predominant mode of comedy found on-screen, but by the mid-1910s longer film lengths and the growing reliance on intertitles for jokes allowed for more complicated plots and comedy based more on situation than on gags and stunts. This shift coincided with the film industry's drive for respectability, as slapstick was generally seen as lowbrow, especially when compared to light comedy.[120] Just as the attractions-based cinema of the early twentieth century was eclipsed by longer narrative films, and the shocks and thrills of the serial-queen melodramas eventually fell out of style, slapstick routines were largely absorbed into situation-based comedies, although this process was neither uncomplicated nor complete. Writing about slapstick shorts in the 1920s, Donald Crafton describes a "calculated rupture" between narrative and gags, "designed to keep the two elements antagonistically apart," as the gags served to disrupt and subvert the larger narrative.[121] Henry Jenkins and Tom Gunning see a less fraught relationship between gags and narrative, as Gunning argues that "gags become absorbed into the narrative economy of most films, marking perhaps an excess, but an excess that is necessary to the film's process of containment."¹²² This symbiotic relationship between gag and narrative is evidenced by the fact that both male and female comics continued to incorporate physical comedy into their films throughout the 1920s, although by the late 1910s comediennes were increasingly vocal about their desire to leave slapstick for "comedy-drama," or "comedies with a little drama, a laugh, followed by a tear perhaps, and capped with a laugh."¹²³ While the popularity of comediennes in the 1910s proved that audiences would accept women performing slapstick, by the end of the decade many female comics were clearly interested in finding a way to reconcile their comedy work with popular conceptions of femininity.

Comediennes frequently referred to "refinement" and "dignity" when discussing their preference for comedy-drama over slapstick. Mabel Normand explained in 1916 that "she wants to be a trifle more serious and dignified than they have allowed her to be in the Keystone comedies. She says comedy does not altogether consist of falling downstairs and throwing custard pies, and she believes that she can be just as funny in more dignified situations."¹²⁴ Dorothy Devore echoed this sentiment when she explained that "a starring comedienne cannot afford to be anything but a perfect lady," and "the kicking, punching and slapping which an audience 'eats up' when a man is the purveyor or recipient just doesn't go with a leading woman on the screen."¹²⁵ Both Normand and Devore position slapstick comedy as undignified and unladylike, recalling debates about whether physical comedy was appropriate for women and whether lowbrow humor had a place in refined cinema. The much-maligned pie became a symbol for coarse and unseemly humor: the extent of comediennes' opposition to broad physical comedy can be seen in Fay Tincher's forceful reply to a reporter who asks if she will make movies "of the 'custard pie' variety."

> "Never!" Fay Tincher declared. "A laugh isn't precious enough to resort to that (and besides I don't think Mr. Hoover would approve of such a waste of pies.) I shall strive to get them—the laughs, I mean, legitimately or not at all. Of course comedy-drama is my aim."¹²⁶

Tincher's response implies that the laughs generated by slapstick comedy are illegitimate and therefore unthinkable for a woman of dignity to pursue. This line of thinking represents a compromise of sorts for female comics. By denigrating slapstick as lowbrow and coarse and simultaneously praising comedy-drama as dignified and refined, comediennes could continue to perform comedy while retaining an acceptably feminine appearance. For comediennes wary about slapstick's link to suspect femininity, light comedy and comedy-drama offered a more refined alternative.

In many cases, the difference between slapstick and comedy-drama was context, as Tincher explained in 1916:

> True comedy . . . [is] just in the situation itself—in the meaning of the situation. For example, there's nothing funny about getting hit in the face with a pie, if there's no reason for it. No, it's the innocent person getting in wrong somewhere thru [*sic*] some blunder he isn't conscious of, but which the audience knows all about, that makes a thing really funny.[127]

Just as narrative was gradually being privileged over thrills in the cinema as a whole, in comedy situation was taking precedence over gags. Anita Loos described this as a "comedy of ideas," in which "the action grows naturally out of the thoughts and emotions of the main characters, as in any literature." Or, as Constance Talmadge put it, "in the old days the best actors were the ones who could climb, and jump, and run best, but now Miss Loos' scenarios let us jump only to conclusions."[128] Loos's reference to literature certainly recalls the ongoing efforts within the motion picture industry to redefine itself as refined entertainment. It's not surprising, then, that comediennes would make a similar move from attraction-based slapstick to narrative-based comedy-drama. While the comediennes who were closely linked to slapstick had a more difficult time leaving their old antics behind—Gale Henry sighed that she was "trying to get away from the pie-throwing type of picture . . . but it seems as if the comedy fan never tires of an artistic fall off a cliff, or a good free-for-all chase"[129]—others were able to easily transition to the "comedy of ideas," and ultimately situation-based comedy-drama would become the dominant mode of comedy.

And yet, as writers, critics, social conservatives, and even some comediennes were debating the range and value of women's humor, many female comics made it clear that they embraced comedy. Newspapers and fan magazines often described comediennes' pleasure in performing comedy and in making people laugh, and, paradoxically, even comediennes who reportedly wanted to abandon comedy in favor of drama were, at times, said to be delighted with comic work. In 1916 Fay Tincher described to *Motion Picture Magazine* the qualities necessary to succeed in the movie business:

> A girl has got to have a sense of humor in order to get into Motion Pictures. No one ever succeeded at the first shot. You have got to keep trying and trying until the ordeal becomes funny, and after a while you'll land. If you take it too seriously, you will find it a cruel experience.[130]

Though a sense of humor could be seen as troublesome for women, as Tincher points out it could also be beneficial. While the most obvious reason for this contradiction has to do with the needs of press agents and studio publicity departments when promoting a new film—an actress's relative love of comedy or drama would certainly rise or fall depending on the genre of her latest picture—it also reflects the broader societal ambivalence surrounding women and comedy. Very few, if any, comediennes were said to be entirely comfortable with comedy throughout their careers. Instead they were generally depicted as conflicted in some way, whether uneasy about performing physical comedy, uncomfortable with their character makeup and costumes, or afraid of looking ridiculous in public. None of this is surprising, given how controversial the discourses surrounding women's humor were. If simply having a sense of humor raised doubts about a woman's femininity, then actively engaging in comic performances could be seen as an affront to and unraveling of traditional gender roles. For the press, fans, and comediennes to show a certain degree of ambivalence or unease about female comics, then, is understandable. At the same time, the fact that many comediennes embraced comedy can be read as an act of rebellion, however minor. Even if their stated love of comedy was followed up, on the release of their next dramatic film, by lengthy discussions of their preference for drama, and even if they were depicted as "clowns with aching hearts" longing to have their dramatic talents discovered, when comediennes were said to enjoy performing comedy they were publicly declaring that women could be unapologetically funny, actively creating humor rather than being the passive butt of the joke. As Tincher's quote illustrates, humor could be an important asset for women.

The image of the "tragic comedienne"—the performer who longs to trade the indignities of comedy for the refinement of drama—was repeated in the press so often that it became a sort of stereotype. As such, the press was quick to draw attention to comediennes who contradicted that stereotype in claiming that they were happy with comedy. Colleen Moore's reported preference for comedy over drama was said to be "reversing the familiar situation which has robbed the comedy concerns of so many of their leading luminaries."[131] In explaining her affinity for comedy, Moore referenced the belief that women were inherently more emotional than men:

> I would rather play comedy than anything else, even if it is more difficult. Practically all women are emotional. They can cry and pound the door and create a rumpus, but few can make people laugh. That is what I want to do. A genuine comedy scene must be studied and worked and felt.[132]

Rather than acquiescing to her "feminine" emotions, Moore embraces the challenge that comedy supposedly presents, and in so doing she disrupts traditional ideas of what women can and can't do. If, as many people thought, women were biologically programmed to be emotional and therefore suited to drama, then Moore's rejection of drama and clear preference for comedy is, ultimately, a rejection of biologically determined gender roles. Moore was clearly aware of the fact that women were supposed to be emotional, and therefore drawn to drama, but by choosing comedy she was refuting that idea. Certainly Moore's stated preference for comedy was not a grand statement in support of women's rights or their changing place in society, and the fact that she performed in light comedies meant that she was already performing a more "properly" feminine mode of comedy than slapstick. It was, however, a subtle but clear message that women didn't have to passively accept the gender roles that were assigned to them and that they could instead create roles for themselves based on their own talents and inclinations.

This is reinforced by other comediennes who similarly expressed a preference for comedy over drama. At the conclusion of a 1920 interview with Gale Henry, a *Photoplay* writer "realized with amazement that the interview seemed to be nearing an end and Miss Henry hadn't said a word about how she longed to make really big, serious pictures. . . . Gale Henry was content to stick to comedy."[133] Another writer noted that Constance Talmadge "refused to live up to the tradition that all motion picture actresses long to make massive productions of the classics" and that she was, as she herself put it, "pretty satisfied with the parts I have."[134] Recalling her beginnings in drama with D. W. Griffith, Colleen Moore said that she "didn't really care for tragic parts":

> I have always believed that laughter is so much greater than tears. It is easy enough to make your audience cry by mere experience and ability, but the gift of humour comes spontaneously and to few. I have always

coveted it for myself. That is why I was glad of the opportunity to put my ambitions to the test under Al Christie, and I enjoyed every moment of my time with him, as a pure comedienne.[135]

Certainly these stories about comediennes who were satisfied with their line of work were complicated by the many stories of comediennes who couldn't wait to leave the genre behind. However, when the press described women who were content to play comedy they often wrote of their personal satisfaction with the genre, an approach that makes sense given the claims of many fan magazines that comedians, both male and female, were born funny. Comedy, in this viewpoint, was a logical and fulfilling mode of expression for people with an innate sense of humor, a view that perhaps seems obvious today but that was somewhat revolutionary for women in the early twentieth century given the very vocal critics who felt that proper ladies couldn't and shouldn't be funny. A declaration by Charlotte Greenwood, then, that "I love my work because I love to hear my audiences laugh and I love to laugh myself" or by Constance Talmadge that the films she wants to make are "Comedies, always comedies"[136] confirms that women could unapologetically enjoy and engage in comedy, despite concerns about dignity and femininity. In fact, as Fay Tincher's quote about needing a sense of humor to succeed in motion pictures indicates, humor could be an effective way for women to face challenges and adversity. Fan magazines encouraged female fans to take their cues from comediennes and similarly see humor as a valuable asset. In a profile of Marie Dressler *Photoplay* told its readers, "If you get depressed because there are wrinkles just beginning to show around your eyes take a look at Marie. Sure, she has wrinkles. They got there from laughing," and *Motion Picture Classic* assured fans that Polly Moran "is a woman who may find it, now and then, tragic to be comic, but who is wise enough to know that it is a good deal more comic to be tragic."[137] By highlighting the fact that many comediennes enjoyed performing comedy and appreciated humor, fan magazines and comediennes themselves were contradicting pervasive sexist discourses about women and comedy and showing fans that a sense of humor was a welcome, and even admirable, quality.

The very presence of women performing comedy onstage and in motion pictures in the first decades of the twentieth century was a strong argument against those who said that women were incapable of understanding and appreciating humor. While some critics used essentialist arguments to prove that women's close link to nature meant that humor was out of their reach, others used those same types of arguments to claim that women's inherent sensitivity and highly charged emotions meant that they could only enjoy refined and gentle humor. Comediennes contradicted both of these notions, as they not only performed comedy, they often performed rough-and-tumble, lowbrow slapstick, the very type of comedy that was assumed to offend women's delicate sensibilities.

By contradicting essentialist notions of what kind of comedy (if any) women were supposed to enjoy, early twentieth-century comediennes were disrupting the familiar narrative about what women were capable of and how they should behave. While the idealized femininity posited by critics of women's humor was dignified and refined, supportive rather than creative, and passive rather than active, the type of femininity that comediennes performed, both on-screen and off, was assertive, intelligent, and unruly. Although many comediennes were said to be ambivalent about comedy, their ambivalence reflected broader concerns in American society about appropriate behavior for women. The fact that so many actresses chose to stay in comedy, despite any concerns they may have had about the genre, would have sent a strong message to fans that women didn't have to restrict themselves to appropriate behavior as defined by others.

2

"An Inferiority Complex in a One-Piece Bathing Suit"

BEAUTY, FEMININITY, AND COMEDY

> Beauty is not essential in a comedienne, it is merely an asset.
> —*Louise Fazenda, 1916*

In a tongue-in-cheek 1928 *Photoplay* interview with Marie Dressler, the comedienne is asked the question "What is beauty?" After several nonsensical answers—"beauty is a second-hand lawn mower—beauty is a pale green ice-cream cone—beauty is a theater ticket without a stub"—she settles on a definition that seems to satisfy her: "'Whoa!' Marie called. 'I've got it! Beauty is an inferiority complex in a one-piece bathing suit!'"[1] What exactly this means is certainly open to interpretation. What is worthy of examination here is the fact that Dressler would be asked this question at all. Like a great many comediennes in silent film, particularly those performing physical comedy, Dressler was not known for her beauty. However, beauty—whether lack of beauty, desire for beauty, or hiding of natural beauty—was a frequent topic in discussions about silent comediennes.

The concepts of beauty and femininity appear in varied and complex ways in popular discourses surrounding silent comediennes. More than in other genres, comedy created a place for women of all physical types to perform in both featured and leading roles. In this way, comediennes offered a model of femininity that ran counter to the narrow images of beauty perpetuated by Hollywood, but the potential was complicated by a number of factors. The type of comedy performed by a silent comedienne was in many ways determined by her appearance, with conventionally attractive comediennes appearing in light comedies and women who were considered less attractive primarily appearing in slapstick comedies or character roles, often in support of "prettier" comediennes, a strategy that reinforced the prevalent stereotype that women could be either pretty or funny but not both. Furthermore, comediennes who were considered less attractive were frequently positioned as worthy of pity because of their appearance, as fan magazines and studio publicity often presented them as tragic figures who suffered greatly because of their inability to fit into popular conceptions of beauty and femininity. In many ways these discourses perpetuate Hollywood's obsession with female beauty and support the idea that "success" as a woman means living up to high standards of feminine attractiveness.

At the same time, comediennes helped put forward the idea that beauty was not an essential component of femininity and furthermore that "typically" feminine traits such as beauty, modesty, grace, and sensitivity were not automatically available to all women. When slapstick comediennes donned outrageous and unflattering costumes and arranged their hair and makeup to emphasize their less attractive features they were embracing their non-normative appearance and complicating the notion that women should aspire to be beautiful. Furthermore, the theme of transformation used in a number of comedies exposes the work required to acquire and maintain beauty and shows that beauty could be a performed, rather than a natural, trait.

"There Isn't Anything Funny in Her Looks at All"

A pervasive stereotype regarding women's comedy is the idea that beauty and a sense of humor are mutually exclusive traits: as Linda Mizejewski puts it, "'pretty' versus 'funny' is a rough but fairly accurate way to sum up the history of women in comedy."[2] This idea is rooted in the perception, discussed in chapter 1, of comedy as a masculine pursuit, at odds with traditional femininity. In this pretty/funny binary, beauty is equated with appropriate femininity and is therefore seen as incompatible with the creation or enjoyment of comedy. In the logic of this dichotomy, pretty women can't be funny, and funny women can't be pretty. The fact that this stereotype persists to the present day indicates, according to Rebecca Krefting, "just how invested we are as a culture in women's beauty and any activities with potential to compromise women's beauty."[3]

In the nineteenth and early twentieth centuries, beauty was seen as a marker of women's inherent moral superiority.[4] This line of thought meant that beauty was, theoretically, available to any woman who lived a pure and honorable life, as feminist historian Lois Banner argues: "The belief in the moral superiority of women—an ideal central to pre–World War I feminism—was closely connected to democratic beauty ideals. Both feminists and beauty experts argued that spiritual qualities were more important to creating and maintaining the appearance of beauty than were physical attributes. Both argued that beauty was potentially available to any woman, if she followed the proper ethical path."[5] The inverse of this reasoning is that women who didn't follow "the proper ethical path"—including those who engaged in traditionally masculine pursuits—would be excluded from beauty. Banner points to "the belief that intellectual women were invariably 'bluestockings,' that they were incapable of keeping their houses and personal appearances in order, that beauty was an attribute they could never possess," while suffragists were often depicted as mannish and unattractive in anti-suffrage illustrations and in films such as *The Strong Arm Squad of the Future* (ca. 1912) and *The Pickpocket* (1913), starring Flora Finch (Figure 2.1). Like intellectuals and suffragists, funny women transgressed gender boundaries and were therefore thought to be lacking in traditional feminine qualities, including beauty. As Rob King argues, "The female clown suggested both a bodily excess (a negation of the spiritual standards that informed sentimental ideals of womanhood) *and* a bodily lack (a failure to match up to normative standards of beauty)."[6] The notion that outer appearance was linked to inner virtue made the film industry's obsession with beauty particularly troubling for comediennes. If a beautiful countenance meant a moral and virtuous soul, what could be said for "fat and sassy" Polly Moran, "beanpole" Charlotte Greenwood, or "elephantine" Marie Dressler? Did the fact of their unattractiveness somehow make them morally inferior to other, prettier women?

Susan Glenn points out that female comics in the theater "arrived on the scene at precisely the moment when beauty was becoming something of a cult in the world of popular entertainment."[7] Around the turn of the century beautiful women gained fame on the stage and in photographs and magazine illustrations just for being beautiful, while stage comediennes served as a counterpoint to the stage beauties. This dynamic could be clearly seen in the Ziegfeld *Follies*, which alternated lavish production numbers showcasing the beautiful Ziegfeld girls with short scenes featuring comics such as Fanny Brice, Eva Tanguay, and Sophie Tucker. The idealized, standardized, and specifically white beauty of the chorus girls was set up in opposition to the disruptive, excessive, and often eth-

Figure 2.1. Suffragists were often depicted as unfeminine and unattractive.

nic appearance of the comics.[8] This division helped cement the demarcation between beauty and comedy in the public consciousness.

This pretty/funny division continued in motion pictures, as the type of comedy women performed in silent film had a great deal to do with their physical appearance: whether a comedienne engaged in slapstick or light comedy was based, to a great extent, on whether she was seen as conventionally attractive. While some comediennes who were considered pretty, such as Mabel Normand, appeared in slapstick, those who were considered less attractive seldom, if ever, appeared in leading roles in light or romantic comedies. Light comedies were considered the privileged form of comedy—they were generally multireel films that foregrounded plot and character, with very little suggestion of physical comedy. Often based on stage plays or novels, light comedies were described as "refined" or "high-class," as opposed to slapstick, which was generally considered to be more lowbrow. The fact that refined comedy was reserved for more attractive comediennes makes sense given that this type of comedy was more in line with "feminine" humor than rough-and-tumble, lowbrow slapstick. The comparatively respectable and refined humor of light comedy was a perfect complement to the conventional beauty of comediennes such as Constance Talmadge or Marion Davies; in both cases, elements of traditional femininity are being reinforced.

Comediennes who were not considered pretty generally played in slapstick or character comedy, often acceding to the stereotype that beautiful women couldn't be funny by donning outlandish costumes and grotesque makeup in their films to accentuate their perceived unattractiveness. Women often downplayed stereotypically feminine traits such as refinement and grace in order to work in comedy, and beauty was another of these traits. Through their use of unflattering costumes, stylized makeup, pratfalls, and gawky gestures slapstick comediennes were effectively "sacrific[ing] all of the vanities of their sex,"[9] as one 1902 article described it, and thereby lessening the potential gender confusion of a "feminine" woman performing "masculine" routines.

Further reinforcing the popular conception that pretty women weren't funny and funny women weren't pretty, many films followed the precedent set by the Ziegfeld *Follies* and placed comediennes who were not considered conventionally attractive alongside acknowledged beauties, as was the case with Mack Sennett's "Bathing Beauties" (Figure 2.2). Hilde d'Haeyere argues that Sennett conceived of the Bathing Beauties as a visual and narrative break from the films' anarchic comedy and comediennes:

> Convinced that pretty girls could not be laughed at, Sennett considered the Bathing Beauties primarily as a "beautiful break" and decided that their physical activities did not necessarily have to be fast and funny. ... They were "splashes of fun and beauty," light-hearted playmates who countered the wildly aggressive comics with serene beauty. The Beauties were presented as counterpoints to the violent slapstick, not as participants in it.[10]

Describing Louise Fazenda's appearance with the Bathing Beauties, one writer explained that "most of them were really pulchritudinous. And one of them was comical,"[11] as if the two qualities were mutually exclusive. Another writer similarly set the Beauties up in opposition to the comics: "Others in the company might have curves or what-not; Miss Fazenda had pigtails."[12] But positioning the beautiful (and passive) Bathing Beauties alongside the less attractive (but active) slapstick comediennes could, paradoxically, serve to both temper and highlight the disruptive potential of the comediennes. Mizejewski argues that "in the historic binary of 'pretty' versus 'funny,' women comics, no matter what

Figure 2.2. Mack Sennett's Bathing Beauties, with Ben Turpin.

they look like, have been located in opposition to 'pretty,' enabling them to engage in a transgressive comedy grounded in the female body—its looks, its race and sexuality, and its relationships to ideal versions of femininity. In this strand of comedy, 'pretty' is the topic and target, the ideal that is exposed as funny."[13] Certainly the Beauties were meant to be models of ideal femininity whose presence emphasized the comediennes' supposed lack of traditional femininity. At the same time, the comediennes were the stars of the films and the protagonists within the films, and at least for some of the women in the audience, their joyfully anarchic antics could seem a more attractive model of femininity than the decorative, passive Beauties.

Although the division of labor between "pretty" comediennes and "funny" comediennes seemed fairly clear-cut, there was not always agreement in the press regarding which women fell into which category. Although there was unanimous agreement that Constance Talmadge, for instance, was beautiful and that Marie Dressler was not, a number of comediennes were considered not-quite-beautiful but not-quite-homely, variously described as pretty or plain depending on the opinion of the writer, the demands of the studio, or the roles they were currently playing. The shifting standards of beauty for comediennes never shifted too far; despite some disagreement over how to classify certain actresses, there was broad agreement over what physical characteristics were necessary to be considered beautiful. However, these disagreements also tacitly challenged beauty standards by publicly questioning the validity of how particular women were classified and, by extension, the very system of classifying women based on physical appearance.

The crowning of Margaret Gorman, a woman who strongly resembled screen beauty Mary Pickford, as the first Miss America in 1921 was part of a move toward a unified vision of beauty for American women. Miss America, like the Ziegfeld Girls and Mack Sennett's Bathing Beauties, represented the possibility of precisely measuring and quantifying women's beauty. Florenz Ziegfeld had very specific ideas about what made a woman beautiful, and newspaper and magazine articles such as "How I Pick My Beauties" and "When Is a Woman's Figure Beautiful? Florenz Ziegfeld Tells How He Judges" passed on these beauty standards to readers, such as Ziegfeld's proclamation that "these are the measurements that I consider about right for the girl of today. Height—five feet, five and a half inches. Weight—one hundred and twenty pounds. Foot size five."[14] Sennett's Keystone had similar beauty requirements for aspiring Bathing Beauties, evidenced by his publicity department's advice to organizers of a local beauty pageant in 1927 (as quoted in d'Haeyere):

> For the judging and measurements of your perfect models: . . . a girl 5ft tall, must weigh approximately 100 pounds, 5 pounds are added for each additional inch over 5ft; features must be attractive, teeth regular, limbs shapely, skin clear; a good carriage and bearing are most requisite.

Homogeneity was key. Indeed, as Hilde d'Haeyere points out, "the Beauties were selected to look like a multiplication of a single type of actress: a young, white, lively, and athletic girl, with a pleasant face, an attractive smile, and a beautifully curved, short body."[15]

This idealized image of femininity was emphatically white. Mizejewski argues "that femininity itself is racialized, and its idealized versions are white, a crucial element in the pretty/funny dynamic of women's comedy."[16] The early twentieth century was a period marked by waves of immigration to the United States, along with a sharp rise in anti-immigrant rhetoric, nativism, and anti-Semitism. The eugenics movement, which peaked in the 1920s and 1930s, held that negative traits including "feeblemindedness" and criminality were inherited and that certain groups of people—including non-northern European immigrants—should be prevented from having children, often through forced sterilization, as these groups had "inordinately high levels of physical and mental hereditary defects that were degrading America's gene pool."[17] The eugenics movement's view of non-white people as genetically inferior meshed well with the mentality of the resurgent Ku Klux Klan, which tied racism to nationalism and stoked fears about the supposed threat posed by immigrants and racial, ethnic, and religious minorities. Viewed in this context, the very specific beauty requirements of the Ziegfeld Girls, the Bathing Beauties, and Miss America, based as they are on northern European traits, clearly have at their core a racist and xenophobic dimension. As Mizejewski argues, "Ziegfeld's promotion of his 'certain girls' as recognizable, standardized 'types' resonated with specific nationalist and racial overtones."[18] This is also true of Sennett's standards for his Beauties, as well as Hollywood's beauty standards in general.

The beauty standards of the film industry were widely discussed in the press, as numerous articles catalogued, in great detail, the physical attributes necessary to succeed in motion pictures. Many of these articles encourage aspiring actresses to assess their own appearance and gauge their chances for success in Hollywood based on how their appearance measured up to established beauty standards. A 1926 article titled "Is Your Face the Type for Film Success?" paints a bleak picture for girls with blue eyes and high cheekbones:

> If you are analyzing the possibilities of some friend or of yourself for the movies consider first this feature of the eyes. You may have large soulful eyes of the right color, deep grey or brown—but they may be hidden under heavy projecting brows. Deep set eyes are shaded by the overhanging brows and lose their beauty and effectiveness. The light blue eye is unphotographic.... There are a few top notchers who possess light blue eyes, but their ascendancy has depended upon some other extraordinary qualities, and in many instances they may have a trace of grey or green in with the blue.
>
> After you have studied the effect of the eyes weigh the other screen requisites of the movie player. High cheek bones, for example, are bad for photographic purposes, particularly when aligned with deep set eyes. A pointed chin is bad. Too large a mouth automatically eliminates the

movie aspirant. All these are bad largely because the motion picture camera is slightly magnifying; it accentuates any prominent feature.

[Lois Wilson's] features are "regular," and if you can apply that adjective to your own face you have the facial requirements of the movie player.[19]

This article—which has the subtitle "If You Have Regular Features, Eyes Which Are Expressive But Not Too Deep Set, a Small Mouth and Shapely Limbs Your Chances in Hollywood are O.K."—presents a fairly narrow and specific conception of beauty. Blue eyes, "heavy projecting brows," and a pointed chin—which are apparently not "regular" features—are all presented here as deal breakers for young women aspiring to become movie stars. This type of very detailed cataloguing of acceptable physical traits could also be found in a 1922 article attributed to Mabel Normand as part of a *Movie Weekly* series, "How to Get into the Movies." In an article titled "Types of Girls That Producers Seek," Normand tells her readers that "the only attributes of which a producer may be positive are the physical. He knows a pretty girl when he sees one, hence she has more in her favor than the girl who is not pretty, even though the latter may have more innate dramatic talent."[20] She then goes on to mention requisite traits: "She must be small, because a small woman is supposed to be more appealing and because she may play youthful roles that a large woman could not"; "She must be young. . . . A woman of thirty should never consider the screen as a career unless she wants to play character roles and even then she hasn't great opportunities"; and "Slenderness is another requisite. Fat is anathema to the screen actress."[21] The article gives an example of the rigid beauty standards placed on actresses:

> I know a beautiful girl who has been playing "extras" for two years. Only recently she secured a small part. Most of the time she was without any sort of work, dependent entirely on the money she received from home. She has an unusually lovely face and a nice personality. Her trouble? She is plump and has thick ankles. If she is able to reduce, the ankles may be forgiven her. But you see how exacting the producer and the camera—can be.[22]

Ultimately, Normand declares, "while a woman need not be beautiful, she cannot be absolutely homely."[23] Articles such as these make it clear that success in Hollywood was largely dependent on appearance and that beauty standards were well-known and very specific, from brown eyes and a small mouth to a slim figure and slender ankles. When studios classified comediennes as "pretty" or "homely," then, and accordingly cast them in either light comedies or slapsticks, they were evidently following these standards. However, what appeared to be a clearly defined set of standards in reality had room for interpretation. Although the press seemed to know exactly what constituted a screen beauty, they often expanded their definition of the term when describing specific actresses.

While some comediennes were consistently described as either beautiful or homely, a number of others apparently defied classification. Much of the press discourse surrounding slapstick comediennes was built around stories of their "tragic homeliness," in which, as I'll discuss later in the chapter, newspaper and magazine accounts detailed the suffering that these women had experienced because they were not beautiful. At the same time, the press frequently insisted that underneath their wild hair and comic makeup they were actually conventionally attractive (Figure 2.3). Descriptions of Polly Moran make it clear that the press was unsure of how to classify her. In a 1915 article announcing that Moran had signed her first contract with Keystone, she is described as "the beautiful and talented singing comedienne" who "represents the typical American beauty, referred to so often by well known artists and illustrators, being tall and willowy, with exceptionally black hair, brown eyes and a stunning complexion" (Figure 2.4).[24] A contradictory description of Moran appeared a few years earlier, however, when a reviewer argued that

> she hasn't a shred of beauty beyond a set of teeth which give her the appearance of being lined with ivory; she has no more voice than the edge of a saw evokes from a log, and, according to her own gleeful admission, she is "fat." But she is alive and sparkling . . . she wins hands down over all the others by being just what she is—a personality, crude, rough, half-refined maybe, but definite, vivid.[25]

The press was clearly divided on whether certain comediennes could be considered pretty. By simultaneously describing women such as Moran as attractive and homely, these discourses point to ruptures in monolithic beauty ideals and opened the possibility that unconventional types could be considered beautiful.

The press wasn't alone in its uncertainty over how to classify various comediennes; the studios also sometimes positioned comediennes as alternately pretty and homely before settling on a type. Fazenda "was a pretty comedienne for quite a while,"[26] appearing in her Keystone films in the same type of slap-

Figure 2.3. "Honest, These Girl Comediennes of the Screen Are Pretty When They're Not on the Movie Screen," *Los Angeles Times*, 4 November 1917.

Figure 2.4. Polly Moran in 1915, and as Sheriff Nell in 1918.

stick-ingénue roles played by Mabel Normand. In *Ambrose's Fury* (1915), for example, she plays a flirtatious neighbor to Mack Swain's Ambrose and spends much of the film cavorting on the beach in a bathing costume[27] and flirting with both Ambrose and a police officer. Especially in her early films, she alternated these types of roles with character roles that featured exaggerated costumes and makeup: in *Willful Ambrose* (1915), made at the same time as *Ambrose's Fury*, Fazenda plays a hick character named Ma, with thick, bushy eyebrows and her hair tied in a wild knot on top of her head, who keeps Pa Ambrose (Swain) in line with the aid of an oversized wooden bat.

Moran generally embraced her "crude, rough, half-refined" image in her films, especially in her series of one-reel comedies playing the rough-and-tumble Sheriff Nell. In the film *Sheriff Nell's Tussle* (1918) she is described ironically as "Triggerville's dainty sheriff" and is paired romantically with the smaller and physically unimposing Ben Turpin, who serves as a counterpoint to her swaggering, cocky Nell. Early in her film career, however, it's clear that the studio had not yet settled on her image, as she, like Fazenda, played slapstick-ingénue roles. In *Love Will Conquer* (1916), for example, she plays a vamp who seduces Ambrose (Swain) and drives men to duel over her, although in *Her Painted Hero* (1915), she is a rough-and-tumble stagestruck girl who aggressively pursues a matinee idol (Hale Hamilton) with whom she is infatuated.

This disagreement in both the press and in the films themselves over the relative beauty of various comediennes was due, in part, to the fact that comedy didn't have the same demands for beauty as did other genres. As a result, a wider range of physical types appeared in comedy, many of which fell outside the contemporaneous standards of screen beauty. This was certainly true in the case of slapstick comediennes such as Marie Dressler, Gale Henry, and Charlotte Greenwood, who were, among other things, older, heavier, skinnier, and/or taller than the requirements of the screen dictated. But it was also true for some of the light comediennes, who were closer to the ideal but still not considered beauties. One reviewer said that Dorothy Devore's "nose suggests the up-tilt, which probably explains one reason she has been cast in comedy roles," and another claimed that Mabel Normand was "too durned [sic] plump and easy to gaze upon to be considered one of those ethereal, spiritual gooks who imagine things."[28] Although most writers described Dorothy Gish as pretty, one article stated bluntly that she "isn't at all beautiful. She has a little girl's figure, but her wistful heart-shaped little face doesn't follow any of the popular ideas of beauty." The writer concluded that Gish "would never win a prize were she to compete with a group of Follies girls."[29] When the popular press disagreed over who was or wasn't beautiful, despite its own awareness of the very specific ways that the motion picture industry defined beauty, it indicated a crack in the unified vision of beauty represented by Miss America, the Bathing Beauties, and the Ziegfeld Girls. Rather than relying on the film industry or press to declare who was or wasn't beautiful, then, these contradictory accounts gave fans license to draw their own conclusions about feminine beauty.

Discussions of Colleen Moore often dwelled on the fact that she was attractive, but not beautiful, "a charming actress without being a stunning beauty, as it were."[30] In fact, a large part of the appeal of Colleen Moore, and many screen comediennes, was precisely the fact that they were not impossibly beautiful. Compared to widely heralded (and often foreign) beauties such as Greta Garbo, Pola Negri, and Jetta Goudal, all of whom appeared primarily in dramatic films, the all-American, girl-next-door "cuteness" of Colleen Moore or Dorothy Devore seemed more accessible and less threatening, especially when considered in the context of the racialized beauty standards of the period (Figures 2.5 and 2.6). Moore was pretty but not *too* pretty, wild but not *too* wild:

> A typical American girl of the "cutie type," the bobbed-hair ingénue. But not one to win beauty contests, although there is undenied attraction. A popular type just now. Wild, vivacious, sprightly and easily roused to incontrolable [*sic*] anger—in her pictures, of course.[31]

Moore's beauty—and her personality—is playfully fun, nonthreatening, and all-American, a distinct counterpart to the foreign (or perhaps "foreign") vamps prowling the screen in dramas and melodramas.

The accessible nature of Moore's beauty was, in fact, explicitly mentioned by the press as a part of her attraction:

> Colleen's success is ample proof that doll-like beauty and high-hat airs are not necessary to stardom. Her triumphs are a result of "being herself." Miss Moore is pretyy [*sic*] to be sure—but her beauty is such as might be found in thousands of other girls.
>
> "I always try to portray characters that are within the scope of every girl," declares Colleen. "Also I insist that my stories tell a tale of everyday life. They must be full of reality—not absurd, improbable yarns."
>
> In that paragraph Miss Moore sums up the "why" of her popularity.

Figure 2.5. Greta Garbo, Jetta Goudal, Pola Negri.

Figure 2.6. Colleen Moore, Constance Talmadge, Dorothy Devore.

> It is a simple matter for her followers to vision themselves in her shoes. And they flock to see her pictures that they may enjoy an hour and 15 minutes of this blissful imagination.[32]

Not everyone found Moore's safe brand of femininity reassuring—it could also be seen as bland, as was the case with this reviewer who determined that audiences liked Colleen Moore because her own Cinderella-type rise from obscurity made her sympathetic to audiences, despite the fact that she possessed "the very smallest equipment in physical attractiveness and in talent for make-believe":

> Perhaps it is simply that Colleen Moore is one of those perfectly safe players who may be counted upon not to do anything which seems far away from our own experience, who will flaunt no charms and graces to which the most obscure may not aspire. That must be the explanation of her vogue. There is no other.[33]

Even this unenthusiastic assessment reinforces the idea that the type of beauty and femininity portrayed by Moore in her films was within reach of movie fans. Unlike the exotic and impossible-to-achieve beauty of Garbo or Goudal, Moore's appearance was familiar and attainable.

Interestingly, a number of articles use the not exactly cutting-edge sciences of physiognomy and phrenology to describe, in great deal, how Moore's all-American, girl-next-door features indicate an all-American, girl-next-door personality. A 1923 article pointed to "the bony formation of the face and head, the shape of the nose, and mouth," and her "wide lips" and "bright eyes" as proof that Moore was just as vivacious, spontaneous, quick-witted, and lovable as the characters she played in her films.[34] A similar article appearing the following year (possibly derived from the same studio source as the previous article) found "good imagination and constructive ability" in Moore's nose and an affinity for music and dancing above her eyes. This writer concluded that Moore

> has enthusiasm, an active nature, good mentality, is industrious, persistent, determined, has good judgment, and an all-absorbing interest in her work. She is self-confident and, above all, has the courage of her convictions. There are initiative, thoroness [sic], patience, carefulness, ability to master details, and dramatic sense. She has vivid mental pictures of the things she desires to do, and usually accomplishes that which she attempts.[35]

The personality traits evident in Moore's face—enthusiasm, industriousness, confidence—are, like the characters she played, typically American. This positions Moore in contrast to exotic foreign vamps and reinforces the fact that her type of beauty was familiar and attainable to certain women in the audience, specifically women who were white and middle class. A movie fan from Dubuque or Sacramento might experiment with imitating the mysterious otherness of Garbo's mannerisms or Negri's appearance, but the exotic beauty and personae of these actresses and the characters they played would have been far removed from the everyday lives of most white American spectators.[36] Moore, however, comes across as a feminine embodiment of the well-worn Horatio Alger myth, a Cinderella figure both on-screen and off, whose rags-to-riches background would likely be comfortably familiar to American audiences raised on countless incarnations of those stories in books, plays, and movies. If Moore's appearance signaled a solidly American personality, then it's possible that American girls could see themselves in her place. The fact that Moore, like a great many comediennes, may not have been a "stunning beauty" added to her appeal, making her familiar and accessible compared to the mysterious and glamorous beauty of many dramatic stars.

The disagreements in the press and the studios over the relative attractiveness of Louise Fazenda or Colleen Moore point to wider tensions regarding the validity of Hollywood's beauty standards. These standards are further questioned in the press in articles about screen comediennes that celebrate, albeit prematurely, the industry's rejection of its beauty standards in favor of brains, personality, and talent. By downplaying the importance of beauty for actresses, these discourses in some ways contradict the many articles that described in detail the physical traits necessary to succeed in motion pictures, and yet the two stances on beauty work in tandem, especially in fan magazines. While articles that reinforced beauty standards might induce readers to buy the beauty products advertised in the magazine, articles that deemphasized beauty in favor of brains or personality, along with the articles that presented comediennes' type of beauty as accessible and attainable, could encourage movie fans to imagine motion picture stardom for themselves.

In a 1921 newspaper article titled "Beauty and Personality," readers were informed that beauty in the movies was becoming passé:

> Beauty, sacred these years in the films, is being humbled by the latest vanity-wrecking efficiency movement. In the new arrangement of qualifications of screen luminaries beauty is shoved far down the list, with personality exalted to the highest requisite. Beauty, if accompanied by intelligence and a charm that survives the photographic processes, is still very desirable. But beauty, just for beauty's sake alone, is no longer being done in pictures.[37]

The article argues that "personality"—described here as largely made up of intelligence—has become more important to producers than beauty both onstage and in the movies and points to Colleen Moore as the perfect combination of personality and beauty. Another article from the same period quotes Moore, who declares that "beauty is not enough" in Hollywood, that "it must be augmented by personality and brains."[38] The series of articles attributed to Mabel Normand detailing "how to get into the movies" also addressed this topic, telling readers that "the pretty face has been tried and found wanting." As in the other articles, intelligence was mentioned as an essential accompaniment to beauty:

> Of a young girl who flashed for a moment into prominence and then disappeared, I heard a director remark:
> "Yes, she is a beauty—but what a dumbbell!"
> I don't pretend to claim that an actress must know scientific and algebraic formulas or other subjects of higher education. I only say that she must have an alert, comprehending mind that can grasp the information which she requires and adapt it to her work.[39]

The emphasis on intelligence in these articles is especially interesting given the fact that excessive intellect was not considered appropriately feminine. Normand excuses women from being *too* intellectual—the type of knowledge that her article advocates is based more in instinct and natural ability than education—but still argues that intelligence, like beauty, is essential to actresses. A similar argument was made by Fay Tincher in 1916:

> Beauty counts; but it is only a parlor ornament if your luxuriant auburn hair and dreamy eyes don't take their root in gray matter. Beauty without brains is unmarketable; brains without beauty is a gambling chance; but brains and beauty combined are a dandy working partnership. With Old Experience taken into the firm, you are on the high-road to a successful studio career.[40]

Like Normand and Moore, Tincher emphasizes the importance of brains as well as beauty for actresses. While none of the articles dismisses beauty entirely, the fact that they wed it to what many considered a masculine trait echoes the way that comediennes themselves combined the apparently opposing traits of beauty and a sense of humor. Arguments that intelligence was as important to actresses as beauty, then, much like the image of a woman performing comedy, served to blur the boundaries created by rigid gender roles by combining traditionally masculine and traditionally feminine traits.

Along with insisting that beauty was out and intelligence was in, the press also tried to reassure fans that compared to screen beauties, actresses who were considered unattractive often led happier, more fulfilling lives in spite of, or even because of, their lack of beauty. A *Motion Picture Magazine* article from 1928, titled "It Pays to Be Homely," argued that "we buck-toothed people have just as much chance for happiness in life as our fancier brethren and sistren; that it isn't necessary to look like a magazine cover" to find true love. While Clara Bow had not yet been married, and Constance Talmadge had been married and divorced several times, the article points out, Louise Fazenda, "the homely girl, has won out where the beauties have failed. For a year she has been married to the good-looking and popular Hal Wallis."[41] A profile of Charlotte Greenwood follows the same logic, claiming that "Charlotte may not have a face like a magazine cover, but she has a fan following which would compare very well with Clara Bow's. And she points to her own good-looking husband as proof positive that it isn't only the girls with bud-like mouths and big blue eyes who have romances."[42] Marie Dressler was similarly positioned as a valued companion: "Marie may not be the World's Sweetheart. But she is the World's Best Friend. And the world knows it. Sweethearts may come and go, while true friendship goes on forever."[43] Like that of Fazenda and Greenwood, Dressler's worth, according to this article, is based on deeper qualities than beauty.

The premise behind this thinking, as spelled out by *Motion Picture Magazine*, was that "when a man marries a girl for her looks she has to worry the rest of her life for fear someone more beautiful will win him away from her—as one usually does. But when a man falls in love with a charming personality, and a sense of humor, his wife is safe. She can trust him every evening at gatherings of Hollywood's most practiced sirens."[44] However patronizing this logic may be, it's not inconceivable to think that it may have been reassuring to some readers. Certainly fans who felt inferior to glamorous movie stars and their idealized beauty could seize on this idea that the stars' lives were not necessarily happy and perhaps feel better about their own lives. When magazines described less conventionally attractive comediennes as having happier home lives because of their appearance, they were contradicting the popular perception, supported (and to some extent created) by advertisements that ran in the same magazines, that beauty was the surest path to happiness.

Articles that downplay the importance of beauty for actresses provide an interesting counterpoint to the ubiquitous insistence that movie stars not only had to be beautiful but also had to fit a very specific and well-defined standard of beauty.

It's significant that these articles are specifically tied to comediennes because comedy allowed for a broader range of physical types, and so fans could more easily see themselves reflected in the faces and bodies of comedy stars than in the perfect beauty of glamorous tragediennes. For the press to point to comediennes as proof that the impossible-to-achieve beauty of most dramatic actresses was "no longer being done" in Hollywood, that brains, personality, and talent were gaining prominence, and that homely women were happier than pretty ones indicates that magazine writers and studio press departments may have understood that fans needed to feel that stardom could, conceivably, be within their reach.

Most strategies used by the popular press to convince fans that they, too, could be movie stars were centered on consumption and transformation, from advertisements for makeup and articles about stars' clothing to fan magazine–sponsored beauty contests. As Banner argues, the idea that women's beauty stemmed from their innate moral superiority fell out of favor by the 1920s.

> But the possibility that every woman might be beautiful, once raised, did not disappear. With its powders and lotions, its cosmetics and hair dyes, the commercial culture of beauty then became the major claimant to the means of beauty for all women. When in the 1920s women no longer were seen as possessing a superior spirituality, their outward appearance could be viewed as more important than their inner character, and external means could become central to improving their looks.[45]

Newspaper and magazine ads assured readers that looking like a movie star was within their reach, as long as they bought the right product. The Bathing Beauties were emblematic of this new focus on commercialism. According to King,

> Beauty, which, in the case of Mabel Normand, had formed part of a pervasive hybridization of classical attractiveness and grotesque physicality, was, in the case of the Bathing Beauties, hypostasized as a spectacular commodity, something to be attained though rigorous physical training. Increasingly, beauty shed its qualitative nature and became a quantifiable possession to be compared across different women.[46]

And yet articles that deemphasize the importance of beauty in Hollywood somewhat avoid this consumerist drive and instead seem to optimistically advance the idea that women should be rewarded for their accomplishments and abilities rather than solely for their appearance. Furthermore, by using such vague terms as "personality," "brains," "accomplishments," and "qualifications," as opposed to very specific lists of required beauty traits, more women could see themselves in these magazine descriptions. After all, while not everyone was 5' 3" with pale skin, brown eyes, and slender ankles, most anyone could be said to have at least some manner of brains or accomplishments. In fact, many of the discourses about how comediennes measured up to Hollywood's beauty standards—including disagreements about who was or wasn't pretty, comparisons to glamorous dramatic actresses, and insistence that beauty was not the most important trait for actresses—were implicitly sympathetic toward female spectators who themselves didn't measure up to those standards. This was, of course, complicated by the fact that these same magazines and newspapers advertised products that tried to convince women that the key to self-worth was achieving beauty by buying the right kind of stockings or face powder. However, comediennes at least presented an alternative model of beauty to female spectators who could not, or would not, emulate Hollywood's narrow beauty standards.

"Graceful Awkwardness"

The tensions regarding Hollywood's beauty standards that circulated in press discourses were also evident in comediennes' performances. Comediennes who were said to fall outside the film industry's conception of normative beauty—even those who were sometimes described as pretty—frequently ignored beauty standards on-screen and made their characters as unattractive as possible. This was accomplished in large part through costuming, as comediennes designed outfits, makeup, and hairstyles for their characters that were funny by virtue of being ill-fitting, outmoded, and unflattering. Comediennes further emphasized their appearance through performances in which they used the physical traits that set them apart from normative femininity as sources of comedy, from Marie Dressler performing an inability to control her excessive body to Charlotte Greenwood kicking her remarkably long, limber legs over her head. Furthermore, comediennes whose bodies were tall, heavy, or otherwise excessive were often paired with smaller, and often submissive, leading men in order to highlight and draw laughs from the reversal of gender positions hinted at by the discrepancy in male and female sizes. In many ways, then, comediennes embraced and emphasized the traits that set them apart from acknowledged screen beauties such as Greta Garbo and Jetta Goudal and reveled in their supposed homeliness. Although their strategy of using self-deprecating humor and inviting audiences to laugh at their physical shortcomings was problematic in many ways, they were also complicating Hollywood's beauty standards by willingly defying cultural expectations that women should be—or at least should strive to be—beautiful and instead made themselves unattractive in the name of comedy.

Female comics working in the theater in the early twentieth century frequently made the "flaws" in their appearance a central element of their acts, establishing a tradition that would be continued by film comediennes. Especially on the vaudeville and burlesque stages, comediennes saw these supposed flaws not as impediments but as a source of comedy. Overweight comediennes such as Stella Mayhew, May Irwin, Sophie Tucker, and Trixie Friganza drew attention to their size through their songs and costumes. Tucker sang a song titled "Nobody Loves a Fat Girl," for example, and Friganza wore layers of costumes that added to her girth and saw her weight as a positive, asking at one point, "Is it surprising that the actress, whose breadth is her meal-ticket, wants to make the most of that asset?"[47] Tall, skinny, and angular comedienne Fanny Brice would emphasize these physical characteristics through awkward dancing and costumes, and she was known for performing roles that made a joke of this awkwardness, as in her parodies of the ballet and of famous sex symbols (Figure 2.7). "Cyclonic Comedienne" Eva Tanguay similarly used her excessive body as a centerpiece in her vaudeville act. She would frequently appear onstage wearing costumes that were deliberate parodies of those worn by burlesque and Follies chorines, dripping with feathers, beads, furs, and sequins (Figure 2.8). Her body, however, was not like anything found in Ziegfeld's chorus, with "bosoms bursting out of bras and thighs rippling with fat."[48] Tanguay put her body on display, mocking the unwritten rule that women who did not adhere to idealized beauty standards could not be objects of sexual spectacle. Photographs of Tanguay frequently show her in revealing costumes, unapologetically displaying her body, and, most important, laughing.

What these stage comediennes have in common is an embrace of their excessive, plain, and/or unruly bodies and an active incorporation of their non-normative appearances into their acts as a source of comedy. Screen comediennes, especially those who appeared in slapstick, continued this tradition of making their perceived unattractiveness and unwillingness or inability to conform to popular beauty standards an integral part of their comedy. Rather than attempting to "pass" as beautiful through attractive costumes, makeup, and appropriately "feminine" physicality, many comediennes instead used these same elements to make themselves look as awkward and homely as possible, often

Figure 2.7. Fanny Brice.

Figure 2.8. Eva Tanguay.

drawing attention to physical characteristics—such as their height, weight, or specific features—that most differentiated them from stage and screen beauties. In this way, many comediennes on both the stage and screen performed an active, embodied mode of comedy, in which their physical appearance was used to tacitly critique accepted beauty ideals.

One strategy that screen comediennes used to make themselves look comically unattractive was their use of costumes, makeup, and hairstyling. Slapstick comedians, both male and female, typically wore outlandish costumes, makeup, and hairstyles to enhance and accentuate their characters. Like Charlie Chaplin's too-tight jacket and oversized pants and shoes that immediately undermined his Tramp character's attempts at dignity, and Harold Lloyd's horn-rimmed glasses and straw hat that positioned him as an everyman in impossible situations, slapstick comediennes also designed costumes and makeup that visually represented the comic personae they had created. These costumes were almost always unflattering, too large or too small, mismatched and out of date, with makeup that served to draw laughs rather than enhance their appearance. Gale Henry's costumes were often poorly fitting, with too-short sleeves and skirts to emphasize her long and lanky body, and she generally wore her hair in a tight, unflattering bun, with stiff bangs jutting over her angular face, and an absurd straw hat perched on top of her head (Figure 2.9). One interviewer described Henry fixing up her hair by "massaging her outstanding bangs with a cake of wet, yellow soap" and pointed out that "she buys her clothes at the Salvation Army rummage sales, and has to alter them very little."[49] Louise Fazenda's standard costume with Keystone, developed around 1918, consisted of an unflattering gingham dress and pantalettes, with her hair pulled back into severe pigtails—that Mack Sennett famously had insured for $10,000[50]—and one big curl in the center of her forehead (Figure 2.10). Fazenda explained that she designed her character's hair and makeup to deliberately draw attention to a physical trait that she concealed offscreen:

> I have a very high forehead—so high that off-stage I wear my hair so as to cover it. I pulled the hair straight back on my head like a little girl's and looking into the glass, found that it gave me a very bizarre appearance. Then I put a thin circle of black around each eye and assumed a vacant expression. The effect was startling! I hardly knew myself.
>
> Mr. Sennett was delighted with my appearance and gave me a leading part right away. My make-up proved so popular that it was utilized for every comedy thereafter in which I appeared.[51]

Figure 2.9. Gale Henry.

Figure 2.10. Louise Fazenda.

There is an implicit rejection of popular beauty standards in the way that Henry and Fazenda—as well as Alice Howell, Polly Moran, and numerous other slapstick comediennes—made a point of using their costumes, makeup, and hair to emphasize their physical "flaws" rather than attempting to conceal these traits to more closely resemble Hollywood beauties. When Henry draped ill-fitting secondhand clothes over her thin frame or Fazenda pulled her hair off her high forehead and placed a spit-curl in the center like a target, they were refusing to hide their supposed "flaws"; instead they were using them as a source of comedy.

Along with using costumes, comediennes also used physical humor to accentuate their physical appearance. Marie Dressler, whom the press described as "homely," "elephantine," and "as plain as an old size-eight shoe,"[52] used physical comedy to highlight her size and admitted homeliness (Figure 2.11). In many of Dressler's films her appearance is the source of numerous gags, as her characters try to maintain their dignity while being thrown around and roughly mistreated. Dressler's gags are frequently centered on her inability to contain her tremendous size, as she inadvertently collides with, gets stuck in, or knocks over anything in her path. Victoria Sturtevant notes that "Dressler's body is the site of considerable emphasis in her films. Her trademark slapstick comedy is based on an athletic and fearless physicality that foregrounds her size and flouts rules of feminine comportment."[53] Indeed, according to Sturtevant, Dressler's "performances tend to reject the ethereal light-and-shadow femininity of the conventional star, insisting instead on the mass, the texture, the volume, the velocity, and the dignity of her body."[54] In *Tillie's Punctured Romance* (1914), Dressler's Tillie is constantly knocking people over or falling down and taking anyone in close proximity with her. A running gag involves Tillie knocking people over with her behind; at one point she playfully bumps Charlie Chaplin's character, knocking him off his feet, and later she bends over and inadvertently takes out several members of the police force. The payoff of this gag comes at the end of the film, when Tillie herself is knocked in the behind by a police car, causing her to fall off a pier into the ocean. The joke here is that Tillie's body is so large that the front half doesn't know what the back half is doing, and that it takes something as large as a car to knock her off her feet. Dressler enthusiastically plays Tillie as unruly and out of control, making use of her large body and accentuating her homeliness with her costumes, makeup, and frequent doleful expressions.

Charlotte Greenwood, whose long, limber arms and legs earned her fame in vaudeville and musical theater, used these assets to her advantage in her si-

"An Inferiority Complex in a One-Piece Bathing Suit"

Figure 2.11. Marie Dressler in *Tillie's Punctured Romance* (1914).

lent films. Greenwood's stage act was built around her "gracefully awkward"⁵⁵ dancing and her ability to "[kick] up each foot on each side—not in front—of her body until the toes were on a level with her shoulders, alternately."⁵⁶ As one reviewer described her performance in the Broadway production of *So Long Letty* (1916–17), "In her own simple way, Miss Greenwood swings an arm or a leg upon an innocent bystander when she has nothing else to do."⁵⁷ She continued to emphasize her gangliness and "graceful awkwardness" in her films, as reviews of her 1915 debut film, *Jane*, pointed out that "Greenwood is her usual angular self"⁵⁸ and that "Miss Greenwood is probably the most grotesque of the numerous Janes . . . whom we have seen in the character." The reviewer goes on to add that "the elongated Charlotte is always good for a laugh when it is handy. In this picture she confines her gymnastic eccentricities and facial grimaces to the character of the maid . . . and she makes Jane an amiable if amusing female 'boob.'"⁵⁹

Twelve years later, when Greenwood was back in Hollywood filming *Baby Mine* (1928), her limber legs were still an important part of her act: a publicity photo of the comedienne nonchalantly reading a book while resting her foot

Figure 2.12. Charlotte Greenwood on the set of *Baby Mine* (1928), *New York Evening Journal*, 1 November 1927, Charlotte Greenwood clipping file, NYPL.

against a camera, well over her head, appeared in newspapers with a caption stating that "She kicks exactly six feet high between scenes in *Baby Mine*" (Figure 2.12). This photo is especially interesting in its attempt to make Greenwood's signature move appear non-performative—she's not in front of an audience but instead appears to be relaxing between takes—a strategy that makes her pose seem even more bizarre. According to this photograph Greenwood's high kick was not just a part of her act, it was something she did off-stage and out of character, seemingly without thought or purpose. As such, it implies that this trait that marked her deviation from normative beauty—her unusually long and limber arms and legs—was not something that she performed but was rather a part of who she was. This image of Greenwood complicated articles that assured fans that she was not gangly or unusually built in any way and instead insisted that her long legs and flexibility were simultaneously remarkable and unremarkable—while they were unusual traits, they were apparently regarded with indifference by Greenwood.

Like Greenwood, Gale Henry also played up her gawkiness on-screen, using her elastic face to comic effect, with exaggerated grimaces and mugging aiding her wild gestures and pratfalls. In a poem that appeared in *Moving Picture Weekly*, she described her appeal: "Leading woman of the Jokers, I'm as thin as twenty pokers. When it comes to face-distortion, I'm the one and only Caution."[60] Henry frequently based her comedy on the gap between her characters' attempts at stereotypical femininity and the reality of their decidedly unfeminine appearance. In the film *Mighty Like a Moose* (1926), she plays a homely wallflower in pursuit of Charley Chase's character, who calls her Floradora and then refers to her as "one of the Mayflower girls," ironic references to both the renowned sextet of beautiful chorines who gained fame in the turn-of-the-century musical *Floradora* and "a quartet of four fascinating young women" who appeared in the 1925 musical *Mayflowers*.[61] An ad for the film *Art Arches* (1917) also used this strategy of setting Henry up in comic opposition to classic beauties. Henry stands on a pedestal wearing classical garb in front of a background that resembles paint strokes while beneath her is the caption, "December Afternoon, Posed by Gale Henry, the Funniest Woman on the Screen" (Figure 2.13). This ad, like the references to the *Floradora* and *Mayflowers* chorus girls, focuses attention on the fact that Henry doesn't fit the beauty standards presented in classical art and personified by Broadway chorines. But like Greenwood, Henry uses her appearance as a source of comedy, rather than attempting to make herself appear beautiful or remaining out of sight altogether. Henry, like Greenwood, Dressler, Louise Fazenda, Polly Moran, Alice Howell, and numerous others, made her appearance an integral part of her comedy, foregrounding traits that directly contradicted popular conceptions of beauty. In this way, these comediennes subtly challenged Hollywood's beauty standard by parodying, rather than praising, beauty.

Comediennes who were tall or overweight, such as Dressler, Greenwood, and Moran, were frequently positioned opposite smaller leading men in their films, making them appear even larger and more ungainly than they actually were. As Sturtevant notes, "Dressler was particularly skilled at using the contrast between her body and the bodies of those around her (short men, thin women, children) to reverse generic norms, particularly the ideological conventions of sentimental melodrama. Often paired with the diminutive Joe Weber, Dressler perfected a comedy style based on her ability to tower over the smaller man."[62] In *Tillie's Punctured Romance*, for example, Dressler is paired with Charlie Chaplin, and while she was likely only an inch or two taller than he was she clearly outweighed him. The disparity in their sizes was emphasized by her broad, unrestrained performance: while Chaplin keeps his movements relatively small, Dressler charges through each scene with physical abandon, knocking

Figure 2.13. Gale Henry in *Art Arches* (1917), unsourced, ca. 1917, Gale Henry clipping file, NYPL.

over anyone and anything in her path. Dressler is larger than life in this film, turning every appearance on-screen into a whirlwind of chaos and anarchy, often because of Tillie's inability to control her excessive body. The fact that Mabel Normand's character in the film is generally referred to as "little"—"the little girl crook," Charlie's "little playmate"—further accentuates Tillie's size and sets her apart from acceptably feminine traits.

Charlotte Greenwood's partner from vaudeville and Broadway, Sydney Grant—who was described by *Moving Picture World* as "Greenwood's comical little partner"[63]—also appeared in *Jane*, continuing his stage role as a comic foil to Greenwood. The disparity in their sizes, highlighted by photographs and illustrations that show Greenwood towering above Grant, further accentuated the lankiness and gangliness that were the central focus of Greenwood's comedy both on stage and on film (Figure 2.14). Just as Dressler's pairing with smaller leading men drew attention to her excessive weight, Greenwood's pairing with Grant made her height a source of comedy in their act. A similar dynamic was present in the pairing of Flora Finch, who was tall and extremely thin, with overweight comedian John Bunny in a series of films from 1910 to 1915, as Finch seemed even more skinny and angular next to her rotund partner. Other slapstick comediennes, including Polly Moran and Louise Fazenda, similarly appeared with smaller and/or less imposing leading men, such as Ben Turpin and Jack Ackroyd, who served as comic counterpoints to their large or unruly characters. These pairings emphasize and draw humor from the very physical traits that exclude these comediennes from Hollywood's beauty standards and at least to some extent mock those standards and question their validity. Although fan magazines told readers that a proper motion picture star must be short and slender, Greenwood and Dressler made their height and weight a central part of their stardom, creating enjoyment for viewers from these supposedly "unattractive" traits and allowing similarly tall, overweight, or unruly women in the audience a chance to imagine stardom for themselves. The coupling of larger women with smaller men in comedies also points to tensions over changing gender roles in the early twentieth century, as the image of women towering over men and dominating them physically certainly reflects anxieties over women's increased social and political power. At the same time, the fact that the interactions between these characters were played for laughs could ease some of these tensions by presenting inverted gender roles as comical rather than threatening.

Comediennes' use of costumes, physicality, and casting to create self-deprecating comedy had complex and contradictory meanings. Certainly the fact that comediennes made jokes about the ways in which they supposedly fell short of the feminine ideal tempered their impact somewhat. By framing their appearance in terms of difference, they were allowing their audiences to think of them as second-class women, displaying a femininity that was inherently different from and perhaps inferior to the type of femininity possessed by Ziegfeld's and Sennett's beauties. However, when comediennes called attention to their appearance, they were demanding visibility in a society that placed a premium

Figure 2.14. Greenwood and Grant. *Chicago Tribune*, 6 June 1915.

on feminine attractiveness. These women were refusing to remain out of sight; instead they were insisting on being seen and on controlling the terms on which they were seen. Dressler, Moran, and other overweight comediennes demonstrated that there was a place for larger women within the concept of femininity, while Henry, Greenwood, and Fazenda showed that grace was not an inherently female quality. The fact that these women embraced their non-normative bodies, putting them on display rather than attempting to make them conform to popular beauty standards, can be read as a subtle challenge to those standards.

"A Pretty Girl Can Afford to Play Homely Parts"

In the 1927 film *The Red Mill*, Marion Davies plays Tina, a "drudge" in a Dutch inn and tavern. With her crooked braids and her face scrubbed free of makeup, Tina is mousy and unassuming, a far cry from the vivacious and beautiful movie-star image of Davies. Tina befriends Gretchen (Louise Fazenda), a rich woman staying at the inn, and the two switch places so that Gretchen can elude her father and tryst with her beau. While waiting in Gretchen's room for her to return, Tina regards herself idly in the mirror, and then notices a jar of "Mud Massage Face Beautifier"—"one application guarantees perpetual beauty"—on the counter. After applying some to her face, she peels off the mask and is transformed, complete with flawless makeup and flattering soft focus; she then lets down her braids and runs a brush through her hair, ending up with perfect curls (Figure 2.15). The scene is not only a wonderful comic moment, it also offers a commentary on Hollywood's laughably unrealistic beauty standards and a glimpse of one way that comediennes drew attention to and challenged those standards. The tropes of transformation and of adopting alternate identities are frequently used by comediennes to advance the idea that beauty wasn't automatically available to all women but rather required a certain amount of work to achieve. Whether in the form of makeover stories or the idea of disguising oneself as either pretty or plain, the notion of transformation informed much of the work of and discourses about comediennes and served as a means of questioning the concepts of idealized beauty and femininity.

The makeover as a plot device, in which homely or unruly women learn how to be "appropriately" feminine, was popular in silent comedies. While the makeovers are not usually as straightforward or as uncomplicated as the type of transformation parodied in *The Red Mill*, in these films characters who are mannish, rowdy, unattractive, or otherwise unladylike are transformed into proper ladies through the use of fashion and makeup. But despite seeming to reinforce the idea that the key to a woman's happiness could be found in the most up-to-date fashions and the perfect lip color, these films offer multiple and often contradictory messages about consumerism and gender roles. Certainly beauty and traditional femininity are presented as desirable goals, and the key to achieving these

Figure 2.15. Tina (Marion Davies) finds "perpetual beauty" in a jar in *The Red Mill* (1927).

goals is often shown to be consumer goods, whether a new wardrobe or the latest beauty product. At the same time, the transformations are often shown to remain on the surface, as temporary performances of femininity that don't completely transform the characters but instead allow them to try on feminine attributes while still holding onto their "unfeminine" qualities. These scenes also lay bare the device of femininity by exposing the tremendous amounts of effort, preparation, and deliberation involved in achieving and maintaining idealized beauty. Makeover films, then, present femininity and beauty as performative rather than natural and automatically available to all women, and in this way they challenge the idea that either trait is essential for women.

A remarkably comprehensive makeover, at least in terms of surface qualities, occurs in *The Clinging Vine* (1926). A. B. Allen (Leatrice Joy), assistant to the president of a paint company, is the epitome of a mannish, overly intellectual professional woman—she even describes herself as "a sexless, loveless machine" (Figure 2.16). The opening scenes of the film show that A. B. essentially runs the company for her absentminded boss, T. M. Bancroft, and the ineffectual (all-

"An Inferiority Complex in a One-Piece Bathing Suit"

Figure 2.16. Leatrice Joy as A. B. Allen in *The Clinging Vine* (1926).

male) board of directors. A. B. is shown to be an astute and capable businesswoman but a miserable failure as a feminine woman—her short, slicked-back hair, thick eyebrows, absence of makeup, and masculine suit and tie (with a skirt instead of trousers, in her only nod to her gender) are evidence of the fact that she has actively rejected all trappings of femininity, as does an intertitle saying that she "hired, wired and fired men—but had never kissed one." Even her name—A. B.—is a rejection of femininity, as she chooses gender-neutral initials over her presumably female given name. While on a business retreat at Bancroft's country estate A. B. overhears his spoiled grandson, Jimmie (Tom Moore), refer to her as a "flat-chested, flat-heeled, flat-headed Amazon" and consequently allows Bancroft's wife (referred to only as "Grandma" [Toby Claude]) to give her a makeover. Grandma buys a new wardrobe for A. B., and teaches her to pluck her eyebrows, curl her hair, and bat her eyelashes (Figure 2.17). Grandma's take on love is fairly cynical—as she tells A. B., "A man wants beauty, not brains. His task is to find a woman pretty enough to please him and dumb enough to love him." In short, Grandma tells A. B., men want "a clinging vine." After learning

Figure 2.17. *The Clinging Vine* (1926): "Woman, wouldst thou have Beauty? Cry and get it!"

how to "twitter," and being assured that the only phrases she needs are "Do go on!" and "Aren't you wonderful!" A. B. is introduced to Grandma's guests, wearing an absurdly over-the-top outfit adorned with yards of ruffles, flounces, and bows (Figure 2.18). The transformed A. B. looks like a parody of Little Bo Peep, and, accordingly, the men follow her like a flock of sheep. Even Jimmie—who has never before met A. B. in person—is smitten, and despite Jimmie's many shortcomings A. B. decides that she wants to marry him.

Although A. B. gamely plays along with what Grandma has taught her about femininity, it's clear that the "new" A. B. is a performance. This is evidenced when A. B. uses her business sense to simultaneously save Bancroft's guests from a con artist, her company from financial ruin, and Jimmie from his own inexperience and naiveté. While she is playing the part of the flirtatious and empty-headed "ideal" woman, A. B. loses none of her business acumen and is ultimately able to find a happy medium between the extremes of mannishness and hyperfemininity. A. B. begins the film as a humorless, sexless businesswoman, a caricature of everything social conservatives feared women would become if they were granted increased social and political power, and is

"An Inferiority Complex in a One-Piece Bathing Suit"

Figure 2.18. *The Clinging Vine* (1926): "Who dressed A. B. up like a girl?"

then molded into a vapid, vacuous creature who epitomizes an old-fashioned model of femininity that feminists were eager to leave behind. Neither role suits her—she is unhappy in her initial guise but uncomfortable with abandoning it entirely—but she is able to find a way to combine elements of both positions, to be smart and capable as well as conventionally beautiful and "feminine," to wear the ribbons and bows while also standing up to her boss. In this way, *The Clinging Vine* offers an interesting commentary on women's changing roles in society, one that is echoed in a newspaper commentary by columnist Dorothy Dix that was published shortly after the film was released:

> And where would you go to look for a clinging vine in this day and age? You remember the gentle little feminine thing who rolled her eyes and asked every man she met what he thought she thought, and who was so frail and delicate she looked as if she was about to pass away at any time?
>
> . . . She thought politics perfectly horrid and believed that woman's place was the home. She didn't know which was the business end of a check. She didn't know how to buy a railroad ticket or check a trunk, and

as a wife she meekly did as John told her and began every statement with "John says."

Perhaps a few specimens of the clinging vine still survive in remote rural communities, but you never see one in cities. Every flapper can drive a car and play as hard a game of golf and tennis as her brother....

The great majority of young women earn their own living, and the only thing they cling to is their jobs. And when they marry they are far more likely to tell their husbands where they get off than to listen to such advice themselves.[64]

The Clinging Vine is vague on exactly how much of a clinging vine A. B. will remain after she marries Jimmie, but like the modern young women Dix refers to, A. B. is smart, capable, and tough, and the film implies that she will retain these qualities, along with her flowing dresses and plucked brows, after her marriage.

Irene (1926), like *The Clinging Vine*, features a character who submits herself to a makeover in order to appear appropriately feminine. Irene (Colleen Moore) is a working-class girl who attracts the attention of a rich young man named Donald Marshall (Lloyd Hughes). Donald gets Irene a job as a model in a modiste shop run by his business partner, an effeminate man called Madame Lucy (as he explains, "I inherited my aunt's business and her name"). Madame Lucy (George K. Arthur) is doubtful about Irene's modeling potential—he tells her that he's "seen sausages with more style than you"—but he nevertheless attempts to transform her. He begins by fitting a dress on her, but she can't stand still; she fidgets, sneezes, clowns around, and complains that the dress is too tight and the pins are poking her. Irene is not a static, classical beauty; instead, she is a fully embodied woman who acknowledges and addresses her bodily needs and functions. This is further illustrated when Madame Lucy removes Irene's bra straps, and Irene clutches the top of the dress to keep it up, drawing attention to the fact that the demands of beauty sometimes conflict with the demands of the body—in this case, the fact that gravity trumps fashion (Figure 2.19). Madame Lucy's other attempts to transform the lively and playful Irene into a stuffy, decorative fashion model are similarly unsuccessful: when he shows her how to strike a pose she makes a joke of it, and when he passes out books to Irene and her friends while teaching them how to walk, the other women place the books on their heads while Irene opens hers and begins to read (Figure 2.20).

Like *The Clinging Vine*, *Irene* shows the work behind beauty and femininity. Irene doesn't automatically know how to wear fashionable clothes or "ooze

"An Inferiority Complex in a One-Piece Bathing Suit"

Figure 2.19. Colleen Moore and George K. Arthur in *Irene* (1926): "I've seen sausages with more style than you."

along" while walking; she needs to be taught these things. The fact that she learns femininity from an effeminate man recalls the strategy of pairing larger comediennes such as Marie Dressler and Charlotte Greenwood with smaller leading men. In fact, a number of makeover films feature effeminate men as supporting characters, including Snitz Edwards as both a timid board member in *The Clinging Vine* and a valet in *The Red Mill*. By pitting the comediennes' characters against these men the films highlight the women's inadequate femininity, as they end up looking more masculine by comparison. Ultimately, although Irene learns a few tricks from Madame Lucy (and is a hit at the Technicolor fashion show that is the film's climax), she largely retains the playful and spontaneous aspects of her personality. *Irene*, then, like *The Clinging Vine*, argues for finding a balance between feminine and "unfeminine" traits, as Irene is able to successfully combine unruliness and beauty.

Although Marion Davies was widely regarded as beautiful, in *The Red Mill* she plays a plain kitchen drudge, wearing a frumpy dress, crooked braids, and

Figure 2.20. Irene (Colleen Moore) reads a book in *Irene* (1926).

no makeup. In fact, quite a few comediennes who were considered attractive played characters who were homely, performing a version of the makeover stories in reverse and furthering the idea of beauty and femininity as artifice. By moving easily between pretty and plain roles, comediennes such as Davies, Colleen Moore, and Constance Talmadge blurred the lines between those classifications somewhat, and by playing sympathetic, albeit homely, heroines they demonstrated that other qualities—such as kindness, intelligence, and a sense of humor—were more important and useful to women than beauty. At the same time, audiences knew that underneath the dowdy costumes and messy hair were attractive women, and as a result their performance of homeliness could in some ways be read as a type of slumming, of playing at being unattractive but returning to the safety of their own beauty when the cameras stopped rolling. In an interview with Talmadge, the comedienne describes her willingness to appear in unflattering roles because she knew that there wasn't much at risk: "I don't want to be a pretty-pretty actress. I am very willing to

"An Inferiority Complex in a One-Piece Bathing Suit"

Figure 2.21. Constance Talmadge, publicity still from *Her Night of Romance* (1924).

be as ugly or as funny looking as the part demands, for the public knows how I look anyhow, and after an ugly part they may think me prettier than I really am, through pure contrast!"[65]

In *Her Night of Romance* (1924), she got the chance to play an "ugly part" of sorts, as a character disguised as a country schoolteacher, alternating in the film between "the flippant flapper and the bleak schoolma'am" (Figure 2.21).[66] Similarly, when Davies played homely or plain characters she was providing an in-joke to audiences who were well aware of her offscreen beauty. Although Colleen Moore inspired some debate about whether she was beautiful, the press generally agreed that she was attractive and therefore paid attention when she played homely characters, such as in *Ella Cinders* (1926) and *The Wall Flower* (1922). The press noted that Moore was "willing to sacrifice appearances for 'art'" in her performance of "a horrid little unkempt, unwashed slavey" in *Ella Cinders*, and after her turn in *The Wall Flower* as Idalene Nobbin, "a weed in a garden of roses . . . a wistful figure, awkward and

Figure 2.22. Colleen Moore in *The Wall Flower* (1922).

pigeon-toed," the press remarked that "a pretty girl can afford to play homely parts" (Figure 2.22).[67]

In fact, these films often made a point of reminding audiences that the homely parts were being played by pretty girls. This was certainly the case in films involving transformations or makeover plots, as the unattractive characters eventually become as beautiful as the actresses playing them. Even in films in which there is no transformation for the heroine, there is sometimes a scene that showcases her beauty. In *Suds* (1920), for example, Mary Pickford plays a shabby, working-class laundress who fantasizes about a fictional rich and titled family. Although Pickford's character is never made over in the film, a fantasy sequence allows the audience to get a glimpse of her as a beautiful princess, complete with her trademark curls (Figure 2.23).

When attractive comediennes played unattractive characters in their films, they were offering mixed messages. By cheerfully appearing on-screen in outmoded and unflattering costumes and makeup, they were doing some of the same work as slapstick comediennes who also donned grotesque character cos-

"An Inferiority Complex in a One-Piece Bathing Suit"

Figure 2.23. Laundry worker Amanda (Mary Pickford) dreams of a better life in *Suds* (1920).

tumes in their films, such as Louise Fazenda and Alice Howell. In both cases, the comediennes were deemphasizing beauty and instead putting the focus on their characters' other qualities and personality traits, such as their humor, intelligence, compassion, and resourcefulness. However, the effectiveness of this act is tempered by the fact that the homely characters generally underwent transformations to make them beautiful and by the audience's knowledge that Talmadge, Davies, and other comediennes were not really as unattractive as the characters they were playing.

The idea of transformation at work here—the idea of plain characters becoming beautiful or beautiful actresses becoming plain—both draws from and challenges Hollywood's beauty standards. Press discourses, studio publicity, and films that feature physical transformations—from homely to pretty, from unruly to feminine—necessarily set up an idealized concept of beauty or femininity as the ultimate goal of the transformation. When Marion Davies's Tina becomes beautiful in *The Red Mill* her success is measured against idealized standards and in turn reinforces those standards. At the same time, these standards are challenged when they're shown to be impossible or undesirable to achieve. In makeover films, idealized beauty and femininity are frequently presented as unsatisfying, as the heroines find happiness only when they embrace their unruly and unfeminine traits along with their newfound beauty and femininity.

"Is It Tragic to Be Comic?"

A common theme found in discourses surrounding comediennes was the tragedy behind their comedy, the fact that they were "clowns with aching hearts." Numerous articles, interviews, movie reviews, and press releases described the difficulties comediennes faced in coming to terms with their natural comedic abilities and the sacrifices they had to make to be funny. According to many of these discourses, one of the greatest sacrifices a comedienne could make was to hide her natural beauty beneath grotesque makeup and unflattering costumes, just as slapstick comediennes did in their films. Despite the fact that most slapstick comediennes designed their own costumes and makeup in a calculated effort to draw humor from their appearance, numerous press discourses imply that these comediennes were victims, both of the demands of the genre and of their own comic bent, as they had to hide what the press insisted were their naturally pretty faces and forms and subject themselves to unladylike situations. At the same time, newspapers and fan magazines offered contradictory readings of comediennes, arguing that they were not beautiful but in fact had suffered greatly throughout their lives because of their unattractiveness. These articles often point to homeliness as a reason for their turning to comedy rather than drama, echoing the assumption, discussed in chapter 1, that women became comediennes because they were unsuited for drama, not because of a specific desire to do comedy. In both cases women were said to resort to comedy rather than drama because they were not appropriately feminine, recalling the division between pretty and funny women that was reinforced by the press and by the studios through casting. Still, the simultaneous positioning of these women as pitiable both because they're attractive and because they're not attractive coincides with disagreements over the relative beauty of various slapstick or light comediennes, indicating cracks in the film industry's seemingly monolithic beauty standards.

A 1931 profile of Polly Moran titled, fittingly, "Is It Tragic to Be Comic?" asked, "Wouldn't any woman rather be known for her beauty than for her wit? When woman's whole aim in life is to be attractive, how must it feel to play the buffoon?"[68] This combination of bewilderment that a woman would choose to make herself a buffoon and sympathy for those who must sacrifice their "whole aim in life" is common in writings about female comics. The idea that women don't like to make themselves appear unattractive, and that this accounted for the supposed scarcity of female comedians in both motion pictures and theater, was repeated often. Charlotte Greenwood is quoted as saying that "the reason so few women on the stage are genuinely funny . . . is that they refuse to be or to look ridiculous."[69] Similarly, in a 1918 article Louise Fazenda "remarks truly" that "there aren't many girl comics. . . . I think it must be because girls like pleasing surroundings with pretty clothes and hate to be laughed at."[70] Another article noted that "about the hardest thing a pretty woman can do is to make herself look ridiculous. . . . When a woman can sacrifice her vanity on the altar of art she must be a true artist."[71]

The press treated comediennes who supposedly "sacrificed their vanity" reluctantly with sympathy. Louise Fazenda was typically described as one who dreaded making herself appear unattractive for laughs. Many articles pointed out that Fazenda had to hide her natural beauty, that "her career has been built upon a systematic suppression of personal charm, on bumps and bruises. Following out the paradoxical intent of her existence, she has risen in spite of her femininity rather than because of it."[72] Saying that she was "heartbroken" the first time she had to play an unattractive character role, one interview quotes her as saying, "It always hurt me to look homely and grotesque, and to have some comedian like Mack Swain or Chester Conklin kick me. . . . No one has ever known this, but I've said prayers before a scene to give me the strength to be humble enough to go through with it."[73] In another interview, Fazenda complained that she was "tired . . . of being homely."

> I always have a part in Sennett comedies where I have to make up to look like last year's bird's nest. From now on, after every picture, I'm going to buy about a million dollars' worth of new clothes and furs and get all calsomined and permanently marcelled and pulled in at the right places and let out at other places, and put on uncomfortable shoes and dazzle 'em for a few days, just to restore my self-respect.[74]

Fazenda's uneasiness with her dowdy costumes and homely characters, and her desire to appear beautiful on-screen, was endlessly discussed in articles, interviews, and publicity releases. More than any other slapstick comedienne, Fazenda's issues with her appearance formed an integral part of how the public understood her.

Articles about Louise Fazenda frequently foregrounded her beauty issues, with titles such as "You Don't Have to Be Beautiful," "Plain or Pretty as You Will," and "It Pays to Be Homely."[75] In these articles, Fazenda frequently discusses her dissatisfaction with wearing grotesque costumes and makeup. In a typical quote, she describes her ambivalence toward her slapstick roles:

> It is pleasant to a comedienne to hear herself laughed at, and I used to see every comedy of mine at the Los Angeles theatres just to hear the audiences laugh at me. But after a time that laughter grew rather tiresome. I wearied of being considered a poor boob and longed for a chance to show my face on the screen without that wild makeup.[76]

In another article, she laments her comedic fate:

> I'm feminine—and I'm human. I love to be dressed in laces and velvets and flowers. Do you suppose that I wouldn't give anything in the world to be a romantic type—and dress like one? Do you suppose that I enjoy wearing my hair skinned back into a towering pompadour, or enjoy wearing funny clothes and taking funny falls and making funny faces? I remember—too well—when I first began to do comedies. I looked upon them as something temporary; I had other ambitions.[77]

These articles positioned comediennes—primarily those whose attractiveness was tentative to begin with—as tragic victims, cruelly forced to sacrifice their vanity and dignity to get laughs. Significantly, attractive comediennes such as Constance Talmadge and Marion Davies were not shown to have the same distaste for assuming character costumes and makeup in some of their films. Certainly the fact that slapstick comediennes wore character garb in the majority of their films, at least in the 1910s, while light comediennes only played homely characters occasionally was a factor in their disparate treatment. It's also likely that by performing physical comedy slapstick comediennes were already considered dangerously unfeminine, a position that would only be reinforced when they made themselves appear unattractive. It's understandable, then, that the press and the studios would want to reassure fans that Louise Fazenda's or Polly Moran's performance of transgressiveness was a reluctant sacrifice rather than a joyful embrace of deviant femininity.

Comediennes who willingly, even cheerfully, made themselves unattractive on-screen, however, were viewed by many in the press with consternation. Alice Howell was particularly perplexing to the media because of her seeming disregard for the trappings of conventional femininity. A 1917 profile of Howell

"An Inferiority Complex in a One-Piece Bathing Suit"

drew attention to her unflappable attitude toward both her dowdy costumes and violent routines:

> When beauty persists in disguising itself in rags and indulging in comedy of the brand known as slapstick, the public's impatience for an explanation of such proclivities reaches a hectic pitch. It cannot conceive of any one enjoying being dumped from a motor car into the sea from the top of a cliff or being dragged all over a lot by the hair or being thrown from the roof of a house. Especially is this true when the subject is possessed of beauty and is young and talented enough to aspire to heroine roles where even the leading man must keep his distance until beckoned to. Alice Howell is the unusual young person who would rather be slung around by the hair than be made love to. She says that she not only has no prejudice against such things, but she actually prefers such work to all other in pictures. And yet it does seem a pity to put stove polish and biscuit dough on such a skin and to use such wonderful golden hair simply to haul one on and off the screen. "It makes it easier to toss me about," said Miss Howell as she shook down her hair which comes nearly to the bottom of her gown. "I don't care what they do with that but confidentially I don't care much about stopping pies in mid-career with my face."[78]

Describing the "public's impatience for an explanation" as to why a woman would prefer to work in knockabout slapstick films that require her to cover herself in "stove polish and biscuit dough," the author seems genuinely at a loss. Howell herself clearly was comfortable with her slapstick persona and in fact sent out publicity photos of herself in her character costume and makeup rather than studio portraits in more fashionable clothing.[79] Frankly confounded by Howell's indifference to presenting herself as the beautiful young woman that the press insisted she was, *Moving Picture World* printed a picture of her without her character costume or makeup, accompanied by the following explanation:

> Alice Howell does herself such perpetual injustice while she is making her fortune and winning fame as a screen comedienne, that the publicity agent of Century Comedies submits a picture of this clever girl unsullied by greasepaint and divested of the unsightly makeup she affects for busi-

ness reasons only. Reckless and daring in her conduct before the camera, Alice Howell is docile and domestic when off duty.[80]

By insisting that she donned the costume "for business reasons only" and that offscreen she was "docile and domestic," the writer was reclaiming for Howell the normative femininity that she herself seemed indifferent to. In another article from 1917, the author describes Howell's preference for unflattering slapstick roles (this preference had become a standard part of her persona) and ends by expressing her "hope, some day, to see Miss Howell in a picture where this pillorying of her fresh young charm will be unnecessary."[81]

Similarly, an article on Beatrice Lillie describes how she laughingly drew attention to her long nose, thus deflecting criticism about her appearance: "And, I beg of you, what other actress on the screen, over whose somewhat imperfect features the producers are worrying, would say, when profile shots are being taken, 'Get all of my nose in this scene, boys. Don't forget!'"[82]

While the press was prepared for women like Fazenda or Greenwood—women who longed to be pretty and feminine but reluctantly sacrificed their femininity for their comedy—they didn't know what to make of Alice Howell or Beatrice Lillie, who were seemingly content to embrace their unconventional appearances. The press and studios were clearly more comfortable with comediennes who longed to fit into Hollywood's beauty standards (of course, whether this longing was real or manufactured as a part of their public persona is unknowable) because, among other reasons, cosmetics, clothing, and personal hygiene industries were dependent upon a similar desire among female fans. But when women such as Howell and Lillie showed a casual indifference to those standards, they challenged the necessity for beauty standards and presented fans with a model of femininity that wasn't tied to physical appearance.

At the same time that the press was insisting that slapstick comediennes really were beautiful underneath their grotesque costumes and makeup and that they had to sacrifice their natural beauty in order to be funny, seemingly contradictory stories were circulating describing how these same comediennes had suffered greatly in their lives because of their lack of physical beauty. In these stories comediennes tell of their painful first discoveries that they were not beautiful, recalling stories, discussed in chapter 1, about their unhappy discovery that they were funny. Charlotte Greenwood tells of the "bitter" tears she cried before coming to terms with her appearance. She describes "the saddest blow of all" as a time when a friend suggested they form a vaudeville act together, with Greenwood acting as a comic foil to her friend's beauty. "Now think of that . . . and I had never dreamed that I was not beautiful—I who had dreamed of the day when I would Sarah-Bernhardt and Olga-Nethersole all over the stage!"[83] At the same time that some writers were praising Louise Fazenda's offscreen beauty, others were describing her disappointment in being homely and her desire to be pretty. In a *Motion Picture Classic* article attributed to Fazenda, she claims that "the worst bump of my life was when I found I was not pretty." She describes her assessment of her appearance after making that discovery at a school dance:

> I wasn't like those girls out there. My eyes were neither veiled nor mischievous—they were round and frankly stared at a then unfriendly world; my hair fell in limp, drab folds—it was hair and that's all; my mouth was neither pouty nor cupid-bowed—it was something to put food into; of my nose, the less said the better; and my forehead and ears, exposed nakedly to the public, gave me a horrid, undressed feeling. I was not pretty. Only a girl can realize what a terrible realization that must be.[84]

Fazenda's heartbreaking discovery of her own plainness and her plaintive longing for beauty were the topic of numerous articles in newspapers and magazines, such as this 1928 profile in *Motion Picture Magazine*:

> Louise Fazenda has gone through life getting her feelings hurt about her looks. According to the standards set by Venus and Ziegfeld, Louise's features don't quite jibe. She's had that brought home to her almost all her life. . . . Louise is the first to admit that her teens were not a lovely age. She was an ungainly kid with large wrists and a mouth that spread too far when she laughed; and funny, rather crinkly eyes in place of large, dreamy ones. When she grew a little older and went into pictures, the bathing beauties over at Sennett's used to refer to her as the homely girl. It hurt at first. It hurt something awful, as it always does with girls with hearts as lovely as Louise's and exteriors that don't match. Even after she became famous on the screen with her comedy antics, there were dark days and nights when Louise wondered if life with its lovely gifts of love and happiness was going to pass her by because she didn't look the part.[85]

One writer found in her homeliness the root of her comedy: "What girl ever lived who sincerely wanted to be called a good sport? Clowning was her 'cover-up.'. . . . The ugly duckling was to become a bird in calico comedy, winging its message to hungry souls."[86] In a profile of Fazenda titled "You Don't Have to Be Beautiful," the writer states flatly:

> It has never occurred to me to think that Louise is not a pretty girl. She offers so much that mere beauty seems a trivial matter. I doubt if the fans pause to notice this lack. Yet, any analysis shows that she does not measure up to the accepted standards of beauty. . . . [S]he has proved that beauty is not necessary for success on the screen. . . . But, she says, she would like to be beautiful.[87]

The contradictions in this quote—that, on the one hand, beauty is unnecessary and unimportant to the fans, while on the other hand not being pretty means not "measur[ing] up"—mirror the contradictions evident in the discourses about the relative beauty of screen comediennes. Ultimately these stories served to make their subjects sympathetic to audience members who may have had similarly contradictory and ambiguous feelings toward their own appearance. The heart-wrenching descriptions of Fazenda, Greenwood, and others trying to come to terms with what amounts to a failure to live up to normative standards of beauty would certainly have been familiar, on some level, to a great many women. As physical beauty was becoming ever more important in American society, and as idealized standards of beauty were narrowing, it's conceivable that women would take comfort in the knowledge that their film idols struggled with the same body and appearance issues as they did.

Surprisingly, similar stories about growing up homely were circulated regarding some comediennes who were considered conventionally attractive. Constance Talmadge described her younger self as "an overgrown, gawky kid" who was too "little and skinny" to follow her famous sister Norma into dramatic films.[88] Although she was only seventeen years old and already quite pretty when she made her debut in films, Talmadge describes her entrée into motion pictures, which came about while visiting Norma at her studio: "One day I heard them say they were looking for a homely, skinny little girl to play a bit. My vanity was all gone by that time. . . . They told me I was a bit too homely and too skinny, but I might try."[89]

Similarly, Adela Rogers St. Johns speculated that Marion Davies's "desire to be an actress came partly from the fact that she was a very plain little girl who only blossomed into a beauty when she had gone through all the hurts and slights of a plain little girl."⁹⁰ Like the stories about "homely" comediennes' childhoods, stories that positioned attractive comediennes as gawky, plain, insecure little girls certainly allowed fans to relate to them. At the same time, these kinds of discourses fed into the theme of transformation found in many of the light comediennes' films (as well as the strategies of the burgeoning cosmetics industry) by assuring fans that beauty was available to every woman, that even the ugliest of ducklings could become a swan.

Stories about comediennes' tragic plainness often included mention of the fact that many of these women turned to comedy because they were not considered attractive enough for dramatic roles. Charlotte Greenwood's description of her dramatic ambitions is typical: "I wanted to be a great dramatic star or prima donna, but all that time I was fighting against nature. It took me all that time to realize that I wasn't built to shine as Ophelia or the Merry Widow."⁹¹ Gale Henry took a more cavalier approach to her comedic fate. When asked by an interviewer if she liked comedies, she laughingly replied, "Do I like 'em? . . . I *have* to like 'em! Can you imagine me as the heroine of a melodrama?"⁹²

Louise Fazenda similarly claimed that she had had her heart set on becoming a dramatic actress and the "accidental" start to her comedy career became an important part of her studio publicity. In one article, Fazenda describes the "terrible irony of fate if you began with the aspirations of a Bernhardt and ended as a clown," and remarks that "when it came to ingénues, I couldn't 'inge' worth a cent." She concludes the article by saying that she "did have a few faint yearnings toward drama, but have reconciled myself with the thought that every one has a hard luck story and to create smiles was worth any sort of sacrifice."⁹³ As Fazenda's realization that she was not beautiful was presented in tragic terms, so was her inability to fulfill her dramatic aspirations. In language that echoes the heartbreaking stories of her childhood as an ugly duckling, a 1925 *Motion Picture Magazine* article argues that Fazenda was "one of the most unhappy" people in Hollywood:

> She is the greatest girl comedian in the world: but she doesn't want to be a girl comedian. The ambition of her life has been to play tragedy. And they will not let her. Louise once told me that she never saw Lillian Gish in a big tragic picture that she didn't go home and cry her eyes out to think it could not be she doing it.⁹⁴

Just who "they" are—those who refuse to let Fazenda play tragedy—is unclear. While this article doesn't question the system that insists on separating the beautiful tragediennes from the homely comediennes, another asked, "Why must a capable actress like Charlotte Greenwood work only in comedies where she sits in mud puddles instead of playing the heroine who gets wooed and won by a hero who hasn't a Greek-god profile?"[95] As Greenwood insightfully pointed out to her interviewer,

> the only women who get courted, kidnapped, insulted, endangered, hired as secretaries, kissed, plotted against, left a fortune, compromised, fought for or married are the young and beautiful ones. All the others presumably live in boarding houses, teach school, and botanize for excitement.[96]

When comediennes are presented as unable to perform dramatic roles—because of their appearance or their natural proclivity for comedy—the implication is that they are unable to perform "ideal" femininity. For Fazenda, her awkwardness and lack of "feminine wiles" conspire to make her a spectacle even when she is trying to behave like a lady. Her fans are clearly meant to find her inability to perform drama as sympathetic, and fan magazines and studio publicity reported on roles that she played that fell closer to her dramatic ideal. Upon the release of her 1924 film *The Lighthouse by the Sea*, one article commented on the fact that Fazenda "plays, for the first time in her long screen career, the heroine who marries the hero,"[97] and in an article titled "Slow Music for Louise at Last," her opportunity to play a death scene in an upcoming film is described with a proud enthusiasm most often reserved for winners of beauty pageants: "In all her eight years of acting she never realized this great moment would ever come."[98]

For "homely" actresses such as Fazenda, Greenwood, and Henry, comedy is presented as their only choice. These discourses, then, simultaneously reinforce and draw attention to the stereotypical division between beauty and comedy. By pointing out that many actresses are prevented from working in drama only because of their appearance, these articles question the usefulness and validity of that system. At the same time, by presenting these comediennes as longing, but unable, to play dramatic roles these articles continue the longstanding tradition of situating comedy as inherently inferior to drama.

The popular discourses surrounding silent comediennes, then, were often paradoxical, framing these women simultaneously as too beautiful for comedy and too plain for drama. What they had in common, however, was the notion that comediennes had to sacrifice a great deal—including their vanity and their dramatic aspirations—to succeed in comedy. Ultimately what they were seen as sacrificing was their femininity, as their lack of traditional feminine qualities paired with their inability to succeed as dramatic actresses was described as tantamount to an inability to succeed as women. Stories that focused attention on comediennes' relative beauty, or lack thereof, served to feed Hollywood's obsession with female beauty while simultaneously furthering the longstanding stereotype that women could be either pretty or funny but never both.

Either as the beauty who courageously hides her attractiveness for the camera or as the tragic ugly duckling longing to be beautiful, comediennes were frequently presented in a way that called attention to their appearance and made it an integral part of their personae, and stories that positioned comediennes as tragic figures in many ways advanced the idea of Hollywood's beauty standards as an unrealistic ideal that many women couldn't live up to. When Louise Fazenda catalogues her physical deficiencies, she sets herself up in opposition to a feminine ideal created by the media, with "veiled" and "mischievous" eyes, "pouty" and "cupid-bowed" lips. Instead of these attributes, she describes eyes that "frankly stared" at the world and a mouth made "to put food into." She is not a passive, mysterious beauty; instead, she investigates the world with her "round" eyes and consumes with her mouth. She is a part of the world, a human being rather than an impossible ideal. Similarly, when Marie Dressler laments that she was born homely, or when Charlotte Greenwood insists that she was not fated to play glamorous ingénue roles, they draw attention to the fact that ideal beauty is out of reach for many women.

Stories about comediennes' lack of success in dramatic roles can be seen in this same light. As I discuss in chapter 1, these discourses complicate the idea that women are naturally sensitive, that they are instinctually drawn to the higher art forms. The notion that many comediennes turned to comedy because they were unable to perform drama functions in the same way as stories about their lack of natural beauty: in both cases, they are unable to perform conventional femininity. The element of pathos in these stories—the idea of a woman who desperately wanted to be a beautiful tragedienne and ended up a homely comedienne—would certainly have resonated with women who similarly had difficulty conforming to societal gender expectations. The fact that both of these themes resurface time and again in a wide variety of newspaper and magazine articles as well as studio publicity and films indicates that this element of pathos was an important part of comediennes' appeal to fans. Whether these comediennes celebrated or lamented their unconventional femininity, they functioned as a reminder that conventional femininity was an ideal that was difficult for many women to achieve.

Not only do these comediennes draw attention to the film industry's impossibly high standards of beauty, they also reveal the artifice behind idealized beauty and femininity. This is something that the popular press also understood: in a 1925 profile of Louise Fazenda, Adela Rogers St. Johns simultaneously exposes and perpetuates the constructed nature of Hollywood beauty:

> Louise is no beauty, but I sometimes think that she might have been made into a beauty as well as some others I have seen on the screen. She has as much to start with—glorious, curly, thick hair, in shades of golden brown. Intelligent eyes. And a figure so excellent that she has posed a number of times for famous sculptors. But if there was ever a woman indifferent to her personal appearance, it is Fazenda. Just the same I cling to my hunch that if as much time and money and attention had been spent on Louise as has been spent upon certain other stars, she might have been called a beauty.[99]

St. Johns frankly affirms that Hollywood actresses are only as beautiful as the studios made them and that even someone like Fazenda, who is "no beauty," and whose heartbreaking homeliness was an integral part of her persona, could have been just as beautiful as other stars.

The supposed sacrifices made by comediennes and detailed by fan magazines and studio publicity—covering their beauty and giving up their dramatic aspirations—while presented as tragic, were also transgressive. Susan Glenn argues that

> to sacrifice femininity, even in the name of artistic devotion, was really to emphasize it by calling attention to the difference between sanctioned and unsanctioned female behavior and looks. . . . Specifically, it allowed funny women . . . to make common cause with the funny (excessive) women in the audience, women who were unable or unwilling to fit within the established beauty and behavior standards of their time.[100]

What comediennes offered was an alternate conception of beauty and femininity as performance, something that is not inherently possessed by all women but something that can be played with, appropriated, or discarded, and even rejected. If these comediennes were conventionally attractive—and many of them are presented this way in studio portraits—then their appearance in films wearing unflattering costumes and harsh makeup can be seen as a rejection of

"An Inferiority Complex in a One-Piece Bathing Suit"

Figure 2.24. Alice Howell: "Look at her as she really is."

physical beauty in favor of laughs. Furthermore, the fact that they were able to switch between plain and beautiful shows that neither category is fixed, that women can inhabit both positions at will.

A perfect illustration of this can be found in the many newspaper and magazine articles that printed pictures of comediennes in character next to glamorous studio portraits. These photo juxtapositions further emphasize the ease with which women can slip back and forth between gender extremes—as conventional beauties or unconventional grotesques. Numerous articles claim to show actresses "as they really are," as if the highly controlled and posed portraits are any closer to the reality of these women's lives than the character shots. These photographs insistently assert that offscreen slapstick comediennes are not as grotesque, and therefore not as threatening, as they appear on-screen. On-screen, they may break every law of society and physics as they roughhouse with men and throw themselves about with reckless abandon. But offscreen, these pictures tell us, they are refined and dignified, and are even a little bewildered by their own on-screen antics (Figures 2.24 and 2.25).

Figure 2.25. Gale Henry: "Off the screen she is a most attractive young woman."

As Kathleen Rowe argues, "The body that 'refuses to be aestheticized,' that does not control its 'grotesque, offensive, dirty aspects,' can . . . communicate resistance to social discipline."[101] At a time when highly visible and unruly women were challenging social and political structures and demanding enfranchisement, these photographs could serve to aestheticize comediennes and reassure fans that their idols were really proper ladies. At the same time, just as in comedies that feature transformation themes, these photographs show that beauty is largely performative and that women could "pass" as either pretty or plain (within limits, of course). Furthermore, the fact that these women were celebrated for qualities other than their beauty makes these other qualities—such as their talent, humor, and intelligence— seem more valued, a fact that is visually represented by the pictures in these articles. Not only are the character images much larger than the studio portraits, the fact that they feature the full body of each actress, as well as the actresses' activity and interaction with other (male) characters, points to the fact that the comic characters are embodied and fully participating in the world, as opposed to the beautiful but static and isolated portraits. These photographs seem to be saying that the portraits may be pretty, but the comic figures are having fun.

Comediennes offered an alternative model of femininity that countered the ideal image of beauty found in other film and stage genres. When comediennes emphasized their non-normative physical traits in their acts, they were rejecting the notion that excessive, homely, or unruly women should attempt to conform to popular standards and were instead embracing their "deviant" appearance. And when comediennes engaged in on-screen transformations, either as homely characters who turned beautiful or beautiful actresses who turned homely, they were showing that an acceptably feminine woman could have an unruly edge. Finally, by showing the work required to achieve and maintain beauty, comediennes demonstrated that beauty is not something innate to all women but rather something that can be created, manipulated, and even rejected altogether. Overall, comediennes modeled a type of femininity that wasn't dependent on beauty or an idealized image of femininity and argued that brains, personality, and a sense of humor were as important to a woman as how she looked.

3

"Cupid Lips and an Ungodly Appetite"

SENSUALITY, SEXUALITY, AND DESIRE

In a scene from the 1927 film *It*, shopgirl Betty Lou Spence (Clara Bow) sees her new boss across a crowded room and determines on the spot to win him over. Like a cat stalking her prey, Betty Lou fixes her gaze on her intended, as her initially tender expression changes from barely contained lust to plaintive longing. After filming the close-up the film's director, Clarence Badger, asked Bow to explain her look:

> "Well," she came back, "if you knew your onions like you're supposed to, you'd know that first expression was for the love-sick dames in the audience, and that the second expression, that passionate stuff, was for the boys and their paps, and that third expression—well, Mr. Badger, just about the time all the old women in the audience had become shocked and scandalized by that passionate part, they'd suddenly see that third expression, become absorbed in it, and change their minds about me having naughty ideas and go home thinking how pure and innocent I was; and having got me mixed up with the character I'm playing, they'd come again when my next picture showed up."[1]

Bow's description of her various expressions and their likely appeal to different segments of the audience indicates a savvy understanding of how a comedienne could effectively portray sexuality on-screen. In silent-era drama and melodrama female sexuality was generally depicted as dangerous, as vamps and other sexually knowing women, played by stars such as Theda Bara, Pola Negri, and Greta Garbo, left a path of ruined lives in their wakes. In a great many of these films female sexuality is punished, often with the death and/or insanity of the "fallen woman," her lover, or both.[2] In *The Devil's Daughter* (1915), for example, Theda Bara plays a vengeful beauty who drives her lover mad after crippling his wife and finally succumbs to madness herself. Greta Garbo's *The Temptress* (1926) similarly ends with the title character on the brink of madness, and in *Flesh and the Devil* (1926) Garbo's character causes the death of her first husband and drives her second husband and her lover to the brink of duel before she herself dies. Several film adaptations of Andre Dumas's novel *La Dame aux camélias* were made in the silent era, each ending with the death of the "courtesan" Camille, either in her lover's arms or alone.[3]

This trend toward punishing female sexuality was not generally found in comedies; sexuality was contained at the end of comedies, usually through marriage, but women were generally free to express their sexuality in myriad ways with no ill consequences. Certainly silent comediennes never wrought the kind of personal destruction that the melodramatic vamps did, but they were nonetheless frequently depicted as desiring and often sexually knowledgeable figures. This is most clearly evident in flapper films, where characters played by Clara Bow, Louise Brooks, Colleen Moore, and Joan Crawford danced, smoked, petted, schemed, and always emerged triumphant. The light comedies of "virtuous vamps" Constance Talmadge, Dorothy Gish, and Marion Davies similarly feature women who flirt with illicit sexuality and are still rewarded with happy endings. Collectively, these films make an argument for female sexuality as fun and natural, in fact, an essential tool for getting and keeping a mate.

Flappers and virtuous vamps were not the only comediennes to play with issues of female sexuality in their films. Slapstick comediennes played with sexuality and sensuality in a variety of ways. Although they were not presented as overtly sexual as flappers or light comediennes, slapstick comedy presented women with an opportunity to test the boundaries of socially acceptable relations between the sexes and revel in bodily pleasures in ways unseen in other genres.

Comediennes, then, afforded women many ways to express sexuality on-screen. Flirtation in comedies highlighted the inherent fun in sexual relations while simultaneously suggesting that romantic relationships could be fluid rather than stable. In films where comediennes were called upon to enact aggressive sexuality they were calling attention to and questioning behavioral standards that required women to be demure and reserved. Comediennes also presented a powerful endorsement of female sensuality in their films, as they reveled in the bodily pleasure of physical comedy. Finally, cross-dressing comedies, which drew from the long tradition of male impersonation in vaudeville and burlesque, tested the boundaries of acceptable sexuality and presented the possibility of homosexual desire. Male impersonation in films and onstage allowed comediennes the opportunity to play with traditional gender roles while simultaneously allowing audience members to enjoy the illicit sexuality that these films presented.

Respectability and Audiences

The tremendous popularity of fallen women and vamp films is an indication of public nervousness surrounding women's increased presence in the public sphere after the turn of the century. Whereas in the previous century middle-class women were not supposed to return a man's gaze, by the late 1800s many adopted a "directness of gaze," making eye contact not only with husbands and family members but also with strangers on the street.[4] This newfound directness, coupled with an increased presence in public and changes in makeup and clothing, made it increasingly difficult to determine at a glance whether a woman was "respectable."[5] As the twentieth century drew near, "an ethic of leisure gradually emerged as an acceptable strand of modern life. This ethic encouraged the pleasures of leisurely shopping and consumption, as well as the pastimes of dancing, movies, and amusement parks."[6] By the 1890s, an active, independent, and assertive model of femininity would emerge to question and challenge societal expectations of the proper role for women: as Rob King argues, "as America moved into modernity, a sentimental ideology of female dependence thus shifted to a cultural image of female autonomy."[7] The rise of the New Woman ideal coincided with a more generalized relaxation of gender roles around the turn of the century. Alison Kibler describes a "sexual revolution" that took place between 1890 and 1920, in which both women and men "experimented more with sexuality outside of marriage and adopted more assertive sexual styles of dress and behavior in public."[8] Dating, which in the Victorian era had been seen as a precursor to marriage, became a recreational activity that was an end in itself. This increased sexual freedom, combined with women's intensifying demands for suffrage and equal rights, led some to predict that the New Woman would bring about the demise of the nuclear family.[9]

At the same time, female theater- and cinemagoers in the late nineteenth and early twentieth centuries were negotiating a difficult set of new roles. On the one hand, changing standards of respectability in legitimate and motion picture theaters meant that audiences were required to sit quietly and passively enjoy the entertainments. On the other hand, loosening restrictions concerning gender roles meant that women could attend the theater on their own or with other women and could participate in a level of heterosocial mixing that was unheard of in the nineteenth century. Theater owners and managers made a specific appeal to female spectators, hoping that the presence of women in the audience would dignify their entertainments.[10] However, despite the industry's desire for feminized respectability, female spectators were not always as demure and passive as theater owners desired. As Alison Kibler points out,

> It is particularly important to remember the multiple ways women took power in vaudeville: through the codes of the female censor (set and reinforced by male managers) and through the appropriation of more masculine behaviors. Although accounts of women's uproarious (masculine) behavior appeared less frequently in [theater] managers' reports and in the published descriptions of vaudeville, this avenue of power for women reminds us that women did not simply pacify the vaudeville audience and that their role was not limited to exerting moral and aesthetic influence. Their pleasures and power in vaudeville were not wholly contained in the role of female censor prescribed for them by managers.[11]

Furthermore, the types of entertainments that women actually enjoyed were often far from dignified: in fact, women were largely responsible for the popularity of strongman performers such as Eugene Sandow, whose act consisted of showing off his considerable muscles while wearing little more than a fig leaf.

A major element in theater's drive to respectability in the nineteenth century was making the theatrical experience less interactive. Formerly boisterous audiences were trained to sit quietly and passively watch the show, without participating in the entertainment. Similarly, actors were expected to observe the fourth wall, and to avoid directly interacting with the audience, but a great many comedians, both male and female, disregarded this new theatrical convention. Many comediennes' acts involved directly addressing the audience, specifically recalling the days before the "feminization" of theater when actors and spectators worked together to create the entertainment. These interactions with the audience were frequently loaded with sexual overtones, as female performers would flirt with men in the audience, often to the embarrassment of the men and the consternation of the theater managers. The Faber Sisters, a singing and dancing team whose repertoire included the playfully suggestive song "How'd You Like to Be My Daddy?" were ordered by one manager to cut their "reference to becoming better acquainted with one of the men in the audience," and another manager chastised comedienne Lillian Shaw's habit of talking to patrons seated in the boxes, saying, "You would think that a girl who had been on the circuit as long as she has would know better."[12] Engaging the audience was a way for female performers to gain more power onstage, as interacting with the audience effectively removed the performers from the position of passive receiver of the spectators' gaze, a position that characterized the chorines of the Ziegfeld *Follies* (and later Mack Sennett's Bathing Beauties). The effect of the suggestive lyrics of their songs combined with an assertive delivery was that the performers appeared in control of their own sexuality, as well as in control of the men in the audience.

As spectators in legitimate and motion picture theaters women were able to envision alternate roles for themselves and vicariously experience transgressive behaviors. In the safety of the darkened theater, women could watch female performers engaging in wild, anarchic behavior and questioning the validity of women's assumed place in society. Female spectators seemed to be particularly delighted by acts that questioned or complicated traditional gender roles and hierarchies. Many popular female performers in vaudeville, for example, challenged the Victorian ideal of women as pure and passive through their aggressive and sexually suggestive songs and routines. Many of the song titles of the period exemplify this performance style, for example, Nora Bayes's "I Work Eight Hours a Day, I Sleep Eight Hours a Night, That Leaves Eight Hours for Lovin'" (1915), Sophie Tucker's "When They Get Too Wild for Everyone Else, They're Perfect for Me" (1922), Eva Tanguay's "It's All Been Done Before But Not the Way I Do It" (1913), and Irene Franklin's Prohibition era song about men who carry hip flasks, "What Have You Got on Your Hip? You Don't Seem to Bulge Where a Gentleman Ought To." These unruly performances made vaudeville theaters "places where women in the audience could fantasize about other possible lives, imagine alternatives to Victorian refinement, and unleash any anger at the limitations in their own lives."[13] While it is impossible to know precisely how audiences reacted to specific performers or acts, there is ample evidence that female spectators enjoyed acts that challenged gender roles and allowed them to flirt with forbidden sexuality. The theater afforded women a place to safely experiment with rebellion and to try on new gender roles. Female spectators could see that there was the possibility for sexual pleasure outside of marriage and that independence and personal fulfillment were accessible to women as well as men.

Public attitudes toward actresses were complex and still somewhat negative in the early 1900s. In the mid-1800s, the link between actress and prostitute was still very clear, as Robert Allen points out:

> The phenomenon of independent, working-class women engaging in commerce in a working-class theatrical space was perceived by those in a position to make laws as tantamount to criminal sexuality.... In the 1850s, "prostitution" meant not so much literal sexual commerce as a whole symbolic constellation of qualities attendant upon the working-class woman's economic and social independence from her family and resistance to or distance from patriarchal control.[14]

The rise of female audiences and the resultant feminization of the theater meant that by the early twentieth century actresses were regarded in a somewhat better light. However, many held that the theatrical profession was inherently immoral and that women who made their living onstage were somehow wicked. In 1899, English drama critic Clement Scott commented that "it was nearly impossible for a woman who adopts the stage as a profession to remain pure."[15] This statement sparked a great deal of controversy in both England and the United States—comedienne May Irwin denounced him as a "hypocrite, a journalistic vampire—a man so low, so vile, that he can see nothing but vice wherever he may look"[16]—but nonetheless it is likely that Scott was not alone in his opinion. Even those who allowed that actresses could manage to remain pure were frequently of the opinion that "women onstage were vain and frivolous, not truly artistic and professional."[17] The widely reported extravagances and luxuries of many actresses, which may have been appealing to some aspiring performers, were seen by many as evidence of women's naturally frivolous nature. Whereas actresses were thought to be interested only in wealth and status, actors were assumed to be interested in the artistic merits of the theater.

If actresses were thought to be vain and frivolous, chorus girls were seen as a much more serious threat. In the early 1900s, "the chorus girl came to be viewed as a social problem, one that seemed to threaten, along with woman suffrage, the very foundation of traditional gender relations."[18] On the one hand, the chorus girl was stereotyped as a Cinderella character who rose from poverty to achieve economic and professional success and occasionally married a rich admirer. Conversely, the chorus girl was frequently portrayed as a heartless gold digger who ruthlessly took advantage of lovestruck men, draining their bank accounts and their self-respect. As actresses on the legitimate and vaudeville stages were breaking away from their longstanding association with prostitution, chorus girls were increasingly identified as "working girls." The gold digger myth was a way of punishing actresses for their economic independence and their perceived sexual transgressions. Chorus girls were commonly thought to be loose and immoral, in part because, according to Susan Glenn, "Broadway producers and performers stimulated fantasies about the sexual desirability and perhaps even the accessibility of theater women. Actresses of all kinds were implicated in the fantasy, but none more so than chorus girls."[19] Adding to the chorus girl myth were popular books such as Anita Loos's *Gentlemen Prefer Blondes* (1925) and plays such as Avery Hopwood's *Gold Diggers* (1919), which portrayed Broadway chorines as alluring and manipulative women who used their sexuality to have their way with unsuspecting men. For women who wanted to find a career in the theater, the chorus offered tremendous possibilities. However, "no profession except for prostitution so stigmatized women. To interrogate this paradox is to reveal much about the history of women's curious entrapment between the empowering potential of performance and its equally powerful potential to immure."[20] The independence and equality that women found in the Broadway chorus often translated into negative stereotyping resulting from conservative backlash.

While film actresses generally were not perceived to be as immoral as the stage actresses of the nineteenth century or the gold-digging chorus girls of the early twentieth century, they were still a part of this tradition. Many actresses used this stereotype to their advantage—not just those who made a career out of playing vamps and dangerous women but also comediennes, especially flappers and light comediennes. Constance Talmadge explicitly referenced the association between acting and prostitution in a *Photoplay* article titled "Why Men Fall in Love with Actresses":

> Men in droves "fall" for actresses more readily than for other women because the actress has the advantage—if you want to call it an advantage—of the tradition, accumulating in weight for hundreds of years, that

all actresses are naughty. They aren't, but that doesn't make any difference. The tradition is there. And Thomas and Richard and Henry like naughty women. Or they think they do.

I have watched men falling over each other in a wild rush to become acquainted with an actress, simply because her press agent had carefully painted a picture of her as a wicked woman—and have then seen these same men dropping her like a hot cake when they discovered that she actually was no more wicked than a bowl of crackers and milk.[21]

Talmadge draws attention to the stereotype that "actresses are naughty" and then deftly deflects any negative connotations by insisting that, in fact, the tradition is inaccurate and by pointing out that men only *think* they want a woman who is "naughty." This image of the "good little bad girl" or the "virtuous vamp"[22] is found in a great many of the films of Talmadge and other light comediennes: in these films, the heroine gets involved in complicated and compromising situations, but her innocence is always confirmed at the end of the film.

Like those of light comediennes, flapper comediennes' personae were frequently crafted with the actress-as-promiscuous tradition in mind. Clara Bow, especially, was portrayed in the press as somewhat loose: "Amoral, and not immoral," as *Motion Picture Magazine* described her.[23] Numerous newspaper and fan magazine accounts breathlessly described her affairs with Gary Cooper, Victor Fleming, Harry Richman, Rex Bell, and various other men.[24] One article argued that "her thirty-six thousand fan letters last month proved that she is the kind of girl that men like to remember,"[25] and another article revealed that "every year, she entertains the whole University of Southern California team *en masse* at her home. Now and then, a few of them individually. Football coaches don't approve."[26] *Motion Picture Magazine* concluded that its own publicity could mean that Bow would have a hard time finding a husband: "She knows that no 'nice man' would be very likely to marry her—now. 'Nice men' are squeamish about newspaper stories and reputations all messed up and untidy."[27]

Rather than hurting Bow, however, this type of publicity helped to more closely align her with the sexually adventurous flappers she played in her films. As the quote that began this chapter illustrates, Bow was aware of and played with her promiscuous image, directing "passionate" looks to the "boys and their paps" in the audience and then changing her expression to appease the "old women" who might be "shocked and scandalized by that passionate part." Bow's reference to these old women confusing her with her character and going to see more of her pictures is telling, as she clearly understood that she needed to maintain a balance between the desirable and desiring flapper and the innocent girl in order to appeal to different segments of the audience. While the actress-as-whore reputation certainly sold magazines and more than a few tickets to their films, this image, for Bow and other comediennes, needed to be tempered by an image of the actress as innocent girl next door. This duality made it possible to present potentially dangerous and illicit sexuality to a broad audience, all in the safe confines of film comedy.

"I Never Flirted in My Life—Unless It Was Absolutely Necessary"

Silent comediennes frequently played with flirtation in their films. Whether as a means of snaring an on-screen mate or as an end in itself, flirting could be a powerful tool for comediennes, who flirt with friends, neighbors, and even complete strangers with joyous abandon. Men in silent comedies routinely ditch their wives to follow attractive young girls who smile at them, and women are shown to enjoy creating havoc with a passing glance. The flirtations in these films foreground anxieties about women's increased presence in the public sphere and the increasing popularity of heterosocial interactions, including unchaperoned dating and companionate marriage. At the same time, they showcase a world in which women are in control of social and sexual situations, where romance and sex are fun and exciting rather than obligatory and, perhaps most revolutionary, where relationships are fluid and swapping partners is a playful alternative to monotonous monogamy.

Slapstick comedies very frequently feature situations in which playful flirtations lead to chaos and mayhem. In these flirtation comedies, the comediennes by and large control not only the narrative but also the men around them. In *The Water Nymph* (1912), Mabel Normand is told by her boyfriend, played by Mack Sennett, that "Papa feels younger today, vamp him at the beach." Mabel happily obliges, smiling seductively at Papa (Ford Sterling) as she passes him, and Papa—who is described in an intertitle as "a faithful husband when locked in at home"—immediately responds by sneaking away from his wife to join Mabel for a swim. The bathing costume that Mabel wears—a highly controversial one-piece style popularized by Australian swimmer Annette Kellerman—positions

Figure 3.1. Mabel Normand in her one-piece "Kellerman" bathing costume.

her as daring and confident, especially when contrasted to the other women in more traditional bathing costumes (Figure 3.1). For many women wearing a Kellerman, as the one-piece suits were popularly known, was tantamount to making a political statement; although the suits were less restrictive than traditional costumes and allowed for freer movement while swimming, women could be arrested for indecent exposure when wearing them in public.[28] Rob King points out that

> the figure of the bathing girl that played such a central role in working-class perceptions of New Womanhood was far from being an innocent or consensually unproblematic category. The key to its popularity arguably depended on its capacity to address different needs based on gender and sexuality—both working women's desire to assert their modernity and working men's heterosexual interests—and to unite them in a figure firmly grounded in the vibrant plebeian culture of beaches, burlesque, and amusement parks.[29]

When Mabel appears in a Kellerman while "vamping" her boyfriend's father she is making a complicated and contradictory statement: on the one hand, she is presenting herself as an object of desire, to be looked at not only by Papa but by everyone else at the beach. At the same time, Mabel isn't passive; after stripping down to her Kellerman, she immediately goes to a diving board and performs a series of athletic dives, reminding the viewers that the original purpose of the one-piece costume was not sexual display but rather the feminist desire for more practical, less restrictive clothing for women.[30]

Just as her wearing of a Kellerman suit can be read in contradictory ways, so can her enthusiastic agreement to vamp her boyfriend's father for fun. She is simultaneously making a sexual spectacle of herself and making a statement about proper feminine behavior. While she flirts with Papa and allows him to gaze lasciviously at her in her bathing costume, she is entirely in control of the situation, leading Papa along even though she knows she is not interested in him romantically. Sex is presented as sport, no different from Mabel's athletic dives.

In light comedies and flapper films, as in slapstick comedies, when women flirt with men they are in control of the sexual situation. Clara Bow was especially known for her playfully flirtatious roles, and in fact this characterization became a part of her persona. A 1928 *Motion Picture Classic* description of Bow reinforced this image:

> Clara Bow. Plump, red-head, cat eyes. Has Cupid lips and an ungodly appetite. Begins to flirt with you after the second cocktail. After the fourth begins to flirt with the saxophone player or the fellow who beats the drum. Knows some good stories, but doesn't always get them straight.[31]

In *Mantrap* (1926), Clara Bow plays with her flirtatious image as Alverna, a manicurist who uses her feminine wiles to get everything and everyone she desires. She is introduced in the film climbing out of an elderly man's car in front of her workplace, saying "So long, Sweet Man—thanks for the buggy ride." When Joe Easter (Ernest Torrence), a small-town man visiting the big city, spots her in the salon in which she works, she convinces him to get a manicure by stroking his hand and telling him that "I just love working on a real he-man's hand—for a little change!" For Alverna, flirting is the currency she uses to get what she needs, whether that means a ride to work or a customer. Even after Alverna marries Joe and moves with him to the backwoods Canadian village of Mantrap, her flirting doesn't stop. Setting her sights on a visiting lawyer from New York named Ralph

Prescott (Percy Marmont), she convinces him to take her back to the city and ultimately gets him to propose. On their way back to the city Alverna and Ralph get lost in the wilderness and are discovered by a forest ranger; hoping to procure some food Alverna smiles and winks at the ranger and is then chastised by Ralph for flirting. Alverna points out that "to get the eats one of us had to flirt with him—and it couldn't be you, could it?" Later she insists that "I never flirted in my life—unless it was absolutely necessary." The idea of flirting as *necessary*, as the best (and in some cases only) way for a woman to get what she wants, is notable, as it introduces the idea of sex as currency, something that women can exchange to fulfill other needs.

It's useful to compare Clara Bow and her use of flirting to Constance Talmadge in *A Virtuous Vamp* (1919).[32] For Talmadge's Gwen Armitage, described as a "congenital vamp," flirting is almost reflexive, something she does automatically. Throughout the film she is able to drive men to distraction simply by smiling at them. The scenario by Anita Loos indicates that Gwen is aware of her power over men, but seldom in the film does she use this power for material gain. In fact, her smiles cause her more trouble than anything else, as she tries to hold a job as a stenographer but continually runs across bosses with more than dictation on their minds. While the film is lost, and therefore unavailable for viewing, it's safe to assume based on her work in other films that Talmadge infused her performance with an active and playful flirtatiousness. Describing Talmadge's performance in this film, one reviewer noted,

> Her methods are of a kind known to most every woman under the sun, though seldom practiced by a girl of breeding such as she is supposed to be. Just naturally she looked upon every man in sight as rightful prey, soulfully gazing into his eyes as she jotted down dictation. She being pretty and ultra feminine in appeal, the most sluggish imagination will be able to picture the consternation that soon reigned.[33]

If Gwen is "soulfully gazing" at her "prey" that certainly indicates that she is actively plying her feminine wiles. Like Bow's Alverna and Mabel Normand's Water Nymph, Gwen uses flirtation to maintain control over sexual situations and the men around her. Unlike Alverna, however, Gwen is, as the title makes abundantly clear, *virtuous*. Whereas Alverna's flirting carries with it the promise and potential of sex, Gwen is indignant when her smiles are met with a pass. When a boss, overcome with desire, proposes to her, Gwen is outraged, exclaiming that she is "surprised that you should so presume on our business relationship." The script describes the exchange that follows:

> He says, "Business relationship? What are you talking about?" and rises to his feet. "Haven't you led me on to think that you cared for me?" She says she certainly has not done anything of the kind. He says, "Well, what have you meant every day when you smiled at me, when you let me hold your hand, when you did everything you could possibly do to let me think you cared for me?" Then she says, "Mr. Bell, you are insulting me. I have done nothing of the kind. If I have smiled at you it has been entirely in a business way."[34]

This is very different from Alverna, who is not only happy to drive men to propose but also gladly takes them up on their propositions.

Light comedies and flapper films contain traces of a tension between Victorian era respectability and modern liberation not found in slapstick. Morality is generally not at issue for slapstick comediennes engaging in flirtations; the films are more concerned with setting up the gag than with commenting on women's proper sexual role. In light comedies and flapper films, however, comediennes were presented as good girls at heart regardless of how much illicit behavior they engaged in over the course of the film. Constance Talmadge's 1926 film *The Duchess of Buffalo* was one of many films that positioned her as an essentially good girl who got herself into and out of compromising situations. In this film she plays Marian Duncan, an American dancer in love with a Russian soldier named Vladimir Orloff (Tullio Carminati); to protect her lover, Marian finds herself forced to seduce his commanding officer, the Grand Duke (Edward Martindel). The seduction scene is played for laughs—at one point Marian jumps into the Grand Duke's lap to prevent him from leaving the room, and he responds by enthusiastically bouncing her on his knee; later, she clasps his head to her breast to prevent him from spotting Orloff, much to the Grand Duke's delight. As with Alverna, flirting for Marian is a necessity, a means to an end. Both Alverna and Marian understand that the most expedient way to get what they want is by manipulating men and bending them to their will. In Marian's case, however, it's clear that she's not really a vamp at heart. She is, like Gwen, a "virtuous vamp," a woman who can use but not compromise her sexuality. *The Duchess of Buffalo* ends in much the same way as many other light comedies and flapper films, with the marriage of the young lovers, leaving the spectators with the reassuring image of contained female sexuality.

Silent comedies, then, often feature women who are in control of sexual situations and who derive pleasure from testing the boundaries of heterosocial interactions. These films present flirtation and romance as fun and exciting, an enjoyable sport rather than a means to an end (marriage). Furthermore, and perhaps more telling, many of these films also present pre- or extramarital flirtation as preferable to the monotony and even misery of marriage. In the 1915 Keystone short *Ambrose's Fury*, dreary, loveless marriages are contrasted with the excitement and pleasure of illicit romance. Ambrose (Mack Swain) is married to a stern, domineering wife (Alice Davenport); his emasculation is made evident as soon as he is introduced, cleaning the house in a frilly apron as his wife barks orders. When Ambrose tries to chat up the maid his wife physically separates them, pushing Ambrose across the room. Glancing out the window, Ambrose spots his neighbor (Louise Fazenda) hanging laundry, and he goes outside to join her (Figure 3.2). As the two laugh and flirt in front of the clothesline and make plans to meet later at the beach, the disparity between married and single life is clear. This illicit flirtation provides an escape from their dreary lives, represented by the laundry drying behind them. Marriage for Ambrose and Louise means drudgery and overbearing spouses; flirtation means excitement, escape, and release. Interestingly, although Louise's husband is jealous and even violent, she is shown to have the upper hand in their marriage. After her husband catches Louise flirting he attempts to drive Ambrose away, only to be cuffed into submission by his much larger rival. When in an attempt to chastise Louise for her indiscretion he meekly slaps her across the face, she responds by soundly belting him and then indignantly walking away. Although she is positioned as a more acceptable feminine model than Ambrose's bossy, mannish wife, Louise is not a shrinking violet: she is independent and refuses to be bullied by her husband.

Another film that argues for extramarital flirtation as an alternative to joyless marriage is *Tillie Wakes Up* (1917).[35] In this film Marie Dressler plays Tillie, a neglected wife whose husband married her for her money and now shuns physical contact with her. Tillie reads a newspaper article by "Beetrees Flarefacts" titled "How to Hold Your Husband's Love," which encourages wives to find a "Romeo of your own even if you have to pay him a salary. Show your husband that you are human and he will begin to suspect that you are." Tillie is not sold on the idea of sparking an affair: a title tells us that "Tillie could not see that

Figure 3.2. Louise (Louise Fazenda) and Ambrose (Mack Swain) plan a trip to the beach in *Ambrose's Fury* (1915).

Romeo idea. In the first place she was overweight for Juliet and in the second place she was afraid something might happen." However, she decides to take a chance with her neighbor, a henpecked husband named J. Mortimer Pipkins (Johnny Hines). Tillie and J. Mortimer encounter each other on the landing between their apartments and flirt clumsily but eagerly with one another (according to an intertitle, "In thirty seconds J. Mortimer had made good with the old one about 'You have beautiful eyes' and Tillie felt she was fast becoming a *Regular Devil*"). As they stand in the darkened hallway talking and laughing, they are framed in close-up with nothing but darkness visible behind them (Figure 3.3). The landing becomes a secret, unreal space where they are alone and can throw away rules concerning propriety and societal expectations. Even in a crowded apartment building in New York they are in their own private world, free to engage in secret flirtations. Tillie's plan works: after she and J. Mortimer spend a day cutting loose at Coney Island, their neglectful spouses track them down and, realizing the error of their ways, reaffirm their love for Tillie and J. Mortimer. The experience has clearly had

Figure 3.3. Tillie (Marie Dressler) and J. Mortimer (Johnny Hines) conspire to make their spouses jealous in *Tillie Wakes Up* (1917).

an effect on Tillie, however, as she and J. Mortimer steal a wink and a smile at each other while in their spouses' arms.

The end of *Tillie Wakes Up* finds Tillie back in the arms of her husband, with order between sexes and spouses seemingly restored. However, her last smile and wink at J. Mortimer, as well as her lingering glances at the well-built lifeguards who have rescued her from the ocean, indicate that Tillie is not completely reformed (Figure 3.4). Similar endings are found at the ends of numerous comedies. Although most romantic comedies and many slapsticks end with marriage or reconciliation, the final pairings are not always convincing when the heroine has spent the previous reels engaging in—and enjoying—flirtation. In fact, these films demonstrate the difficulty inherent in trying to reconcile the impression created by the comediennes' flirtation with the generically necessary ending of heterosexual union. In *Mantrap*, the impossibility of this reconciliation is made clear in the last scene. After leaving her husband for a handsome lawyer, and then abandoning both men for the big city, Alverna finally decides

Figure 3.4. Tillie steals a glance at her rescuer in *Tillie Wakes Up* (1917).

to return to her husband. As they embrace, a young Mountie walks through their door. Alverna's eyes widen as she looks him up and down. After a moment she looks back to her husband, and says, "Hang on to me, Joe—I'm slipping just a little." Clearly marriage will never change Alverna—the desire to "slip" back into her old habits will always be strong—as Joe puts it, "She'll flirt as long as she breathes."

The real-life marriages of many flapper comediennes were discussed in the press in terms of containment, in much the same way that their characters were ostensibly contained in their films. An article about Joan Crawford that begins by stating that "she receives all her telephone calls while in the bathtub" goes on to describe how domestic and settled down she's become since her well-publicized marriage to Douglas Fairbanks Jr.: "Joan, in the early days, had been somewhat of a play girl, winning many cups and trophies at dance contests. When she became Mrs. Douglas Fairbanks Jr., she settled down into a sedate matron."[36] Here, Crawford's life follows the same trajectory as that of many of the characters she played. Just like in her films, Crawford had been tamed and rewarded with marriage.

Clara Bow received similar treatment in the press after marrying Rex Bell in 1931. Interestingly, although she is described as settling down and becoming domesticated, as in her movies her containment is neither complete nor entirely convincing. One press account of the newly married Bow pointed out that "once upon a time Clara would have been delighted to oblige the greeting horde of photographers by dancing atop a table if they asked her. Today she insisted on being pictured gazing wistfully out her hotel window at the Sunday traffic on the boulevard"[37]—the implication being that Bow's insistence on a demure, thoughtful pose has as much to do with her carefully constructed image as her earlier, table-dancing days. Even Bow herself implicitly acknowledged that marriage couldn't contain her. In an article titled "Hot-Cha Life Doesn't Pay, Says 'It' Girl," Bow is quoted as saying: "I have found out that hot-cha doesn't pay. I'm young, but I'm getting older. I'm going to lead a quiet life. Just like a nice married girl." However, she then adds: "Of course, I've still got a lot of pep. But I'll take it out in dancing."[38] So, in her life as well as in her movies, marriage won't entirely contain the "It" girl.

Comediennes, then, made use of flirtation in their films for a number of reasons and with varying results. When used by film comediennes, flirting showcased situations where women were in control of and enjoyed their sexuality and in some cases represented an alternative to joyless monogamy. And although many films made clear that the comediennes were essentially good girls at heart, and attempted to contain their characters' sexuality by the end of the film, these comedies still presented audiences with an example of female sexuality that was a far cry from the passive and reserved sexuality that had long been the feminine ideal.

"When I'm on the Make for a Man, I GET HIM!"

Flirting was just one of many ways that comediennes enacted sexual desire on-screen. The comically aggressive sexuality of slapstick comediennes, the innocent desire of the light comediennes, and the carnal lust of the flappers all showcased female sexual desire as not only acceptable but also enjoyable. The ideal woman of the early 1900s was supposed to be sexually attractive but not sexually aggressive. As women increasingly eschewed traditional female traits and took on attributes that had previously been associated with men they inspired anxieties in conservative society about appropriate female sexuality. By the 1910s, acknowledgment of women's sexual drives was a standard element of feminist discourse, and despite creating new fears about the "Pandora's Box" of female sexuality, the topic found its way onto the stage and screen.[39] Unlike the passive availability of the Ziegfeld Girl, female performers in vaudeville, burlesque, and nightclubs exhibited aggressive sexuality and tacitly argued that women could take just as much pleasure in sex as men could. Screen comediennes followed the lead set by their stage counterparts by enacting aggressive sexual desire in their films.

Sex was a popular topic on the vaudeville stage despite Tony Pastor and B. F. Keith's efforts to make vaudeville a refined entertainment, suitable for the delicate sensibilities of women and children. Performers such as Mae West, Sophie Tucker, Lillian Shaw, and Eva Tanguay pushed limits with racy songs and patter and a suggestive delivery. Theater managers were often torn between censoring the "blue" material and leaving it in because it was popular with audiences. Audiences and critics seemed similarly divided, both praising and condemning risqué acts. In 1915, for example, *Variety* reported an incident in which Eva Tanguay's publicity posters in Syracuse, New York, were deemed immodest by local authorities:

> Miss Tanguay's popularity in town was given a wide local sphere when Commissioner of Public Safety Hitchcock developed a sudden sense of modesty last week requesting Manager Kallet of the Grand to remove all of the Tanguay "one-sheets" from the billboards and stores. The posters had been up for three days before action was taken by the Commissioner, who said he had received a complaint.
>
> The newspapers printed the story with the result the Grand has been besieged by crowds wanting the lithos.[40]

Tanguay was known for her revealing costumes—described by one reviewer as "the usual tight Tanguay thing-ums"[41]—and one can assume that the censored posters featured one of these costumes. Tanguay was also known for her masterful use of public relations and publicity, and it is entirely likely that the poster incident was orchestrated by Tanguay herself. Whether or not this was a publicity stunt is almost beside the point, however. What is most telling in this instance is the fact that the removal of the posters resulted in the theater being "besieged" by fans seeking copies for themselves. In her act as well as in her publicity, Tanguay appealed to the prurient interests of the audience and was rewarded for it throughout her career. The incorporation of highly sexual material into her acts helped make her the highest-paid and most popular star in vaudeville throughout the 1910s and 1920s. Theater managers knew that raciness was central to her act's appeal and were reluctant to censor her: as one manager wrote in 1909, "She was a veritable riot to-day.... Certainly a phenomenal drawing card, and while we might like to make some changes in her material, still I think the fact that it is Tanguay makes the people forget what in another might offend."[42]

Other comic performers similarly used risqué material in their acts, employing an aggressive sexuality that was at odds with the image of ideal womanhood exemplified by the Ziegfeld Girl. Sophie Tucker was famous for her suggestive songs and colorful language; as one writer put it, "Her exuberance and racy songs made people feel wicked without the wear and tear of being so."[43] Tucker's songs "[had] to do with sex, but not with vice,"[44] and her lyrics were filled with racy double entendres aided by a smoldering delivery, causing songs such as "Who Paid the Rent for Mrs. Rip Van Winkle (When Rip Van Winkle Went Away)" to be censored in some cities. In later years, the transgressiveness of Tucker's sexually charged delivery was tempered by her weight, as critics could dismiss her as non-sexual and therefore unthreatening. However, early in her career she was considered conventionally attractive: in a 1909 *Variety* review of her vaudeville act, for example, it was reported that "the young woman has a way of ingratiating herself at once, and possesses not alone good looks, but magnetism to back it."[45]

When Tanguay, Tucker, and numerous other female performers made use of sexually aggressive material in their acts they were challenging the dominant conception of women as passive and refined. They were demanding that women be seen as sexual beings, and not just as homemakers and moral compasses, and their performances were in line with feminists' demands for a recognition of female sexuality. Furthermore, incorporating risqué material into their acts made them immensely popular. Certainly many people were offended by their acts, and they faced ongoing battles with censors. But the fact remained that they frequently played to standing room only houses, earned top salaries, and enjoyed long careers. Clearly their acts, although they employed "immodest material," struck a nerve with audiences who were open to seeing an alternative type of femininity represented onstage.

While flirtation comedies frequently show women who are self-assured and even a little brazen in their playful flirtations with men, many slapstick comedies follow the lead of unruly stage comediennes and position women as sexually aggressive, hunters who will stop at nothing to get their prey. Polly Moran, especially, was presented as a man-hungry aggressor in many of her comedies. In her earlier films she sometimes played slapstick-ingénues and vamps, but she soon became known for playing rough-and-tumble women such as Sheriff Nell in a series of shorts in the late 1910s and early 1920s. A 1918 *Motion Picture Magazine* piece titled "She Insisted on Idealizing Her Man" confirms her aggressive persona. Alongside a photo of Moran in her Sheriff Nell costume, complete with guns drawn, is a description of her ideal mate:

> These are the specifications for my ideal man:
> HE MUST NOT—
> Talk about himself when I want to talk about myself,
> He must not blacken his tan shoes,
> He must never call me "Lovey." I could stand for "Dearie" or "Honey" or even "Angel," but I firmly draw the line at "Lovey."
> He must not eat dill pickles or wear spats.
> Have gold front teeth.
> HE MUST BE ABLE TO DO THE FOLLOWING THINGS:
> Change an automobile tire without swearing,
> Be bored to death by all females except me,
> Drink nothing but water.
> Here's hoping from
> POLLY MORAN[46]

The idea of Moran *insisting* on idealizing her man, combined with her assertive pose in the accompanying photo and the laundry list of attributes that she will and will not put up with, positions her as a determined woman who knows what she wants and will do what's needed to get it. The demure "Here's hoping" that ironically ends the piece stands in contrast to the musts and must nots that precede it. By the end of the silent era Moran's image as a sexual aggressor was solidified, as in this article from 1931: "When I'm on the make for a man, I GET HIM! I make wisecracks, but not too many, and subtle ones, *you* know.... I act coy... like this... I... oh, *you* know."[47]

This image can be found in her films as well as in her publicity. In *Her Painted Hero* (1915) Moran plays a "Matinee Idoler" who is in pursuit of a handsome leading man (Hale Hamilton). After inheriting a fortune she agrees to marry a stagehand from the local theater but invites the Matinee Idol in the hopes of winning him over. When she spots him chatting with a group of girls, Polly darts across the room and jumps on his back in greeting, then drags him outside to be alone with her. When the groom tries to keep her away from the idol, she clocks him and runs off. This film references the tradition of stage-struck (and later movie-struck) girls, young women who were demonstrative in their adoration of handsome leading men and entertained dreams of stardom for themselves. Stage- and movie-struck girls disrupted the classical mode of viewing: rather than passively absorbing the spectacle on stage or screen, these young women wanted to be a part of the spectacle, narcissistically imagining a place for themselves on stage or screen.[48] Stage-and movie-struck girls exhibited the same kind of frank sexuality that Moran enacts in *Her Painted Hero*. In referencing and exaggerating the perceived threat of these young women, Moran allows audiences to laugh at what many felt was "the worst aspect of the female audience."[49]

When comediennes in these films enact comically aggressive sexuality they become unruly women, unable to contain their passions. Kathleen Rowe describes how the unruly woman contrasts with the "well adjusted woman," who is "static, silent, invisible—'composed' and 'divinely' apart from the hurly-burly of life, process, and social power."[50] In *Her Painted Hero*, Polly Moran's stagestruck girl is the epitome of the unruly woman: the well-adjusted women at her wedding are content to passively admire the matinee idol, whereas Polly, unwilling to sit by and let the man take the lead, physically accosts him. She eventually strikes a deal with her idol—"Make me your leading lady and I'll back your show"—in essence purchasing the opportunity to satisfy not only her sexual desires but also her dramatic aspirations.

Light comediennes' performance of desire was often contradictory and complex, frequently combining the comically aggressive sexuality of the slapstick comediennes with the blatant lust of the flappers. As with their use of flirtation, light comediennes were careful to maintain a balance between sex and virtue, frequently mitigating their desire by making their characters childlike. In *The Red Mill* (1927), Marion Davies plays Tina, a Dutch girl who does drudge work at an inn. While looking out her window she spots Dennis (Owen Moore) and is immediately smitten; she rushes outside and stands awkwardly in front of him, grinning. After entering—and winning—an ice-skating contest for which the winner has been promised a kiss from Dennis, Tina is full of joyful expectation; she is crestfallen when he leaves town without delivering her prize.

Tina's childishness is emphasized at the beginning of the film by the fact that Davies wears very little makeup, with her hair in pigtails. She is awkward when she meets Dennis, standing close to him and smiling expectantly rather than flirting or making any move to win him (Figure 3.5). This scene stands in contrast to both the aggressive sexuality of Polly Moran's characters and the skillful flirtation found in *The Water Nymph*, *A Virtuous Vamp*, *Mantrap*, and other films. Tina doesn't know how to use her "feminine wiles" to get a man—she is much too naïve and innocent to understand the laws of sexual attraction. She does, however, understand her own desire, and although she doesn't know what to do with that desire, she knows that she wants to act on it. When she finally gets her kiss, she has already begun her transformation from innocent girl to desiring woman (evidenced by the fact that she is now wearing makeup and has her hair down), and the realization of her desire completes her transformation. As Dennis kisses Tina, we see a close-up of her hand on his arm as she feebly tries to push him away; after a few moments he starts to pull away, but she forcefully pulls him closer to extend their clinch. The film ends with Dennis promising to make Tina "an Irish Princess," and the two imagine an elaborate setting, with servants standing in a line holding jewels, perfume, gowns, and food while an elegantly dressed Tina and Dennis lounge on a bed of pillows (Figure 3.6). Tina's sexual desires are realized by the end of the film, but the fantasy suggests a catalogue of material desires as well.

Other light comedies similarly counteract the potency of female desire by emphasizing the childishness of the heroine. Although Mary Pickford plays an adult in the film *Suds* (1920), her character, a laundry slavey named Amanda, is like a child in her innocent simplicity; at one point in the film Amanda rescues a neighborhood horse from the glue factory and brings him home to her second-floor apartment, where she spends the night curling the horse's mane and tail. Amanda has built up an elaborate fantasy surrounding a man named Horace (Albert Austin) who has left a shirt at her laundry, and she insists to the other laundresses that he will return to rescue her from her life of drudgery. As with Tina, Amanda's sexual and romantic desire is tempered by her childishness—her adoption of the horse, her detailed fantasy based on one brief encounter with Horace—as well as her appearance—she wears slavey makeup and her trademark curls are tucked into a messy bun. Because of this she is not positioned as a sexual subject; instead, Pickford's mature femininity is defused by Amanda's youthful androgyny.

Mabel Normand takes this to an extreme in *What Happened to Rosa?*

Figure 3.5. *The Red Mill* (1927): Tina (Marion Davies) spots the object of her desire (Owen Moore) . . .

(1920). In an effort to get close to Maynard Drew (Hugh Thompson), a doctor with whom she has fallen in love, Mayme (Normand) hijacks a neighbor boy's clothes, muddies her face, and fakes a collision with a pushcart. When Dr. Drew asks where it hurts, she points first to her rear; then, thinking twice about what body part she wants the doctor to examine, points to her face. At this moment in the film when she is boldly acting on her desires, her very convincing urchin-boy costume mitigates the power of her actions and ultimately defuses the transgressiveness of a sexually mature, desiring woman. Like Tina and Amanda, Mayme has the potential to be a powerful, even threatening, sexual symbol. As single women living alone and working and playing in heterosocial urban settings, they represent the increasing numbers of independent women similarly testing new social and sexual boundaries. This new independence added to active female desire was a potent combination and the source of a great deal of concern among social conservatives who may have been worried about a perceived increase in immorality among young women. As one writer in 1925 lamented:

Figure 3.6. . . . and the objects of her desires.

The age of innocence is gone. Blame it on the war, blame it on bobbed hair, blame it on our prodigiously increasing national wealth, blame it on radio, on automobiles or any other means of making life wise and uniform by communication—young America is speedily taking on the sophistication of old Europe.[51]

This anxiety was most clearly found on-screen in the character of the vamp, a man-hungry parasite who would drive a man to ruin and then glibly move on to her next victim. Certainly Tina, Amanda, Mayme, and other childlike characters played by light comediennes were not meant to be as threatening as vamps; however, they nonetheless reflect cultural anxieties over women's sexuality. Whereas vamps indicate the destructive side of female desire, these childlike characters show a way in which women's desire and sexuality can be rendered nonthreatening. Additionally, the placement of these characters in the "safe" genre of comedy can be seen as further eroding their potential threat, although ultimately these comedies may have made female desire more palatable to audiences.

Figure 3.7. Clara Bow in *Mantrap* (1926).

Screen flappers, like light comediennes, performed a mixture of active desire and essential virtue. Like those of the stage comediennes before them, screen flappers' performances were often boldly, aggressively sexual—they knew what and who they wanted, and they knew how to get it. Flapper films presented their heroines as mature, desiring women rather than the desexualized childish figures of the light comedies. At the same time, flapper films took a cue from light comedies by insisting that their heroines were really good girls and that their sexual needs would be fulfilled by marriage to the right man.

Flapper comediennes are frequently presented as the romantic aggressors in their films, acting on desire and lust. Clara Bow, especially, was famous for portraying barely contained lust in her pictures. Her typical characters in the 1920s were wild young things who burned with desire for the man (or in some cases *men*) they wanted to possess. Bow's performance of desire was not deflected or mitigated as in the light comedies; on the contrary, in many of her films it is emphasized by lingering close-ups on her face as she gazes lustfully at the objects of her passion (Figures 3.7 and 3.8). The scene from *It* described at the beginning of this chapter provides an excellent example of Bow's performance

"Cupid Lips and an Ungodly Appetite"

Figure 3.8. Clara Bow in *It* (1927).

of desire. In this scene, department store lingerie salesgirl Betty Lou has just spotted Mr. Waltham (Antonio Moreno), the new boss. Betty Lou is immediately struck, and a close-up reveals her chest heaving as she pleads, "Sweet Santa Claus, give me *him*!" Betty Lou is so focused on Waltham that she doesn't seem to notice the other salesgirls who have gathered around her to join in gawking at the new boss. This shot is framed so that Betty Lou is the apex of a triangle: behind her, the other shopgirls represent the life of department-store drudgery that faces her if she can't win her man; in front of her, the bits of silky lingerie strewn about the counter provide a suggestion for how she might achieve her goal (Figure 3.9). As Lori Landay has argued, "Bow's active gaze accentuated the erotic possibilities of modern femininity."[52] Bow's glance was an outward manifestation of her inner sexual desires, a way of telegraphing to the object of her gaze as well as to audiences that her characters were comfortable with and confident in their sexuality. These close-ups serve to draw audience members into Bow's act and make them the unwitting objects of her performed sexual desire, much like the interactive performances of stage comediennes. Furthermore, these glances represent a break from an earlier time when women were expected

Figure 3.9. *It* (1927): "Sweet Santa Claus, give me *him*!"

to hide baser passions such as longing and lust.[53] Of course, Bow and other flappers are removed from the film audience, providing that audience safety from their transgressiveness through distance. Still, the very presence on-screen of desiring women who are not punished for their blatant desire is notable.

Not surprisingly, the on-screen antics of Bow and other flappers as sexual aggressors were attributed to their offscreen lives as well. After marrying Rex Bell, one newspaper claimed that "Miss Bow said she was really the huntress in pursuing Bell, who was an obscure figure in the screen world compared to her."[54] Similarly, an article about Joan Crawford claimed that "across a luncheon table she is as anatomically seductive as she has ever been when doing her carnal darndest in a screen sex orgy typical of our modern maidens and dancing daughters."[55] These instances are notable because they implied that there was some truth to the characters played by Bow and Crawford, that the desiring, possibly threatening woman found on-screen had a basis in reality.

In a 1925 magazine article a writer pointed to the new moral terms of the 1920s, describing how the innocent, virtuous image associated with Mary Pickford had been eclipsed by the shrewd worldliness of Gloria Swanson:

The moral offered by Gloria is infinitely more attractive than the one advanced by Mary. Mary's amounted to: "Be good and you'll wear rags," but Gloria's is: "Be good and you'll preen in duvetyn."

The problem for the flapper is how to be good yet fashionable. She doesn't care to be listed as an abandoned soul simply because she bobs and lipsticks and lingeries. Gloria does not list her so. Gloria bobs and rouges and lingeries, yet always defeats the villain's ends—even though he supplied her with the rouge and the lingerie.

Thus, the young female of the hour looks upon Gloria as possessing greater finesse than the little girl who sacrifices home and honor before getting so much as a beaded bag. Gloria is a positive good woman; the old heroine was a passive good one. I leave it to you which the girl of today is.[56]

As this article makes clear, sexual desire for the flapper figure was often conflated with material desire. Tina's final fantasy in *The Red Mill* showed that she was content to wait until after marriage before realizing her material fantasies, but flappers, on the contrary, preferred to fulfill their material and sexual desires at the same time. In a great many flapper films (as well as light comedies) class is an integral issue, as working women—shopgirls, telephone operators, secretaries—fall in love with and eventually marry rich men. Although women in these films are shown to desire the man, and not his bank account, the leading man's money and status are often what draw the attention of the working girl in the first place. In *It*, Betty Lou doesn't notice Mr. Waltham until a coworker exclaims "Hot socks—the new boss!" Although the look she gives Mr. Waltham is one of pure lust, it's not clear whether she's initially attracted to his looks, his position, or his bankroll.

Orchids and Ermine (1927) spells out the flapper's materialist leanings with the first title card of the film: "Every girl of today loves fine feathers, but only one in a thousand can find the right bird." The film then introduces Pink Watson (Colleen Moore), who "was willing to fall in love if she could fall on fine feathers." Pink so desperately longs for the trappings of wealth, symbolized by orchid corsages and ermine coats, that she rescues a discarded orchid from the middle of the street and then, throwing her cat around her shoulders, poses with her own low-budget version of luxury. When she does meet a millionaire, Richard Tabor (Jack Mulhall), he has switched identities with his valet to avoid the attentions of gold diggers, and so she believes him to be poor. While Pink

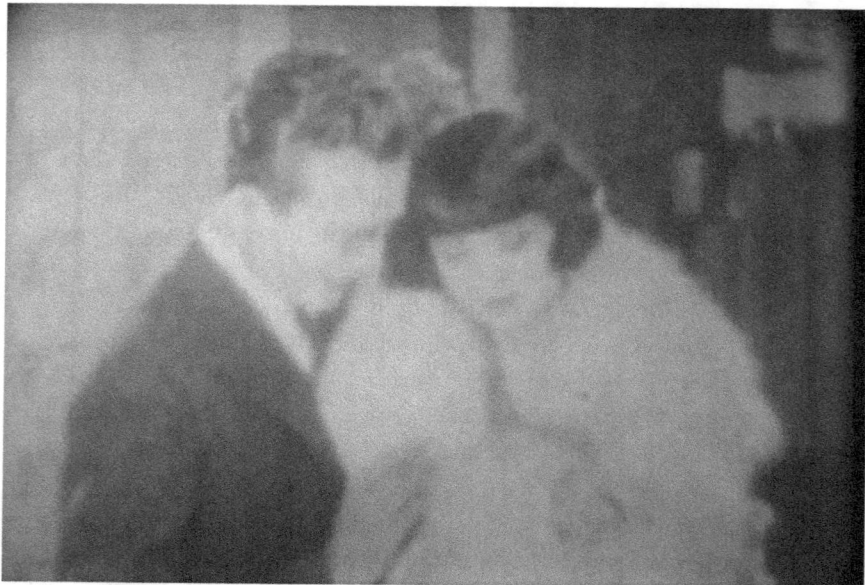

Figure 3.10. Pink (Colleen Moore) enjoys the culmination of her desires in *Orchids and Ermine* (1927).

pursues rich men, she is pursued by Richard. Pink ultimately learns the lesson "that a poor girl can be happy—but a happy girl isn't poor," and agrees to marry Richard, who immediately confesses his real identity and, instead of kissing his new fiancée, announces that he's taking her to "the finest modiste shop in town." Pink's expression in anticipation of their shopping spree is far more passionate than her expression when being proposed to. This moment marks the culmination of Pink's desires—she has found a man to love who will buy her everything she desires. Their orgy of consumption at the dress shop takes the place of sex for Pink and Richard; instead of kissing or embracing to consummate their engagement he wraps her in decadent clothes and runs his hands over her fur-draped shoulders, as the ermine coat becomes the object of their displaced sexual desire (Figure 3.10). A similar conflation of sexual and material desires can be found in many light comedies, although the comediennes in these films don't portray desire as frankly as the flapper comediennes. While the heroines of light comedies were happy to wait until after marriage to have their material or physical desires fulfilled, for flapper characters making bank was almost as important as making love.

Physical Comedy and Bodily Pleasure

Perhaps the most interesting way that comediennes addressed sexuality and sensuality on-screen was in their depiction of the bodily pleasure inherent in physical comedy. Comediennes reveled in the sheer joy of their physical interaction with the world around them. As Rob King argues, "The New Woman had defined herself, in large part, by reclaiming the right to her own embodiment against the morally and spiritually defined—hence quintessentially *dis*embodied—ideal of true womanhood."[57] Whereas the feminine ideal of the nineteenth century was passive and polite, keeping herself removed from the possibility of contact with the public sphere, comediennes, as exemplars of New Womanhood in the early twentieth century, fully interacted with the people and places around them. In so doing, they revealed the sensual pleasure inherent in physical activity.

Movie theaters in the 1910s, following the lead of legitimate theaters at the end of the nineteenth century, attempted to create an atmosphere of "refinement" by taming the rowdy, vocal, and active crowds of the nickelodeon years and encouraging passive spectatorship.[58] As film historians have shown, this transition was not brought about smoothly, as many audiences continued to respond to films in ways that ran counter to the theater owners' preferred "feminized" mode of viewing. This could include physical reactions to the films. Shelley Stamp refers to "the intense physiological sensations and unaccustomed mental states audiences experienced watching astonishing serial exploits enacted on screen,"[59] pointing out that "adventuresome, suspenseful antics on film also seem to have produced boisterously enthusiastic crowds, whose reported behavior was at odds with the visual inscription of female fans in ads that pictured decorous, stylishly dressed, middle-class women, patrons from whom such immodest behavior would not have been expected."[60] Jennifer Bean has similarly commented on the bodily reactions of spectators to adventure serials, such as *The Perils of Pauline* (1914) and *The Hazards of Helen* (1914–17).[61] Spectators could experience similar physical reactions to comedies.[62] According to Lauren Rabinovitz,

> Even after movies adopted distinct storytelling features of psychologically motivated characters, cause-and-effect plots, and dramatic crises, slapstick comedy preserved a particular inscription of the cinematic body both as the spectacular figure-in-motion and as the laughing spectator

in all her or his presence in the theater. Slapstick sustained a more carnal spirit and upheld an enlarged sense of corporeal delight even during the era when the experience of watching movies became increasingly proscribed by Aristotelian categories associated with "the higher senses." Beginning around 1909, slapstick comedies intertwined bodies (both onscreen and off) with those effects of cinema that produce celebration in the physicality of one's own body.[63]

Numerous silent films feature scenes of theater and cinema audiences enjoying comedy performances with their whole bodies. Without fail, these audiences—men and women alike—are shown doubled over with laughter, stomping their feet, throwing their hands in the air, slapping their knees, and in all ways behaving the exact *opposite* of the passive audiences promoted by theater owners. In *That Ragtime Band* (1913), one of many Keystone shorts that take place in a theater, the audience at an amateur vaudeville show starts out laughing hysterically and eventually becomes so boisterous that they start throwing food and other objects at the performers. Similarly, King Vidor's drama *The Crowd* (1928) ends in a vaudeville house: the final shot of the film is a tracking shot of row after row of spectators convulsed with laughter, rocking back and forth in their seats.

Just as in adventure genres, this kind of physiological reaction to comedy films could have been seen as threatening. Reviewing *Tillie's Punctured Romance* (1914), the first feature-length slapstick comedy, a reviewer for the *New York Daily News* wondered if audiences were physically prepared for ninety minutes of laughter: "It is difficult to keep an audience in continuous laughter through six reels of film; facial muscles rebel and demand a rest."[64] As Victoria Sturtevant argues, "If sensationalism is the film's ability to produce a shock in the body of the audience, this slapstick comedy channels that shock into comic violence, with a similarly depleting physical effect on its spectators."[65] Apparently, comedy could even kill. A spate of reports of women who literally died from laughter appeared in newspapers during this time, providing the "disciplinary warning that women were too fragile and vulnerable to experience exuberant joy."[66]

If audiences were reacting physically to comedies and adventure films, then the genres' appeal was clearly sensual as well as intellectual, a threatening proposition at a time when the motion picture industry was trying to reposition itself as a refined entertainment.[67] Rob King frames this embodied spectatorship in terms of cultural and class divisions:

> From the belly laugh of variety entertainment to the "blood and thunder" scenes of cheap melodrama, from the thrills of the amusement park ride to the physical contact of the dance hall, popular forms thus reflected a hunger for intense bodily stimulation that, to genteel tastes, was the very definition of vulgarity. An interest in physical spectacle and stimulation made sensationalism an aesthetic mode that corresponded to an emphasis on laboring bodies and the "embodied relationships that workers have to power." . . . The slapstick humor of vaudeville's "nut acts," "bone crunchers," and "facial" and "knockabout" clowns was a part of this culture of sensationalism; and, if its pleasures contradicted genteel emphasis on transcendence, they nonetheless crystallized the embodied orientation of working-class culture and experience.[68]

According to King, the popularity of these sensationalist entertainments reveal a broader trend toward corporeal engagement with popular culture, driven, at least in part, by the tastes of working-class audiences and indicative of a break with the genteel restraint that defined the Victorian era culture. Lauren Rabinovitz similarly sees these dynamics occurring in turn-of-the-century amusement parks, arguing that "what matters most is that this kind of physiologically engaged spectator who mimics the parkgoer's equally engaged experience—even without actual traveling motion—participates in a new delighted corporeal relationship to technological modernity."[69] A parallel can be drawn between the unruly audiences watching comedies and the unruly women appearing in the comedies. Mary Russo argues that the "grotesque body is opposed to the classical body, which is monumental, static, closed, and sleek, corresponding to the aspirations of bourgeois individualism; the grotesque body is connected to the rest of the world."[70] The classical body is controlled by intellect; the grotesque body succumbs to the sensual pleasure of laughter. Women on-screen, like women in the audience, were expected to fit the mold of the classical body and not the grotesque.

Physical comedy, when performed by women, could be read as an endorsement of female sensuality and bodily pleasure. While for most comediennes this tended to represent implicit rather than overt sexuality, it is a representation and celebration of sexuality nonetheless. As Kathleen Rowe has argued, "The grotesque body breaks down the boundaries between itself and the world outside it."[71] In many comedies, the comediennes interact endlessly with their surroundings with physical abandon. They are not refined or reserved. They venture into the modern world, with its inherent shocks and dangers, and they connect with and ultimately triumph over their surroundings. Ben Singer has pointed out that the rise of modernity brought with it anxieties about urban living, including fears of bodily peril, sudden and violent deaths caused by increased traffic, falls from great heights, and other elements of the modern city.[72] Many of these anxieties are addressed in comedies, especially slapstick comedies, as comediennes are subjected to and conquer the many dangers of the modern city, and even find physical pleasure in the thrills and excitement of modernity.

Comediennes interacted with the world around them, and their enjoyment of this physical interaction is often palpable. Perhaps the clearest example of this dynamic can be found in amusement park comedies, which "foreground an exaggerated corporeal body while maintaining amusement park spectacle in order to depict relaxation of Victorian codes of conduct, changing gender roles, and comic critique of the institution of marriage."[73] Amusement parks such as New York's Coney Island featured rides that allowed visitors to safely flirt with danger, while the relaxed atmosphere at the parks presented an opportunity for visceral pleasures and heterosocial mixing: "Coney Island plunged visitors into a powerful kinesthetic experience that, like the surf itself, overturned conventional restraints, washed away everyday concerns, buoyed and buffeted participants as they submitted to its sway."[74] Numerous silent comedies take place in amusement parks, and in these films we can see comediennes enjoying the bumps, jolts, and thrills of modernity. Their delight in the physical sensations found on the rides and attractions represents a more general enjoyment of bodily pleasure, as the rides stand in for the modern city. In *Tillie Wakes Up*, Tillie's outing with her neighbor ends up at Coney Island, where she tries out various rides such as the Witching Waves, the Barrel of Fun, and the Human Pool Table. Although Tillie is at first unsure of these rides after being roughly tossed around, she comes to enjoy these new physical sensations, as an intertitle tells us that "Tillie was willing to try anything once, for she was having the *time* of her *Young Life*." Tillie's growing enjoyment of the physical thrills at Coney Island coincides with her burgeoning understanding of her own sexual powers: as she loosens up and enjoys her illicit outing with J. Mortimer, she more fully enjoys the bodily pleasures of the amusement park. Tillie's experience can be contrasted with that of Ambrose's wife in *Ambrose's Fury*. In an attempt to ditch his wife so that he can meet his neighbor at the beach, Ambrose tricks her into getting on a roller coaster and then runs off once she is secured in the car. The wife is shown sitting in the front of the roller coaster, screaming unhappily and berating the ride operator. In contrast to Tillie, Ambrose's overbearing, killjoy wife is incapable of enjoying the sensual thrill of the roller coaster, offering an explanation for why Ambrose would be tempted by his fun-loving neighbor. Rabinovitz and King both argue that amusement parks and slapstick comedies helped ease contemporary fears about modernity, recasting machinery and technology as pleasurable rather than threatening and further differentiating modern audiences from their Victorian predecessors. With this in mind, we can see that Tillie is firmly aligned with modern, working-class audiences, whereas Ambrose's wife is positioned as hopelessly old-fashioned and out of touch with modern pleasures.

The sensual pleasures of the amusement park are even clearer when Clara Bow is involved. In *It*, Betty Lou and Mr. Waltham go to Coney Island on a date, and Betty Lou goes on many of the same rides as Tillie did years earlier. With Bow, however, there is a level of flirtatiousness and frank sexuality absent from Dressler's performance. Like Tillie, Betty Lou enjoys the physical thrills of the amusement park rides, and we frequently see her laughing heartily as she's tossed about. Unlike Tillie, Betty Lou sees the amusement park as a way to get closer to her date; while Tillie and J. Mortimer's physical contact is friendly and platonic, Betty Lou looks for excuses for romantic contact with her date, at one point telling him to "hold [her] tight" and then wrapping his arms around her before heading down a slide.

Both Tillie and Betty Lou ride the Barrel of Fun, which turns them head over heels and allows the audience generous views of their undergarments. At least one reviewer commented on this scene in *Tillie Wakes Up* by asking, "What would any show of Miss Dressler's be, minus her preposterous display of nether-nether-nether lands?"[75] The description of Dressler's display of "nether-nether-nether lands" as preposterous indicates the likelihood that the audience would have read this scene as comedic rather than sexual, and certainly the views of Tillie's voluminous petticoats and sizable cotton bloomers, along with her vain efforts to maintain her dignity, are very comical. In *It*, on the other hand, shots of Betty Lou's abbreviated silk undergarments and lacy garters, shown in great detail, are certainly meant to highlight the considerable sexual appeal of Betty Lou and, by extension, Bow (Figures 3.11 and 3.12).

In both of these films, the amusement park is a place to explore exciting, illicit sexuality, and an essential component to this is the sensual thrill offered by the rides. Lauren Rabinovitz has pointed out that "the amusement park invited women to find sensual pleasure in their own bodies as it simultaneously trans-

Figure 3.11. Betty Lou (Clara Bow) cuts loose at Coney Island in *It* (1927).

formed them into spectacles."[76] Certainly, Betty Lou and Tillie are both offered up as sexual spectacles, to the other amusement park patrons as well as the films' spectators. While Tillie is unsure of her new role as sexual spectacle—she struggles to keep her "nether-nether-nether lands" covered—Betty Lou is clearly not bothered by the prospect of putting herself on display. What the two women share is a thorough enjoyment of relinquishing bodily control to the rides. Rabinovitz describes the "young female bodies" in an early amusement park comedy as "acted upon, out of control, and given over to shaking and jerking movements that produce a kind of unrestrained, sensual motion *of* the body rather than of individual will or subject control. As park pleasure-seekers, the boarding school girls have shed their ladylike demeanor and self-control for an unrestrained, unfettered display of physical expression."[77] In the case of Betty Lou and Tillie, it's important to note their enjoyment of the sensual experience. On one level they are sexual spectacles, but the fact that they are deriving physical, sensual pleasure from the rides complicates the idea of sexual display.

Physical enjoyment wasn't just found at the amusement park; it could also

"Cupid Lips and an Ungodly Appetite" 169

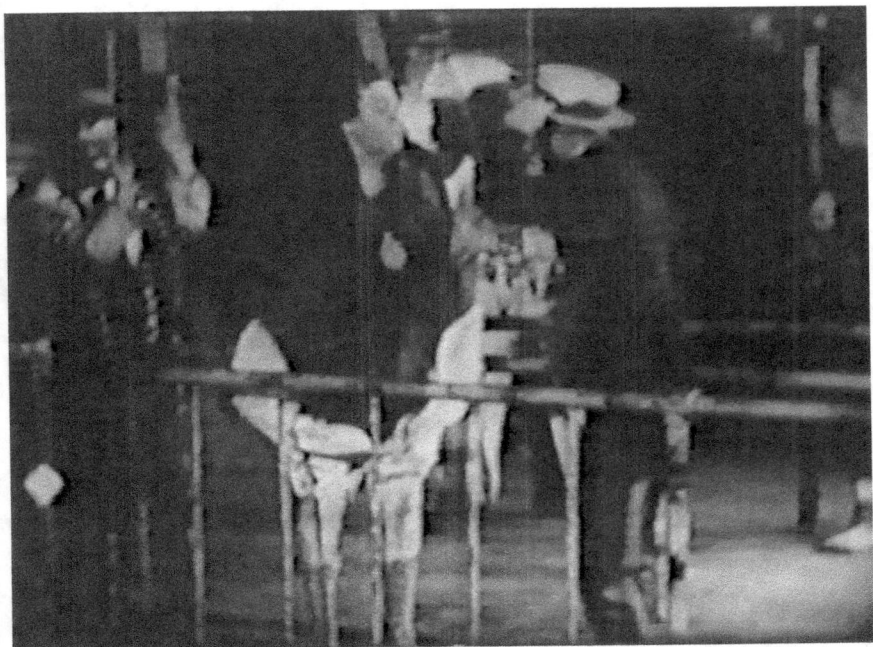

Figure 3.12. Tillie (Marie Dressler) displays her nether-nether-nether lands in *Tillie Wakes Up* (1917).

be found in ostensibly private moments. Mabel Normand combines bodily pleasure with bodily display in her 1918 film *Mickey*. In this film Normand plays a young tomboy raised in a remote mining community. Mickey is introduced as a childlike character, a tomboy with an affinity for animals and a penchant for stirring up trouble. Normand's positioning in this film as half woman, half child is reminiscent of films featuring Constance Talmadge, Mary Pickford, Dorothy Gish, and other light comediennes.[78] However, Mickey's childish asexuality is contrasted suddenly and starkly with a scene in which she swims in the nude. As surveyor Joe Meadows (George Nichols) looks on, an undressed Mickey makes a perfect dive off a cliff into a lake and then runs back to the top of the cliff, joyously waving her arms and legs, and jumps again. The scene is highly voyeuristic, as we see Mickey in a long shot through Joe's telescope (Figure 3.13); only after Joe has turned his telescope away do we see a close-up of Mickey's face, as she exuberantly emerges from the lake after her second dive (Figure 3.14). This scene certainly recalls Normand's earlier film, *The Water Nymph*, as a showcase of both her athletic ability and her figure. However, the context has

Figure 3.13. Mickey (Mabel Normand) dives off a cliff in *Mickey* (1918).

changed—in *Mickey*, she is watched without her knowledge, the classic recipient of the male gaze. Like the glorified American girls in the Ziegfeld *Follies*, Mickey is beautiful, passive, and nonthreatening. Mickey is unaware that she is being watched and so has no control over how her image is interpreted; in *The Water Nymph*, on the other hand, she is putting on a show, fully aware of and in control of how others are viewing her. However, despite her more passive position in the scene from *Mickey*, she still demonstrates a sensual enjoyment of her body that is very powerful. As she dances on top of the cliff, spinning around and throwing her arms and legs wildly about, she is clearly completely absorbed in the physicality of the moment—the feeling of the sun on her skin, the cold water, the freedom of leaping from the cliff. The fact that she is being watched makes this moment *sexual*, but it's her own enjoyment of her bodily sensations that makes this moment *sensual*.

Perhaps not surprisingly, Normand's nude scene in *Mickey* was mentioned in many reviews as a selling point for the film. *Motion Picture Classic* pointed out that "Mabel does high dives from distant rocks apparently minus all Kellermanns [*sic*]. Which, as they say in the classics, is important, if true,"[79] and

Figure 3.14. Mickey (Mabel Normand) goes for a swim in *Mickey* (1918).

Wid's Daily mentioned that "there was one sequence in which we saw Mabel doing some Annette Kellerman stuff, dressed as Eve without even a fig leaf, and this was not only pretty and nicely handled, but will, of course, be an added attraction if carefully handled in the advertising."[80] By drawing attention to the nude scene—including *Wid's* recommendation that exhibitors refer to it in advertising for the film—the press was helping to foreground Normand's sexuality, despite the efforts of the film to mitigate this sexuality by making the character childlike.

A somewhat similar presentation of bodily pleasure is found in Clara Bow's *Hula* (1927). Bow's Hula Calhoun shares some similarities with Mickey: she is a tomboy living in a remote and "uncivilized" location (in Hula's case, Hawaii), and she is linked to nature and animals, both of which serve to highlight her youth and immaturity. Like Mickey, an early shot of Hula finds her bathing in the nude. However, unlike Mickey, Hula appears in close-up, and she remains unobserved within the diegesis. Hula is introduced in the film lying on her back in a shallow pool of water, surrounded by vines and tropical flowers, an Eve all alone in her Eden. As she lounges in the pool, a close-up of her face shows her

Figure 3.15. Hula (Clara Bow) enjoys a private moment in *Hula* (1927).

delighted smile as she throws her head back to more fully experience the feel of the water (Figure 3.15). Spotting a flower near her foot, she grabs it with her toes and brings it to her hands, in the process exposing most of her leg. Her pleasure is ruined by a bee stinging her thigh, shown in extreme close-up.

Rather than resembling a Ziegfeld chorine, like Mickey, Bow in this scene resembles a burlesque stripper, showing us exactly what she wants us to see, while teasing us with the prospect of more. Bow owns her sexuality in this scene; even the stolen glimpse of her thigh as the bee stings her is happily repeated by her later in the film when she shows the sting to her nursemaid and later to handsome engineer Anthony Haldane (Clive Brook) (Figure 3.16). Where Normand takes Freud's classic female position in smut, as the innocent and embarrassed object of the joke, Bow is the instigator of her own joke and is entirely in on the fun.[81] Despite the differences in the way these scenes impart their characters' presentation of their sexuality, they have in common an endorsement of female sensual pleasure. In *Mickey*, the potential objectification of Normand's character is mitigated by her bodily pleasure; similarly, Hula's sensual enjoyment

Figure 3.16. Hula (Clara Bow) shows Anthony (Clive Brook) her bee sting in *Hula* (1927).

of her swim indicates an ownership of her body and her sexuality, one that is further reinforced when she shows Anthony her "hurt," in a move that's both childishly naïve and playfully sexual.

Another way of showing the sensual pleasure of physical activity was through dance. Especially for flapper comediennes, dancing could be a frank expression of sexuality, a way of releasing sexual energy while showcasing athletic ability and bodily pleasure. Dance was a common element in many vaudeville and burlesque comediennes' acts, often an extension of the brazen and aggressive sexuality found elsewhere in their performances. Dancing was certainly linked in the public imagination to sex, and many saw dance as a sexual outlet for women:[82] in 1894, Havelock Ellis claimed that dancing enabled women "to give harmonious and legitimate emotional expression to this neuromuscular irritability which might otherwise escape in more explosive forms."[83] Female comedians in vaudeville and burlesque used dance as a means of sexual expression, which, along with their suggestive songs and sensual delivery, helped position them as sexually assertive, transgressive, and unruly.

The screen flappers, like the unruly stage comediennes before them, used their bodies to exude sexuality, and nowhere is this more evident than through dance. Whether Clara Bow is dancing the hula or Joan Crawford is dancing the Charleston, dance is very clearly used as an outlet for their characters' pent-up sexuality. In *Hula*, Bow's character uses dance to draw in the object of her affection: after her married lover tells her that they can't see each other anymore, she performs an energetic hula dance at a luau. Her plan works, as Anthony is unable to control himself and carries her away. Bow makes similar use of dance in other films: in *Mantrap*, for example, Alverna stages an impromptu dance at her home in order to entice a visiting big-city lawyer, and in *The Plastic Age* (1925) Cynthia Day performs a suggestive shimmy while dancing with a new conquest. In these and other scenes dance is not a performance per se; rather, it's an expression of the characters' sexuality. For Hula, Alverna, and Cynthia the most effective way to convey their complex feelings is physically, through dance. As modern women, it's not surprising that these characters would find expression in movement, in what Lori Landay calls "the kinaesthetic pleasures of modernity."[84] Dancing in these films is another way in which comediennes showcased the sensual pleasure in physical activity, and another way in which comediennes perform sexuality in their films.

"This Young Fellow Is My Wife": Male Impersonation and Gender Confusion

Comedies that featured cross-dressing—particularly male impersonation—both reflected and defused anxieties over sexuality and changing gender roles in the early twentieth century. Male impersonation was a form of entertainment well known to audiences of the silent era. Nineteenth-century actresses found tremendous success appearing as men in vaudeville, burlesque, minstrel shows, and melodrama. By the early twentieth century, however, the popularity of male impersonators had begun to wane; this was due to increased anxiety over gender and sexual roles, and new research on homosexuality.[85] Homosexuality was defined at this time by social practices rather than sexual practices,[86] and it was thought that any woman who rejected the trappings of True Womanhood and instead desired a place on the public stage was likely to be a lesbian. Late nineteenth-century sexologist Richard von Krafft-Ebing believed that the female invert, or lesbian, was, in fact, a man trapped in a woman's body and that this would cause these women to "act like men" in a variety of ways, from taking a job or becoming involved in politics, to carrying on romantic relationships with other women, to wearing men's clothing. Krafft-Ebing's contemporary Havelock Ellis agreed that cross-dressing was frequently indicative of inversion and went on to claim that professional women and actresses were likely to be lesbians.[87]

In spite of this volatile cultural climate, cross-dressing is a familiar trope in silent film, although Laura Horak has shown that male impersonation in early twentieth-century film was not necessarily linked to deviant sexuality but was instead considered "wholesome entertainment." In fact, Horak argues, "the American moving picture industry used cross-dressed women in the 1910s to help the medium become respectable and appeal to audiences of all classes. Cross-dressed actresses embodied turn-of-the-century American ideals of both boyhood and girlhood."[88] However, compared to the instances of male impersonation in the sentimental melodramas and westerns that Horak examines, in silent comedies these moments were often more sexually charged and frequently had overtly homosexual overtones. These films, no matter the genre, also allowed audiences to vicariously experience and enjoy queer moments, as both male and female spectators could entertain same-sex attractions. While heterosexual audiences could be secure in the knowledge that the gender confusion would right itself by the end of the film, homosexual spectators were able to revel in the cracks and fissures of normative heterosexuality that these performances highlighted.

Numerous silent comedies bear a resemblance to what Chris Straayer calls "temporary transvestite" films, in which a (presumably heterosexual) character cross-dresses as a disguise.[89] Although Straayer's work doesn't specifically address silent-era films, her theories can be applied to early twentieth-century works, as many of the same dynamics are in place. Both men and women cross-dress in these temporary transvestite films; however, while the female impersonations are largely played for broad laughs, the male impersonations, like those found onstage in the early twentieth century, showcase both skillful imitation and sexual display. A fairly typical example of female impersonation in silent comedy can be found in the 1915 Keystone comedy *Miss Fatty's Seaside Lovers*. In this film Roscoe Arbuckle appears as a woman vacationing at a seaside resort who must ward off men who mistakenly believe that she is an heiress. Interestingly, in this film Arbuckle does not play a man who cross-dresses as a woman; rather, he simply plays a female character. With his large frame dressed in long skirts and a hat decorated with flowers and bows, Arbuckle makes an unconvincing woman. Much of the comedy in the film comes as Miss Fatty overpowers her would-be suitors in the typical Keystone knockabout style.

While female impersonation on-screen, as well as onstage, was primarily played for broad comedy, male impersonation could be more subtly subversive, in that homosexually charged moments were often implicit and sometimes even exploited by the filmmakers. Temporary transvestite films frequently feature moments that are simultaneously hetero- and homosexually charged. Straayer argues that these films "often support heterosexual desire at the narrative level and challenge it at a more ambiguous visual level where other desires are suggested."[90] This commonly occurs through what she terms the paradoxical bivalent kiss. These kisses take place under one of two circumstances: in one, different-gendered characters appear to be in a homosexual situation because one of the characters is cross-dressed; in the other, characters of the same sex are involved, but heterosexuality is implied because of costuming.[91] In both of these instances, the "properly" gendered characters know, or believe, that they are engaging in a heterosexual romance. An example of the latter situation occurs in the Keystone film *Hearts and Flowers* (1919). Phyllis Haver, a Sennett Bathing Beauty, cross-dresses in order to woo a flower girl, played by Louise Fazenda, away from Haver's love interest. Disguised as a man, Haver flirts with Fazenda's flower girl and then kisses her. After the kiss, the flower girl pauses a moment and then goes in for another one. When her boyfriend appears and breaks up the clinch, the flower girl kisses him on the forehead and sends him on his way before turning back to her new "boyfriend." As the two women embrace, an intertitle appears, reading "Woman against woman" (Figure 3.17). In this instance the characters (with the exception of Haver's temporary transvestite) believe that a heterosexual romance is taking place, while the audience knows that they are witnessing a homosexual moment. The opposite situation takes place in the Christie comedy *Know Thy Wife* (1918). In this film Bob (Earle Rodney) returns home from school with his new wife, Betty (Dorothy Devore), disguised as a man so as not to upset his parents, who are unaware of his marriage and have picked out another woman for him. Wearing a suit and hiding her long hair under a short wig, Betty is welcomed as her husband's college roommate. When Betty and Bob find a moment alone they share a kiss, only to be interrupted by Bob's mother, who looks away in embarrassment and confusion, finally remarking that "you boys are certainly fond of each other" (Figure 3.18). Later the masquerade is ended when Betty removes her wig to reveal her long hair, and Bob explains to his parents that "this young fellow is my wife."

Figure 3.17. *Hearts and Flowers* (1919): "Woman against woman."

A more subtle example of the dynamics of simultaneous hetero- and homosexual moments involved in paradoxical bivalent kisses occurs when the film's hero finds himself sexually attracted to the heroine while believing that she is a man. In comedies such as *The Ragged Earl* (1914) and *The Dream Lady* (1918) male characters are drawn to female characters disguised as men, and although the "male" characters are revealed to be women before the pairs can be united, the films offer moments of intriguing queer possibility. These comedies are analogous to what Horak calls range romances, westerns that feature women who cross-dress in order to work or live on a ranch or other predominantly male space and then fall in love with a male coworker. Horak writes that "cross-dressed frontier girls allowed these men to keep their orientation toward hyper-masculinity even as they were assimilated into heterosexuality. The sleight of hand that turned the boy into a girl made visible same-sex desire even as it was dissolved."[92] The *audience* knows that the beautiful young man is actually a woman, but the male character who is attracted to her doesn't know this. Although the possibility of the leading man's homosexuality is left unspoken in these films, its presence is felt.

178 CHAPTER 3

Figure 3.18. *Know Thy Wife* (1918): "You boys are certainly fond of each other."

Temporary transvestite comedies of the silent era invariably end with "proper" gender roles restored. But before everything is returned to heterosexual normalcy at the end, audiences are given the opportunity to vicariously transgress sexual roles. The spectatorial pleasures of these films are manifold. All viewers, regardless of their gender or sexual identity, could derive pleasure from watching gender and sexual boundaries stretched to their limits. Women might savor the potential freedom represented by male impersonators, who could move about in masculine spaces with impunity. Gay and lesbian audiences could take pleasure in seeing queer moments, including implied homosexual behavior on-screen, while straight audiences, both male and female, could experience the thrill of illicit, potentially deviant sexuality, comfortable in the knowledge that all would be righted in the end. This restoration of traditional gender roles would have been especially reassuring to viewers who were anxious about continually shifting social and sexual roles.

As reassuring as the endings of these comedies may have been to some viewers, it is difficult to claim that they feature a *complete* return to normalcy given the fact that the universe of silent comedy is anything but normal. Is it even possible to talk about what's traditional or conventional in a filmic world of chaos and anarchy, where anything is possible? *Hearts and Flowers* ends with a heterosexual marriage, but the ceremony is preceded by a would-be suitor being thrown and batted around the corridor like a baseball. Why should we believe that these newlyweds will assume conventional gender and sexual roles when other characters in the story can't even be bothered to abide by the laws of gravity? In *A Florida Enchantment* (1914), a woman swallows seeds from a mysterious African "Tree of Sexual Change" and is transformed into a man; her maid and fiancé are similarly transgendered after swallowing the seeds, and all three engage in cross-dressing and manic flirtations with members of what had been the same but are now the opposite sexes. Although the "natural" order is restored at the end of the film by the revelation that it was all a dream, it doesn't entirely erase the impact of the alternate universe created in the preceding reels. Even after these comedies have ended, audiences are left with the impression that gender is fluid and unstable, a proposition that likely would have been thrilling to some spectators and horrifying to others. In the anarchic worlds created by silent comedies, where comedians defy the laws of physics and logic in every reel and "normal" is relative, the restoration of traditional gender and sexual roles at the end of the film can only be assumed to be temporary and incomplete.

While male impersonation may have been considered wholesome, respectable entertainment in certain genres, silent film comedies highlighted the most subversive aspects of these performances. Horak argues that cross-dressed women in film were not explicitly linked to lesbianism until the 1920s: "it took much longer for sexually deviant women to become legible in American popular culture than sexually deviant men. Even after the 'pansy' had become a recognizable urban type, women in men's clothing were not automatically under suspicion."[93] However, silent comedies that featured male impersonation exploited homosexual subtext with a knowing wink at the audience, placing cross-dressed women in situations that were certainly meant to be interpreted by the audience as queer moments. The scene from *Know Thy Wife* offers an example of this, as the kiss between Bob and his "roommate" is certainly interpreted by his mother as a homosexual moment, and her obvious distress over her son's apparent proclivities is played for laughs. In *Hearts and Flowers*, the title card that reads "Woman against woman" emphasizes the fact that the audience is, indeed, witnessing two women locked in a kiss, and the flower girl's rejection of her male suitor and seeming preference for a cross-dressed woman is a joking reference to the scene's lesbian connotations. An even more blatant example of this dynamic can be found in *Behind the Screen* (1916). Desperate to break into motion pictures, a woman (Edna Purviance) disguises herself as a man and joins the stagehands in the studio. One of the stagehands (Charlie Chaplin) meets her, and after discovering that she is a woman, he kisses her. Another stagehand (Eric Campbell) witnesses the kiss and teases the couple, dancing and skipping about the sound stage and wagging his finger at Chaplin (Figure 3.19). These actions are a clear indication that the filmmakers knew that this kiss would be read as a homosexual moment by audiences and that these moments were meant to be read as homosexually charged. In fact, Horak points out that the industry's censorship board, the National Board of Review of Moving Pictures (NBRMP), wanted Chaplin "to cut the manager's intertitle, 'Oh! Mercy! and 'the action of the fat man imitating a sissified character,' particularly when he 'switches [*sic*] up and down the room.'"[94] Interestingly, the cross-dressing and the actual kiss were inoffensive to the NBRMP; it was Campbell's reaction to the kiss, and its explicit framing of the moment as homosexual, that raised objections. Alison McMahan has argued that director Alice Guy Blaché was similarly aware of and deliberately exploited the homosexual subtext in her cross-dressing comedies.[95] Whether other filmmakers also made a conscious decision to exploit homosexual themes is unknown, although in silent comedies homosexuality is among the many social transgressions and taboos that are playfully satirized. This is perhaps surprising, given the fact that homosexuality was considered by many to be perverse and immoral. Comedy, however, has always been a "safe" place to play out cultural anxieties. The fact that silent comedies included these queer moments speaks to comedy's ability to address contentious topics and make them acceptable, and even enjoyable, for a mass audience.

For comediennes, cross-dressing meant an opportunity to perform masculinity with the freedom and license that entails. Even if just within the confines of the film shoot, actresses who impersonated men could explore masculine spaces, and women in the audience could experience these spaces vicariously through them. Male impersonators who appeared onstage had to worry that they would be labeled "mannish" at best and immoral or homosexual at worst. On-screen, however, the threat inherent in male impersonation was mitigated by the fact that the cross-dressing was only temporary and the knowledge that the actresses who appeared in these roles would likely be performing "proper" femininity on-screen in their next film. Whereas male impersonators onstage built their entire careers around dressing and acting like men, the cross-dressing

Figure 3.19. *Behind the Screen* (1916): "Oh! Mercy!"

that screen actresses engaged in was brief and temporary and therefore more acceptable to audiences.

Comediennes' performances of sexuality and sensuality on-screen were as diverse as the comediennes themselves. Through their enactment of flirtation, desire, bodily pleasure, and gender confusion, comediennes helped broaden and complicate notions of female sexuality and allowed a space for women to own their own desires and bodies. Certainly comediennes' enactment of sexuality was not without problems. Slapstick films often present female sexuality as comic rather than something to be taken seriously, and comediennes were often presented as sexual spectacles, so that even though they appeared in control of their own sexuality, they were still ultimately defined in terms of sex. Perhaps most problematic was the fact that the desires they were enacting and encouraging, which were, ultimately, desires for political and social equality, for freedom from oppressive familial and social systems, from systematic sexism and oppression, were presented as easily fulfilled through consumerism and, especially, through marriage. So while comediennes often helped women give voice to the dissatisfaction they felt in their lives, their films simultaneously implied that buying a new dress or marrying the boss would bring them the happiness they sought. Despite these complications, comedy gave women the opportunity to experiment with sexuality in ways unseen in other genres. Unlike the heroines of drama and melodrama, comediennes could revel in their own desires and pleasures without being punished at the end of the film. Ultimately, comediennes provided audiences with important and highly visible examples of healthy and enjoyable sexuality.

4

"Ever on the Move"

MODERNITY AND THE NEW WOMAN

When a 1917 magazine article wanted to know "who is the most strenuous [woman in] the photoplay?" the obvious answers of serial queens such as Pearl White and Helen Holmes were quickly dismissed. "No, no, no! You're all wrong," the writer insisted.

> Diving out of a balloon and flicking a speeding freight train isn't at all strenuous as Polly Moran knows the word. And Polly, we venture, is the most strenuous thing in or out of skirts. If you want to see the wild, wild woman of the screen, you want to see Polly.
>
> She rides a horse with the reckless abandon that would make Bill Hart look like a nursery jockey. Upstairs, downstairs, over cliffs, from one towering ledge to another—that's the sort of horse tricks she executes. And she can wield her fists as fast and as effectively as any man you ever saw. She has no aversion to leaping head foremost into a crowd of some twenty gangsters and then cleaning out the entire set. And she can handle a lariat with dexterous skill. Does she rope one object at a time? She does not! She ropes twenty and thirty with one movement, and just to demonstrate her strength, she pulls them all through the city streets and lodges them in jail.[1]

Looking past the tongue-in-cheek hyperbole of this article (almost certainly written by a studio publicist), one finds a description of a very modern woman. Polly Moran is figured here as strong, assertive, independent, intelligent, and athletic, able to hold her own alongside men. Her character, Sheriff Nell, was a working woman holding a traditionally masculine job, and Moran herself was known as a gifted and hardworking comedienne. Moran, and comediennes more generally, in many ways were the personification of modernity, with its speed, thrills, energy, and vitality. Whether performing wild and dangerous stunts or embracing athletics and automobiles, comediennes' activities both on-screen and off linked them to the thrilling and lively modern city and to the iconic figure of the New Woman. Comediennes also made a strong case for the malleability of personal identity, the ability to choose one's personality and type and to change it at will, an appealing prospect in a time when everything from fashions to technology to social values was changing at lightning speed. Comediennes further cemented their link to modernity and to New Womanhood by virtue of their position as working women, both in the film industry, where they served as actors, writers, directors, and producers, and in their films, where they played shopgirls, secretaries, waitresses, and other working-class heroines. Finally, by bobbing their hair and appearing in comedies that blurred the line between traditionally masculine and feminine roles, comediennes questioned strict gender roles and instead promoted women's social and political power.

In these ways comediennes provided a highly visible example of women who successfully negotiated the modern world, with its constantly changing landscape. These women were often progressive and forward-looking, breaking with the past as they gave female spectators a model for modern femininity. Just as Louise Fazenda was said to have "clubbed her path-way to success, leaving behind her a pallid mass of shocked and bleeding traditions,"[2] comediennes showed women that they didn't need to be demure and conventionally feminine to succeed—in fact, comediennes seemed to suggest that just the opposite qualities were needed for the New Woman to engage fully with the modern world.

Comediennes and the Modern World

The New Woman was as much cultural construct as lived reality. As a site of struggle over changing gender roles the New Woman was, as Ben Singer describes her, "a particularly striking example of modernity's characteristic cultural discontinuity."[3] She was a product of her time. According to Maggie Hennefeld, her break from prior iterations of femininity, including the ideal of True Womanhood, was driven by encroaching modernity, as "modern culture—with its overwhelming crowds, anarchic mass politics, proliferation of distracting images, and hyperstimulating new technologies—severed women's experiences from traditional ideals of femininity."[4] The label "New Woman" was applied to disparate groups of women in the late nineteenth and early twentieth centuries with differing and sometimes contradictory goals. The first generation of New Women advocated for women's political, social, and sexual equality, while emphasizing social service. The second generation of New Women similarly fought for women's equality but placed greater emphasis on self-expression and self-fulfillment. Both generations rejected traditional Victorian gender expectations, however the first generation was much more aligned with bourgeois values whereas their daughters "fought not in the name of a higher female virtue ..., but for absolute equality.... Not one shred of the Cult of True Womanhood remained to cloak their life style in the symbols of respectability."[5] Originally figured as an antidote to the True Woman, the New Woman came to embody the complex changes taking place in women's lives in the early twentieth century. She was fashionable, young, healthy, attractive, and vivacious when figured by Charles Dana Gibson, Howard Chandler Christy, and Ziegfeld's chorines; she was mannish, overbearing, sexually ambiguous, dangerously overeducated, and inexcusably neglectful of her husband and children when represented by antisuffragists and social conservatives (Figure 4.1). She was, in short, a catch-all symbol for the anxieties and fears that many were feeling as women increasingly made their mark on the public sphere—holding jobs, mixing in heterosocial company, and making ever more vocal demands for equality and enfranchisement.

The character types that comediennes played on-screen often mirrored these divergent images of the New Woman, from light comediennes and slapstick-ingénues such as Colleen Moore and Mabel Normand to unruly knockabout types such as Marie Dressler and Alice Howell (Figure 4.2). However, rather than simply confirming popular stereotypes about New Women, comediennes defused their perceived threat through their comic portrayals. Furthermore, unlike action heroines who typically portrayed one type of New Womanhood—active, young, and attractive—comediennes portrayed a wide range of femininities, from comically overbearing or gawky to young, pretty, and effervescent. As such, they helped broaden the popular conception of the New Woman and showed audiences that "New Woman" was a much more inclusive category than many believed.

Just as the icon of the New Woman was gaining prominence in the early twentieth century, a new type of comedy was similarly displacing older forms. This comedy was tantamount to performed modernity, full of speed and

Figure 4.1. Gibson Girl and suffragist.

Figure 4.2. Divergent images of the New Woman: Mabel Normand (1915) and Marie Dressler, with Charlie Chaplin in *Tillie's Punctured Romance* (1914).

thrills. The "New Humor" was, as Susan Glenn describes it, "a visceral, fast-paced, direct, physically demonstrative, and sometimes violent style of comedy. In contrast to more cerebral, thoughtful and didactic forms of narrative humor, the new humor created joking and laughter for its own sake."[6] This new style of comedy found its way into vaudeville and motion picture theaters in the form of slapstick and eccentric comedy, which was violent and anarchic and concerned with disorder and inversion. New Humor wasn't universally embraced: as Anke Brouwers points out, "proponents of a more restrained and 'thoughtful' type of comedy that required at least moderate intellectual or cognitive activity had been vehemently opposed to the crude and vulgar shocks of vaudeville and burlesque later adopted by slapstick."[7] Rules of acceptable behavior were acknowledged and then broken, as comedians, both male and female, pushed the limits as far as they could. Rick DesRochers describes the interactive nature of this mode of comic performance:

> Comic vaudevillians courted audience response by working very close to the edge of the stage—if not in the auditorium itself—for maximum contact with spectators. . . . Complicity between comedian and spectator developed as performers addressed their audiences directly and

made them feel as if they were in on the jokes. The vaudeville performers reached their audiences in a visceral, direct way; distinguishing themselves from their competition obligated them to push the boundaries of middlebrow propriety, sometimes encouraging youthful rebellion among their patrons. The rowdiness and call-and-response with the audience created an atmosphere that not only broke the rules of the legitimate stage but was feared it would permeate the rules of behavior in American society as well.[8]

This new type of comedy is perfectly illustrated in a routine performed in the Ziegfeld *Follies* by Eva Tanguay, described by a reviewer as "a mimic ball game in which she and the audience pelted each other with soft balls, and for a few minutes the fun is fast and furious."[9] Comedy of the 1910s, just like comediennes, New Women, and the modern world itself, demanded attention; it was not content to sit quietly and demurely on the sidelines.

In many ways, comediennes were uniquely equipped to confront the modern world. Armed with a new style of humor (and perhaps a few soft balls), comediennes engaged in and ultimately triumphed over the shocks and thrills of the modern landscape. As Ben Singer, Jennifer Bean, Lauren Rabinovitz, Rob King, and others have argued, the turn of the twentieth century was a time of tremendous anxiety, as rapidly changing technologies, expanding cities, and increasing immigration brought about a displacement of nineteenth-century lifestyles and culture.[10] The Second Industrial Revolution helped drive a migration from rural to urban areas, and technological advances meant that

> labor and production associated with manufacturing, transporting, and selling goods of all kinds moved from the self-enclosed system of the "agrarian form" to the factory and store, thus turning men and women into wage laborers and women into consumers for their families' needs. The household became transformed into a site of consumption rather than of production, and labor itself became a process measured in hours and minutes rather than by the results of what it produced.[11]

New technologies such as telegraphs, telephones, electric lights, moving pictures, and automobiles drastically altered the way Americans worked, communicated, traveled, shopped, and spent their leisure time. These changes were unsettling to many, as King argues that "modernity appeared to many much in the guise of a juggernaut, a runaway engine of uncontrollable power that crushed all that stood before its onrush."[12] The big city itself was fraught with peril. In the city, Singer points out, there was a "sense of a radically altered public space, one defined by chance, peril, and shocking impressions rather than by any traditional conception of continuity and self-controlled destiny."[13] Crossing the street could mean risking one's life, as out-of-control trolleys collided with horse-drawn carriages, and the brand-new menace of automobiles mowed down everyone and everything in their way. Horrible accidents were breathlessly reported in the popular press, adding to the sense of danger from all sides. Headlines such as "A Falling Man Kills a Boy," "Horse Smashed Cable Car Window," and "Child Choked by a Transom" reinforced the ubiquitousness and unpredictability of violent death in the city.[14] Even comedy could kill in these troubling times: Hennefeld describes a rash of women in the late nineteenth and early twentieth centuries who reportedly died of laughter, linking these incidents to "the dually exhilarating and destructive encounters between women's bodies and modernity's cult of entertainment."[15]

    The anxieties that the tremendous scale and rapid pace of these transformations provoked in many Americans could be ameliorated to some extent by the vast array of new popular amusements, and specifically by their presentation of technology as exciting rather than scary. Moving pictures and amusement parks such as Coney Island allowed audiences to experience and master the shocks and jolts of modern technologies. King has argued that a major reason for the popularity of Keystone's slapstick comedies was their ability to refigure machines as objects of pleasure and amusement rather than trauma, "offering carnivalesque images of out-of-control machinery that bracketed off the more distressing aspects of American culture's encounters with the machine."[16] Similarly, Rabinovitz shows how mechanized rides at amusement parks gave visitors a safe thrill, allowing them to interact with and conquer the shocks and excitement of modernity.[17] Hennefeld sees similar dynamics played out in specifically gendered terms in early film comedies, which feature endless variations of women being dismembered, blown up, miniaturized, and generally mistreated for laughs: "laughter and terror provide coconspirators for spectators to embrace the underlying instabilities of historical change—and women's mangled, dismembered, and incinerated bodies were among the principle protagonists in this endless cycle of looming catastrophe and uproarious release."[18]

    Anxieties about modern urban living, including fears of bodily peril and sudden and brutal deaths, are frequently acted out in comedies, especially slapstick comedies, with their violent and chaotic situations. In fact, early cinema in general had what Bean describes as a "unique capacity for giving aesthetic expression to the very crisis of which it is a part; that is, to embrace disruption and discontinuity as a premise for titillation."[19] While a number of early genres—especially action and chase films—embraced disruption and discontinuity, comedy foregrounded these tropes and played them for laughs. A comparison can be drawn between the expression of modernity in action serials and in slapstick comedies. In action series and serials, the commonly used devices of runaway trains, careening cars, and malfunctioning telephones and telegraphs point to the instability and unreliability of modern technology, "its potential to backfire, to generate a world of blind chance."[20] The restoration of order, however temporary, at the end of each film/episode provides reassurance to the audience that the problems of the modern world are fixable. These films allow audiences to revel in the shocks and thrills of modernity at its most chaotic and then safely return to normalcy.

By contrast, in slapstick comedy unreliable technology is just one of many unstable factors to be reckoned with. The volatility and disorder at play in slapstick are presented as fundamental elements of the larger world. In the comedy universe *everything* is unstable, including technology, industry, institutions such as marriage and family, the government (particularly the police), and even the laws of physics and physiology. While these films may have provided audiences with a temporary respite from the stresses of the modern world, nothing is restored at the end of a slapstick comedy because there is no "normal" world to return to. The comedy universe is, indeed, one where machines, order, and society itself regularly break down. As such, comedy is the perfect generic parallel to modernity. As much as audiences might like to believe that the restoration of order and stability found at the end of action films was possible in real life, the change and upheaval begun in the late nineteenth century instead continued unabated throughout the 1910s and 1920s.

Of course, the expression of modernity that appeared in comedy was an extreme version. In *Manhandled* (1924), shopgirl Tessie McGuire (Gloria Swanson) struggles with the challenges of the modern city. After emerging from the hectic department store basement where she works, Tessie stands momentarily on the busy sidewalk and is promptly splattered with mud from a passing car. Her difficulties continue on the subway, as she has to fight her way through the mass of commuters to get on her train, and after narrowly escaping being crushed by the subway doors she is instead crushed between two large men as she rides.

After emerging from the train she heads to the exit but trips over a barricade and lands on her rear. Another run-in with public transit can be found in the Hal Roach comedy *Anything Once!* (1927), in which Mabel Normand plays a laundry employee charged with delivering a voluminous gown to a client. As she attempts to board a crowded trolley with her massive package she is bumped and jolted, and forced off the trolley and into the street. When she finally manages to board, an annoyed passenger throws the oversized box out the window, at which point it's promptly run over by a passing horse-drawn carriage; jumping out of the trolley to save the dress, Mabel herself is almost run down by a passing car. Chase films also show out-of-control traffic, such as in Keystone's *Love, Loot and Crash* (1915), in which a wild chase involving two cars and a motorcycle winds through the city streets, demolishing a pushcart and a fence before ending with the cast and their vehicles plunging into the Pacific Ocean.

Traffic and transit aren't the only elements of the unruly modern world featured in silent comedies. *A Strong Revenge* (1913) follows a pair of immigrants—Schnitz (Mack Sennett) and Meyer (Ford Sterling)—as they attempt to assimilate into American society and woo Mabel Normand's character. Crime is featured in numerous silent comedies, and the success of the criminals coupled with the incompetence of the police (especially the Keystone Kops) adds to the notion of the modern city as a place of anarchy and lawlessness. Even the widespread fear of danger from above—evidenced by repeated news stories of objects and people falling from overhead[21]— shows up in silent comedy. *Hold Your Breath* (1924) includes a scene of an airplane spiraling out of control and falling in the middle of a crowded city street, and Harold Lloyd in *Safety Last* (1923) and Dorothy Devore in *Hold Your Breath* themselves risked falling from great heights as they scaled the sides of buildings. Rooftop chases also figure prominently in silent comedies: in films such as Keystone's *Fatty's Faithful Fido* (1915) and Buster Keaton's *The Three Ages* (1923), the heroes either chase or are chased across the tops of buildings. In a gag that echoes newspaper headlines that warned of big-city dangers, a chase in *Court House Crooks* (1915) includes a pair of policemen on foot running into a ladder on which a house painter is perched. The painter falls on top of the policemen, who knock him around before they continue their chase.

The language used in the popular press to describe comediennes—volatile, topsy-turvy, impulsive, impudent—was similar to the language used to describe the modern experience. Comediennes were, in many ways, the embodiment of modernity, with their frantic pace, limitless energy, and unbounded optimism. In a 1915 review of vaudeville star Eva Tanguay's act, for example, a writer claims that she "admirably personifies the American ideals of hurry, assurance and impudent disregard for conventions" and then continues:

> The songs are, after all, inconsequential. They are merely lines upon which the electricity travels. . . .
>
> Miss Tanguay, we have said, is the spirit of the subway rush. But she's more than that. She is Personality tearing through the line of Art for a touchdown. She is Excitement knocking a homerun in the ninth, with Hysteria on third. She is a Krupp howitzer of Restlessness hurling a 42-centimeter shell into Poise. *She is—Eva Tanguay.*[22]

Stage and screen comediennes were icons of the new modern world. The traits that made a successful comedienne—pep, vitality, energy, an effervescent personality—were ascribed both to the New Woman and to the modern city. And so Dorothy Gish is described as "a little dynamo of energy" and "a rag-time comedienne, with all the pep of a jazz band,"[23] Mabel Normand is "a dancing mouse, whirling madly all the time, but without purpose,"[24] and Dorothy Devore is "a 'Go-Getter' of the real kind."[25] Likewise, Constance Talmadge is "the female exponent of pep, so delightfully and naughtily sophisticated, so pretty, so charming, so approximate to mere man's idea of a mate to lay his slippers out for him at night; but then Constance Talmadge would never lay out his slippers—no, she'd be dragging him off to the theater, then to supper, cabaret, and all."[26]

Along with language indicating energy and effervescence, writers frequently used electricity as a metaphor to describe comediennes. Regarding Colleen Moore, one writer claimed that "her conversation kind of sizzles. She gives a remarkably good imitation of an electric spark." Another wrote that "Colleen has always been about as calm and reflective as electric current. She goes rushing around all the time you are talking to her and her conversation sizzles. There are no cobwebs in her mind."[27] A newspaper illustration from around 1927 pictures Moore as a live wire, her body coursing with so much "pep" and energy that three large and gruff-looking women have to hold her down until the director is ready for her (Figure 4.3).[28] Comediennes are closely aligned with modernity in these examples, as they are said to be infused with the same energy, electricity, and excitement as the modern world. A typical article describes Constance Tal-

Figure 4.3. "Colleen Moore's Vim and Vitality," unsourced, Colleen Moore scrapbook #2, AMPAS.

madge, who was perhaps closest of all the screen comediennes to the ideal of the pretty and vivacious New Woman in the late 1910s and early 1920s, in this way:

> A saucy, inconsequent little baggage, ever on the move, is Constance, and possessed of an illusive fascination that's quite irresistible. She races her car like mad—only last week she killed a Ford—and she takes long walks through the Hollywood hills, swims like a fish, sails a boat like an old salt, dances like a nymph—anything as an excuse to be forever on the move.[29]

Just like the thrilling modern city and the lively and adaptable New Woman who inhabited it, Talmadge is "forever on the move," her restless energy a perfect companion and complement to the comedies she appeared in.

Far from being threatened or made vulnerable by the dangers of the modern world, comediennes epitomize the spirit of modernity with their energy and activity, and they revel in the sheer joy of their interaction with the world around them, engaging their surroundings with physical abandon. They are not refined or reserved. They venture into the city with its inherent shocks and dangers, and they connect with and conquer their surroundings. Their ability to successfully negotiate these spaces is indicative of their ability to negotiate the modern world in general. In *Hold Your Breath*, Dorothy Devore plays Mabel, an aspiring reporter who ventures out into the city in search of a story. Her first few attempts fail; she chases a fire engine only to watch it return to the station, and when she races back to her editor with news of a plane crash on Broadway she discovers that another reporter has beat her to the story. Finally, Mabel is assigned an interview with a wealthy collector about his acquisition of a $50 million bracelet. While inspecting the item in the collector's hotel room, an organ grinder's monkey darts into the window and swipes the bracelet. The collector accuses her of theft, prompting her to duck out the window and scale the side of the building in pursuit of the monkey. As Mabel climbs from ledge to ledge she encounters a variety of obstacles, and several times she slips, only to have her falls broken by awnings, flagpoles, and other protrusions. Mabel ultimately catches the monkey, returns the bracelet to its owner, and clears her name, and then immediately renounces her career as a reporter in favor of marriage to her long-suffering beau (played by Walter Hiers).

While the ending of this film is somewhat unsatisfying, as the scrappy and resourceful Mabel declares of her fiancé, "I guess I'll let him do the reporting—and I'll do the wife-ing," the audience is still treated to the spectacle of Mabel fearlessly taking on the city. After her first failed attempt to find a story, a dejected Mabel tells her boyfriend, "I guess I'll never be a reporter, dear. Perhaps it's better that we get marri—." Before she can finish her thought she sees an airplane fall from the sky, and she immediately dashes to the scene of the accident, leaving her beau behind. As she tries to fight her way through the crowd she is pushed over into a baby carriage, which gets hooked onto the back of a car. Mabel is pulled down the street and then thrown roughly from the carriage as the car turns. Undaunted, she leaps to her feet, runs back to the plane crash, interviews the pilot, and runs to her editor to tell him the story. Interestingly, she is scooped by another reporter who telephoned in the details of the accident while Mabel was heading to the office on foot. Mabel's link to modernity doesn't come through technology—especially passive devices such as the telephone. Instead, she *embodies* the rush and excitement of the city. She runs from story to story, even wearing out the man her boyfriend hired to follow her and keep her out of trouble. When she decides to chase the bracelet-stealing monkey, she doesn't rely on elevators, stairs, or ladders; instead, she chooses the most physically demanding route, pulling herself up by her fingertips and swinging her legs up and over ledge after ledge. The policemen following her are unable to keep up with her acrobatic and fearless pursuit and instead continue their chase from the interior of the hotel. Mabel embodies modernity, and therefore she is able to connect with the city in a way that other characters cannot.

Other films similarly highlight comediennes' affinity to the modern city. In *Mabel's Dramatic Career* (1913), Mabel Normand plays a small-town cook who is engaged to her employer's son (Mack Sennett). After catching Mack flirting with a girl "*Fresh* from the city," Mabel throws a violent fit and chases after the two of them while brandishing a stick. Mabel is summarily thrown out—"Driven out into the cruel world"—and she lands in the city and eventually at the Keystone Studio. Seeing a pair of actors mock-strangling each other on set, Mabel cheerfully determines that this is the job for her. The explosive violence and energy exhibited by Mabel—chasing her beau and her rival, beating them with a stick, wringing their necks—are unacceptable in the small town but are the keys to Mabel's success in the big city: the actions and traits that cause her to be thrown out of her small town are the very traits that allow her to flourish in the "cruel world" of the city. Not only does Mabel get a job at Keystone, she becomes a star. When Mack sees one of her films years later, he is unfamiliar with moving pictures and believes that the villain on-screen is actually threatening his Mabel. Mack pulls a gun and shoots at the screen and then goes to the actor's house, only to find that the "villain" and Mabel are married, with two small children. Mack is clearly at odds with the modern world; whereas Mabel is able to use her unruly and energetic personality to thrive in the city, Mack fails to understand simple (and, by 1913, ubiquitous) motion picture technology, and after losing both the city girl and Mabel ends up all wet, both figuratively and literally—as he peers into Mabel's window, a bucket of water is dumped on him from an upstairs window.

The athleticism, personality, and adventurousness ascribed to female comedians showed up in their films in the form of daring stunts and perilous gags. Slapstick and some light comediennes engaged in on-screen stunts and acrobatics that rivaled the exploits of action heroines, including scaling buildings, diving off piers, racing cars, flinging pies, and chasing, and being chased by, all manner of people and animals. Press accounts of their offscreen physical accomplishments such as swimming, running, driving, and dancing were received along with films that included their daring on-screen stunts, with the result that fans understood many comediennes to be exceptionally gifted and courageous athletes.

Jennifer Bean has described how discourses surrounding action heroines worked to "enhance the believability of real peril to the players' body"[30] by, among other things, emphasizing the very real risks the stars took when executing their stunts. Similarly, press reports and studio publicity pointed out that comediennes, too, did their own stunt work and that they were often put in peril and even injured. The press let readers know that "Miss [Alice] Howell's art is not of the make-believe kind" and that Gale Henry was working closely with a live bear in a 1920 film.[31] As with action heroines, stories about broken bones and other on-set mishaps were widely reported. In 1919, *Photoplay* reported that "after stopping stove lids, runaway flivvers, rabid motorcycles and fire engines with various parts of her anatomy for two years without even sustaining a bruise, Polly Moran, Keystone comedienne, has finally reached the hospital" after falling off a horse and breaking her arm while performing a stunt.[32] Another press item told fans about an on-set accident involving Mabel Normand: "You will be glad to know that this clever little comedienne has recovered from a severe accident. A blow from the heel of a shoe, thrown in a comedy rehearsal, fractured her skull, and for a time threatened to prove fatal."[33] *Photoplay* related the tragic story of Louise Fazenda's "terrific longing for a baby" and "the bitterest moment of her life when . . . a physician told her gently one day that motherhood would probably never be for her" because of an old slapstick injury. The article describes how "she was carried from the studio, agonized with pain. There was a brief recuperation, then she went back to her clowning."[34] In discussing action stars, Bean argues that articles that draw attention to on-set accidents and the very real dangers inherent in stunt work posit the star as an "exceptional subject of modernity." The action star, and, I would argue, the comedienne, "not only experiences accident but, more importantly, survives and, better yet, thrives on it—her persistence in the face of ceaseless catastrophe raises the threshold of commonly held psychical, physical, and conceptual limits of human motility."[35] In making a career out of performing stunts that the public knew to be dangerous, and succeeding, both physically and financially, these stars were providing a powerful counterargument to those who claimed that modernity brought about a rise in neurasthenia, shock, eyestrain, nervous stimulation, and other physical and mental disorders.[36] The idea that modern life was draining the populace—and especially the *female* populace—of energy, virility, strength, and mental abilities was forcefully disputed by films that showed women scaling buildings and riding horses over cliffs. That comediennes were risking life and limb in the service of comedy added an element of playful flippancy—not only were these women willingly putting themselves in harm's way, they were doing so for a laugh.

In fact, despite the various broken bones and run-ins with wild animals, comediennes were said to cheerfully take on the wildest stunts, a logical extension of the good humor required to succeed in comedy. Dorothy Devore, then, "neither balks at dancing on the ledge of the 27th floor of the Paramount Building, nor hesitates in jumping off a fast-moving train,"[37] Fay Tincher "never balks nor protests no matter how difficult her Komic comedy assignment may be,"[38] and readers are told of Mabel Normand that "fearlessness is one of her characteristics. When a thrill is required in a picture nothing daunts her."[39] One reviewer even admitted that "one is forced to admire the nerve of Marie Dressler. For a woman as large as she is and one who has lost the resiliency of youth she takes some risks that are thrilling and nerve wrecking to say the least."[40] This is certainly evidenced in *Tillie Wakes Up* (1917), in which Dressler's Tillie is thrown unceremoniously around the rides and attractions of Coney Island like a rag doll but gamely submits to the inevitable bruises to her body and dignity.

As I discussed in chapter 3, comediennes' engagement in physical comedy can be read in terms of sensual pleasure, as an endorsement of finding enjoyment in purely physical sensation. The public's interest in accounts of comediennes performing thrilling and dangerous stunts and gags can also be seen as a response to what philosopher Martin Heidegger described as the "lostness" of the present in the modern world, the idea that awareness of a moment only comes after the moment has passed, and therefore it is impossible for cognition and sensation to occur in the same moment. Physical sensation, however, is experienced in the moment, and therefore, as Leo Charney explains it,

> the present's lostness could be partly redeemed by valorizing the sensual, bodily, prerational responses that retain the prerogative to occupy a present moment. To say we cannot recognize the present inside the moment of presence is not to say that the present cannot exist. It is merely to say that it exists as felt, as experienced, not in the realm of the rational catalog but in the realm of the bodily sensation.[41]

Heidegger posits the "possibility of a sensual present as antidote to the alienation of modernity,"[42] and while he is referring to the sensation of vision it seems clear that other bodily sensations would similarly work to dispel modern alienation. Therefore, when comediennes use their bodies to take a pratfall, dive off a cliff, tangle with amusement park rides, or take a pie to the face, they are fully experiencing the moment. The fact that they are said to perform these dangerous stunts willingly, even cheerfully, despite possible harm aligns them more closely with "sensation" rather than "cognition"—after all, a reasonable person would not "[stop] stove lids, runaway flivvers, rabid motorcycles and fire engines with various parts of her anatomy," but Polly Moran gladly performs these acts every day.

Spectators, then, could vicariously experience the sensual moment through the performances of Moran and other comediennes. Watching them perform wild stunts and gags, audiences could see an alternative—however extreme—to the "lostness" of the present moment and the alienation brought about by modernity. But even more than this, audiences could experience a sensual present while watching the films, as they laugh and thrill along with the comediennes. A *Moving Picture World* review of a Polly Moran film describes possible audience reactions: "In *Roping Her Romeo* Miss Moran does more stunts on horseback than the average comedienne can accomplish upon her own feet. While the spectators are being convulsed with laughter they will also be thrilled at her daring feats."[43] While spectators are both spatially and temporally removed from the on-screen moment, given that the films were shot weeks or months in advance, their own sensual reaction to the film—whether being "convulsed with laughter" or feeling "thrilled" by the action on-screen—can enable them to fully experience the moment while watching the film.

Comediennes' athleticism connected them to the modern world, but this was not the only trait attributed to them. A 1916 description of Constance Talmadge reveals the characteristics that were essential to the New Woman as personified by the screen comedienne: "She is decidedly athletic, splendidly built and has the grace and freedom of movement that comes from muscles in perfect condition. She can run like a deer, dive and swim, and handle her own car, and she is as quick of wit as she is of movement."[44] The inclusion of "quick wit" among the standard list of New Woman qualities of athleticism, daring, and grace highlights the fact that a sense of humor was an important trait for the comedienne-as-New Woman. In other articles Talmadge is described as having "the comedy spirit and the rare facility of spoofing herself"[45] and possessing "never-failing wit and delightful good humor."[46] In fact, humor is seen as a specifically modern trait: "The Perfect Flapper of 1924 is exactly what her grandmother would like to have been, could she have dared to laugh as heartily at her sweetheart's whiskers as they deserved."[47] The freedom to laugh, then, is seen as the difference between the modern girl of 1924 and her Victorian grandmother. Dorothy Gish's sense of humor also linked her to the modern world, as her pep and vitality are attributed to her good humor: "Perhaps Lillian Gish appropriated a trifle more than her share of girlish beauty, but Dorothy sure did get even by grabbing a big piece out of the family funny-bone and keeping it for her very own. It runs all through her anatomy and just won't let her arms or legs behave."[48] When describing the personality traits important to a comedienne, Louise Fazenda understandably included humor, but the rest of her description of an ideal comedienne is strikingly similar to the popular conception of the "ideal" New Woman: "Personality, adaptability, quickness to grasp the situation, keen insight and a sense of humor to me appear to be the principal requirements, and, of course, a girl has got to take lots of chances, especially in 'slap' comedy, and must be a pretty good athlete."[49] It's certainly reasonable that a sense of humor would be among the traits required of a comedienne. That humor would be an essential trait of the modern woman is perhaps not surprising either. Given the frantic pace of the modern world and its ubiquitous shocks, anxieties, and nervous ailments, the ability to laugh at oneself and the world at large would be a singularly effective coping strategy.

Some writers even saw humor as a trait unique to the specifically *American* New Woman. A Boston writer, defending comedienne Charlotte Greenwood from charges of vulgarity in her vaudeville act, argued at length that Greenwood's humor, far from being vulgar, is in fact distinctly and proudly American:

> The quality in American girls which makes Europeans eye them askance is their chummy "open-faced" manner. . . . [The American girl] is not a snob; she is as willing to be chummy with a count as with a cabby. To her, anyone who enjoys a joke needs no introduction; she takes the whole world into her confidence, thanks to her sense of humor, yet never loses her individuality and her underlying dignity. Her mother would have been gracious to the men she met and excoriated them behind their backs; *she* tells them what she thinks to their faces. She is not at all the typical "summer girl," who is athletic and "free" as a ruse to attract men. Still less is she the "mannish" girl, who slaps young men on the back and calls them "Old Sport." She is, rather, the girl who, when she discovers that the family expects her to be the same fudge-making little miss that she was in short dresses, goes out and finds a "job," and keeps it, makes all men respect her, and those few who she cares about love her. Her frankness is amazing; it is one of her chief assets.[50]

Frankness, athleticism, affability, good humor—these are the traits of the American New Woman and the American comedienne, as interpreted by the popular press.

Comediennes were further linked to modernity and typed as New Women through their hobbies, as reported in the press and through studio publicity. Many of the comediennes' reported hobbies involved sports, travel, dancing, and driving, all of which emphasized women's increased presence in the public sphere and took advantage of the technological and social advances brought about by modernity. Stories about comediennes dancing the night away, swimming for exercise (most likely in one-piece suits), and enjoying the mobility provided by their cars reinforced the notion that the modern woman could, and did, mix freely in heterosocial society without fear of reproach or reprisal.

A tremendous amount of press was given to comediennes' love of fast cars and reckless driving. This further linked them to New Women because, as Eileen Bowser points out, "to drive a car became a symbol of the New Woman's emancipation, and the movie star led the way on and off the screen."[51] A 1914 article titled "Movies' Speed Queens Hurl Auto Defis" declared that Mabel Normand and Marie Dressler would settle a rivalry by means of a car race, with Normand in her Stutz and Dressler in her Fiat, and "each claim[ing] her car is faster than that of the other." The article reports that when Normand proposed the race, Dressler "laughed joyously and accepted the challenge,"[52] a response that highlights the comedienne's humor as well as her love of thrills. Other comediennes also were said to enjoy the speed and excitement that came with driving, and the press discourses invariably described them as reckless thrill seekers. Constance Talmadge reportedly "races her car like mad—only last week she killed a Ford,"[53] and Louise Fazenda sped about town in a car called "the coop," one that "travels at an incredible rate of speed for so ancient and battered a car, and Louise manoeuvers it through mazes of intricate traffic in a fashion which must be cited as masterly."[54] Of course, these driving habits would eventually catch up with some of them: Bebe Daniels was reported to have spent ten days in jail after being arrested for speeding, although vast numbers of visitors and many comforts from home no doubt helped ease her time behind bars.[55]

Comediennes were also said to be avid swimmers, hikers, dancers—anything involving speed, energy, and athleticism. Marie Prevost was "a daring and skilled athlete, particularly in water sports like swimming and surf board riding,"[56] and Louisa Fazenda claimed, "I'm fond of swimming, dancing and driving a car, and when I'm fifty I'll still be enjoying dance-music, sea-bathing and automobiles—or maybe air-planes!"[57] Constance Talmadge "is the best ballroom dancer, according to masculine report, among the screen stars. She plays a rattling good game of golf and swims like a fish"[58] and "is one of those slim, clean-limbed girls who can ride a horse, drive a car, sail a boat, and do everything else a good, healthy, out-of-door girl can do,"[59] while Charlotte Greenwood "is an athlete from every point of view. . . . She drives her own touring car, wins her own tennis matches and swims, dances, golfs and bowls."[60] Colleen Moore was said to swim year round and "claims that the only objection she has to motion pictures is that they interfere with her outdoor life."[61]

The emphasis on female stars' athleticism and love of speed and thrills was certainly not unique to comediennes, nor were all comediennes described in these terms (some were said to prefer more traditional activities such as sewing, cooking, and keeping house). However, these discourses firmly aligned comediennes with both the New Woman and the modern world. As in their films, comediennes engaged in energetic, exciting activities (with the exception of Alice Howell, who obstinately replied to a fan magazine's questionnaire by saying that her hobby was "not filling in questionnaires").[62] The activities that comediennes were said to enjoy—swimming, dancing, driving, even surfing—were the same as those enjoyed by the stereotypical New Woman. In fact, Colleen Moore's description of "The American Girl of Today" is indistinguishable from a typical fan magazine description of a day in the life of a movie star:

> Getting up late, they begin the day with the lip stick. Afterward they play a round of tennis or golf or ride horseback. After lunch they read the latest books and get a thrill out of them. In the afternoon they may sit in on a game of Mah Jongg or bridge. Then have tea and converse freely on psycho-analysis and love. Possibly a drink now and then but that's just a pose. Being able to order a dinner for two or a brunch. Dance the latest dances all night without getting tired. Drive a car and be up-to-date on all the latest styles. Believe me—it's not easy![63]

Mary Pickford also understood the link between an active lifestyle and the modern woman. In a published plea to her fans to let her trade her famous curls for a more practical bob, Pickford argued that

> in these outdoor days of swimming, golf, and motoring, a woman is relieved of that constant nagging anxiety of how her hair is standing the strain. Her hair, so to speak, is no longer on her mind to the exclusion of possibly more important matters. . . . We are more mobile, more active

and alert. Short hair fits our new character as gracefully as long hair crowned the more dignified behavior of our ancestors.[64]

In this view, the revolutionary trend of bobbing hair (which, as I will discuss, was as much a feminist as a fashion statement) goes hand in hand with an active lifestyle; in other words, letting go of past fashions and, presumably, conventions is an important precursor to engaging in many of the comediennes' favorite activities. As Rob King argues, "For young women across the social spectrum, the growth of female physical culture not only provided a means to keep healthy, it became a way of affirming their refusal of traditional gender norms and participating in a modernizing process. Women's sporting activities thus came to imply solidarity with cultural narratives of female modernity."[65] These activities were not only associated with the New Woman; they were also activities that, like the comediennes themselves, epitomized modernity. Comediennes didn't just drive cars; they drove fast and recklessly. Their physical activities put them in close contact with men (dancing) or on public display (swimming) and emphasized the speed, energy, and mobility that were essential elements of the modern world.

The Comedienne as Mimic and the Fluidity of Modern Identity

The modern city was the perfect place for a young woman to reinvent herself. Rising populations afforded city dwellers a level of anonymity not found in small towns, and even women in rural areas could emulate society women by wearing the latest fashions, thanks to the mass-produced, ready-to-wear versions sold through the Montgomery Ward and Sears-Roebuck catalogues.[66] These and other changes meant that class and societal boundaries were not as clearly demarcated as they had been in the nineteenth century. In this new world identity was fluid, and "personality" could be appropriated and discarded at will. Comediennes reinforced this notion in their publicity and in their films, which often figured them as expert mimics, able to change identities frequently and with ease.

Susan Glenn has shown that imitative comedy was used by a great many female comedians onstage in the early twentieth century.[67] Impersonators such as Elsie Janis and Cecilia Loftus were tremendously popular in vaudeville and revues, and Janis was able to parlay her stage success into a moderately successful screen career. The type of impersonations performed by Janis and Loftus onstage relied as much on voice as on appearance; in a typical Elsie Janis act, for example, the impersonations were based around musical numbers with Janis performing as "Leonore Ulric singing a jazz song; Beatrice Lillie doing a sentimental sob-ballad; Jeanne Eagels singing a hot popular tune; John Barrymore doing 'Yes, We Have No Bananas,' and Fanny Brice doing 'Peter Pan,' dialect and all."[68] Although voice wasn't a factor in silent film, screen comediennes could make use of appearance and mannerisms in their impersonations, and they used these tools to work imitations of well-known celebrities as well as more generalized character types, such as vamps or aristocrats, into their films. Whether imitating Lillian Gish or a fictitious duchess, when comediennes used impersonation they were demonstrating the malleability and fluidity of identity and making an argument that women could change their personality at will.

An example of a comedienne imitating both actual celebrities and more generalized character types occurs in *The Patsy* (1928). Pat (Marion Davies) decides that she needs to "get a personality" in order to get the man of her dreams to notice her. After reading a few self-help books she decides to try on a new personality, peppering her conversation with "interesting" sayings, such as "Many a live wire would be a dead one if it wasn't for his connections" and "Always remember—Nature gives us many of our features but she lets us pick our own teeth." When this first attempt at "personality" falls short—her odd behavior causes her mother (Marie Dressler) to think she's crazy—her father invents a ruse based on a movie he saw the night before about a girl who "sure knew her onions." Pat heads to the house of a well-known playboy named Billy Caldwell and plays the role of a wild flapper in an attempt to get him to seduce her, but she's unable to rouse any interest from the very drunk and nearly unconscious man. Seeing framed pictures of several movie stars in Billy's living room, Pat puts on an impromptu show, impersonating Mae Murray, Lillian Gish, and Pola Negri. Pat's attempts to try on different personalities—the "fascinating conversationalist," the carefree flapper, and the movie star personae of Murray (the party girl), Gish (the demure virgin), and Negri (the dangerous vamp)—make an argument for the ease with which women can appropriate different identities to suit their needs. While Pat's impersonations fail within the context of the plot, as comedic performances they are utterly successful. Davies's skillful impersonations of other stars are a highlight of the film and even formed a part of the film's publicity: a fan magazine photo layout that appeared shortly before the film's release featured pictures of Davies as Gloria Swanson, Mary Pickford, Greta Garbo, Gish, Negri, and Murray and told readers that Davies is "always the life of the party—and her impersonations are partly the reason why" (Figure 4.4).[69] A similar photo spread appeared in a fan magazine featuring Colleen Moore, "a born mimic," imitating Douglas Fairbanks, Charlie Chaplin, Lillian Gish, Mary Alden, and Werner Krauss as Dr. Caligari.[70] These photo layouts suggest that identity is a guise and that adopting different personalities could be fun and playful. Just as Mary Ann Doane discusses "womanliness" as "a mask which can be worn or removed,"[71] these imitative performances suggest that identity itself is a similar type of masquerade.

Comedies that featured impersonation gave audiences the vicarious thrill of temporarily abandoning societal restrictions to cross gender, sexual, and class boundaries. This is certainly the case in cross-dressing comedies, discussed in chapter 3, which allowed audiences to enjoy queer moments and question strict gender roles. Other types of imitation that were frequently found in silent comedies include women posing as vamps (crossing sexual boundaries) and women posing as aristocracy (crossing class boundaries). In the first type of film, the comedienne generally poses as a vamp either to pursue a man or to cut loose and have fun. In *The Cardboard Lover* (1928), Marion Davies plays Sally, a vivacious coed whose friend Andre (Nils Asther) is hung up on a duplicitous vamp named Simone (Jetta Goudal). In order to get Andre to forget Simone, Sally puts on a vamp act for him, telling Andre "you're not really cured . . . until you want to kiss someone else." In *Exit Smiling* (1926), Violet (Beatrice Lillie) is similarly called on to rescue her would-be boyfriend, Jimmy (Jack Pickford), from trouble. As the "drudge" of a traveling theater troupe, Violet does the cooking and plays an occasional maid but longs for the chance to play the vamp onstage. When Jimmy is threatened by a blackmailer, Violet dons a vamp costume and attempts to distract the blackmailer by acting out the seduction scene from the company's play in his living room. Although she is not terribly effective as a vamp—at one point her necklace breaks and spills beads all over the floor, attracting the attention of a playful cat—she succeeds in keeping the blackmailer at bay and saving Jimmy's reputation. Even innocent Mary Pickford has a shot at a vamp scene in *My Best Girl* (1927). When shopgirl Maggie (Pickford) becomes romantically involved with department store heir Joe (Charles "Buddy" Rogers), Joe's father grows concerned about the match and offers Maggie $10,000 not to marry his son. Maggie loves Joe, but understanding the potential damage to Joe's reputation if he marries beneath him, she tries to convince him that she was only in it for the money,

Figure 4.4. Marion Davies: "always the life of the party—and her impersonations are partly the reason why." "Stars in the Film Firmament," January 1928, Marion Davies clipping file, AMPAS.

telling him he was an "easy mark . . . for a gold digger like me." Putting on a jazz album, Maggie paints her lips, lights a cigarette, and performs a frantic Charleston, exclaiming, "That's me all over—a red hot mama!" In each of these instances the women play with their identity, assuming the character of a sexual aggressor in order to achieve their desired outcome. Although their results are mixed—Sally and Maggie win their men, Violet does not—they still get to experiment, however briefly, with dangerous and illicit sexuality.

Mabel Normand has a different reason for putting on a vamp act in *What Happened to Rosa?* (1920). Normand plays Mayme, a hosiery salesgirl in a department store and "a dreamer whose dull, drudging life has never been brightened by a single gleam of romance." When a psychic tells her that she is inhabited by the spirit of a beautiful Spanish woman—and "You need only to smile, and men will obey your slightest wish!"—Mayme takes her words to heart and starts acting the part. Her first test comes when she boards a streetcar without the money to pay the fare. As the conductor reprimands her, Mayme decides "to try her powers of fascination" and, batting her eyes at the conductor, tells him, "I no got ze money. You let me ride, plees?" Her ploy works, and, pleased with her success, she dives into character, digging up a Spanish dress her mother had worn as a vaudeville dancer and insisting that she is Rosa Alvaro. Mayme's impersonation of Rosa is a response to and escape from her dreary modern life. Her job is stressful—the first title card of the film tells us that "Bargain Monday at Friedman's [is] heralded as the most ruthless carnage of regular prices in the history of retail drygoods," followed by a shot of throngs of shoppers clamoring to save a nickel on silk hose—and her life outside of work is bleak. Impersonating Rosa gives Mayme an opportunity to live out a fantasy of romance, exoticism, and intrigue, tinged with the illicit excitement of crossing ethnic, as well as sexual, boundaries. She has a chance to make her romantic fantasy a reality when she meets Dr. Maynard Drew (Hugh Thompson), whom she believes to be the "handsome, dark complexioned young man" the psychic predicted she would meet, but worried that he would be unimpressed by an ordinary shopgirl, Mayme sets out to seduce him as Rosa. Mayme's plan works a little too well; when she finally confesses her impersonation to the doctor, he exclaims, "To me you will *always* be Rosa Alvaro!" Her attempt to blur the lines between fantasy and reality through playful impersonation lands her the man but at the cost of potentially having that fantasy take over her life. Mayme's stunned expression at Dr. Drew's declaration, followed by a backward swoon, indicates that she is not thrilled at the prospect of playing Rosa indefinitely. Her impersonation was a temporary thrill, a way to step out of herself and her "drudging" life (the word "drudging" is used multiple times to describe Mayme). The notion of her temporary fantasy becoming a permanent reality is more than she can handle.

Comediennes didn't only play with sexual boundaries in their films; they also played with class boundaries. A great many comedies feature working-class characters—including shopgirls, waitresses, and maids—who long for a better life, and this desire to rise above their station often leads them to impersonate upper-class women, particularly royalty. *Her Wild Oat* (1927) features an elaborate scheme by Mary Lou (Colleen Moore), a lunch cart owner, to break into high society. After working hard and saving her money for five years, she decides to indulge in a stay at an exclusive seaside resort. Mary Lou is well aware of the fact that she won't fit in among the elite, and so she asks her friend, a cabaret dancer named Daisy (Gwen Lee), to teach her how to be elegant. Daisy is a thinly disguised prostitute—she is described as "One of those Iowa girls—'Iowa month's rent, Daddy'"—and while her idea of elegance may seem chic to humble Mary Lou, the ruffles and feathers she dresses Mary Lou in are loud and garish compared to upper-class fashions. After a run-in with the resort's house detective who thinks that she, too, is a prostitute, Mary Lou turns to her friend Tommy (Hallam Cooley), a lifestyle reporter who straddles upper- and lower-class spaces. Tommy finds some new clothes for Mary Lou and encourages her to pass herself off as the fictitious "Duchesse de Granville." The ruse works, and soon the same people who had previously snubbed Mary Lou are desperate to meet her. For Mary Lou, as for Mayme, her impersonation allows her an escape from her life of drudgery. The opening scenes of Mary Lou hard at work on her lunch cart from early morning until late at night provide a striking contrast to the life of luxury she experiences as the Duchesse de Granville (Figures 4.5 and 4.6).

A similar rags-to-riches impersonation occurs in *Cinderella Cinders* (1920), which features Alice Howell as Cinderella, a hardworking fry cook and server in a greasy-spoon diner. When her union goes on strike, Cinderella takes a job as a cook for a wealthy family and is asked to pose as a countess at a party given by the family when the real countess is unable to attend. Cinderella and the butler (posing as the count) are continually betrayed by their working-class manners, despite their best attempts to act dignified. Their efforts are further hampered when they unknowingly drink spiked punch, although even drunk they maintain the haughty demeanor and stiffly formal expressions that they associate with the upper class. When Mabel Normand's "Girl Bandit" passes for high class in *Should Men Walk Home?* (1927), she does so for decidedly sinister means—to rob the home of a society couple throwing a party. She and her partner are able to fool the guests at the party, but they can't escape the suspicions of the detective, a working-class man who recognizes his own class. In all of these instances the characters are able to slip (mostly) undetected into high society and for a short time escape the harsh realities of their own lives. Continued drudgery presumably awaits Mary Lou and Cinderella after their

Figure 4.5. *Her Wild Oat* (1927): Colleen Moore as Mary Lou Smith . . .

stints as royalty are over, and while it's assumed that the Girl Bandit will continue her life of crime, her introduction in the film—hitchhiking on the side of the road—indicates that she has not had a great deal of success in her chosen career. While their daily lives involve a struggle to make ends meet, for a brief time they are waited on by others and treated with deference not usually shown to working-class women.

Whether impersonating vamps or duchesses, the heroines of these films always discover that they're best served by remaining true to who they are. At the same time, the films offer the underlying message that crossing boundaries is uncomplicated and rewarding. This idea could be unsettling to some, however, as Susan Glenn has argued: "In the era of the New Woman, the idea that individuals were always in flux, and always susceptible "to influence of others," threatened to undermine any claims for a stable, autonomous self, and suggested the possibility of endless gender permutations. Even a concept as previously unassailable as sexual difference might be threatened by theories of the imitative self."[72] If personality, as these films suggest, is something that a woman can

Figure 4.6. . . . and the Duchesse de Granville.

easily put on and discard to suit her needs, what does that say about the stability of social roles and, more generally, personal identity? If a servant can pass herself off as a duchess, or an otherwise "virtuous" woman can come across as a sexual aggressor, then that calls into question the rigid gender, class, and social boundaries that purportedly divided people into neat groups in the nineteenth century. While this concept would certainly have been threatening to some, for many the prospect of crossing boundaries would have been exciting. Film fans were encouraged to experiment with identity not just by the films but also by fan magazines and advertisers. The notion of identity as malleable, of personality as masquerade and artifice, is apparent in fan magazines in promotions such as *Motion Picture Classic*'s Fame and Fortune contest, which promised to transform a lucky young woman into a glamorous international movie star. In magazine advertisements, too, readers were presented with the idea of both appearance and personality as changeable, as they were encouraged to adopt the looks and attitudes and appearances of the screen stars. The idea of a woman being able to experiment with a whole new personality simply by changing her makeup, hair, or clothes was certainly something that advertisers would want to encourage, as was the concept of "developing a personality" through imitation. Fan magazines ran countless advertisements that featured the trope of personal transformation, of using lipstick, silk stockings, toothpaste, and other products to become someone else. Ads that featured celebrity endorsements invited readers to imitate their favorite stars, in the hopes of emulating the glamorous lives that the stars were supposed to have led.

Faced with encouragement from films, fan magazines, and advertisements to reinvent themselves some movie fans were glad to try out different personalities, much like the comediennes who performed imitations and boundary crossing in their films or who starred in the makeover comedies discussed in chapter 1. One fan described her attempts at developing a "coquettish" personality, in an echo of Pat's attempts to foster "personality" in *The Patsy*:

> When I discovered I should like to have this coquettish and coy look which all girls may have, I tried to do it in my room. And surprises! I could imitate Pola Negri's cool or fierce look, Vilma Banky's sweet but coquettish attitude. I learned the very way of taking my gentlemen friends to and from the door with that wistful smile, until it has become a part of me.[73]

Other viewers similarly cultivated personalities they had seen in the movies. One young woman admitted, "Clara Bow has been my ideal girl, and I have tried to imitate some of her mannerisms.... I have learned from the movies how to be a flirt, and I have found out that at parties and elsewhere the coquette is the one who enjoys herself the most."[74] Another girl pointed out, "It seems on the screen that the wild girl or the one that pets gets the one she loves. I am now trying that method and am going to see how it will work.... The movies give one many ideas and I'm going to try this one. Time will tell."[75] For these girls, a personality is something that can be tried on as easily as a new coat and discarded just as easily if it doesn't fit.

"The Work Is as Strenuous as a Laundry Girl's"

One of the most visible ways in which comediennes symbolized the modern world, both on-screen and off, was simply by doing their job. As working women comediennes could be role models for the vast numbers of women entering the workforce in the early twentieth century. Stage and screen actresses from all genres were very public examples of women who had achieved the social autonomy and mobility that feminists were fighting for. Acting was one of the few professions in which women could achieve career parity with men, with the opportunity for equal pay and equal opportunities. Furthermore, many comediennes were involved in other aspects of film production, including writing, directing, and producing, and a number of them ran their own production companies. Much of the discourse surrounding motion picture acting points out the difficulties of the profession, including long hours, tedious work, and the dangers involved in performing stunts and physical comedy. At the same time, comediennes are very frequently presented as capable businesswomen for whom film work is not a hobby but rather a fulfilling career.

Although actresses faced many risks and hardships, a career as an actress offered women opportunities not found in other professions. Writing in 1909, a British playwright claimed that "the actress has long appeared to the crowd as the ideal image of freedom and spontaneity, and indeed as a pioneer of public work and wages for women . . . free from many old-fashioned crampings and conventions."[76] The potential for high salaries, economic and social independence, and equality with men existed in movies and theater and made acting an attractive career for many women. Performers were paid according to talent and popularity, regardless of gender, and female headliners appearing in first-class vaudeville theaters could earn $1,000–4,000 a week, compared to the $5–15 a week earned by the average female worker in the 1910s. Even non-headliners' salaries could be high in vaudeville, ranging from $200 to $500 a week.[77] At first motion picture salaries were, on average, lower than theater salaries, but as *Variety* pointed out, "the figure they command is good the whole year round and that is more comfort than working the legitimate stage at a bigger salary for a short season."[78] In 1913 Mabel Normand was one of the highest-paid women in the movies; by 1914 her salary was reported to be $1,500 a week, and ten years later it had risen to $5,000 a week.[79] Even this impressive amount seemed small when compared with Mary Pickford's earnings; in 1916 she took in $10,000 a week and 50 percent net profits on her films, giving her an annual salary almost seven times higher than that of then-president Woodrow Wilson. Studio publicity described Pickford's salary as "the largest salary ever paid to any woman in the world."[80]

Comediennes were frequently involved in aspects of film production besides performing, and their involvement in writing, directing, and producing was widely reported in the popular press. Constance Talmadge, Mabel Normand, Fay Tincher, Alice Howell, Mary Pickford, Gale Henry, Dorothy Devore, and Dot Farley are among the many comediennes who ran their own, often self-named, production companies. While their duties varied and some were production heads in name only, many took an active role in producing their films, making decisions on everything from budgets to scripts to casting. Mary Pickford's behind-the-scenes acumen was well known to film fans, as fan magazines and newspapers frequently reported on her business dealings. One magazine speculated that Pickford could "become one of the greatest producers the screen has known. And what's more to be desired?" The writer further predicted that if Pickford left acting, "she may progress to a higher plane as a creator."[81] Like Pickford, Fay Tincher was also described in the press as a skillful businesswoman, capable of running her own production company:

> Fay Tincher is very businesslike, tho [sic] she looks like the most feminine of her sex. She is highly intelligent, thinks quickly, expresses herself very clearly, has a fine flow of language and has learnt from every one of her varied experiences. She is self-reliant, knows the Motion Picture business thoroly [sic], and is confident that she will succeed as head of the Fay Tincher productions.[82]

When the press detailed the business acumen of Pickford, Tincher, and other comediennes, it was celebrating highly visible women who were in positions of power and authority. Fan magazines were uniformly positive in their discussions of women's power in Hollywood, telling their largely female readership that these well-paid and highly respected positions were both exciting and rewarding for the women who held them. Although comediennes' production companies were almost always subsidiaries of larger studios, and as such comediennes only had control over their own films—and not always complete control—the fact that these women were, at least to some degree, their own bosses was seen as tremendously positive by the popular press. As *Moving Picture World* said about Dorothy Devore, "What gives her the great kick is that this June she will practically be her own boss."[83] In these discourses, the prospect of being one's own woman, not controlled by men, is highly appealing.

Along with acting in and in some cases producing their films, many comediennes were also writers and directors. Film fans knew that Mabel Normand directed many films at Keystone, including some of Charlie Chaplin's earliest work.

In 1915 she was "reputed to be the only actress director in the country today," and two years later *Moving Picture World* proclaimed her "the first woman director of comedies."[84] Gale Henry was a writer as well as an actor and director, and her 1929 Paramount biography highlighted her career trajectory, pointing out that she "entered Century Comedies as a starring comedienne. For four years she was starred by this company; and then she turned producer herself. In one year, she wrote, directed, produced, and starred in twenty-six two-reel comedies."[85] Fan magazines let readers know that Louise Fazenda "has worked upon scenarios and has a sense of plot development that many students of photoplay writing would give much to acquire" and that Dot Farley "has written more than 200 photoplays all of which have been produced on the screen."[86] Slapstick comediennes were also known to invent their own gags, an important form of authorship in films that, in the 1910s, had little or nothing in the way of written scripts. Victoria Sturtevant has argued that although Marie Dressler didn't write her own screenplays, she shaped the narrative and genre of her films through her performance:

> It was much more common for comic stars of the studio system, like Charles Chaplin, Buster Keaton, or Mae West, to take on an authorial function relative to their films, because they understood better than anyone else how to showcase their particular comic skills. The same logic that permitted Fred Astaire to choreograph his own dances permitted Marie Dressler to design her own outlandish costumes and improvise her physical comedy, as well as some lines. She understood the comic potential of her own face and body, and she came to that understanding through her training on Broadway and vaudeville stages.[87]

Louise Fazenda acknowledged the hard work involved in inventing gags, a process that could be quite stressful for performers. "We start a picture with only the thinnest frame-work of a plot," Fazenda revealed, and the actors were often under pressure to supply the comic situations.

> Sometimes the director sits with his arms folded on his chest and an I'm-from-Missouri-expression on his face and says, "Well, be funny. Make me laugh, why don't you?" And you try all the gags you've thought of, and they don't look as funny as they might—I tell you, it's no joke! Even if I did go to a convent for a little while, this work has given me some very original ideas on religion. For instance, my idea of heaven is

anywhere that there isn't such a thing as a gag you have to think of yourself; and my idea of hell is a studio where you have to spend all eternity thinking up gags that nobody laughs at.[88]

As early as 1915 *Photoplay* was crediting Mabel Normand with being an integral part of Keystone's creative team—"Always brim-full of new ideas and ever creating new scenarios she helped Sennett make moving picture history out there in Edendale, Calif."—and Normand discussed how audience reaction would shape the creative process: "I make it a part of my daily work . . . to attend theaters where they show Keystone pictures. I listen eagerly for criticisms among the audience and many times get good ideas in this way. But I do not confine myself to my own pictures either. I see everybody's. That is the only way I can keep in touch."[89] Whether producing, directing, writing scenarios, or authoring gags, comediennes were actively involved in the creation of their films from both sides of the screen. Through their involvement in the creative elements of their films, many comediennes could control, at least to some extent, the structure and content of their films and thereby control their representation, image, and identity. Furthermore, the publicity given to comediennes' behind-the-scenes work meant that the general public could see these women as serious professionals and capable businesswomen.

This image was reinforced by stories that emphasized the long hours and difficult work involved in making films. Fay Tincher summed up the disconnect between the public's perception and the reality of motion picture work.

> The trouble with most girls is—and I have talked to hundreds of them in the studios—that they seem to think Motion Pictures are a combination picnic-ground, dream-world and short-cut to fame. They are anything but that. The work, to talk plain English, is as strenuous as a laundry girl's; the hours are long, there is very little time for outside pleasures, and your E-string must be kept twanging at concert pitch all the time.[90]

Colleen Moore agreed that making movies was more work than glamour, saying, "I don't know whether there's a short cut to stardom or not . . . whatever I've done has been through hard work, study, and not playing about, but sticking on the job all the time."[91] In a 1924 article, Louise Fazenda made it clear that her success was due to her own hard work:

> I got what success I have by sheer concentration. For five years I toiled in obscurity, as patiently as any clerk on a ledger; was just a bathing girl at Mack Sennett's. Then I planned in my own mind the gingham dress, the pigtails and the square-toed shoes, and the comedy that went with them. In a way, it's just as a man builds a house. Of course, you modify it as you go along, but what I [want] to stress [is] this, the comedy is made from the gray matter of the brain and it's much harder than it looks.[92]

Mary Pickford compared motion picture work to retail sales when she spent a day working in a five-and-dime to prepare for her role in *My Best Girl*. Pickford claimed that "it wasn't nearly as hard work as some of my own work in pictures. . . . Of course, it might get monotonous if you had to do it every day, but I'm not a bit tired. I wouldn't have missed it for anything."[93] While some shopgirls might take exception to the idea that their work wasn't that hard, stories about comediennes' difficult rise to the top of their profession and the hard work involved in a motion picture career helped confirm their image as serious professionals. Furthermore, these stories provide evidence of another way that comediennes are linked to, and ultimately triumph over, modern life. While a great many women entered the workforce in the early twentieth century, either because of financial need or desire for a career, there was a great disparity in the types of jobs held by women as compared to men and the salaries they received. When comediennes succeeded in business, functioned as their own bosses, and achieved at least some parity with men they were providing an example of women who successfully negotiated the changing social and financial landscape and came out on top.

Of course, the financial and business success enjoyed by motion picture actresses was not accessible to all women. Large numbers of women in the workforce in the early twentieth century worked long hours in service jobs for low pay. This reality was reflected in comedies, as comediennes frequently portrayed working-class girls such as shopgirls, servants, secretaries, telephone operators, and waitresses. While the real-life problems of these women were complicated and not easily resolved, the films almost always presented a happy ending, which usually included marriage, often to the boss or to a handsome young millionaire. Although these films are sympathetic to the plight of the working girl, she is by and large figured as a modern-day Cinderella waiting for her prince to rescue her from the world of paid labor rather than as an ambitious businesswoman hoping to work her way to the top. The Cinderella trope is evident in many of

Colleen Moore's films, to such an extent that the press was often critical of the similarity between her roles. One writer cynically proclaimed that "some day Colleen Moore is going to play the part of a rich spoiled little girl, instead of a downtrodden, hard-working girl, and then the millennium will have arrived," and another writer postulated that Moore's popularity with fans was due to the fact that "the Cinderella legend is dearest to our hearts of all the stories in the world. Miss Moore's career dramatizes that story. She has come up from the ranks of the extras and she has come with the very smallest equipment in physical attractiveness and in talent for make-believe."[94] Moore's Cinderella persona is reflected in her films, most notably in *Ella Cinders* (1926), in which she plays an abused stepchild yearning for a movie career, but also in her other films such as *Her Wild Oat* and *Orchids and Ermine* (1927). Mary Lou, the lunch cart owner in *Her Wild Oat*, and Pink, the telephone operator in *Orchids and Ermine*, long for lifestyles beyond their means but are unable to achieve their dreams despite the long, hard hours they work. Mary Lou points out that she's slaved day and night for five years, working toward her goal of leaving her job in the lunch cart, while Pink hopes to snare a rich man to take her away from her drab job. Mary Lou and Pink are both shown to be hard workers, and the former is presented as an especially good businesswoman, as she runs her lunch cart on her own, deftly handling finances, customers, and competition from other lunch cart owners. Despite Mary Lou's shrewd business sense, or Pink's aptitude for answering busy phone lines and interacting with the public, neither is shown to be especially ambitious in terms of career. For these women, work is something to be done until one can find a husband. As one reviewer described the trajectory of Moore's characters, "Colleen, as usual, starts as a 'poor working girl' and ends in a palace—or the American conception of whatever that is."[95] According to these films, the perfect outcome for a working-class Cinderella was a rich suitor and an escape from the labor force. Although these films seem to deny the possibility of female ambition in the workforce, for working women who held demanding and stressful jobs, and who found it difficult or impossible to compete with male coworkers and find success in the working world, these Cinderella stories could be attractive escapist fantasy.

Shopgirls are especially sympathetic characters in silent comedies, as their chaotic jobs and impoverished home lives are the subject of both comedy and pathos. Gloria Swanson (*Manhandled*), Mabel Normand (*What Happened to Rosa?*), Clara Bow (*It*), and Mary Pickford (*My Best Girl*) are among the comediennes who played women working in retail settings. In *Manhandled* Gloria

Swanson plays the socially ambitious salesgirl Tessie, introduced as "one of the mob" of retail workers. Tessie's social position is illustrated by her physical position at work, in the basement of Thorndyke's department store. As she emerges from the chaos of Thorndyke's basement after work she stops on the sidewalk to enjoy the sunlight and air, and is promptly splattered by mud when a car drives through a puddle in front of her. Descending once more underground, Tessie is jostled and abused as she rides the subway to her home, a depressing one-room apartment that is a perfect architectural manifestation of her dead-end life. Tessie desperately longs for escape from her dreary life and she pleads with her boyfriend, Jimmy (Tom Moore), to take her dancing, telling him, "I'm so sick of Thorndyke's—and bargain hunters, and pawed-over goods. I just got to have some fun!" Mabel Normand similarly seeks escape from her life of drudgery in *What Happened to Rosa?* as her Mayme masquerades as the romantic and exotic Rosa Alvaro. While at work, Mayme, like Tessie, has to deal with disapproving bosses and demanding customers, whose frenzied hunt for bargains resembles a brawl (Figure 4.7). Both Tessie and Mayme retreat from their hectic and unrewarding jobs and dreary apartments through fantasy. While Mayme impersonates Rosa to create some excitement and attract the attention of Dr. Drew, Tessie has a more ambitious exit strategy. Tagging along to a party with a coworker, Tessie meets a sculptor who invites her to be his model for $60 a week—a marked improvement over her $18 weekly salary at Thorndyke's. Tessie takes the job but quits when the sculptor tries to force himself on her. She then meets the owner of a tea room, who offers her a full $75 a week to pose as a Russian countess while serving tea in his restaurant. He, too, makes a pass at her, and Tessie ultimately realizes that her happiness lies with Jimmy, who has conveniently struck it rich as an inventor. When Tessie and Mayme engage in class- and nationality-crossing impersonations—Tessie as a Russian countess, Mayme as a Spanish noblewoman—they are appropriating identities that are as distant from their working-class lives as possible and using these identities as a way out of their everyday existence. This type of fantasy would certainly have resonated with motion picture fans who, as Herbert Blumer showed in his landmark 1933 study *Movies and Conduct*, engaged in similar fantasies inspired by the movies. One young movie fan described how she "particularly liked pictures in which the setting was a millionaire's estate or some such elaborate place. After seeing a picture of this type, I would imagine myself living such a life of ease as the society girl I had seen. My day-dreams would be concerned with lavish wardrobes, beautiful homes, servants, imported automobiles, yachts, and countless

Figure 4.7. Shoppers hunt for bargains in *What Happened to Rosa?* (1920).

handsome suitors."[96] Even movie fans who were not, themselves, working girls could understand the concept of fantasy and role-play as an alternative to reality.

While some shopgirl characters are portrayed as desperately longing to escape their lives, others are shown to be cheerful, scrappy, and resourceful, making the best of their lowered economic and social situations, using their limited means to care for others, and enjoying the excitement of the modern city. In *It*, Betty Lou (Clara Bow) works at the lingerie counter at Waltham's department store where, a title tells us, "In a shopgirl's day, the first thousand customers are the crabbiest." Despite the pressures of her job, Betty Lou is consistently energetic and optimistic. She shares her apartment—located "in that fashionable downtown suburb—Gashouse Gables"—with a sick shopgirl friend (Priscilla Bonner) and the friend's baby, and when her friend expresses remorse for not being able to contribute financially, Betty Lou just smiles and tells her that she "won't go back on a pal." *My Best Girl*'s Maggie is also the chief caretaker for her household, a ramshackle Victorian situated on a busy street corner—"the swellest house on Goat Hill"—that she shares with her ailing parents and party-girl sister. After working a long day as a stock clerk and salesgirl in Merrill's five-and-dime store, Maggie goes home to cook dinner, wash the dishes, and settle family disputes. Maggie doesn't complain about her tough life and is in fact a passionate defender of her family, telling Joe that they "live a sort of quiet life"; later, when her sister is dragged into night court, Maggie tearfully pleads with the judge to let her go, telling him "we're such a happy family." Whether Maggie genuinely believes this to be true is unclear, but what is clear is that she loves her family and is, for the most part, happy to care for them. Betty Lou and Maggie, then, both face their challenges without complaining and make the best of their economic and social situations. Neither resorts to the sort of escapist fantasy that Tessie and Mayme indulge in. While both Betty Lou and Maggie ultimately live out the Cinderella fantasy by marrying the boss's rich son, their romantic interest is not financial, as Maggie is initially unaware of Joe's real identity and Betty Lou's interest in Mr. Waltham seems to be primarily based on sexual desire.

Perhaps not surprisingly, Betty Lou and Maggie demonstrate a greater level of comfort with modern life than does Tessie. Tessie struggles against the modern city, and the city seems to have declared war on her, as a passing car covers her with mud, a subway door closes on her, and she's almost crushed by the horde of commuters riding the subway (Figure 4.8). The fantasy world that Tessie takes refuge in is decidedly old-fashioned, as she first strikes classical poses for a sculptor and then masquerades as a member of the deposed Russian aristocracy. Betty Lou and Maggie, on the other hand, seem to thrive on the excitement and activity of the big city. Betty Lou is especially attuned to modern life; with her energy and restlessness she is the embodiment of modernity. When Mr. Waltham's friend, Monty (William Austin), asks Betty Lou if she'd like a ride home from work, she playfully agrees but only if they take *her* car—a double-decker bus packed with commuters. As she herds Monty up the stairs to the upper deck, his obvious discomfort is met with her laughter; the upper-class Monty is ill at ease riding public transit, while Betty Lou is entirely at home in the middle of a crowd. Like Betty Lou, Maggie is comfortable navigating the city. Maggie saves bus fare by riding home in the back of a delivery truck, and in an attempt to pull Joe's attention from some flirtatious women outside the store she "accidentally" drops her purse just as the truck is pulling away—an update of the familiar feminine gesture of dropping a handkerchief that makes use of her urban surroundings. Joe picks up the purse and darts through traffic to catch up to her; as soon as he does, she playfully knocks another package off the truck,

Figure 4.8. Tessie (Gloria Swanson) struggles against hordes of commuters in *Manhandled* (1924).

prompting him to chase her again until he finally jumps on the back of the truck and joins her on her ride home (Figure 4.9). Both Maggie and Betty Lou are energized by the modern city, and the city plays an important role in their courtships. Betty Lou takes Mr. Waltham to the epicenter of modernity, Coney Island, on their date, while Maggie and Joe spend their first date wandering the city streets, fully at ease despite the rushing traffic, throngs of pedestrians, and pouring rain (Figure 4.10). Betty Lou and Maggie are less at ease when in the more formal haunts of the upper classes. The normally confident Betty Lou becomes self-conscious about her appearance while dining at the Ritz, altering her dress to fit in with the wealthy and elegant women surrounding her, and Maggie refuses to let Joe take her to a posh restaurant and is nervous and jumpy when he takes her to dine at his mansion (although she's still unaware that it's his home and thinks that they're crashing the boss's house). The staid and formal environs of the well-to-do are too far removed from the energy and excitement of the city for Betty Lou and Maggie; they are much more comfortable enmeshed in the

Figure 4.9. Maggie (Mary Pickford) gets Joe (Charles "Buddy" Rogers) to pursue her in *My Best Girl* (1927).

thrilling modern city. This alignment with modernity serves these women well in the workplace, as they're able to face the bumps and bruises of their hectic jobs with much more resiliency than Tessie, who can only dream of escape.

Whether appearing offscreen as successful actors, writers, producers, and directors or on-screen as shopgirls, servants, or secretaries, comediennes as working girls were absolutely identifiable to female spectators. Colleen Moore, who was the prototypical Cinderella on-screen, claimed that she was "just like ten thousand other girls," and Alice Howell, who often played servants, drew from her own past experiences of financial need in creating characters that working girls would recognize: "I often felt then like the down-trodden, put upon, much abused slavies that I struggle to portray humorously to-day. Most of my scenes are broad farce, of course, but when I get an opportunity I try to register faithfully the character of such a girl."[97] Marie Dressler introduced what would become her signature song, "Heaven Will Protect the Working Girl," in the 1910 Broadway production of *Tillie's Nightmare* and solidified her position as a

Figure 4.10. The city plays an important role in Maggie and Joe's courtship in *My Best Girl* (1927).

champion of working girls in her movies, which "always held this populist note and associated her with the working classes, the marginalized people of the city."[98] Comediennes could serve as role models for spectators as real-life examples of women who succeeded in business. They could also be objects of identification for working-class women who fantasized about escape from their difficult lives or aspired to find a way to coexist with and even thrive in the modern city.

"When Women Will Wear Mustaches"

In 1928, eight years after F. Scott Fitzgerald's Bernice bobbed her hair, and five years after Colleen Moore created a sensation in *Flaming Youth* (1923) with her new pageboy cut, Mary Pickford had to plead with her fans to allow her to cut her hair. In an article titled "Please May I Bob My Hair?" she made the case for cutting off her famous curls, saying that "comfort and beauty are not necessarily irreconcilable qualities." The thirty-six-year-old Pickford announced that she was "now planning to play slightly older roles, and if I am going to represent the

Figure 4.11. Mary Pickford: bobbing her hair gave her the freedom to play more mature roles.

modern girl I must look like her" (Figure 4.11).[99] Bobbed hair was more than a fashion statement; it represented a break from earlier styles and values and an embrace of a modern, more active lifestyle. When Pickford cut off her curls she stepped into a public debate that many other comediennes had already entered into, as their flapper characters popularized a hairstyle that many found to be unattractive at best and immoral at worst.

When Colleen Moore started in films she had the same curls as Mary Pickford and played similar ingénue and girl-next-door roles, but by the early 1920s she began to feel a disconnect from those wholesome, old-fashioned characters. She first began to form an idea of a more fitting character type when she met her brother's college-age girlfriends, women Moore felt "represented the wave of the future." Moore describes how she "shared their restlessness, understood their determination to free themselves of the Victorian shackles of the pre–World War I era and find out for themselves what life was all about."[100] Understanding that she was not an ingénue type, Moore cut off her curls and lobbied her studio for the flapper lead in *Flaming Youth*. The film was a tremendous success, prompting young women across the country to copy Moore's Dutch bob and adding fuel to a national debate that had already been smoldering. The tenor of this debate can be seen in opposing letters that were printed in *Photoplay* accompanying a picture of Moore that showcased her short hair:

> Bobbed hair—and particularly this new method of shingling it—is another defi [*sic*] that the girls of today are hurling into the teeth of their elders. They've been telling us for five years that it is their self-expression that counts, and they've sneered at the delicate, feminine instincts that distinguished their grandmothers. And to back up their arguments about being intellectual equals of men, they shave their necks. It's barbaric.
>
> Dean Marion Talbot
> Women's Department, University of Chicago
>
> ********
>
> Long hair can carry germs and, undoubtedly, it often does. It naturally collects more dust and dirt than the shorter hair, which can be more easily covered and washed.
>
> Dr. F. J. Monaghan
> Health Commissioner of New York[101]

Bobbed hair became a national obsession. A Los Angeles–area drugstore ran a contest offering $150 in gold for writers of the best arguments for and against the bob (the "for" letters outnumbered the "against" by more than a two-to-one margin), local theaters ran beauty contests for women with bobbed hair, and the press speculated about the expenses of maintaining a bob (estimates ranged from $5 a week for Colleen Moore to $18 a day for Mae Murray—reduced to $15 a week when she wasn't working on a film).[102] Bobbed hair became the required look for comediennes who played in flapper films and light comedies, such as Clara Bow, Constance Talmadge, and Betty Compson, as their modern characters demanded a modern look (Figure 4.12).

Underlying this anxiety over bobbed hair was the concern that women were losing their femininity, that short hair on women would further blur the constantly changing boundaries between male and female. Writing on "The American Girl of Today," Colleen Moore acknowledged that "some people will say the flappers today are too masculine in their manners" but went on to say, "I can't see where womanhood is turning to the masculine trend in mannerisms, except

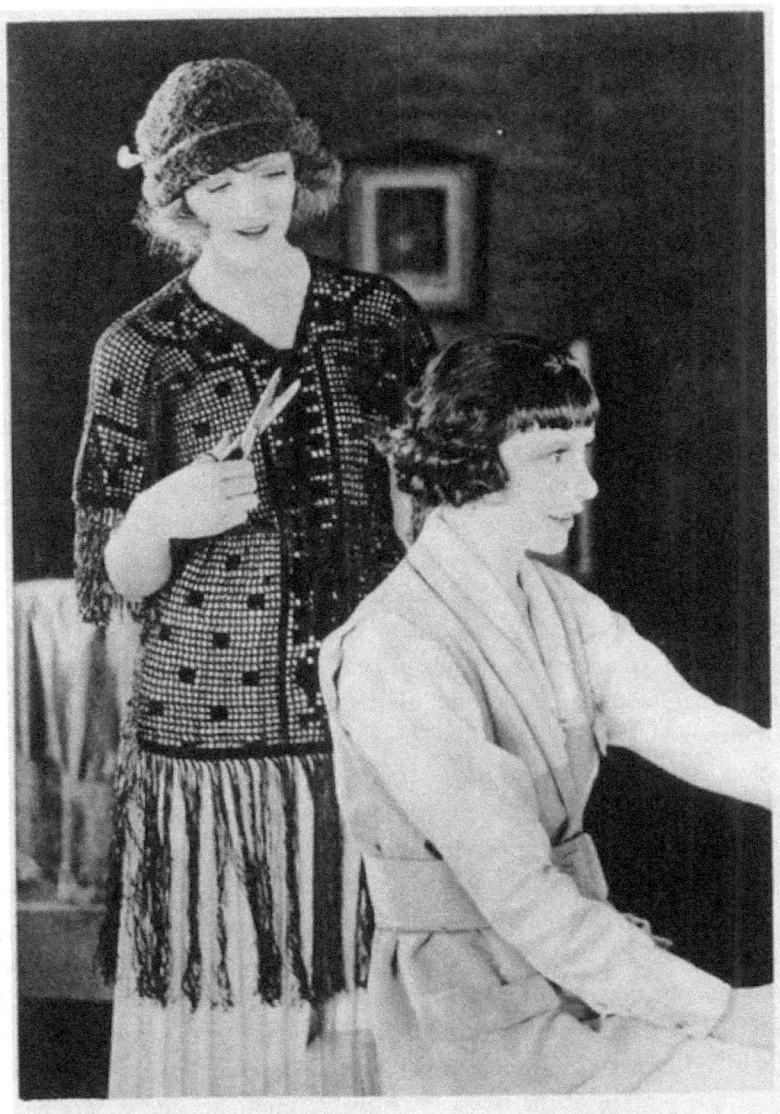

Figure 4.12. Constance and Natalie Talmadge: "Constance Talmadge caught at her favorite indoor sport: bobbing."

for bobbed hair."¹⁰³ Despite Moore's protestations that women were not becoming more masculine, many understood that bobbed hair was one of many symbols of women's increasing move toward social and political equality with men.

In the years leading up to the passage of the Nineteenth Amendment the question of what would happen if women gained the equality they were seeking frequently cropped up in films, live theater, and the popular press. One joke reprinted in a newspaper has Miss Strongmind explaining to Mr. Meekly that she wouldn't "want the word 'obey' omitted from the marriage service" but "merely transferred so that the man will say it."¹⁰⁴ Another joke claims that when women rule, detective forces will suffer because "we can't find anyone who is willing to be a plain clothes woman."¹⁰⁵ A 1911 cartoon shows a woman passing by a line of male wallflowers at a dance because "when women rule, some girls will be revenged"; another cartoon from 1913 has men contentedly flying into outer space as the Earth is overrun by female voters and their candidates (Figure 4.13).¹⁰⁶

Anxiety over the increasing "masculinization" of women played out in comedies that imagined societies where women's and men's social roles were reversed. Unlike the utopia imagined by Charlotte Perkins Gilman in her 1915 novel *Herland*, where a race of women has evolved beyond the need for men, gender-reversal comedies present these societies as places of chaos and anarchy, where the natural order has been hopelessly disrupted. These texts imagine two clearly defined, essentialist positions for men and women, with little room for deviation. An example of this occurs in the 1912 vaudeville skit titled *In 1999*, which presented a futuristic society in which women have become the dominant sex, taking over men's jobs and social roles, while men are forced to stay at home and do housework. In describing the audience's reaction to the skit (which was written by Cecil B. DeMille's brother, William), one vaudeville theater manager stated: "The idea of social conventions, customs, etc. applying to the man instead of the woman is the nucleus from which are evolved any number of laughs. The acts seemed to find instant favor with both sexes, and the women were especially delighted." Another manager claimed that the playlet appealed to "particularly the feminine portion of the house."¹⁰⁷ Other comic plays and vaudeville skits such as *When Women Rule, or A.D. 1956* (1915) and *The Mayoress* (1910) similarly satirized the inevitable chaos that would ensue if women were to come to power.

In 1920 the topic of possible gender reversal in the future was addressed in the Gale Henry film *Her First Flame*. The opening title sets the scene for the audience: "Just suppose this were the year 1950—and the occupation of the sexes were reversed—the women earning the bacon while the men take care of the

Figure 4.13. "When Woman Rules the World," *San Francisco Chronicle*, 19 January 1913, 31.

offsprings." This is followed by scenes of a "female 'Speed Copess'" writing out a speeding ticket for a male motorist (and then tearing up the ticket when the driver starts to cry) and a "Lady Trampess" menacing an aproned man hanging laundry in his yard (Figure 4.14). In the film—which involves an election for fire chief with Minnie Fish (Phyllis Allen) and Lizzie Hap (Henry) as the candidates— each gender performs as caricatured stereotypes of the other gender. The men in the film are shown wearing aprons, pushing baby carriages, and coyly flirting with women while the women use their positions of authority to dominate the men. At one point Lizzie breaks up a crowd of men listening to Minnie's speech by sending a wind-up mouse into their midst. The men scream and faint, and when Lizzie "kills" the mouse with a stick the men gratefully follow her to hear her speech. Later, after Lizzie has won the election, she finds her firefighters (all young and attractive women) gambling and leering at pictures of men. This trope of the women as sexual aggressors continues throughout the film: at one point Lizzie gives her boyfriend, Willie, a box of chocolates and steals a kiss from him, and later Minnie attempts to seduce Willie by plying him with sarsaparillas and then luring him to her apartment, where she locks him in and kisses him.

Other films paint a similar picture of what would happen should women come to power. Like *Her First Flame*, *What's the World Coming To?* (1926) is set in the distant future—"one hundred years from now when men have become more like women and women more like men." In this film Claudia (Clyde Cook), a

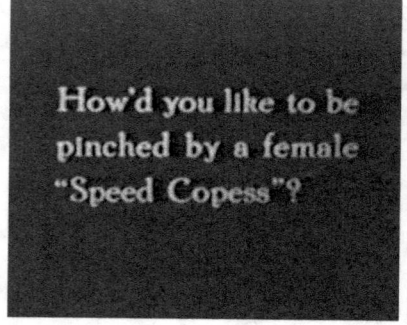 

Figure 4.14. *Her First Flame* (1920).

"blushing groom," is unhappily married to a playgirl named Billie (Katherine Grant) and pursued by a female lothario named Lieutenant Penelope. While Billie stays out all night, Claudia is left at home with his meddling father, who urges him to leave his wife and "live on the alimony." Claudia is presented as an excessively feminine man, wearing ruffled silk shirts, curlers in his hair, and lacy bloomers under his long robe and swooning over flowers and jewelry (Figure 4.15). Like the women in *Her First Flame*, Billie and Penelope occupy the masculine position of sexual aggressor, as Billie spends her nights out on the town, presumably chasing other men, and Penelope moves in on Claudia, the passive object of both women's desire. The film *A Lively Affair* (ca. 1912), although not specifically set in the future, also shows women who have become unforgivably masculine. In their rush to attend a "Suffragette Club meeting"—which turns out to be an excuse for a card game—they abuse their husbands and neglect their families, and one woman even steals a bicycle from a little girl. The card game eventually devolves into a brawl, and the would-be suffragettes end up behind bars, "sadder but wiser."

The humor in these scenarios is obviously based on prevailing sexist stereotypes of women's behavior, presenting women as too preoccupied with trivial matters such as appearance, gossip, and petty jealousies to effectively take men's place. At the same time, it's telling that in many of these scenarios women's first order of business after coming to power is to subjugate men, often by forcing them to wear skirts or to become financially or emotionally dependent on their wives. A comic article from 1909 that describes the "Scene in Congress When Men Lose Their Votes" has the all-woman Congress of the future stopping their chatty discussion of clothes and housekeeping to pass a law:

Figure 4.15. *What's the World Coming To?* (1926).

> It is provided
> Herein that from this date divided
> Skirts shall be worn by every man.
> To rigidly enforce this plan
> The penalty affixed for each
> And every trouser worn in breach
> Of law is seven months in jail.
> Hard labor washing dishes, bail
> To be refused in every case![108]

The fear inherent in these gender-inversion scenarios—that men would be forced to submit to the drudgery and indignity that women faced on a daily basis—seems to include a tacit acknowledgment that women were justified in their quest for equality, as well as a profound uneasiness among men about what women would do if they succeeded in gaining equality

The comically anarchic gender reversals found in these plays and films, then, are symptomatic of generalized anxiety felt by many as women were gaining more social, financial, and political power. These and other comedies addressed this anxiety just as comedies often do: by making fun of it and therefore defusing the threat. By showing the absurdity of societies in which gender roles are reversed, the comedies were making an argument for maintaining traditional gender roles, at least to some extent. Inherent in both gender-reversal comedies and the cross-dressing comedies discussed in chapter 3 is some measure of reassurance for audiences that the gender upheaval evident on-screen was both fictional and containable. The "distant future" setting of many gender-inversion comedies highlighted the fact that traditional gender roles were still in place for contemporaneous audiences, and temporary transvestite comedies invariably ended with "proper" gender roles restored. At the same time, these messages were undermined by a number of factors. In films that featured popular comediennes, such as *Her First Flame*, the performances and personas of the stars would likely affect the audience's reading of the film. While Lizzie Hap may be a dismal failure as a fire chief, Gale Henry is a resounding success as a comic performer, and, as I discussed earlier, as an athlete and a businesswoman. Certainly audiences could laugh at Lizzie's comic attempts to woo her boyfriend or put out a fire, but these same audiences would also be familiar with Henry's well-publicized success as a writer, director, and producer, her impressive abilities as an athlete, and her strong comic performance in this and other films. The message in these films, then, would be mixed at best, as the diegetic argument against powerful women is complicated by the extradiegetic endorsement of these same women. Furthermore, the sheer absurdity of some of these predictions could cause audiences to see through the gloom-and-doom predictions of some social conservatives. A tongue-in-cheek newspaper article from 1924 illustrates this point. Titled "Here Is Peep into Future When Women Will Wear Mustaches," the article is accompanied by doctored photos of female actresses with different types of mustaches. According to the writer,

> There will be as many women as men with beards and mustaches if women persist in bobbing their hair the physician declares. The beauty specialist adds that if women won't let the hair grow on their heads, it will grow on their faces and arms. That is what happened to men, he says. And it will happen to women....
>
> Cute mustaches for flip flappers! Dignified Van Dyke beards for professional women and society leaders. Full-grown beards for matronly

women. Dashing mustachios for the adventuress and the athletic girl. Why not? . . .

Step by step women have been advancing in the freedom enjoyed by men. They cast the vote. They affect knickers. They cut their hair and smoke cigarets [*sic*]. . . .

But think of the thousands of men who will be affected by women raising beards. The men will be the real victims.

With the barber shops adopting the ship slogan of "Women and children first" in hair cuts now, men are hard put for a place to have their locks shorn. The long-haired sheik is the logical result.

What will the condition be when women's order includes a shave or a beard marcel as well as a haircut? One may look for a return in Biblical hair fashions for men.

A permanent wave in the Van Dyke as well as in the bob would put a decided crimp in the purse of husband and dad.[109]

This article takes the prevalent question of whether the trend of bobbed hair would rob women of their femininity and carries it to an extreme. But readers would certainly understand that bobbing hair wouldn't really cause women to grow facial hair, and the overblown hyperbole in this article, as well as in films such as *Her First Flame* and *What's the World Coming To?*, might cause audiences to question hyperbolic statements in the type of socially conservative rhetoric that opposed women's enfranchisement and equality with men. In gender-reversal comedies, on film, onstage, or in print, the consequences of women's increased mobility and power is an extreme restructuring and rearticulation of gender roles, with women wearing mustaches and seducing men, while men cry on cue and faint at the sight of a mouse. As comedies, these texts can present and play with these issues, allowing audiences to laugh at the absurdity of these situations while questioning the implication that the futures they posit could in fact become reality. As the article points out, barbers "report that the number of women having their hair cut increases daily, despite the fact that the women might increase their orders to 'haircut and a shave' within a few years." In spite of the possibility of a complete reversal of gender roles, women were still willing to take their chances with bobbing their hair, going to work, voting, and fully participating in modern life.

Conclusion

Contrary to popular mythology, the introduction of sound technology didn't bring about a drastic overnight change to the motion picture industry. Synchronous sound was seen by many inside as well as outside of the industry as a fascinating, if temporary, fad, and silent films continued to be made for several years after the 1927 release of *The Jazz Singer*, typically regarded as the "first" feature film with synchronous sound.[1] At the same time that the film industry was transitioning to talking pictures, the United States was undergoing dramatic transformations, presaged by the stock market collapse in 1929. Silent performers, then, not only had to contend with changing technology, they also had to adjust to changing cultural expectations and mores. While some silent performers were able to reinvent themselves and flourish in the new climate or successfully transfer their silent-film personae to talking pictures, a great many silent actors retired from motion pictures, unable or unwilling to adapt to the new demands of the industry.

The end of the silent era brought obstacles and opportunities for performers from all genres. Up-and-coming young stars such as Carole Lombard, Gary Cooper, William Powell, and Norma Shearer benefited from the fact that their screen identities were not completely set and created new personalities to carry them into the 1930s. Some performers who were already stars in silent films—including Joan Crawford and W. C. Fields—managed to reinvent themselves to suit the new technology and social climate, and other stars—including Greta Garbo, Stan Laurel, and Oliver Hardy—had screen identities that transferred readily to sound film with minimal retooling.

Comedians, both male and female, had a fair amount of difficulty transitioning to talkies, perhaps more so than actors in other genres. Whereas dramatic actors could move from silent to sound films with only minor adjustments to their performance style, comedians specializing in physical comedy would have to make wholesale changes to their routines, gags, and essential personae to succeed in talking pictures. Adding to the problem for comedians was the fact that the bulky cameras and microphones used in early sound technology tended to limit motion and inhibit spontaneity, as all on-screen activity needed to be meticulously blocked to accommodate the movement of boom microphones and cumbersome cameras that were initially encased in soundproof booths. While most comedy production had moved away from the technique of early Keystone shorts in which actors were free to invent their own gags, there was still a fair amount of freedom and spontaneous movement in later silent comedy that was inhibited in early sound films. The coming of sound also meant that stage comedians whose routines were based in verbal gags and language play, such as Mae West, the Marx Brothers, and George Burns and Gracie Allen, found success in Hollywood and provided competition for established film comics.

Silent comediennes approached talkies in a number of ways. Some, like Constance Talmadge, retired from acting without ever making a sound film. Although Anita Loos claims that Talmadge "abandoned her career for marriage," it seems unlikely given her previous insistence, repeated after her divorces in 1922 and 1927, that women should not let marriage interfere with their careers: after her first divorce she explained that her husband "wanted me to give up my movie career. But I cherish that career as I do life itself. He wanted me to give it up and merge my individuality with his. Of course, I refused. So in course of time there must be a divorce."[2] When Constance's sister Norma's speaking voice was criticized by the press after her first appearance in a sound film, Constance cabled her to "quit pressing your luck, baby. The critics can't knock those trust funds Mom set up for us,"[3] indicating that the Talmadges' personal wealth lessened their financial incentive to stay in motion pictures. The criticism of Norma's voice also leads one to wonder whether the sisters' Brooklyn accents were insurmountable in talking pictures. Constance Talmadge was not the only comedienne to leave pictures at the dawn of the sound era: Dorothy Devore and Fay Tincher both made their last films in 1930, and Dorothy Gish abandoned Hollywood for the stage after making her first sound film, although she would eventually return to the screen and work in movies, theater, and television until the 1960s.[4]

Flapper actresses were not only challenged by the new technology, they were also handicapped by the fact that they represented an earlier era, one that increasingly seemed out of place. The two most successful flappers of the 1920s—Clara Bow and Colleen Moore—tried their hand at sound film, but each eventually left acting after making a few unsatisfying films. Clara Bow was at the height of her popularity when she made her first talkie, *The Wild Party*, in 1929, but in the rush to release the film she wasn't given time to rework her performance style to accommodate the new demands of the medium; as biographer David Stenn claims, "In two weeks' time, Clara was expected to transform herself from a visually to a verbally communicative actress. To an innate talent without theatrical training or studio support, it was all overwhelming."[5] Bow's "mike fright," along with a string of scandals (some of which were capitalized on in her films)[6] and her increasingly fragile mental state, led to her retirement from pictures in 1933 at the age of twenty-eight. Colleen Moore also had difficulty adjusting her acting style for talking pictures, resulting in a first effort that she described as "the longest, slowest, dullest picture ever made."[7] Her later films include dramatic turns as Spencer Tracy's long-suffering wife in *The Power and the Glory* (1933) and Hester Prynne in a 1934 remake of *The Scarlet Letter*, her last film. Neither Bow nor Moore was able to translate her flapper stardom into success in Depression-era cinema, and, unable to transform their earlier unruly personae, they retired from the screen.

Mary Pickford, easily one of the biggest stars of the silent era, also had trouble adjusting to the new medium. Significantly, Pickford's first sound film was also the first film in which she appeared wearing her newly bobbed hair, signaling a complete departure from the innocent little girl characters that had made her famous. The film, *Coquette* (1929), presents her in a very different role from the feisty waifs and noble working girls she played in her silent films. Instead, *Coquette* features Pickford as a flirtatious southern belle who becomes engaged in a sordid affair that ends with her father murdering her lover and then committing suicide. Although Pickford received good reviews (and the Academy Award) for her performance, the cumulative effect of her new, startling image, her bobbed hair, and her uneven southern accent was too much for some of her fans. Like the flappers, Pickford's familiar screen persona was hopelessly out of date by the 1930s, and, like Bow and Moore, she simply wasn't able to remake herself in a way that resonated with fans. Pickford made a total of four talking pictures before retiring in 1933.

Marion Davies had a longer sound career than Pickford, starring in fifteen sound features before her retirement in 1937, although it's impossible to know how long her career would have lasted without the backing of Hearst-owned Cosmopolitan Pictures. Many of Davies's sound films feature her in the same type of light comedy roles that she played in the silent era, including turns as a chambermaid posing as the most beautiful woman in Hollywood in *Page

Miss Glory (1935), a waitress-turned-dancer-turned-waitress in *Cain and Mabel* (1936), and a scatterbrained fiancée in *Not So Dumb* (1930), a remake of Constance Talmadge's 1923 film *Dulcy*. As in her silent films, Davies alternated light comedies with melodramas and historical dramas, and in at least two films—*The Floradora Girl* (1930) and *Blondie of the Follies* (1932)—her early years as a chorus girl in the Ziegfeld *Follies* are referenced. Davies's retirement at the age of forty was voluntary; as she recalled, she "just didn't want to work in pictures anymore. I'd been working awfully hard for a long time. At that time Mr. Hearst was about seventy-eight or so, and I felt he needed companionship."[8]

Interestingly, the comediennes who had the longest careers after the introduction of sound were often slapstick performers. Louise Fazenda made close to sixty sound shorts and feature films, playing mostly supporting and character roles in genres ranging from musicals to melodramas to comedies, before her retirement in 1939. In her sound films, as in her silent films, she was not strictly limited to one type of role; instead, she played a range of parts from businesswomen and society matrons to unglamorous roles as servants, shopgirls, and waitresses, and she would revisit her farm girl role in several sound films, including two from 1938, *Down on the Farm* and *Swing Your Lady*, in which she played a wrestling blacksmith from the Ozarks. She received top billing in most of the shorts and B-movies that she made during this period; however, in her A-movies from this time she appeared almost exclusively in character or supporting roles, often as comic relief.

Polly Moran also made numerous sound shorts and features, including a series of films with Marie Dressler. Like Fazenda, Moran primarily appeared in supporting roles in her feature films, and, like Fazenda, she played a wide variety of mostly working-class characters (frequently named Polly), in both comedy and drama films, including a maid in *The Unholy Night* (1929), a wardrobe mistress in *Chasing Rainbows* (1930), a schoolteacher in *Two Wise Maids* (1937), and the Dodo bird in Paramount's star-studded 1933 production of *Alice in Wonderland*, which also featured Fazenda as the White Queen. Moran's last film was in 1950, two years before her death.

Marie Dressler, who was a star on Broadway before finding limited success in motion pictures in the 1910s, had perhaps the greatest career resurgence of any silent comedienne after the introduction of sound. Dressler spent much of the 1920s struggling to find work on stage or screen, but her career was revived when she was offered a pivotal role in the 1930 adaptation of Eugene O'Neill's play *Anna Christie*. Although the film garnered tremendous attention as Greta

Garbo's first talkie, Dressler's performance was widely heralded and led to a career revival that made her a top box-office draw until her death in 1934 and earned her a Best Actress Oscar for *Min and Bill* (1930). Although Dressler's role in *Anna Christie* was largely dramatic, she continued to play comedy roles in her films with Polly Moran, as well as in some of her features, including *Let Us Be Gay* (1930) and *Dinner at Eight* (1933).

The fact that some slapstick comediennes were able to find a measure of success in talking pictures speaks to the flexibility and fluidity of their screen personalities. Flapper and light comediennes had a much narrower range of roles that they could play, due in large part to the fact that those roles were often tied to their youth and beauty. Because most flapper and light comediennes were so strongly associated with a small range of eternally young and beautiful characters—the wild coed, the irrepressible waif, the vivacious dancer, the feisty shopgirl—it was difficult to create new, more suitable roles that took into account their age, the changed social conditions of the 1930s, and the demands of sound film. Furthermore, in the silent era comediennes such as Bow, Moore, and Talmadge appeared almost exclusively in starring roles in films that were written specifically for their talents, and so taking on supporting or character roles in sound films that showcased other actresses would have been an unacceptable step backward in their careers. Slapstick comediennes, however, had already been playing a broad range of characters and types throughout their careers—for example, Fazenda, who was only a year older than Constance Talmadge, was playing mothers of adult children when she was barely twenty years old—and so were more readily able to accept the servant and spinster aunt–type supporting roles that were available to them in talking pictures.

Despite the limited success of silent-era comediennes in talking pictures, their impact could be felt long after the advent of sound. The 1930s brought a new group of comediennes to Hollywood and new types of film comedy, from daring pre-code comedies starring Mae West and Jean Harlow to anarchic screwball comedies starring Katharine Hepburn, Myrna Loy, and Jean Arthur. These films were often quite different from the slapstick and light comedies of the silent era, and yet the comediennes in these later films in many ways drew from and continued the cultural work begun by the comic actresses of the 1910s and 1920s. Clara Bow's performance of playfully aggressive sexuality can be seen as a precursor to Harlow's more blatantly seductive characters, and Marion Davies's quirky characters bear more than a passing resemblance to the screwball heroines of the late 1930s.

Like comediennes in the silent era, comediennes in the 1930s and beyond presented a version of femininity that questioned and challenged the concept of ideal femininity. Certainly the early twentieth-century image of the ideal woman as refined, beautiful, chaste, and domestic has changed substantially over the last hundred years, and comediennes have adapted their performances to suit their own cultural moment. Depression-era comediennes reacted to the chaos and disorder in the world around them by incorporating these tropes into their performances, embracing unruliness and anarchy and eschewing refinement and staid domesticity. Early television comediennes such as Lucille Ball and Gracie Allen used their comedy to reflect societal ambivalence over traditional masculine and feminine roles, as their characters feigned submissiveness to their husbands while simultaneously asserting their own independence and power—a dynamic that was reinforced by the fact that Desi Arnaz and George Burns played straight man to their wives, who were the stars and the comedic centers of their shows. Stand-up comediennes and sit-com and variety show stars of the 1960s and 1970s, including Phyllis Diller, Joan Rivers, Totie Fields, Jackie "Moms" Mabley, Mary Tyler Moore, Bea Arthur, and Carol Burnett, played with societal expectations for women and acknowledged the struggles and goals of second-wave feminism in their performances.

Present-day comediennes continue to use humor to question gender roles. While the specific elements of "ideal" femininity may have changed since the early twentieth century, the media still promote standards of femininity that are, for many women, unattainable or undesirable, and female comics still challenge those standards. Roseanne Barr's crass and unruly "domestic goddess" character forcefully contradicted the idea of women as naturally refined and domestic, while Whoopi Goldberg's early character comedy—particularly her self-titled, one-woman stage show from the early 1980s—echoed the tropes of transformation, mimicry, and mutability found in silent comedies and highlighted the instability of both racial and gender roles.[9] Although her methods are certainly different from those of silent comediennes, Sarah Silverman's combination of a sweetly innocent persona with crude language and provocative subject matter demonstrates a way that contemporary comics challenge cultural expectations about appropriate behavior for women. Other women today similarly continue the trend, found in the silent era, of using comedy to draw attention to, and make fun of, societal restrictions and expectations for women. Amy Sedaris cheerfully dons fat suits and unflattering hair and makeup in her film and television work, and subversively slips a prosthetic arm into what is otherwise a typical "cheesecake" photo. Margaret Cho bases much of her comedy on her appearance, including her attempts to lose weight in order to more closely fit Hollywood's beauty standards; in a stage performance, however, she embraces her figure by appearing nude. Like Sedaris, Cho doesn't simply display her body; instead, she creates dissonance by showcasing, rather than hiding, her belly fat and by attaching a phallus to her G-string. Tina Fey contradicts the stereotype that women—particularly attractive women—can't be funny through her very successful work as a comedy writer and performer. Like the silent comediennes who came before them, present-day female comics continue to break boundaries by questioning, challenging, and mocking social and cultural expectations of gender roles.

Silent comediennes were, of course, products of their own historical moment, and their performances and personae reflected contemporaneous social, cultural, and political discourses. As women in the early twentieth century fought for the right to vote and work outside the home, for reproductive and sexual rights, and for equitable legal and economic treatment with men, the popular understanding of "femininity" was increasingly a source of anxiety and debate. This anxiety can be traced in the films of silent comediennes and the popular discourses surrounding these women.

In this book I have argued that silent comediennes played an integral role in helping to reconceptualize notions of femininity and womanhood in the early twentieth century. Of course, women's lived experience of femininity was always multiple and variable—there was never just one way to be a woman—and yet numerous traits were commonly held to be essential elements of the ideal woman. By being bold and unruly instead of restrained and passive, homely instead of beautiful, aggressively sexual instead of demure and chaste, and relentlessly visible and modern instead of homebound and conservative, comediennes were demonstrating that there was more than one way to be feminine. While this certainly wasn't news to women, in forcefully and convincingly repeating this argument every time they appeared in films, in magazines, or in public, comediennes were chipping away at narrow and restrictive conceptions of femininity that would keep women socially and politically subordinate to men.

Certainly comediennes were only one of many groups of women who were helping to break boundaries at this time. Suffragists and other political activists, social workers and reformers, female daredevils and barnstormers, and athletes and stuntwomen all contributed in major ways to changing views of femininity. Perhaps, compared to Alice Paul, Emma Goldman, Jane Addams, Bessie "Queen Bess" Coleman, and Gertrude Ederle, the impact of a slapstick clown such as Polly Moran or a light comedienne such as Constance Talmadge may seem insignificant. And yet, like other barrier-breaking women, silent comediennes were a vital factor in questioning, challenging, and redefining what it meant to be a woman in early twentieth-century America.

Abbreviations

AMPAS	Academy of Motion Picture Arts and Sciences, Margaret Herrick Library
BFI	British Film Institute, London
GEH	George Eastman House
LOC	Library of Congress
MOMA	Museum of Modern Art, New York
NYPL	Billy Rose Theater Collection, New York Public Library
UCLA	University of California, Los Angeles

Appendix: Selected Filmographies

Following are brief biographies and selected filmographies for key comediennes discussed in this book. This list is by no means comprehensive; I have included only surviving films (unless noted with an asterisk) and primarily (although not exclusively) comedies made during the silent era. The information given here is intended to provide the reader with an overview of each comedienne and a starting point for further viewing.

Films discussed in this book are marked in **bold**.

Clara Bow (b. 1905, Brooklyn, NY; d. 1965, West Los Angeles, CA)

> Bow was the only magazine beauty contest winner to achieve significant success in Hollywood. She came to be associated with flapper characters and other vivacious, free-spirited types and was known as the "It Girl" after appearing in the film version of Elinor Glyn's short story "It."

Parisian Love (B. P. Schulberg Productions, 1925). Dir. Louis Gasnier. Cast: Clara Bow, Donald Keith. Archive: UCLA, LOC.

***The Plastic Age* (B. P. Schulberg Productions, 1925)**. Dir. Wesley Ruggles. Cast: Clara Bow, Donald Keith, Mary Alden. Archive: LOC, UCLA, AMPAS.

The Primrose Path (Arrow Pictures, 1925). Dir. Harry O. Hoyt. Cast: Clara Bow, Wallace MacDonald, Arline Pretty. Archive: GEH, UCLA.

Dancing Mothers (Famous Players-Lasky, 1926). Dir. Herbert Brenon. Cast: Clara Bow, Alice Joyce, Conway Tearle. Archive: LOC, GEH, UCLA, AMPAS.

Kid Boots (Famous Players-Lasky, 1926). Dir. Frank Tuttle. Cast: Clara Bow, Eddie Cantor, Billie Dove, Natalie Kingston. Archive: GEH, LOC, MOMA.

***Mantrap* (Famous Players-Lasky, 1926)**. Dir. Victor Fleming. Cast: Clara Bow, Ernest Torrence, Percy Marmont. Archive: LOC, GEH, UCLA.

My Lady of Whims (Dallas M. Fitzgerald Productions, 1926). Dir. Dallas M. Fitzgerald. Cast: Clara Bow, Donald Keith. Archive: LOC, UCLA, AMPAS.

***Hula* (Paramount Famous Lasky Corp., 1927)**. Dir. Victor Fleming. Cast: Clara Bow, Clive Brook. Archive: LOC, UCLA, GEH.

***It* (Famous Players-Lasky, 1927)**. Dir. Clarence Badger. Cast: Clara Bow, Antonio Moreno. Archive: LOC, UCLA, AMPAS.

***

Mae Busch (b. Annie May Busch, 1891, Melbourne, Victoria, Australia; d. 1946, San Fernando Valley, CA)

> Known as "the versatile vamp," Busch played in vaudeville before making a string of comedy shorts with Keystone. In the late 1910s and 1920s she appeared in numerous features, both comedies and dramas, as well as in a number of Laurel & Hardy shorts for Hal Roach. Busch worked steadily in sound films throughout the 1930s and 1940s.

A One Night Stand (Keystone Film Co., 1915). Dir. Horace McCoy. Cast: Mae Busch, Charles Murray, Chester Conklin. Archive: LOC, AMPAS.

Wife and Auto Trouble (Keystone Film Co., 1916). Dir. Dell Henderson. Cast: Mae Busch, William Collier, Blanche Payson, Alice Davenport. Archive: GEH, LOC, MOMA, AMPAS.

Souls for Sale (Goldwyn Pictures, 1923). Dir. Rupert Hughes. Cast: Mae Busch, Eleanor Boardman, Barbara La Marr, Richard Dix. Archive: MOMA.

Fools of Fashion (Tiffany Productions, 1926). Dir. James C. McKay. Cast: Mae Busch, Marceline Day. Archive: BFI.

Love 'Em and Weep (Hal Roach Studios, Inc., 1927). Dir. Fred L. Guiol. Cast: Mae Busch, Stan Laurel, Oliver Hardy. Archive: LOC, MOMA, UCLA, AMPAS.

***

Betty Compson (b. Eleanor Luicime Compson, 1897, Beaver City, UT; d. 1974, Glendale, CA)

> After beginning her career in vaudeville—billed as "The Vagabond Violinist"—Compson signed with Al Christie and made a series of two-reel comedies with him in the 1910s. She continued making comedies, along with dramas, melodramas, and westerns, until the late 1940s.

Inoculating Hubby (Cub Comedies, 1916). Cast: Betty Compson, Neal Burns. Archive: LOC.

Almost a Bigamist (Christie Film Co., 1917). Dir. Al Christie. Cast: Betty Compson, James Harrison, Eddie Gribbon. Archive: LOC.

Betty's Big Idea (Christie Film Co., 1917). Cast: Betty Compson, Jay Belasco. Archive: LOC.

Selected Filmographies

Her Crooked Career (Christie Film Co., 1917). Dir. Al Christie. Cast: Betty Compson, Eddie Barry, Neal Burns. Archive: LOC.
The Enemy Sex (Famous Players-Lasky, 1924). Dir. James Cruze. Cast: Betty Compson, Percy Marmont. Archive: LOC.
Paths to Paradise (Famous Players-Lasky, 1925). Dir. Clarence Badger. Cast: Betty Compson, Raymond Griffith. Archive: LOC, UCLA, GEH.

***

Bebe Daniels (b. 1901, Dallas, TX; d. 1971, London, England)

Known as "the good little bad girl of the screen," Daniels appeared as Harold Lloyd's leading lady in a series of "Lonesome Luke" shorts then went on to play in light comedies and comedy-dramas throughout the late 1910s and 1920s. She appeared in several musicals in the 1930s and eventually starred in a radio show, *Life with the Lyons*, with husband Ben Lyon.

All Aboard (Rolin Film Co., 1917). Dir. Alfred Goulding. Cast: Bebe Daniels, Harold Lloyd, "Snub" Pollard. Archive: MOMA, UCLA, GEH.
The Dancin' Fool (Famous Players-Lasky, 1920). Dir. Sam Wood. Cast: Bebe Daniels, Wallace Reid, Raymond Hatton. Archive: MOMA.
Why Change Your Wife? (Famous Players-Lasky, 1920). Dir. Cecil B. DeMille. Cast: Bebe Daniels, Thomas Meighan, Gloria Swanson. Archive: GEH, MOMA, AMPAS.
The Affairs of Anatol (Famous Players-Lasky, 1921). Dir. Cecil B. De Mille. Cast: Bebe Daniels, Wallace Reid, Gloria Swanson. Archive: GEH, LOC, UCLA.
*The Speed Girl (Realart Pictures, 1921). Dir. Maurice Campbell. Cast: Bebe Daniels, Theodore von Eltz, Frank Elliott.
Monsieur Beaucaire (Famous Players-Lasky, 1924). Dir. Sidney Olcott. Cast: Bebe Daniels, Rudolph Valentino, Lois Wilson. Archive: LOC, MOMA.
Miss Bluebeard (Famous Players-Lasky, 1925). Dir. Frank Tuttle. Cast: Bebe Daniels, Robert Frazer, Raymond Griffith. Archive: GEH, UCLA.
The Campus Flirt (Famous Players-Lasky, 1926). Dir. Clarence Badger. Cast: Bebe Daniels, James Hall. Archive: UCLA.
Feel My Pulse (Paramount Famous Lasky Corp., 1928). Dir. Gregory La Cava. Cast: Bebe Daniels, Richard Arlen, William Powell. Archive: LOC.

***

Marion Davies (b. Marion Douras, 1897, Brooklyn, NY; d. 1961, Hollywood, CA)

Davies began her career as a dancer in Broadway musicals and the Ziegfeld *Follies* before making her first film in 1917. Although the majority of her films were dramas (possibly at the urging of William Randolph Hearst, with whom she had a thirty-four-year relationship), she made a number of light comedies throughout the 1920s and 1930s and was widely regarded as a gifted comedienne.

Getting Mary Married (Cosmopolitan Productions, 1919). Dir. Allan Dwan. Cast: Marion Davies, Norman Kerry, Matt Moore. Archive: LOC.

When Knighthood Was in Flower (Cosmopolitan Productions, 1923). Dir. Robert G. Vignola. Cast: Marion Davies, Forrest Stanley. Archive: LOC.

Tillie the Toiler (Cosmopolitan Productions, 1927). Dir. Hobart Henley. Cast: Marion Davies, Matt Moore. Archive: GEH.

***The Red Mill* (Cosmopolitan Productions, 1927)**. Dir. Roscoe Arbuckle (as William Goodrich). Cast: Marion Davies, Owen Moore, Louise Fazenda. Archive: LOC.

The Fair Co-Ed (MGM, 1927). Dir. Sam Wood. Cast: Marion Davies, John Mack Brown, Jane Winton. Archive: GEH, LOC.

***The Patsy* (MGM, 1928)**. Dir. King Vidor. Cast: Marion Davies, Orville Caldwell, Marie Dressler, Jane Winton. Archive: GEH, LOC, UCLA.

***Show People* (MGM, 1928)**. Dir. King Vidor. Cast: Marion Davies, William Haines, Dell Henderson, Polly Moran. Archive: LOC, MOMA, UCLA.

***The Cardboard Lover* (Cosmopolitan Productions, 1928)**. Dir. Robert Z. Leonard. Cast: Marion Davies, Niles Asther, Jetta Goudal. Archive: LOC, UCLA.

***

Dorothy Devore (b. Anna Inez Williams, 1899, Fort Worth, TX; d. 1976, Woodland Hills, CA)

Devore started out as a singer at a Los Angeles café before signing with Al Christie's studio in 1918. She made a series of one- and two-reel light comedies with Christie in the late 1910s and early 1920s before signing with Warner Bros. and eventually producing films through her own company, Dorothy Devore Comedies, in conjunction with Educational Pictures. Although she appeared in light comedies, Devore often incorporated a great deal of physical comedy and stunts into her films.

***Know Thy Wife* (Christie Film Co., 1918)**. Dir. Al Christie. Cast: Dorothy Devore, Earle Rodney, Leota Lorraine, Archive: AMPAS.

A Flirt There Was (Christie Film Co., 1919). Cast: Dorothy Devore, Lucille Hutton, Jay Belasco. Archive: MOMA.

Kiss the Bride (Christie Film Co., 1919). Cast: Dorothy Devore, Bobby Vernon. Archive: LOC.

Should Husbands Dance? (Christie Film Co., 1920). Dir. Al Christie. Cast: Dorothy Devore, Neal Burns, James Harrison. Archive: LOC, GEH, MOMA, AMPAS.

Nearly Newlyweds (Christie Film Co., 1920). Cast: Dorothy Devore, James Harrison. Archive: LOC.

The Tomboy (Chadwick Pictures, 1924). Dir. David Kirkland. Cast: Dorothy Devore, Herbert Rawlinson, James Barrows. Archive: LOC.

Hold Your Breath **(Christie Film Co., 1924)**. Dir. Scott Sidney. Cast: Dorothy Devore, Walter Hiers, Tully Marshall. Archive: UCLA.

***

Marie Dressler (b. Leila Marie Koerber, 1868, Cobourg, Ontario, Canada; d. 1934, Santa Barbara, CA)

> Dressler was a major star on Broadway and in vaudeville before coming to Hollywood to star in Keystone's landmark six-reel comedy *Tillie's Punctured Romance* in 1914. After making a few other films in the late 1910s, Dressler returned to the stage, but by the mid-1920s she had difficulties finding work in either theater or film. Dressler made a series of comedies with Polly Moran in the late 1920s and early 1930s, and after her career was revived by her appearance in *Anna Christie* (1930), she became one of the top Hollywood box-office draws until her death in 1934.

Tillie's Punctured Romance **(Keystone Film Co., 1914)**. Dir. Mack Sennett. Cast: Marie Dressler, Charles Chaplin, Mabel Normand. Archive: LOC, MOMA, AMPAS.

Tillie's Tomato Surprise **(Lubin Mfg. Co., 1915)**. Dir. Howell Hansel. Cast: Marie Dressler, Tom McNaughton, Eleanor Fairbanks. Archive: LOC.

Tillie Wakes Up **(World Film Corp., 1917)**. Dir. Harry Davenport. Cast: Marie Dressler, Johnny Hines, Frank Beamish. Archive: MOMA, UCLA, AMPAS.

The Scrub Lady (Dressler Producing Corp., 1917). Cast: Marie Dressler. Archive: LOC.

The Red Cross Nurse (Dressler Producing Corp., 1918). Cast: Marie Dressler. Archive: UCLA.

The Joy Girl (Fox Film Corp., 1927). Dir. Allan Dwan. Cast: Marie Dressler, Olive Borden, Neil Hamilton. Archive: MOMA.

**The Callahans and the Murphys* (MGM, 1927). Dir. George Hill. Cast: Marie Dressler, Polly Moran.

**Breakfast at Sunrise* (Constance Talmadge Productions, 1927). Dir. Malcolm St. Clair. Cast: Constance Talmadge, Marie Dressler, Alice White.

The Patsy **(MGM, 1928)**. Dir. King Vidor. Cast: Marion Davies, Orville Caldwell, Marie Dressler, Jane Winton. Archive: GEH, LOC, UCLA.

**Bringing Up Father* (MGM, 1928). Dir. Jack Conway. Cast: Marie Dressler, Polly Moran.

APPENDIX

***

Louise Fazenda (b. 1896[?] Lafayette, IN; d. 1962, Beverly Hills, CA)

Fazenda began her career with Universal's Joker Comedy unit before moving to Keystone in 1915 and eventually to Warner Bros. in the mid-1920s. Dubbed "Queen of the Screen Comediennes," she was a tremendously popular performer, appearing in well over two hundred films before her retirement in 1939. Fazenda initially engaged in knockabout slapstick but transitioned to character roles in the late 1920s and 1930s.

Ambrose's Fury **(Keystone Film Co., 1915)**. Cast: Louise Fazenda, Mack Swain. Archive: LOC, UCLA.

Willful Ambrose **(Keystone Film Co., 1915)**. Cast: Louise Fazenda, Mack Swain. Archive: AMPAS.

Hearts and Flowers **(Mack Sennett Comedies, 1919)**. Dir. Edward F. Cline. Cast: Louise Fazenda, Ford Sterling, Phyllis Haver. Archive: MOMA, AMPAS.

Down on the Farm (Mack Sennett Comedies, 1920). Dir. Erle Kenton. Cast: Louise Fazenda, Bert Roach, Harry Gribbon, Marie Provost, Ben Turpin. Archive: LOC, MOMA.

**The Beautiful and the Damned* (Warner Bros., 1923). Dir. William A. Seiter. Cast: Louise Fazenda, Marie Prevost, Kenneth Harlan.

The Lighthouse by the Sea **(Warner Bros., 1924)**. Dir. Malcolm St. Clair. Cast: Louise Fazenda, William Collier Jr., Rin Tin Tin. Archive: GEH, LOC, UCLA.

Footloose Widows (Warner Bros., 1926). Dir. Roy Del Ruth. Cast: Louise Fazenda, Jacqueline Logan, Neely Edwards, Jason Robards. Archive: LOC.

The Red Mill **(Cosmopolitan Productions, 1927)**. Dir. Roscoe Arbuckle (as William Goodrich). Cast: Marion Davies, Owen Moore, Louise Fazenda. Archive: LOC.

The Cradle Snatchers (Fox Film Corp., 1927). Dir. Howard Hawks. Cast: Louise Fazenda, Ethel Wales, Dorothy Phillips. Archive: LOC.

**Tillie's Punctured Romance* (Christie Film Co., 1928). Dir. Edward Sutherland. Cast: Louise Fazenda, W. C. Fields, Chester Conklin, Mack Swain.

***

Dorothy Gish (b. 1898, Dayton, OH; d. 1968, Rapallo, Italy)

Dorothy Gish began her career appearing with her sister Lillian in a number of D. W. Griffith films for Biograph. She soon established herself as a talented light comedienne, although she alternated between drama and comedy throughout her career.

A Cure for Suffragettes (Biograph Co., 1913). Dir. James Kirkwood (?). Cast: Dorothy Gish, Blanche Sweet. Archive: MOMA.

*The Suffragette Minstrels (Biograph Co., 1913). Dir. Dell Henderson. Cast: Dorothy Gish, Gertrude Bambrick.

Liberty Belles (Biograph Co., 1914). Dir. Dell Henderson. Cast: Dorothy Gish, Gertrude Bambrick, Jack Pickford. Archive: LOC, MOMA.

*The Suffragette's Battle in Nuttyville (Majestic Motion Picture Company, 1914). Dir. Christy Cabanne. Cast: Dorothy Gish.

Stagestruck (Fine Arts Film Co., 1917). Dir. Edward Morrisey. Cast: Dorothy Gish, Frank Bennett. Archive: LOC.

*The Hope Chest (New Art Film Co., 1918). Dir. Elmer Clifton. Cast: Dorothy Gish, George Fawcett, Richard Barthelmess, Carol Dempster.

*Boots (New Art Film Co., 1919). Dir. Elmer Clifton. Cast: Dorothy Gish, Richard Barthelmess, Fontine LaRue.

The Country Flapper (Dorothy Gish Productions, 1922). Dir. F. Richard Jones. Cast: Dorothy Gish, Glenn Hunter, Mildred Marsh. Archive: GEH, UCLA, AMPAS.

***

Charlotte Greenwood (b. Frances Charlotte Greenwood, 1893, Philadelphia, PA; d. 1978, Beverly Hills, CA)

> Greenwood was an established star in vaudeville and on Broadway before making her first film in 1915. She based much of her comedy onstage and in motion pictures on her long, limber arms and legs, using gangly mannerisms and high kicks to accentuate her tall and lanky frame.

Jane (Oliver Morosco Photoplay Co., 1915). Dir. Frank Lloyd. Cast: Charlotte Greenwood, Sydney Grant. Archive: LOC.

*Stepping Some (Universal Film Manufacturing Company, 1918). Dir. Lee Moran and Eddie Lyons. Cast: Eddie Lyons, Lee Moran, Charlotte Greenwood. [There is some debate about whether Greenwood appears in this film.]

*Baby Mine (MGM, 1928). Dir. Robert Z. Leonard. Cast: Charlotte Greenwood, Karl Dane, George K. Arthur.

So Long Letty (Warner Bros., 1929). Dir. Lloyd Bacon. Cast: Charlotte Greenwood, Claude Gillingwater, Patsy Ruth Miller, Bert Roach. Archive: UCLA [both sound and silent versions were made].

***

Phyllis Haver (b. Phyllis O'Haver, 1899, Douglass, KS; d. 1960, Sharon, CT)

Haver got her start in film as one of Mack Sennett's original Bathing Beauties. She eventually became a skilled light comedienne, starring in pictures for Christie, First National, and others throughout the 1920s, including a starring turn as Roxie Hart in the 1928 film adaptation of *Chicago*.

***Hearts and Flowers* (Mack Sennett Comedies, 1919)**. Dir. Edward F. Cline. Cast: Louise Fazenda, Ford Sterling, Phyllis Haver. Archive: MOMA, AMPAS.

Love, Honor and Behave! (Mack Sennett Comedies, 1920). Dir. Richard Jones. Cast: Phyllis Haver, Charles Murray, Ford Sterling, Marie Prevost. Archive: LOC.

A Small Town Idol (Mack Sennett Productions, 1921). Dir. Erle Kenton. Cast: Phyllis Haver, Ben Turpin, James Finlayson, Marie Prevost. Archive: GEH, MOMA.

The Perfect Flapper (First National, 1924). Dir. John Francis. Cast: Colleen Moore, Phyllis Haver, Sydney Chaplin. Archive: LOC.

The Nervous Wreck (Christie Film Co., 1926). Dir. Scott Sidney. Cast: Phyllis Haver, Harrison Ford, Chester Conklin, Mack Swain. Archive: GEH.

Up in Mabel's Room (Christie Film Co., 1926). Dir. E. Mason Hopper. Cast: Phyllis Haver, Marie Prevost, Harrison Ford. Archive: MOMA.

The Battle of the Sexes (Art Cinema Corp., 1928). Dir. D. W. Griffith. Cast: Phyllis Haver, Jean Hersholt, Belle Bennett. Archive: GEH, UCLA.

Chicago (De Mille Pictures Corp., 1928). Dir. Frank Urson. Cast: Phyllis Haver, Victor Varconi, Virginia Bradford, Eugene Pallette. Archive: MOMA, GEH, UCLA.

***

Gale Henry (b. Gale Trowbridge, 1893, Bear Valley, CA; d. 1972, Palmdale, CA)

Henry was a leading comedienne in both the Joker Comedy Company and Powers Comedies in the mid-1910s, starring in slapstick shorts including the *Lady Baffles and Detective Duck* series in 1915. She worked steadily throughout the silent era, appearing in leading roles in short films and supporting roles in features. In the late 1910s she produced two-reel movies through her own company, Gale's Model Comedies.

Lady Baffles and Detective Duck in the Great Egg Robbery (Powers Picture Plays, 1915). Dir. Allen Curtis. Cast: Gale Henry, Max Asher. Archive: LOC.

Lady Baffles and Detective Duck in When the Wets Went Dry (Powers Picture Plays, 1915). Dir. Allen Curtis. Cast: Gale Henry, Max Asher. Archive: LOC.

*Art Arches **(Joker Comedies, 1917)**. Dir. William Beaudine. Cast: Gale Henry, Billy Franey, Milburn Morante.

The *Detectress* (Model Comedy Co., 1919). Dir. Bruno C. Becker. Cast: Gale Henry, Milburn Morante, Hap H. Ward. Archive: LOC, AMPAS.
Her First Flame (Model Comedy Co., 1920). Dir. Bruno J. Becker. Cast: Gale Henry, Phyllis Allen, Milburn Morante, Hap H. Ward. Archive: GEH, LOC, AMPAS.
Soup to Nuts (Christie Film Co., 1925). Dir. William H. Watson. Cast: Gale Henry, Neal Burns. Archive: MOMA, UCLA.
Mighty Like a Moose (Hal Roach Studios, Inc., 1926). Dir. Leo McCarey. Cast: Gale Henry, Charley Chase, Vivien Oakland. Archive: AMPAS.
Two-Time Mama (Hal Roach Studios, Inc., 1927). Dir. Fred L. Guiol. Cast: Gale Henry, Vivian Oakland, Anita Garvin. Archive: MOMA.

***

Alice Howell (b. Alice Clark, 1888, New York, NY; d. 1961, Los Angeles, CA)

> A former vaudevillian, Howell appeared in a number of early Keystone shorts—including *Tillie's Punctured Romance*—before moving to L-KO in 1915. She was known for her scrub lady character, an unflappable clown with vacant eyes and a wild mass of hair. Howell primarily performed in slapstick comedies, mostly shorts, throughout her career, although she had supporting roles in a few feature films in the 1920s.

Their Last Haul (L-KO, 1915). Dir. John G. Blystone. Cast: Alice Howell, Hank Mann, Wallace MacDonald. Archive: LOC.
Sin on the Sabbath (L-KO, 1915). Cast: Alice Howell, Billie Ritchie, Louise Orth. Archive: MOMA.
How Stars Are Made (L-KO, 1916). Dir. John G. Blystone. Cast: Alice Howell, Richard Smith, Raymond Griffith. Archive: BFI.
In Dutch (Century Film Corp., 1918). Dir. John G. Blystone. Cast: Alice Howell. Archive: LOC.
Hey, Doctor! (Century Film Corp., 1918). Dir. John G. Blystone. Cast: Alice Howell, Russ Powell, Eddie Barry. Archive: LOC.
***Cinderella Cinders* (Reelcraft Pictures Corp., 1920)**. Dir. Frederick J. Ireland. Cast: Alice Howell, Richard Smith, Rose Burkhardt. Archive: GEH, AMPAS.
Distilled Love (1920). Dir. Vin Moore and Dick Smith. Cast: Alice Howell, Dick Smith, Oliver Hardy. Archive: LOC.
One Wet Night (Universal Pictures Corp., 1924). Dir. William Watson. Cast: Alice Howell, Neely Edwards, Bert Roach. Archive: GEH, AMPAS.
Under a Spell (Universal Film Manufacturing Company, 1924). Dir. Richard Smith. Cast: Alice Howell, Neely Edwards, Bert Roach. Archive: MOMA, GEH, LOC, AMPAS.

That's the Spirit (Universal Film Manufacturing Company, 1924). Dir. William Watson. Cast: Alice Howell, Bert Roach, William Fletcher. Archive: LOC.

Madame Dynamite (Fox Film Corp./Imperial Comedies, 1926). Dir. Zion Myers and Eugene J. Forde. Cast: Alice Howell, Eddie Clayton, Della Peterson. Archive: GEH, UCLA.

***

Leatrice Joy (b. Leatrice Joy Zeidler, 1893, New Orleans, LA; d. 1985, Riverdale, NY)

> Joy often played tough, independent women, both in her comedies and in the dramas she made with Goldwyn Studios and Cecil B. DeMille. Her sometimes mannish characters were signaled by her close-cropped hair—in fact, she was one of the first Hollywood actresses to appear in public with bobbed hair.

Manslaughter (Famous Players-Lasky, 1922). Dir. Cecil B. De Mille. Cast: Leatrice Joy, Thomas Meighan, Lois Wilson. Archive: GEH, LOC, MOMA.

Changing Husbands (Famous Players-Lasky, 1924). Dir. Frank Urson. Cast: Leatrice Joy, Victor Varconi, Raymond Griffith, ZaSu Pitts. Archive: LOC, UCLA.

***The Clinging Vine* (De Mille Pictures Corp., 1926)**. Dir. Paul Sloane. Cast: Leatrice Joy, Tom Moore, Toby Claude. Archive: LOC, UCLA.

Man-Made Women (De Mille Pictures Corp., 1928). Dir. Paul L. Stein. Cast: Leatrice Joy, H. B. Warner, John Boles. Archive: LOC.

***

Beatrice Lillie (b. 1894, Toronto, Ontario, Canada; d. 1989, Henley-on-Thames, Oxfordshire, England)

> Billed as "the funniest woman in the world," Lillie was primarily known for her work onstage in revues and comedies. She was an immensely popular comedienne, although she only made a handful of films (and only one silent film).

***Exit Smiling* (MGM, 1926)**. Dir. Sam Taylor. Cast: Beatrice Lillie, Jack Pickford, Doris Lloyd, De Witt Jennings. Archive: GEH, UCLA.

***

Colleen Moore (b. Kathleen Morrison, 1900, Port Huron, MI; d. 1988, Templeton, CA)

Moore began her career playing bit parts and ingénue roles for D. W. Griffith. After stints with Selig and Christie, Moore signed with First National in the early 1920s. Moore's appearance in the hit film *Flaming Youth* in 1923 made her a star and led to years of typecasting as flappers and other vivacious, fun-loving girls.

*The Wall Flower **(Goldwyn Pictures, 1922)**. Dir. Rupert Hughes. Cast: Colleen Moore, Richard Dix, Gertrude Astor, Laura La Plante.
Flaming Youth **(First National, 1923)**. Dir. John Francis Dillon. Cast: Colleen Moore, Milton Sills, Elliott Dexter. Archive: LOC.
The Nth Commandment (Cosmopolitan Productions, 1923). Dir. Frank Borzage. Cast: Colleen Moore, James Morrison, Eddie Phillips. Archive: LOC.
The Perfect Flapper (First National, 1924). Dir. John Francis. Cast: Colleen Moore, Phyllis Haver, Sydney Chaplin. Archive: LOC.
*We Moderns (John McCormick Productions, 1925). Dir. John Francis Dillon. Cast: Colleen Moore, Jack Mulhall, Carl Miller.
Ella Cinders **(John McCormick Productions, 1926)**. Dir. Alfred E. Green. Cast: Colleen Moore, Lloyd Hughes, Vera Lewis. Archive: GEH, LOC, MOMA, UCLA.
Irene **(First National, 1926)**. Dir. Alfred E. Green. Cast: Colleen Moore, Lloyd Hughes, George K. Arthur. Archive: GEH, LOC, MOMA.
Her Wild Oat **(First National, 1927)**. Dir. Marshall Neilan. Cast: Colleen Moore, Larry Kent, Hallam Cooley, Gwen Lee. Archive: AMPAS.
Orchids and Ermine **(John McCormick Productions, 1927)**. Dir. Alfred Santell. Cast: Colleen Moore, Jack Mulhall, Gwen Lee. Archive: GEH, LOC, UCLA.
Naughty But Nice (John McCormick Productions, 1927). Dir. Millard Webb. Cast: Colleen Moore, Donald Reed. Archive: Cineteca Italiana, Milan.

***

Polly Moran (b. Pauline Moran, 1883, Chicago, IL; d. 1952, Los Angeles, CA)

Moran had a lengthy career in vaudeville and musical theater before making her first film in 1914. In her films with Keystone—particularly her Sheriff Nell films—she generally engaged in rough-and-tumble slapstick. Beginning in the late 1920s Moran teamed with Marie Dressler for a series of short and feature films.

Her Painted Hero **(Keystone Film Co., 1915)**. Dir. F. Richard Jones. Cast: Polly Moran, Hale Hamilton, Charles Murray. Archive: LOC, AMPAS.
Those College Girls (Keystone Film Co., 1915). Dir. Mack Sennett. Cast: Polly Moran, Charles Murray, Mae Busch. Archive: AMPAS.

Love Will Conquer **(Keystone Film Co., 1916)**. Dir. Edwin A. Frazee. Cast: Polly Moran, Harry Gribbon, Fred Mace, Mack Swain. Archive: MOMA.

Cactus Nell (Keystone Film Co., 1917). Dir. Fred Hibbard. Cast: Polly Moran, Wallace Beery. Archive: UCLA.

Sheriff Nell's Tussle **(Keystone Film Co., 1918)**. Dir. William S. Campbell. Cast: Polly Moran, Ben Turpin, Billy Armstrong. Archive: Danish Film Institute, Copenhagen.

*The Callahans and the Murphys (MGM, 1927). Dir. George Hill. Cast: Marie Dressler, Polly Moran.

*Bringing Up Father (MGM, 1928). Dir. Jack Conway. Cast: Marie Dressler, Polly Moran.

While the City Sleeps (MGM, 1928). Dir. Jack Conway. Cast: Polly Moran, Lon Chaney, Anita Page, Mae Busch. Archive: GEH [silent with sound sequences].

***

Mabel Normand (b. 1892, Staten Island, NY; d. 1930, Monrovia, CA)

Known as the "Queen of Comedy," Normand was one of the most successful comediennes of the silent era. She began her career as an artist's model in New York and around 1910 began making movies for Vitagraph and Biograph, shortly thereafter moving to Keystone. Normand soon began directing films for Keystone as well as starring in them and directed several of Charlie Chaplin's early films. Normand made a number of shorts and features into the 1920s, but her career was cut short by a series of scandals, followed by her death in 1930 from tuberculosis.

The Water Nymph **(Keystone Film Co., 1912)**. Dir. Mack Sennett. Cast: Mabel Normand, Mack Sennett, Ford Sterling. Archive: UCLA, AMPAS.

Mabel's Dramatic Career **(Keystone Film Co., 1913)**. Dir. Mack Sennett. Cast: Mabel Normand, Mack Sennett, Alice Davenport, Ford Sterling. Archive: MOMA, UCLA, AMPAS.

That Ragtime Band **(Keystone Film Co., 1913)**. Dir. Mack Sennett. Cast: Mabel Normand, Ford Sterling, Alice Davenport, Roscoe Arbuckle. Archive: LOC.

A Strong Revenge **(Keystone Film Co., 1913)**. Dir. Mack Sennett. Cast: Mabel Normand, Ford Sterling, Mack Sennett. Archive: Lobster Films, Paris.

Tillie's Punctured Romance **(Keystone Film Co., 1914)**. Dir. Mack Sennett. Cast: Marie Dressler, Charles Chaplin, Mabel Normand. Archive: LOC, MOMA, AMPAS.

Mickey **(Mabel Normand Feature Film Co., 1918)**. Dir. Richard Jones. Cast: Mabel Normand, George Nichols, Wheeler Oakman, Minta Durfee, Lew Cody. Archive: LOC, MOMA, UCLA.

What Happened to Rosa? **(Goldwyn Pictures Corp., 1920)**. Dir. Victor Schertzinger.

Cast: Mabel Normand, Doris Pawn, Hugh Thompson, Tully Marshall. Archive: LOC.

***The Extra Girl* (Mack Sennett Productions, 1923)**. Dir. F. Richard Jones. Cast: Mabel Normand, Ralph Graves. Archive: GEH, MOMA, UCLA.

The Nickel-Hopper (Hal Roach Studios, Inc., 1926). Dir. F. Richard Jones and Hal Yates. Cast: Mabel Normand, Theodore von Eltz, Michael Visaroff. Archive: GEH, UCLA.

***Anything Once!* (Hal Roach Studios, Inc., 1927)**. Dir. F. Richard Jones and Hal Yates. Cast: Mabel Normand, James Finlayson, Theodore von Eltz, Nora Hayden.

***Should Men Walk Home?* (Hal Roach Studios, Inc., 1927)**. Dir. Leo McCarey. Cast: Mabel Normand, Creighton Hale, Eugene Pallette, Oliver Hardy. Archive: UCLA.

***

Mary Pickford (b. Gladys Smith, 1892, Toronto, Ontario, Canada; d. 1979, Santa Monica, CA)

Known as "America's Sweetheart," Mary Pickford was one of the biggest stars of the silent era. She began her career onstage and then in 1909 signed with Biograph; in 1916 she formed her own production company and in 1919 formed United Artists with Douglas Fairbanks, Charles Chaplin, and D. W. Griffith. Pickford was primarily known for playing little girl roles, and she continued to play these parts into her thirties.

100% American (Famous Players-Lasky, 1918). Dir. Arthur Rosson. Cast: Mary Pickford, Loretta Blake, Monte Blue. Archive: GEH, LOC, UCLA.

Stella Maris (Pickford Film Corp., 1918). Dir. Marshall A. Neilan. Cast: Mary Pickford, Conway Tearle, Marcia Manon. Archive: GEH, LOC, MOMA.

Johanna Enlists (Pickford Film Corp., 1918). Dir. William Desmond Taylor. Cast: Mary Pickford, Anne Schaefer, Fred Huntley, Monte Blue, Douglas MacLean. Archive: GEH, LOC.

Amarilly of Clothes-Line Alley (Pickford Film Corp., 1918). Dir. Marshall A. Neilan. Cast: Mary Pickford, William Scott, Norman Kerry, Ida Waterman. Archive: GEH, UCLA.

***Suds* (Mary Pickford Co., 1920)**. Dir. Jack Dillon. Cast: Mary Pickford, Albert Austin, Harold Goodwin, Rose Dione. Archive: GEH, LOC.

Through the Back Door (Mary Pickford Co., 1921). Dir. Alfred E. Green. Cast: Mary Pickford, Gertrude Astor, Wilfred Lucas. Archive: GEH, LOC.

Little Annie Rooney (Mary Pickford Co., 1925). Dir. William Beaudine. Cast: Mary Pickford, William Haines, Walter James. Archive: GEH, LOC, AMPAS.

***My Best Girl* (Mary Pickford Co., 1927).** Dir. Sam Taylor. Cast: Mary Pickford, Charles "Buddy" Rogers, Sunshine Hart, Lucien Littlefield, Carmelita Geraghty. Archive: GEH, LOC, AMPAS.

***

Edna Purviance (b. 1895, Paradise Valley, NV; d. 1958, Hollywood, CA)

Purviance was Charlie Chaplin's leading lady from 1914 until 1923. She had starring roles in two movies in the 1920s—*A Woman of Paris*, which was a box-office failure, and *A Woman of the Sea*, which was never released.

The Tramp (Essanay Film Mfg. Co., 1915). Dir. Charles Chaplin. Cast: Charles Chaplin, Edna Purviance. Archive: GEH, LOC, MOMA, UCLA, AMPAS.
***Behind the Screen* (Lone Star Corporation, 1916).** Dir. Charles Chaplin. Cast: Charles Chaplin, Edna Purviance, Eric Campbell. Archive: GEH, LOC, MOMA, UCLA.
A Day's Pleasure (First National Pictures, 1919). Dir. Charles Chaplin. Cast: Charles Chaplin, Edna Purviance. Archive: GEH, UCLA.
The Kid (Charles Chaplin Productions, 1921). Dir. Charles Chaplin. Cast: Charles Chaplin, Jackie Coogan, Edna Purviance, Carl Miller. Archive: GEH, MOMA, UCLA.
A Woman of Paris (United Artists Corp., 1923). Dir. Charles Chaplin. Cast: Edna Purviance, Adolphe Menjou, Carl Miller. Archive: LOC.
**A Woman of the Sea* (Charles Chaplin Productions, 1926). Dir. Josef von Sternberg and Charles Chaplin. Cast: Edna Purviance, Eve Southern, Gayne Whitman.

***

Gloria Swanson (b. 1899[?], Chicago, IL; d. 1983, New York, NY)

Although best remembered as a dramatic actress, Swanson was a versatile comic actress, appearing in everything from slapstick shorts to drawing room comedies directed by Cecil B. DeMille. Even after she became a major dramatic star she still punctuated her later light comedies with moments of slapstick, remnants of her early days at Keystone.

The Danger Girl (Keystone Film Co., 1916). Dir. Clarence G. Badger. Cast: Gloria Swanson, Bobby Vernon, Helen Bray, Mack Swain. Archive: GEH, UCLA, AMPAS.
Teddy at the Throttle (Keystone Film Co., 1917). Dir. Clarence G. Badger. Cast: Gloria Swanson, Bobby Vernon, Wallace Beery, Teddy the Dog. Archive: GEH, LOC, MOMA, UCLA, AMPAS.

The Pullman Bride (Keystone Film Co., 1917). Dir. Clarence G. Badger. Cast: Gloria Swanson, Mack Swain, Chester Conklin, Polly Moran. Archive: GEH, UCLA.

Don't Change Your Husband (Famous Players-Lasky, 1919). Dir. Cecil B. DeMille. Cast: Gloria Swanson, Elliott Dexter, Lew Cody, Sylvia Ashton: Archive: GEH, AMPAS.

Why Change Your Wife? (Famous Players-Lasky, 1920). Dir. Cecil B. DeMille. Cast: Gloria Swanson, Thomas Meighan, Bebe Daniels. Archive: GEH, MOMA, AMPAS.

The Affairs of Anatol (Famous Players-Lasky, 1921). Dir. Cecil B. DeMille. Cast: Gloria Swanson, Wallace Reid, Bebe Daniels. Archive: GEH, LOC, UCLA.

***Manhandled* (Famous Players-Lasky, 1924)**. Dir. Allan Dwan. Cast: Gloria Swanson, Tom Moore, Lilyan Tashman. Archive: GEH, LOC, UCLA.

Stage Struck (Famous Players-Lasky, 1925). Dir. Allan Dwan. Cast: Gloria Swanson, Lawrence Gray, Gertrude Astor, Marguerite Evans, Ford Sterling. Archive: GEH.

*Madame Sans-Gêne (Famous Players-Lasky, 1925). Dir. Léonce Perret. Cast: Gloria Swanson, Emile Drain, Charles De Roche.

***

Constance Talmadge (b. 1898[?], Brooklyn, NY; d. 1973, Los Angeles, CA)

> The youngest of the three Talmadge sisters, Constance Talmadge was the comedienne of the family, while her older sister Norma was the tragedienne. Constance rose to fame as the Mountain Girl in the Babylonian sequences of D. W. Griffith's 1916 epic *Intolerance* and soon made a name for herself in slightly racy light comedies, often written by Anita Loos and John Emerson.

A Pair of Silk Stockings (Select Pictures Corp., 1918). Dir. Walter Edwards. Cast: Constance Talmadge, Harrison Ford, Wanda Hawley. Archive: GEH.

*A Virtuous Vamp **(Constance Talmadge Film Co., 1919)**. Dir. David Kirkland. Cast: Constance Talmadge, Conway Tearle, Harda Daube, Jack Kane.

A Temperamental Wife (Constance Talmadge Film Co., 1919). Dir. David Kirkland. Cast: Constance Talmadge, Wyndham Standing, Eulalie Jenson. Archive: LOC.

In Search of a Sinner (Constance Talmadge Film Co., 1920). Dir. David Kirkland. Cast: Constance Talmadge, Rockcliffe Fellowes, Corliss Giles. Archive: LOC, UCLA.

*Polly of the Follies (Constance Talmadge Film Co., 1922). Dir. John Emerson. Cast: Constance Talmadge, Kenneth Harlan, Billie Dove.

*Dulcy **(Constance Talmadge Film Co., 1923)**. Dir. Sidney A. Franklin. Cast: Constance Talmadge, Claude Gillingwater, Jack Mulhall, May Wilson.

***Her Night of Romance* (Constance Talmadge Productions, 1924)**. Dir. Sidney A.

Franklin. Cast: Constance Talmadge, Ronald Colman, Jean Hersholt. Archive: LOC.

The Duchess of Buffalo **(Constance Talmadge Productions, 1926)**. Dir. Sidney Franklin. Cast: Constance Talmadge, Tullio Carminati, Edward Martindel. Archive: GEH, MOMA, UCLA.

Breakfast at Sunrise (Constance Talmadge Productions, 1927). Dir. Malcolm St. Clair. Cast: Constance Talmadge, Marie Dressler, Alice White. Archive: GEH, LOC.

Venus of Venice (Constance Talmadge Productions, 1927). Dir. Marshall Neilan. Cast: Constance Talmadge, Antonio Moreno, Julanne Johnston. Archive: GEH, UCLA.

***

Fay Tincher (b. 1884, Topeka, KS; d. 1983, Brooklyn, NY)

> Tincher was a star in vaudeville and musical theater before starting in motion pictures in 1913 with D. W. Griffith. In 1914 she starred as a gum-chewing stenographer clad in black and white stripes in the popular "Bill the office boy" series of comedies for Komic. She later signed with Christie, where she blended light comedy with some slapstick in one- and two-reel films. From 1923 to 1928 Tincher starred as Min Gump in "the Gumps" comedy series for Universal.

Leave It to Smiley (Komic Pictures Co., 1914). Dir. Edward Dillon. Cast: Fay Tincher, Tammany Young, Tod Browning. Archive: LOC.

The Housebreakers (Komic Pictures Co., 1914). Dir. Edward Dillon. Cast: Fay Tincher, Tod Browning, Edward Dillon. Archive: LOC.

Bill Spoils a Vacation (Komic Pictures Co., 1914). Dir. Edward Dillon. Cast: Fay Tincher, Tammany Young, Tod Browning. Archive: LOC.

Bill Joins the W.W.W.'s (Komic Pictures Co., 1914). Dir. Edward Dillon. Cast: Fay Tincher, Tammany Young, Tod Browning. Archive: LOC, AMPAS.

*Ethel Has a Steady (Komic Pictures Co., 1914). Dir. Edward Dillon. Cast: Fay Tincher, Tammany Young, Tod Browning.

Music Hath Charms (Komic Pictures Co., 1915). Dir. Edward Dillon. Cast: Fay Tincher, Tod Browning, Augustus Carney. Archive: LOC.

Sunshine Dad (Fine Arts Film Co., 1916). Dir. Edward Dillon. Cast: Fay Tincher, De Wolf Hopper, Chester Withey. Archive: LOC.

Rowdy Ann (Christie Film Co., 1919). Dir. Al Christie. Cast: Fay Tincher, Eddie Barry, Katherine Lewis. Archive: LOC, MOMA, AMPAS.

*Oh! Min! (Samuel Van Ronkel Productions, 1924). Dir. Norman Taurog. Cast: Fay Tincher, Joe Murphy, Jack Morgan.

Andy's Lion Tale (Samuel Van Ronkel Productions, 1925). Dir. Francis Corby. Cast: Fay Tincher, Joe Murphy, Jack Morgan. Archive: LOC, MOMA.

Notes

Introduction

The epigraph is a quote from Bebe Daniels, in Christopher Bram, "Bebe Daniels: The Early Screen Siren at Her Beachfront House," *Architectural Digest* (April 2000), Bebe Daniels clipping file, AMPAS.

1. James Agee, "Comedy's Greatest Era," in *The Film Comedy Reader*, ed. Gregg Rickman (New York: Limelight Editions, 2001), 14–28.
2. Walter Kerr, *The Silent Clowns* (New York: Da Capo Press, 1975).
3. Maggie Hennefeld, "Slapstick Comediennes in Silent Cinema: Women's Laughter and the Feminist Politics of Gender in Motion," in *The Routledge Companion to Cinema and Gender*, ed. Kristin Lené Hole, Dijana Jelaca, E. Ann Kaplan, and Patrice Petro (London: Routledge, 2017), 144.
4. Gail Finney, "Unity in Difference?: An Introduction," in *Look Who's Laughing: Gender and Comedy*, ed. Finney (Langhorne, PA: Gordon and Breach, 1994), 1.
5. See Nancy Walker, *A Very Serious Thing: Women's Humor and American Culture* (Minneapolis: University of Minnesota Press, 1988); Regina Barreca, ed., *Last Laughs: Perspectives on Women and Comedy* (New York: Gordon and Breach, 1988); Frances Gray, *Women and Laughter* (Charlottesville: University Press of Virginia, 1994); and Henry Jenkins, *What Made Pistachio Nuts? Early Sound Comedy and the Vaudeville Aesthetic* (New York: Columbia University Press, 1992).
6. Henri Bergson, "Laughter," in *Comedy*, ed. Wylie Sypher (Baltimore: Johns Hopkins University Press, 1956), 148.
7. Michel Foucault, *The History of Sexuality* (New York: Vintage, 1990).
8. Gray, *Women and Laughter*, 6–7.
9. Ibid., 8, emphasis in original.
10. Rebecca Krefting, *All Joking Aside: American Humor and Its Discontents* (Baltimore: Johns Hopkins University Press, 2014), 118.
11. Ibid., 120.
12. Ibid., 113.
13. Ibid., 2.
14. Walker, *A Very Serious Thing*, 71.
15. Kathleen Rowe, *The Unruly Woman: Gender and the Genres of Laughter* (Austin: University of Texas Press, 1995), 8.

16. Jenkins, *What Made Pistachio Nuts?* 225.
17. Bonnie J. Dow, *Prime-Time Feminism: Television, Media Culture, and the Women's Movement since 1970* (Philadelphia: University of Pennsylvania Press, 1996), 103. For more on comedy and social change, see Geoff King, *Film Comedy* (London: Wallflower Press, 2002), 2; and Hugh Duncan, *Communication and Social Order* (New York: Oxford University Press, 1962), 398.
18. Rowe, *The Unruly Woman*, 3.
19. Regina Barreca, *They Used to Call Me Snow White ... But I Drifted: Women's Strategic Use of Humor* (New York: Penguin, 1991), 26.
20. Tom Gunning, "Crazy Machines in the Garden of Forking Paths: Mischief Gags and the Origins of American Film Comedy," in *Classical Hollywood Comedy*, ed. Kristine Brunovska Karnick and Henry Jenkins (New York: Routledge, 1995), 98.
21. Tom Gunning, "Mechanisms of Laughter: The Devices of Slapstick," in *Slapstick Comedy*, ed. Tom Paulus and Rob King (New York: Routledge, 2010), 138–39.
22. Rob King, *The Fun Factory: The Keystone Film Company and the Emergence of Mass Culture* (Berkeley: University of California Press, 2009), 2.
23. Susan A. Glenn, *Female Spectacle: The Theatrical Roots of Modern Feminism* (Cambridge, MA: Harvard University Press, 2000), 216.
24. Barbara Welter, "The Cult of True Womanhood: 1820–1860," *American Quarterly* 18, no. 2, part 1 (Summer 1966): 152; Kathy Peiss, *Hope in a Jar: The Making of America's Beauty Culture* (New York: Henry Holt, 1998), 24–25; Lois W. Banner, *American Beauty* (Chicago: University of Chicago Press, 1983), 9.
25. Ben Singer, *Melodrama and Modernity: Early Sensational Cinema and Its Contexts* (New York: Columbia University Press, 2001), 174.
26. See Rowe, *The Unruly Woman*; Mary Russo, *The Female Grotesque: Risk, Excess and Modernity* (New York: Routledge, 1994); Natalie Zemon Davis, "Women on Top," in *Society and Culture in Early Modern France* (Stanford, CA: Stanford University Press, 1975); Jenkins, *What Made Pistachio Nuts?*; Robert C. Allen, *Horrible Prettiness: Burlesque and American Culture* (Chapel Hill: University of North Carolina Press, 1991); M. Alison Kibler, *Rank Ladies: Gender and Cultural Hierarchy in American Vaudeville* (Chapel Hill: University of North Carolina Press, 1999); Glenn, *Female Spectacle*; Lori Landay, *Madcaps, Screwballs, and Con Women: The Female Trickster in American Culture* (Philadelphia: University of Pennsylvania Press, 1998).
27. See Laura Mulvey, "Visual Pleasure and Narrative Cinema," in *Film Theory and Criticism*, 4th ed., ed. Gerald Mast, Marshall Cohen, and Leo Braudy (New York: Oxford University Press, 1992), 746–57.
28. Rowe, *The Unruly Woman*, 5.
29. "Redefining Film Preservation: A National Plan: Recommendations of the Librarian of Congress in Consultation with the National Film Preservation Board" (Washington, DC: Library of Congress, 1994).

30. Eileen Whitfield, *Pickford: The Woman Who Made Hollywood* (New York: Faber and Faber, 1997), 370–72.
31. Eric Smoodin, "The History of Film History," in *Looking Past the Screen: Case Studies in American Film History and Method*, ed. Jon Lewis and Eric Smoodin (Durham, NC: Duke University Press, 2007).
32. Ibid., 20–21.
33. Richard deCordova, *Picture Personalities: The Emergence of the Star System in America* (Urbana: University of Illinois Press, 1990).
34. Gaylyn Studlar, "The Perils of Pleasure? Fan Magazine Discourse as Women's Commodified Culture in the 1920s," in *Silent Film*, ed. Richard Abel (New Brunswick, NJ: Rutgers University Press, 1996), 272.
35. DeCordova, *Picture Personalities*, 12.
36. Ibid., 86.
37. Ibid., 87.
38. Ibid., 98.
39. For more on the rise of fan magazines, see Anthony Slide, *Inside the Hollywood Fan Magazine: A History of Star Makers, Fabricators, and Gossip Mongers* (Jackson: University Press of Mississippi, 2010).
40. Eileen Bowser, *The Transformation of Cinema, 1907–1915* (Berkeley: University of California Press, 1990), 179.
41. King, *The Fun Factory*, 11.
42. Richard Koszarski, *An Evening's Entertainment: The Age of the Silent Feature Picture, 1915–1928* (Berkeley: University of California Press, 1990), 175.
43. See Gunning, "Crazy Machines in the Garden of Forking Paths"; Gunning, "Mechanisms of Laughter"; and Jenkins, *What Made Pistachio Nuts?*
44. F. Scott Fitzgerald wrote, "I was the spark that lit up *Flaming Youth*, Colleen Moore was the torch. What little things we are to have caused all that trouble." Quoted in Colleen Moore, *Silent Star* (Garden City, NY: Doubleday, 1968), 141.

Chapter 1

1. Constant Coquelin, "Have Women a Sense of Humor?" *Harper's Bazaar* 34, no. 2 (12 January 1901): 67–69; Christopher Hitchens, "Why Women Aren't Funny," *Vanity Fair* (January 2007): 54.
2. Grace Lee Mack, "The Girl Who Put Stripes in Comedy," *Photo-Play Journal* (June 1919): 37.
3. David Bianculli, "Comedy Turns to Horror as Lewis Pans Female Comics," *New York Daily News*, 15 February 2000, 82; W. Speers, "Jerry Lewis' Odd Remarks about Female Comics," *Philadelphia Inquirer*, 15 February 2000, D02; Michael Posner, "The Day the Clown Bombed," *Globe and Mail*, 19 February 2000, R1.
4. Glenn Collins, "Public Lives," *New York Times*, 18 February 2000, B2; "Names

and Faces," *Washington Post*, 19 February 2000, C03; "For the Kids, This Ladies' Man Is Sorry," *USA Today*, 21 February 2000, 2D.
5. CNN Transcript, *Larry King Live*: Jerry Lewis Discusses Hosting His 50th Telethon, original airdate 1 September 2000, http://www.cnn.com/TRANSCRIPTS/0009/01/lkl.00.html.
6. Ibid.
7. Collins, "Public Lives."
8. William Congreve, "Concerning Humour in Comedy" [1695], in *The Works of William Congreve*, vol. 3, ed. D. F. McKenzie (Oxford: Oxford University Press, 2011), 70.
9. Hitchens, "Why Women Aren't Funny," 54.
10. Jenkins, *What Made Pistachio Nuts?* 256.
11. Dean Burnett, "Why Do People Believe Women Aren't Funny?" *Guardian*, 11 February 2014, https://www.theguardian.com/science/brain-flapping/2014/feb/11/women-arent-funny-why-do-people-believe-this; Olga Khazan, "Plight of the Funny Female," 19 November 2015, http://www.theatlantic.com/health/archive/2015/11/plight-of-the-funny-female/416559/. See also Alison Stevenson, "Why Women Aren't Funny," *askmen.com*, 17 February 2015, http://www.askmen.com/dating/curtsmith_500/594_why-women-arent-funny.html; Kathy Benjamin, "4 Ways We're Programmed to Think Women Aren't Funny," *Cracked.com*, 21 January 2014, http://www.cracked.com/blog/4-ways-were-programmed-to-think-women-arent-funny/; Gabrielle Moss, "A Brief History of 'Women Aren't Funny,'" 29 April 2013, https://bitchmedia.org/post/a-brief-history-of-women-arent-funny; and Jon Miltimore, "Why Women (Still) Aren't Funny," *Intellectual Takeout*, 12 August 2016, http://www.intellectualtakeout.org/blog/why-women-still-arent-funny.
12. *History of the Joke* (Triage Entertainment, 2008).
13. Tina Fey, *Bossypants* (New York: Little, Brown, 2011), 143–44.
14. Dana Goodyear, "Quiet Depravity," *New Yorker*, 24 October 2005, 50+.
15. Welter, "The Cult of True Womanhood," 151–74; Walker, *A Very Serious Thing*, 27.
16. Quoted in Jenkins, *What Made Pistachio Nuts?* 256.
17. Quoted in Linda Martin and Kerry Segrave, *Women in Comedy* (Secaucus, NJ: Citadel Press, 1986), 13.
18. Bergson, "Laughter," 63.
19. Hitchens, "Why Women Aren't Funny," 54.
20. Ibid.
21. Reginald Blyth, *Humour in English Literature*, quoted in *Last Laughs*, ed. Barreca, 4.
22. King, *The Fun Factory*, 221.
23. Maggie Hennefeld, "Death from Laughter, Female Hysteria, and Early Cinema," *differences: A Journal of Feminist Cultural Studies* 27, no. 3 (December 2016): 46.

24. Ibid., 58.
25. Mack Sennett, "The Psychology of Film Comedy," *Motion Picture Classic* (November 1918): 70.
26. Nancy A. Walker, "Toward Solidarity: Women's Humor and Group Identity," in *Women's Comic Visions*, ed. June Sochen (Detroit: Wayne State University Press, 1991), 59.
27. Walker, *A Very Serious Thing*, 43.
28. Bergson, "Laughter," 148, 187.
29. Sigmund Freud, *Jokes and Their Relation to the Unconscious*, trans. and ed. James Strachey (New York: W. W. Norton, 1960), 115, 118.
30. The fact that two articles with this same title appeared a year apart in the same magazine indicates the level of public interest in the question of women's humor.
31. Robert J. Burdette, "Have Women a Sense of Humor?" *Harper's Bazaar* (July 1902): 597–98, quoted in Jenkins, *What Made Pistachio Nuts?* 257.
32. Alan Dale, *Comedy Is a Man in Trouble: Slapstick in American Movies* (Minneapolis: University of Minnesota Press, 2000), 122.
33. Jenkins, *What Made Pistachio Nuts?* 258.
34. "'Comedian' Girls Jump to the Front," n.p., 8 June 1902, quoted in Glenn, *Female Spectacle*, 46.
35. Glenn, *Female Spectacle*, 58–59.
36. George Jean Nathan, "Bea Lillie an Exception to Sad Rule," *Los Angeles Examiner*, 19 October 1952, Beatrice Lillie clipping file, AMPAS.
37. Coquelin, "Have Women a Sense of Humor?" 68.
38. Kibler, *Rank Ladies*, 59; also M. Alison Kibler, "Nothing Succeeds Like Excess: Lillian Shaw's Comedy and Sexuality on the Keith Vaudeville Circuit," in *Performing Gender and Comedy: Theories, Texts and Contexts*, ed. Shannon Hengen (Amsterdam: Gordon and Breach, 1998), 71.
39. J. Francis Perrett, "The Colleen of the Movies," *Extension Magazine*, November 1926, Colleen Moore scrapbook #15, AMPAS.
40. Coquelin, "Have Women a Sense of Humor?" 67.
41. Ibid., 68.
42. Ibid.; Burdette, quoted in Kibler, *Rank Ladies*, 59.
43. Beth Brown, "Making Movies for Women," *Moving Picture World*, 26 March 1927, 342.
44. Sennett, "The Psychology of Film Comedy."
45. Albert F. McLean Jr., *American Vaudeville as Ritual* (Lexington: University of Kentucky Press, 1965), 107.
46. Rick DesRochers, *The New Humor in the Progressive Era: Americanization and the Vaudeville Comedian* (New York: Palgrave Macmillan, 2014), 11.
47. Glenn, *Female Spectacle*, 43.
48. Ibid., 41; Kibler, *Rank Ladies*, 56.
49. For vaudeville's efforts at refinement, see Kibler, *Rank Ladies* and Robert

W. Snyder, *The Voice of the City: Vaudeville and Popular Culture in New York* (Chicago: Ivan R. Dee, 1989). For cinema's drive to respectability, see William Uricchio and Roberta E. Pearson, *Reframing Culture: The Case of the Vitagraph Quality Films* (Princeton: Princeton University Press, 1993); Shelley Stamp, *Movie-Struck Girls: Women and Motion Picture Culture after the Nickelodeon* (Princeton: Princeton University Press, 2000); and Lee Grieveson, *Policing Cinema: Movies and Censorship in Early Twentieth-Century America* (Berkeley: University of California Press, 2004).

50. King, *The Fun Factory*, 3.
51. Mabel Normand, "How to Be a Comedienne," *New York Dramatic Mirror*, 19 June 1920, 1244.
52. Unidentified clipping, 28 October 1916, Charlotte Greenwood clipping file, NYPL.
53. Margaret Denny, "How Fay Tincher Regards Her Profession," *Motion Picture Magazine* (August 1916): 77.
54. Kibler, *Rank Ladies*, 31.
55. For more on the theater and film industries' desire for respectability, see Uricchio and Pearson, *Reframing Culture*; Richard Butsch, "Bowery B'hoys and Matinee Ladies: The Re-Gendering of Nineteenth-Century American Theater Audiences," *American Quarterly* 46, no. 3 (September 1994): 374–405; Kibler, *Rank Ladies*; Stamp, *Movie-Struck Girls*; and Snyder, *The Voice of the City*.
56. Butsch, "Bowery B'hoys and Matinee Ladies," 375.
57. Kibler, *Rank Ladies*, 13.
58. Stamp, *Movie-Struck Girls*, 9.
59. Jolo, "Tillie's Tomato Surprise," *Variety*, 1 October 1915, 19.
60. *Jane* ad, Charlotte Greenwood clipping file, AMPAS, emphasis in original; "'Jane' Next Oliver Morosco Release," *Moving Picture World*, 20 November 1915, 1515.
61. Peter Milne, "Tillie Wakes Up," *Motion Picture News*, 3 February 1917, 759; "Tillie Wakes Up," *Wid's Daily*, 25 January 1917, 60.
62. James R. Quirk, "The Girl on the Cover," *Photoplay* (August 1915): 41.
63. "Experimental Marriage," *Wid's Daily*, 30 March 1919, 16.
64. "The Coming Film Comedy of Ideas," *Christian Science Monitor*, 4 November 1919, 16.
65. Quoted in Laura Frost, "Blondes Have More Fun: Anita Loos and the Language of Silent Cinema," *Modernism/Modernity* 17, no. 2 (2010): 296–97.
66. Ibid., 297.
67. "The Coming Film Comedy of Ideas."
68. Jack Gaines, "Her Wild Oat," *Filmograph*, 3 December 1927, Colleen Moore scrapbook #18, AMPAS.
69. Untitled review, *Judge*, Colleen Moore scrapbook #13, AMPAS.
70. "A Need," *Film Daily*, 3 February 1924, 1.
71. Palmer Smith, "Three Farcical Offerings with Two Good—Hendricks and

Gunboat Smith Emerge—Paul Leni on Production Abroad—The 'Unhappy Ending' Test—First National Shuns the Stage," *New York World*, 14 June 1926, Colleen Moore scrapbook #13, AMPAS.
72. Comedienne-run production companies include Mabel Normand Feature Film Company, Flora Finch Comedy Company, Model Comedy Company (Gale Henry), Constance Talmadge Film Company, Fay Tincher Productions, Mary Pickford Film Corporation, and Marie Dressler Motion Picture Corporation.
73. Celluloid, "Most Screen Comedians Are Sheer Individualists," *Toronto Star*, 16 April 1927, Colleen Moore scrapbook #15, AMPAS.
74. Imitative humor and the idea of the comedienne as mimic will be discussed more fully in chapter 4.
75. "Alice Howell in New Comedies," *Moving Picture World*, 19 May 1917, 1135.
76. Allen Corliss, "Fazenda—Comic Venus," *Photoplay* (April 1918): 67.
77. "Kitchen Komedy," unsourced, 20 March 1918, Louise Fazenda clipping file, Robinson Locke scrapbook, NYPL.
78. Unsourced, January 1917, Polly Moran clipping file, NYPL.
79. Julia Harpman, "The Inside Dope on Movie Stars: Mabel Normand Victim of an Unkind Fate," 29 June 1924, Mack Sennett Collection, Mabel Normand clipping file, AMPAS.
80. "*Automaniacs*," *Photoplay*, June 1918, Alice Howell clipping file, NYPL.
81. Julian Johnson, "The Shadow Stage," *Photoplay* (April 1919): 68.
82. "Ladeez and Ge'men, in This Corner," ca. 1938, Louise Fazenda clipping file, AMPAS.
83. Marquis Busby, "Three's a Crowd," *Photoplay* (June 1930): 77; "Norma's Sister Constance," *Chicago News*, 7 September 1916, Constance Talmadge clipping file, NYPL; "Alice Howell in 'Alice in Society,'" *Moving Picture Weekly*, 28 October 1916, 26; untitled, *Photoplay* (March 1914), Louise Fazenda clipping file, Robinson Locke scrapbook, NYPL; untitled, *Motion Picture Magazine*, April 1917, Louise Fazenda clipping file, Robinson Locke scrapbook, NYPL; untitled, *Morning Telegraph*, 10 December 1910, Charlotte Greenwood clipping file, NYPL; unsourced, ca. 1916, Charlotte Greenwood clipping file, NYPL.
84. Gladys Hall, "Is it Tragic to Be Comic?" *Motion Picture Classic* (May 1931): 91.
85. Unsourced, Louise Fazenda clipping file, NYPL.
86. Cal York, "You Can Never Be an Actor," *Photoplay* (July 1928): 78; *The Patsy* review, *Variety*, 25 April 1928, 28.
87. "Don't Fight against Nature," ca. 1917, Charlotte Greenwood clipping file, NYPL.
88. Helen Carlisle, "Enter and Exit, Smiling," *Motion Picture Magazine* (December 1926): 115.
89. A more detailed discussion of comediennes as working women can be found in chapter 4.
90. Mlle. Chic, "Alice Howell—Funniest Woman in Pictures," *Moving Picture Weekly*, 13 May 1916, 31.

91. "Alice Howell in 'Alice in Society.'"
92. Unidentified clipping, ca. 1922, Charlotte Greenwood clipping file, NYPL.
93. Mabel Normand, "How to Get into the Movies: Part VI, Keep a Diary!" *Movie Weekly*, 25 March 1922, quoted in William Thomas Sherman, *Mabel Normand: A Source Book to Her Life and Films* (New York: New York Times Company, 2004), 345.
94. Constance Talmadge, "The Tragedy of Being Funny," *Motion Picture Magazine* (August 1927): 54.
95. Harry Carr, "Putting the Fizz in Fazenda," *Motion Picture Magazine* (January 1919): 109.
96. Kristine Brunovska Karnick, "Comedy Is Hard: Labor, Beauty and Louise Fazenda" (unpublished paper presented at the Society for Cinema and Media Studies conference, Montreal, 27 March 2015).
97. Normand, "How to Be a Comedienne"; "How to Be Funny," unsourced, 26 August 1915, Polly Moran clipping file, NYPL; Gladys Hall, "Have YOU Got the Makings of a COMEDIAN?" *Movie Classic* (December 1934): 30.
98. Photo caption, *Motion Picture Magazine* (October 1919): 28; unidentified clipping, ca. 1922, Charlotte Greenwood clipping file, NYPL; Moore, *Silent Star*, 174.
99. "Louise Back in Comedy," *Morning Telegraph*, 6 April 1924, Louise Fazenda clipping file, AMPAS.
100. Talmadge, "The Tragedy of Being Funny," 54; Carr, "Putting the Fizz in Fazenda," 109.
101. Unidentified clipping, ca. 1915, Charlotte Greenwood clipping file, NYPL.
102. Regina Cannon, "Quality Street," *New York American*, 25 October 1927, Marion Davies clipping file, NYPL; *Automaniacs* review, *Photoplay* (June 1918), Alice Howell clipping file, NYPL; *Mickey* review, *Moving Picture World*, 10 August 1918, 880; *Exit Smiling* review, *Moving Picture World*, 20 November 1926, 166; Alma Whitaker, "*Ella Cinders* Blends Tragedy with Humor," *Los Angeles Times*, 30 May 1926, C17.
103. "Two-Reel Trip to Joy Planet," ca. 1917, Alice Howell clipping file, NYPL.
104. Hall, "Have YOU Got the Makings of a COMEDIAN?" 30.
105. As I'll discuss in chapter 2, many of the stories about Fazenda's uneasy relationship to comedy had to do with her physical appearance and the fact that her supposed homeliness was emphasized in her comedies.
106. Hall, "Is It Tragic to Be Comic?" 48; Talmadge, "The Tragedy of Being Funny," 54.
107. Hall, "Is It Tragic to Be Comic?" 48.
108. Unidentified clipping, ca. 1916, Charlotte Greenwood clipping file, NYPL.
109. Unidentified clipping, Charlotte Greenwood clipping file, NYPL.
110. Emma Lindsay Squier, "'Pies Is Pizen,'" *Photoplay Art* (September 1918): 4.
111. As I will discuss in chapter 2, discourses about comediennes' shock at discovering they were funny were often accompanied by stories about their unhappy realization that they were not beautiful.

112. "They Both Rebelled," *Photoplay* (June 1920): 28.
113. "Fay Tincher—An Ingenuish Vampire," unsourced, Fay Tincher clipping file, NYPL.
114. Maude Cheatham, "A Toiling Lily," *Motion Picture Magazine* (March 1921): 54; untitled, *Morning Telegraph*, 3 February 1924, Bebe Daniels clipping file, AMPAS.
115. "Comedienne Sighs for Other Worlds," *Los Angeles Times*, 4 May 1924, 24.
116. "Two Weeks," *Dramatic Mirror*, 5 February 1920, 181; "A Look at Mehitabel Lactea," *Cleveland Leader*, 24 June 1917, Gale Henry clipping file, NYPL; "Coiffure Note: Louise Fazenda Still Wears Those Old Pigtails," *Herald-Tribune*, 23 January 1938, Louise Fazenda clipping file, NYPL; unidentified photo caption, Dorothy Devore clipping file, NYPL; Cheatham, "A Toiling Lily," 54.
117. Untitled, *Morning Telegraph*, 3 February 1924, Bebe Daniels clipping file, AMPAS.
118. Talmadge, "The Tragedy of Being Funny," 54.
119. Mulvey, "Visual Pleasure and Narrative Cinema," 746–57. On comedy's inherent aggressiveness, see Rowe, *The Unruly Woman*; Gray, *Women and Laughter*; Barreca, *Last Laughs*; and Walker, *A Very Serious Thing*.
120. Although, as Rob King has shown, Keystone continued to rely heavily on slapstick throughout the 1910s despite its lower-class associations, "flout[ing] the Protestant moralism of genteel culture" (*The Fun Factory*, 12).
121. Donald Crafton, "Pie and Chase: Gag, Spectacle and Narrative in Slapstick Comedy," in *Classical Hollywood Comedy*, ed. Kristine Brunovska Karnick and Henry Jenkins (New York: Routledge, 1995), 107.
122. Tom Gunning, "Response to 'Pie and Chase,'" in *Classical Hollywood Comedy*, 121. See also Jenkins, *What Made Pistachio Nuts?*
123. Mack, "The Girl Who Put Stripes in Comedy." The phrase "comedy-drama" was frequently used in the press to describe light comedies, films that relied more heavily on plot and situation than slapsticks and that blended pathos with comedy.
124. "They Will Not Remain in Comedy," *Film Fun* (May 1916), quoted in Sherman, *Mabel Normand*, 116.
125. "The Big Four of Educational," *Moving Picture World*, 23 April 1927, 709.
126. Mack, "The Girl Who Put Stripes in Comedy."
127. Denny, "How Fay Tincher Regards Her Profession," 78.
128. "The Coming Film Comedy of Ideas."
129. Dorothy Faith Webster, "The Bear Facts about Gale Henry," *Picture Play* (January 1920): 49.
130. Untitled, *Motion Picture Magazine* (October 1916), Fay Tincher clipping file, NYPL.
131. "They Both Rebelled," 29.
132. "Colleen Moore Likes Comedy Best," *Pittsburgh Post*, 21 June 1925, Colleen Moore scrapbook #2, AMPAS.

133. Webster, "The Bear Facts about Gale Henry," 49.
134. "The Coming Film Comedy of Ideas."
135. "A Captivating Colleen," *Pictures and Picturegoer* (October 1924): 41, Colleen Moore scrapbook #2, AMPAS.
136. Unidentified clipping, Charlotte Greenwood clipping file, NYPL; Walter Vogdes, "Twenty Minutes with Constance," *Select Pictures Magazine* 4, no. 11 (ca. 1918): 5, Constance Talmadge clipping file, AMPAS.
137. Katherine Albert, "Two True Troupers—Louise & Marie," *Photoplay* (March 1930): 35; Hall, "Is It Tragic to Be Comic?" 93.

Chapter 2

The epigraph comes from Louise Fazenda, "How to Get in!" *Motion Picture Magazine* (December 1916): 72.
1. Robert Fender, "What Is Beauty?" *Photoplay* (July 1928): 35.
2. Linda Mizejewski, *Pretty/Funny: Women Comedians and Body Politics* (Austin: University of Texas Press, 2014), 1.
3. Krefting, *All Joking Aside*, 132.
4. See Banner, *American Beauty* and Peiss, *Hope in a Jar*.
5. Banner, *American Beauty*, 206.
6. King, *The Fun Factory*, 222.
7. Glenn, *Female Spectacle*, 47.
8. See Linda Mizejewski, *Ziegfeld Girl: Image and Icon in Culture and Cinema* (Durham, NC: Duke University Press, 1999).
9. "'Comedian' Girls Jump to the Front," n.p., 8 June 1902, quoted in Glenn, *Female Spectacle*, 46.
10. Hilde d'Haeyere, "Splashes of Fun and Beauty: Mack Sennett's Bathing Beauties," in *Slapstick Comedy*, ed. Tom Paulus and Rob King (New York: Routledge, 2010), 210.
11. Irene Thirer, "Film Beauts Come and Go—Funny Fazenda Lingers," *New York Evening Post*, 29 April 1936, n.p., Louise Fazenda clipping file, NYPL.
12. "Coiffure Note: Louise Fazenda Still Wears Those Old Pigtails."
13. Mizejewski, *Pretty/Funny*, 5.
14. Florenz Ziegfeld Jr., "How I Pick My Beauties," *Green Book* (February 1914): 212–18; Florenz Ziegfeld Jr., "When Is a Woman's Figure Beautiful? Florenz Ziegfeld Tells How He Judges," *New York Evening World*, 26 December 1922, quoted in Mizejewski, *Ziegfeld Girl*, 112–13.
15. D'Haeyere, "Splashes of Fun and Beauty," 208.
16. Mizejewski, *Pretty/Funny*, 23.
17. Adam Cohen, *Imbeciles: The Supreme Court, American Eugenics, and the Sterilization of Carrie Buck* (New York: Penguin, 2016), 5.
18. Mizejewski, *Ziegfeld Girl*, 115.

19. William Cohill, "Is Your Face the Type for Film Success?" *Des Moines Sunday Register Magazine*, 7 November 1926, Colleen Moore scrapbook #15, AMPAS.
20. Mabel Normand, "How to Get into the Movies: Part II, Types of Girls That Producers Seek," *Movie Weekly*, 25 February 1922, quoted in Sherman, *Mabel Normand*, 341.
21. Ibid.
22. Ibid.
23. Ibid.
24. Unidentified clipping, 5 July 1915, Polly Moran clipping file, NYPL.
25. Frances Wayne, "Pauline Moran Is Fat and Sassy, and Her Personality Leads Orpheum," *Denver Times*, 8 October 1911, n.p., Polly Moran clipping file, NYPL.
26. Ted Le Berthon, "Star Once Sold Newspapers at Arcade Depot," unsourced, 25 June 1930, Louise Fazenda clipping file, AMPAS.
27. Fazenda, however, wears a decidedly more demure bathing costume than the one-piece "Annette Kellerman" type, discussed in chapter 3, that Mabel Normand wore on-screen in such films as *The Water Nymph* (1912).
28. Cheatham, "A Toiling Lily"; Wid Gunning, "Title Wallop Puts over Spy Meller Based on Joan Idea," *Wid's Daily*, 12 May 1918, 29. Gunning is using an older meaning of the word "gook," referring to someone who is foolish or odd.
29. "Dorothy Gish Gratifies Early Stage Ambition," *Philadelphia Inquirer*, 13 April 1930, n.p., Dorothy Gish clipping file, NYPL.
30. Unidentified photo caption, Colleen Moore scrapbook #2, AMPAS.
31. "Two Entrancing Types," unsourced, Colleen Moore scrapbook #2, AMPAS.
32. Dan Thomas, "Daily Movie," *West Palm Beach Post*, 13 October 1925, Colleen Moore scrapbook #15, AMPAS.
33. J. G., "Her Wild Oat," *St. Paul Pioneer Press*, 25 December 1927, Colleen Moore scrapbook #18, AMPAS.
34. "Character Sketch of Vivacious Colleen Moore," *Newark Ledger*, 9 December 1923, Colleen Moore scrapbook #1, AMPAS.
35. Untitled, *Brooklyn Motion Picture Magazine* (September 1924), Colleen Moore scrapbook #2, AMPAS.
36. As I will discuss in chapter 4, fans did in fact play with trying on and discarding personalities they had seen on the screen.
37. "Beauty and Personality," *Washington Star*, 20 November 1921, Colleen Moore scrapbook #1, AMPAS.
38. "More than Beauty Needed, Is Claim," unsourced, ca. 1921, Colleen Moore scrapbook #1, AMPAS.
39. Mabel Normand, "How to Get into the Movies: Part VI, Keep a Diary!" 289.
40. "Fay Tincher," *Motion Picture Magazine* (October 1916): 68.
41. Dorothy Manners, "It Pays to Be Homely," *Motion Picture Magazine* (November 1928): 31.

Notes to Chapter 2

42. Lynn Fairfield, "Why Not Homely Movie Stars?" *Motion Picture Magazine* (December 1927): 54.
43. Jane Kutten, "The World's Best Friend," *Motion Picture Magazine* (January 1931): 31.
44. Fairfield, "Why Not Homely Movie Stars?" 93.
45. Banner, *American Beauty*, 207–8.
46. King, *The Fun Factory*, 244.
47. Archie Bell, "Her Breadth Is Her Meal Ticket, Quoth the Mirthful Trixie," n.p., Trixie Friganza clipping file, NYPL.
48. Anthony Slide, *The Encyclopedia of Vaudeville* (Westport, CT: Greenwood, 1994), 488.
49. Webster, "The Bear Facts about Gale Henry."
50. "Coiffure Note: Louise Fazenda Still Wears Those Old Pigtails."
51. Louise Fazenda, "Plain or Pretty as You Will," *Pantomime*, 5 October 1921, 8.
52. W. Stephen Bush, "Tillie's Tomato Surprise," *Moving Picture World*, 16 October 1915, 463; Kutten, "The World's Best Friend."
53. Victoria Sturtevant, *A Great Big Girl Like Me: The Films of Marie Dressler* (Chicago: University of Illinois Press, 2009), 2–3.
54. Ibid., 4.
55. Unidentified clipping, Charlotte Greenwood clipping file, NYPL.
56. Unidentified clipping (ca. 1914), Charlotte Greenwood clipping file, NYPL.
57. Charles Darnton, "'So Long Letty' Almost as Broad as It Is Long," *New York World*, 1916, Charlotte Greenwood clipping file, NYPL.
58. Thomas C. Kennedy, "'Jane,'" *Motography*, 18 December 1915, 1289.
59. "Jane," *New York Dramatic Mirror*, 11 December 1915, 26.
60. "Gale's Infinite Variety," *Moving Picture Weekly*, 10 March 1917, 15.
61. "*Mayflowers* Bloom with Sweet Tunes," *New York Times*, 25 November 1925, 14.
62. Sturtevant, *A Great Big Girl Like Me*, 16.
63. "*Jane* Next Oliver Morosco Release," *Moving Picture World*, 20 November 1915, 1515.
64. Dorothy Dix, "Vanished Ladies," *Hartford Courant*, 27 September 1926, 8.
65. Constance Talmadge, "Here's How Kid Connie Landed in the Movies," *Toledo Blade*, December 1919, n.p., Constance Talmadge clipping file, NYPL.
66. "How These English Lords Do Suffer," *Hartford Courant*, 7 December 1924, C3.
67. "Another Actress Is Willing to Sacrifice Appearances for 'Art,'" *Cleveland News*, 26 February 1926, Colleen Moore scrapbook #13, AMPAS; *The Wall Flower* advertisement, unsourced, Colleen Moore scrapbook #1, AMPAS.
68. Hall, "Is It Tragic to Be Comic?" 48.
69. "Don't Fight against Nature," ca. 1917, Charlotte Greenwood clipping file, NYPL.
70. "Kitchen Komedy," unsourced, 20 March 1918, Louise Fazenda clipping file, Robinson Locke scrapbook, NYPL.

71. "Alice Howell in 'Alice in Society.'"
72. Willis Goldbeck, "Stuff of Gold," *Motion Picture Magazine* (November 1921): 52.
73. Le Berthon, "Star Once Sold Newspapers at Arcade Depot."
74. Untitled, *Photoplay* (December 1918), Louise Fazenda clipping file, Robinson Locke scrapbook, series 3, vol. 468, NYPL.
75. Marquis Busby, "You Don't Have to Be Beautiful," *Photoplay* (January 1930): 47; Fazenda, "Plain or Pretty as You Will"; Manners, "It Pays to Be Homely."
76. Fazenda, "Plain or Pretty as You Will," 8.
77. Hall, "Have YOU Got the Makings of a COMEDIAN?" 30.
78. "Alice Howell," *New York Tribune*, 2 September 1917, n.p., Alice Howell clipping file, NYPL.
79. "Alice Howell," *Moving Picture World*, 29 September 1917, 1994.
80. "Alice Howell without Make-up," *Moving Picture World*, 15 December 1917, 1625.
81. Carol Lee, "Oddities of Screen Makeup," *Motion Picture Magazine* (May 1917): 33–34.
82. Carlisle, "Enter and Exit, Smiling."
83. Unidentified clipping, Charlotte Greenwood clipping file, NYPL.
84. Louise Fazenda, "Me by Myself: The Confessions of a Comedienne," *Motion Picture Classic* (May 1919): 35.
85. Manners, "It Pays to Be Homely."
86. Myrtle Gebhart, "La Fazenda Tops the Waves," *Picture Play* (October 1930): 55, 110.
87. Busby, "You Don't Have to Be Beautiful."
88. Vogdes, "Twenty Minutes with Constance."
89. Grace Kingsley, "The Wild Woman of Babylon—Oh, Yes! She Has Tame Moments," *Photoplay* (May 1917): 148.
90. Adela Rogers St. Johns, "An Impression of Marion Davies," *Photoplay* (January 1925): 104.
91. "Don't Fight against Nature."
92. Webster, "The Bear Facts about Gale Henry."
93. Fazenda, "Me by Myself," 69.
94. Harry Carr, "No! They're Not Happy Even with Wealth and Fame," *Motion Picture Magazine* (September 1925): 111.
95. Fairfield, "Why Not Homely Movie Stars," 93.
96. Ibid.
97. Unidentified clipping, ca. 1924, Louise Fazenda clipping file, NYPL.
98. "Slow Music for Louise at Last," *Toledo Blade*, 1 February 1923, Louise Fazenda clipping file, NYPL.
99. Adela Rogers St. Johns, "The Most Versatile Girl in Hollywood," *Photoplay* (June 1925): 129.
100. Glenn, *Female Spectacle*, 59.
101. Rowe, *The Unruly Woman*, 62.

Chapter 3

1. Clarence C. Badger, "Reminiscences of My Experiences as Director of the Paramount Motion Picture, *It*," letter sent to George Eastman House, June 1957, excerpted in the 21st Pordenone Silent Film Festival Catalogue, 12–19 October 2002, 49–50.
2. See Lea Jacobs, *The Wages of Sin: Censorship and the Fallen Woman Film* (Berkeley: University of California Press, 1995), and Janet Staiger, *Bad Women: Regulating Sexuality in Early American Cinema* (Minneapolis: University of Minnesota Press, 1995).
3. The 1915 and 1917 versions of *Camille*, starring Clara Kimball Young and Theda Bara, respectively, end with the heroine dying in Armand's arms. In the 1921 and 1927 versions, starring Alla Nazimova and Norma Talmadge, Camille dies rejected and alone. Other silent-era versions of *Camille* were filmed in the United States (1912), Denmark (1907), France (1912), Italy (1909, 1915), and Germany (1917, 1920).
4. Allen, *Horrible Prettiness*, 140.
5. Ibid.
6. Mizejewski, *Ziegfeld Girl*, 67.
7. King, *The Fun Factory*, 213.
8. Kibler, "Nothing Succeeds Like Excess," 61.
9. Shirley Staples, *Male-Female Comedy Teams in American Vaudeville, 1865–1932* (Ann Arbor, MI: UMI Research Press, 1984), 106–10.
10. Kibler, *Rank Ladies*, 29–32.
11. Ibid., 52.
12. Quoted in Kibler, "Nothing Succeeds Like Excess," 64.
13. Ibid., 61.
14. Allen, *Horrible Prettiness*, 76.
15. "Clement Scott Resigns," *New York Times*, 11 December 1898, 1, quoted in Albert Auster, *Actresses and Suffragists: Women in the American Theater, 1890–1920* (New York: Praeger, 1984), 43.
16. *Morning Telegraph*, 26 December 1898, quoted in Auster, *Actresses and Suffragists*, 43.
17. Kibler, *Rank Ladies*, 86.
18. Glenn, *Female Spectacle*, 188.
19. Ibid., 200.
20. Angela J. Latham, *Posing a Threat: Flappers, Chorus Girls, and Other Brazen Performers of the American 1920s* (Hanover, NH: Wesleyan University Press, 2000), 118.
21. Constance Talmadge, "Why Men Fall in Love with Actresses," *Photoplay* (February 1925): 117.
22. Numerous light comediennes were described in the press as "good little bad girls"; *A Virtuous Vamp* (1919) was the name of a Constance Talmadge vehicle,

written by Anita Loos, and the term was subsequently used to describe her in the press.
23. Gladys Hall, "In Defense of Clara Bow," *Motion Picture Magazine* (January 1931): 30.
24. See, for example, Ruth Biery, "The Love Life of Clara Bow," *Motion Picture Magazine* (November 1928): 44–45, 104–6, and Marian Rhea, "Wedded Bliss Is Told by Clara Bow," *Los Angeles Evening Herald and Express*, 19 December 1931, AMPAS.
25. Biery, "The Love Life of Clara Bow."
26. Michael Woodward, "That Awful 'It'!" *Photoplay* (July 1930): 133.
27. Hall, "In Defense of Clara Bow," 30.
28. Latham, *Posing a Threat*, 69.
29. King, *The Fun Factory*, 216.
30. See Latham, *Posing a Threat*, 65–69 and d'Haeyere, "Splashes of Fun and Beauty," 207–25.
31. Untitled, *Motion Picture Classic* (January 1928), AMPAS.
32. Descriptions and quotes from this film, which is not known to survive, are taken from a reproduced scenario in Anita Loos, *The Talmadge Girls* (New York: Viking, 1978), 137–204.
33. Untitled, *Wisconsin News*, 16 November 1919, NYPL.
34. Loos, *The Talmadge Girls*, 165–66.
35. Although *Tillie Wakes Up* is not directly related to Dressler's previous films *Tillie's Punctured Romance* (1914) or *Tillie's Tomato Surprise* (1915), or her Broadway play *Tillie's Nightmare* (1910–11), the title character is clearly meant to recall the slavey character played by Dressler in the earlier vehicles.
36. Louella O. Parsons, "Doug Fairbanks Jr. and Joan Crawford Reveal Separation," *L.A. Examiner*, 18 March 1933, Joan Crawford clipping file, AMPAS.
37. "Clara Bow Demurely Poses in Pensive Vein," unsourced, 23 November 1932, Clara Bow clipping file, AMPAS.
38. "Hot-Cha Life Doesn't Pay, Says 'It' Girl," unsourced, 30 November 1932, Clara Bow clipping file, AMPAS.
39. Nancy F. Cott, *The Grounding of Modern Feminism* (New Haven, Conn.: Yale University Press, 1987), 41–48.
40. "Tanguay's Posters Banned," *Variety*, 10 March 1915, 5.
41. *Dramatic Mirror*, 29 January 1916, n.p., Eva Tanguay clipping file, NYPL.
42. Quoted in Kibler, "Nothing Succeeds Like Excess," 63.
43. Quoted in Slide, *The Encyclopedia of Vaudeville*, 508.
44. Quoted in Mary Unterbrink, *Funny Women: American Comediennes, 1860–1985* (Jefferson, NC: McFarland, 1987), 30.
45. Walt, "Sophie Tucker," *Variety*, 4 September 1909, 14.
46. "She Insisted on Idealizing Her Man," *Motion Picture Magazine* (June 1918): 128.
47. Hall, "Is It Tragic to Be Comic?" 91, 93.

48. For stagestruck or matinee girls, see Butsch, "Bowery B'hoys and Matinee Ladies," 397; for movie-struck girls, see Stamp, *Movie-Struck Girls*, 37.
49. Butsch, "Bowery B'hoys and Matinee Ladies," 397.
50. Rowe, *The Unruly Woman*, 31.
51. Herbert Howe, "Is Mary Pickford Finished?" *Pre-View*, 25 March 1925, 7.
52. Lori Landay, "The Flapper Film: Comedy, Dance, and Jazz Age Kinaesthetics," in *A Feminist Reader in Early Cinema*, ed. Jennifer M. Bean and Diane Negra (Durham, NC: Duke University Press, 2002), 237.
53. See Welter, "The Cult of True Womanhood," 151–74.
54. Rhea, "Wedded Bliss Is Told by Clara Bow."
55. J. H. Keen, "Joan Crawford," *Philadelphia Daily News*, 8 August 1930, AMPAS.
56. Howe, "Is Mary Pickford Finished?" 11.
57. King, *The Fun Factory*, 220.
58. See Miriam Hansen, *Babel & Babylon: Spectatorship in American Silent Film* (Cambridge, MA: Harvard University Press, 1991), 95; Lawrence W. Levine, *Highbrow/Lowbrow: The Emergence of Cultural Hierarchy in America* (Cambridge, MA: Harvard University Press, 1988), 184–98.
59. Stamp, *Movie-Struck Girls*, 114.
60. Ibid., 125.
61. Jennifer M. Bean, "Technologies of Early Stardom and the Extraordinary Body," in *A Feminist Reader in Early Cinema*, ed. Jennifer M. Bean and Diane Negra (Durham, NC: Duke University Press, 2002), 432–37.
62. Much has been written recently about audiences' physical engagement with comedies through laughter. See Hennefeld, "Death from Laughter"; Hennefeld, "Miniature Women, *Acrobatic Maids*, and Self-Amputating Domestics: Comediennes of the Trick Film," *Early Popular Visual Culture* 13, no. 2 (2015): 134–51; Lauren Rabinovitz, *Electric Dreamland: Amusement Parks, Movies, and American Modernity* (New York: Columbia University Press, 2012); and King, *The Fun Factory*.
63. Rabinovitz, *Electric Dreamland*, 137–38.
64. Quoted in Sturtevant, *A Great Big Girl Like Me*, 25.
65. Ibid.
66. Hennefeld, "Death from Laughter," 55.
67. See Uricchio and Pearson, *Reframing Culture*.
68. King, *The Fun Factory*, 11.
69. Rabinovitz, *Electric Dreamland*, 140–41.
70. Russo, *The Female Grotesque*, 62–63.
71. Rowe, *The Unruly Woman*, 33.
72. Singer, *Melodrama and Modernity*, 62–90.
73. Rabinovitz, *Electric Dreamland*, 138.
74. John F. Kasson, *Amusing the Million: Coney Island at the Turn of the Century* (New York: Hill and Wang, 1978), 49.
75. Milne, "Tillie Wakes Up," 759.

76. Lauren Rabinovitz, *For the Love of Pleasure: Women, Movies, and Culture in Turn-of-the-Century Chicago* (New Brunswick, NJ: Rutgers University Press, 1998), 138.
77. Ibid., 163, emphasis in original.
78. Rob King argues that Normand's role in *Mickey* is "divorcing Normand's screen persona from the boisterous physicality of her early roles and tying it to a sentimental emphasis on female sanctity, associated with notions of separate, gendered spheres and essential gender differences" (*The Fun Factory*, 230), part of a larger project at Keystone to reinscribe conservative gender roles and "popularize a consumerist imagery of youthful womanhood that defined women's appropriate role as that of decorative, titillating spectacle" (211).
79. Frederick James Smith, "The Celluloid Critic," *Motion Picture Classic* (October 1918), 47.
80. "Mickey," *Wid's Daily*, 11 August 1918, 4.
81. Freud, *Jokes and Their Relation to the Unconscious*, 117–20.
82. Allen, *Horrible Prettiness*, 229.
83. Quoted in ibid., 229.
84. Landay, "The Flapper Film," 237.
85. See Gillian Rodger, "He Isn't a Marrying Man," in *Queer Episodes in Music and Modern Identity*, ed. Sophie Fuller and Lloyd Whitesell (Urbana: University of Illinois Press, 2008), and Elizabeth Reitz Mullenix, *Wearing the Breeches: Gender on the Antebellum Stage* (New York: St. Martin's Press, 2000).
86. Mullenix, *Wearing the Breeches*, 291.
87. Ibid., 296–98.
88. Laura Horak, *Girls Will Be Boys: Cross-Dressed Women, Lesbians, and American Cinema, 1908–1934* (New Brunswick, NJ: Rutgers University Press, 2016), 2.
89. Chris Straayer, *Deviant Eyes, Deviant Bodies: Sexual Re-Orientations in Film and Video* (New York: Columbia University Press, 1996), 42.
90. Ibid., 54.
91. Ibid.
92. Horak, *Girls Will Be Boys*, 78.
93. Ibid., 96.
94. Ibid., 106. The intertitle was cut, but Campbell's mincing reaction remains in the film.
95. Alison McMahan, *Alice Guy Blaché: Lost Visionary of the Cinema* (New York: Continuum, 2002), 224.

Chapter 4

1. Unidentified clipping, ca. 1917, Polly Moran clipping file, NYPL.
2. Goldbeck, "Stuff of Gold," 95.
3. Singer, *Melodrama and Modernity*, 294.
4. Hennefeld, "Death from Laughter," 82.

Notes to Chapter 4

5. Carroll Smith-Rosenberg, *Disorderly Conduct: Visions of Gender in Victorian America* (New York: Oxford University Press, 1985), 177–78.
6. Glenn, *Female Spectacle*, 41.
7. Anke Brouwers, "Mud Pies and Tears: Little Mary's Funny Side," in *Slapstick Comedy*, ed. Tom Paulus and Rob King (New York: Routledge, 2010), 94.
8. DesRochers, *The New Humor in the Progressive Era*, 48.
9. *Pittsburgh Leader*, 21 March 1910, Eva Tanguay clipping file, NYPL.
10. For discussions of modernity, see Singer, *Melodrama and Modernity*; Jennifer M. Bean, "Bodies in Shock: Gender, Genre and the Cinema of Modernity" (PhD diss., University of Texas at Austin, 1998); Rabinovitz, *Electric Dreamland*; King, *The Fun Factory*; Leo Charney and Vanessa R. Schwartz, eds., *Cinema and the Invention of Modern Life* (Berkeley: University of California Press, 1995); and Kristen Whissel, *Picturing American Modernity: Traffic, Technology, and the Silent Cinema* (Durham, NC: Duke University Press, 2008).
11. Rabinovitz, *Electric Dreamland*, 12.
12. King, *The Fun Factory*, 190.
13. Singer, *Melodrama and Modernity*, 70.
14. Quoted in ibid., 74–89.
15. Hennefeld, "Death from Laughter," 74.
16. King, *The Fun Factory*, 191.
17. Rabinovitz, *Electric Dreamland*.
18. Maggie Hennefeld, "Destructive Metamorphosis: The Comedy of Female Catastrophe and Feminist Film Historiography," *Discourse* 36, no. 2 (Spring 2014): 179–80.
19. Bean, "Bodies in Shock," 55.
20. Jennifer M. Bean, "'Trauma Thrills': Notes on Early Action Cinema," in *Action and Adventure Cinema*, ed. Yvonne Trasker (New York: Routledge, 2004), 20.
21. See Singer, *Melodrama and Modernity*, 82–88.
22. *Dramatic Mirror*, 6 January 1915, Eva Tanguay clipping file, NYPL.
23. *Boots* review, *Wid's Daily*, 28 February 1919, Dorothy Gish clipping file, AMPAS; *The Hope Chest* review, *Wid's Daily*, 12 January 1919, 12.
24. Frederick James Smith, "Mabel in a Hurry," *Motion Picture Magazine* (November 1918): 119.
25. "The Song and Dance Girl," unsourced, Dorothy Devore clipping file, NYPL.
26. *Picture-Play*, April 1920, Constance Talmadge clipping file, NYPL.
27. "A Captivating Colleen"; Helen Klumph, "Flapping Her Way to Fame," Colleen Moore scrapbook #2, AMPAS.
28. Colleen Moore scrapbook #2, AMPAS.
29. Kingsley, "The Wild Woman of Babylon," 81.
30. Bean, "Bodies in Shock," 98.
31. "Alice Howell of L-Ko Makes a Tackle," 15 August 1916, Alice Howell clipping file, NYPL; Webster, "The Bear Facts about Gale Henry."
32. Unsourced, January 1917, Polly Moran clipping file, NYPL.

33. Photo caption, ca. 1915, Mabel Normand clipping file, AMPAS.
34. Edith Meredith, "The Miracle of Louise Fazenda's Baby," *Photoplay* (August 1933): 33. The story has a happy ending; the article was written on the occasion of the birth of Fazenda's son.
35. Jennifer M. Bean, "Technologies of Early Stardom and the Extraordinary Body," in *A Feminist Reader in Early Cinema*, ed. Jennifer M. Bean and Diane Negra (Durham, NC: Duke University Press, 2002), 425.
36. For a discussion of nervous disorders associated with modernity, see Singer, *Melodrama and Modernity*, 59–99, and Bean, "Bodies in Shock," 38–71.
37. Unidentified photo caption, Dorothy Devore clipping file, NYPL.
38. "Fay Tincher Game," unsourced, June 1915, Fay Tincher clipping file, NYPL.
39. Quirk, "The Girl on the Cover," 40.
40. "Feature Films of the Week," *New York Dramatic Mirror*, 6 October 1915, 28.
41. Leo Charney, "In a Moment: Film and the Philosophy of Modernity," in *Cinema and the Invention of Modern Life*, ed. Leo Charney and Vanessa R. Schwartz (Berkeley: University of California Press, 1995), 281.
42. Ibid.
43. *Roping Her Romeo* review, *Moving Picture World*, 13 October 1917, 261.
44. "Norma's Sister Constance," *Chicago News*, 7 September 1916, Constance Talmadge clipping file, NYPL.
45. Vogdes, "Twenty Minutes with Constance."
46. Unidentified clipping, ca. 1922, Constance Talmadge clipping file, NYPL.
47. "Colleen Has Definitions for Flapper," *Los Angeles Examiner*, July 1924, Colleen Moore scrapbook #2, AMPAS.
48. *The Hope Chest* review, *Wid's Daily*, 12 January 1919, 12.
49. Fazenda, "How to Get in!"
50. "Miss Greenwood's Comedy," *Boston Transcript*, ca. 1914, Charlotte Greenwood clipping file, NYPL.
51. Eileen Bowser, "Mack Sennett vs. Henry Ford," in *Slapstick Comedy*, ed. Tom Paulus and Rob King (New York: Routledge, 2010), 107.
52. "Movies' Speed Queens Hurl Auto Defis: Marie Dressler and Mabel Normand to Clash in Big Race Duel," *Los Angeles Evening Herald*, 8 May 1914.
53. Kingsley, "The Wild Woman of Babylon."
54. St. Johns, "The Most Versatile Girl in Hollywood."
55. "Regarding Bebe Daniels in Jail," *Morning Telegraph (New York)*, 1 May 1921, Bebe Daniels clipping file, AMPAS. Daniels's run-in with the law was capitalized on in a film called *The Speed Girl* (1921), in which her character is arrested for speeding and spends ten days in jail.
56. H. C. Carr, "Where Does Mack Sennett Get 'Em?" *Motion Picture Classic* (October 1918), AMPAS.
57. "What They Want to Do When They Are Fifty," *Motion Picture Magazine* (October 1925): 34.

58. Unidentified clipping, ca. 1922, Constance Talmadge clipping file, NYPL.
59. "Convalescing with Constance," unsourced, Constance Talmadge clipping file, NYPL.
60. Unidentified clipping, Charlotte Greenwood clipping file, NYPL.
61. "Movies Spoil Her Outdoor Sport," ca. 1923, Colleen Moore scrapbook #1, AMPAS.
62. "Alice Howell," *Moving Picture World*, 29 September 1917, 1994.
63. Colleen Moore, "The American Girl of Today," unsourced, ca. January 1925, Colleen Moore scrapbook #2, AMPAS.
64. "Please May I Bob My Hair?" *Liberty Magazine*, 30 June 1928, Mary Pickford clipping file, AMPAS.
65. King, *The Fun Factory*, 215.
66. On the rise of ready-to-wear fashion in the United States, see Joshua Zeitz, *Flapper: A Madcap Story of Sex, Style, Celebrity, and the Women Who Made America Modern* (New York: Three Rivers Press, 2006), 161–72.
67. Susan A. Glenn, "'Give an Imitation of Me': Vaudeville Mimics and the Play of the Self," *American Quarterly* 50, no. 1 (March 1998): 47.
68. *New York Telegraph*, 12 December 1925, Elsie Janis clipping file, NYPL.
69. "Stars in the Film Firmament," January 1928, Marion Davies clipping file, AMPAS.
70. "Something Just as Good," *New York Pictureplay Magazine*, April 1922, and "Colleen Moore as Impersonator," unsourced, in Colleen Moore scrapbook #1, AMPAS.
71. Mary Ann Doane, "Film and the Masquerade: Theorizing the Female Spectator," *Screen* 23 (1982): 78–87.
72. Glenn, "Give an Imitation of Me," 67.
73. Herbert Blumer, *Movies and Conduct* (New York: Macmillan, 1933), 34.
74. Ibid., 43.
75. Ibid., 52.
76. Israel Zangwill, "Actress versus Suffraget," *The Independent* 67 (2 December 1909): 1248–50, quoted in Glenn, *Female Spectacle*, 135.
77. Glenn, *Female Spectacle*, 13–14; Slide, *The Encyclopedia of Vaudeville*, 489; Snyder, *The Voice of the City*, 47; Joe Laurie Jr., *Vaudeville: From the Honky-Tonks to the Palace* (New York: Henry Holt, 1953), 254, 247.
78. "What They Get," *Variety*, 10 January 1913, 15.
79. Ibid.; "Dressler in Pictures," *Variety*, 17 April 1914, 20; "Ban Is Extended on Normand Films," *New York Times*, 5 January 1924, 3.
80. Mary Pickford studio biography, ca. 1921, Mary Pickford clipping file, AMPAS.
81. Howe, "Is Mary Pickford Finished?"
82. Fritzi Remont, "Featuring Fay," *Motion Picture Magazine* (August 1918): 29.
83. "The Big Four of Educational," 709.
84. "The Lady on the Cover," *Photo-Play Review*, 23 March 1915, quoted in

Sherman, *Mabel Normand*, 95; G. P. von Harleman, "Motion Picture Studios of California," *Moving Picture World*, 10 March 1917, 1604.
85. Biography of Gale Henry, Paramount, 19 July 1929, Gale Henry clipping file, AMPAS.
86. Goldbeck, "Stuff of Gold"; Richard Willis, "Dot Farley: Comedienne, Tragedienne and Photoplaywright," *Photoplay* (November 1914): 140.
87. Sturtevant, *A Great Big Girl Like Me*, 14.
88. Corliss, "Fazenda."
89. Quirk, "The Girl on the Cover," 41.
90. "Fay Tincher, the Inimitable Comedienne, Thinks It Easy to Imitate Her," Fay Tincher clipping file, NYPL.
91. *Los Angeles Examiner*, 18 September 1921, Colleen Moore scrapbook #1, AMPAS.
92. "Fazenda Would Quit Comedy for Drama," *Brooklyn Daily Eagle*, 10 August 1924, E3.
93. "Mary Doubles in Shop Role," *Los Angeles Examiner*, 18 May 1927, Mary Pickford clipping file, AMPAS.
94. "Ella Cinders," *Liberty Magazine*, 24 July 1926, Colleen Moore scrapbook #13, AMPAS; J. G., "Her Wild Oat."
95. "Colleen at Library in 'Her Wild Oats' [sic]," *Huntington (PA) News*, 29 February 1928, Colleen Moore scrapbook #18, AMPAS.
96. Blumer, *Movies and Conduct*, 64.
97. J. Francis Perrett, "The Colleen of the Movies," *Extension Magazine*, November 1926, Colleen Moore scrapbook #15, AMPAS; "Alice Howell," *New York Tribune*, 2 September 1917, Alice Howell clipping file, NYPL.
98. Sturtevant, *A Great Big Girl Like Me*, 6.
99. "Please May I Bob My Hair?"; unsourced, 25 June 1928, Mary Pickford clipping file, AMPAS.
100. Moore, *Silent Star*, 129.
101. *Photoplay*, ca. 1923, Colleen Moore scrapbook #2, AMPAS.
102. Advertisements for the Owl Drug Co., June 1924; "Flappers in Contest at Olympia," *New Bedford (MA) Times*, 9 September 1924; "Billion for the Bobs: Film Actresses Tell of Enormous 'Overhead' in the Upkeep of Short Hair," *Tacoma (WA) News Tribune*, 28 July 1924, Colleen Moore scrapbook #2, AMPAS.
103. Moore, "The American Girl of Today."
104. "When Women Rule," *Chicago Defender*, 26 July 1913, 2.
105. "In Lighter Vein," *San Francisco Chronicle*, 6 December 1909, 6.
106. "Wall Flowers," *Life*, 25 May 1911, 1036; "When Woman Rules the World," *San Francisco Chronicle*, 19 January 1913, 31.
107. Quoted in Kibler, *Rank Ladies*, 49–50.
108. "When Women Rule," *Boston Daily Globe*, 25 April 1909, SM16.
109. Margrete Daney, "Here Is Peep into Future When Women Will Wear

Mustaches," *Toledo News-Bee*, 11 October 1924, Colleen Moore scrapbook #2, AMPAS.

Conclusion

1. Naming anything the "first," of course, can be slippery. *The Jazz Singer* was one of many films that included synchronous sound sequences in an otherwise silent film. To varying degrees, the technical and box office successes of these films helped convince Hollywood to shift to fully synchronous sound production by the late 1920s. See Donald Crafton, *The Talkies: American Cinema's Transition to Sound, 1926–1931* (Berkeley: University of California Press, 1997), 516–31.
2. Loos, *The Talmadge Girls*, 2; "Lure of Screen Wrecks Romance of Constance and Greek Husband," *Toledo Blade*, 19 November 1921, Constance Talmadge clipping file, NYPL; Helen Louise Walker, "For To-morrow We Die," unsourced, ca. 1927, Constance Talmadge clipping file, NYPL.
3. Loos, *The Talmadge Girls*, 2.
4. Mabel Normand died in 1930 without ever having the opportunity to make a sound film. Alice Howell retired from the screen in 1926, before sound was a factor.
5. David Stenn, *Clara Bow: Runnin' Wild* (New York: Cooper Square Press, 2000), 160.
6. *Her Wedding Night* (1930) was a nod to Bow's numerous sex scandals, and *No Limit* (1931) contained references to her legal entanglement with a Cal-Neva casino owner.
7. Moore, *Silent Star*, 198.
8. Marion Davies, *The Times We Had: Life with William Randolph Hearst* (New York: Ballantine Books, 1975), 261.
9. Goldberg played both male and female characters in her act, as well as characters of various races.

Bibliography

SECONDARY SOURCES

Abel, Richard, ed. *Silent Film*. New Brunswick, NJ: Rutgers University Press, 1996.
Affron, Charles. *Lillian Gish: Her Legend, Her Life*. New York: Scribner, 2001.
Agee, James. "Comedy's Greatest Era." In *The Film Comedy Reader*, ed. Gregg Rickman. New York: Limelight Editions, 2001.
Allen, Robert C. *Horrible Prettiness: Burlesque and American Culture*. Chapel Hill: University of North Carolina Press, 1991.
Auster, Albert. *Actresses and Suffragists: Women in the American Theater, 1890–1920*. New York: Praeger, 1984.
Banner, Lois W. *American Beauty*. Chicago: University of Chicago Press, 1983.
Barreca, Regina, ed. *Last Laughs: Perspectives on Women and Comedy*. New York: Gordon and Breach, 1988.
———. ed. *New Perspectives on Women and Comedy*. Philadelphia: Gordon and Breach, 1992.
———. *They Used to Call Me Snow White . . . But I Drifted: Women's Strategic Use of Humor*. New York: Penguin, 1991.
Bean, Jennifer M. "Bodies in Shock: Gender, Genre and the Cinema of Modernity." PhD diss., University of Texas at Austin, 1998.
———. "'Trauma Thrills': Notes on Early Action Cinema." In *Action and Adventure Cinema*, ed. Yvonne Trasker. New York: Routledge, 2004.
Bean, Jennifer M., and Diane Negra, eds. *A Feminist Reader in Early Cinema*. Durham, NC: Duke University Press, 2002.
Bergson, Henri. "Laughter." In *Comedy*, ed. Wylie Sypher. Baltimore: Johns Hopkins University Press, 1956.
Blumer, Herbert. *Movies and Conduct*. New York: Macmillan, 1933.
Bowser, Eileen. *The Transformation of Cinema, 1907–1915*. Berkeley: University of California Press, 1990.
Butler, Judith. *Gender Trouble: Feminism and the Subversion of Identity*. New York: Routledge, 1990.
Butsch, Richard. "Bowery B'hoys and Matinee Ladies: The Re-Gendering of Nineteenth-Century American Theater Audiences." *American Quarterly* 46, no. 3 (September 1994): 374–405.

Carroll, Noël. "Notes on the Sight Gag." In *Comedy/Cinema/Theory*, ed. Andrew Horton. Berkeley: University of California Press, 1991.

Charney, Leo, and Vanessa R. Schwartz, eds. *Cinema and the Invention of Modern Life*. Berkeley: University of California Press, 1995.

Cohen, Adam. *Imbeciles: The Supreme Court, American Eugenics, and the Sterilization of Carrie Buck*. New York: Penguin, 2016.

Conboy, Katie, Nadia Medina, and Sarah Stanbury, eds. *Writing on the Body: Female Embodiment and Feminist Theory*. New York: Columbia University Press, 1997.

Cott, Nancy F. *The Grounding of Modern Feminism*. New Haven, CT: Yale University Press, 1987.

Crafton, Donald. *The Talkies: American Cinema's Transition to Sound, 1926–1931*. Berkeley: University of California Press, 1997.

Dale, Alan. *Comedy Is a Man in Trouble: Slapstick in American Movies*. Minneapolis: University of Minnesota Press, 2000.

Davies, Marion. *The Times We Had: Life with William Randolph Hearst*. New York: Ballantine Books, 1975.

Davis, Natalie Zemon. *Society and Culture in Early Modern France*. Stanford, CA: Stanford University Press, 1975.

deCordova, Richard. *Picture Personalities: The Emergence of the Star System in America*. Urbana: University of Illinois Press, 1990.

DesRochers, Rick. *The New Humor in the Progressive Era: Americanization and the Vaudeville Comedian*. New York: Palgrave Macmillan, 2014.

Doane, Mary Ann. "Film and the Masquerade: Theorizing the Female Spectator." *Screen* 23 (1982): 78–87.

Dow, Bonnie J. *Prime-Time Feminism: Television, Media Culture, and the Women's Movement since 1970*. Philadelphia: University of Pennsylvania Press, 1996.

Duncan, Hugh. *Communication and Social Order*. New York: Oxford University Press, 1962.

Fey, Tina. *Bossypants*. New York: Little, Brown, 2011.

Finney, Gail, ed. *Look Who's Laughing: Gender and Comedy*. Langhorne, PA: Gordon and Breach, 1994.

Foucault, Michel. *The History of Sexuality*. New York: Vintage, 1990.

Freud, Sigmund. *Jokes and Their Relation to the Unconscious*. Trans. and ed. James Strachey. New York: W. W. Norton, 1960.

Frost, Laura. "Blondes Have More Fun: Anita Loos and the Language of Silent Cinema." *Modernism/Modernity* 17, no. 2 (2010): 291–311.

Fussell, Betty Harper. *Mabel: Hollywood's First I-Don't-Care-Girl*. New Haven, CT: Ticknor and Fields, 1982.

Gehring, Wes D. *Personality Comedians as Genre: Selected Players*. Westport, CT: Greenwood, 1997.

Gish, Lillian. *The Movies, Mr. Griffith, and Me*. San Francisco: Mercury House, 1969.

Glenn, Susan A. *Female Spectacle: The Theatrical Roots of Modern Feminism.* Cambridge, MA: Harvard University Press, 2000.

———. "'Give an Imitation of Me': Vaudeville Mimics and the Play of the Self." *American Quarterly* 50, no. 1 (March 1998): 47–76.

Gray, Frances. *Women and Laughter.* Charlottesville: University Press of Virginia, 1994.

Grieveson, Lee. *Policing Cinema: Movies and Censorship in Early Twentieth-Century America.* Berkeley: University of California Press, 2004.

Grossman, Barbara. *Funny Woman: The Life and Times of Fanny Brice.* Bloomington: Indiana University Press, 1991.

Gunning, Tom. "An Aesthetic of Astonishment: Early Film and the (In)credulous Spectator." In *Film Theory and Criticism: Introductory Readings*, ed. Leo Braudy and Marshall Cohen. New York: Oxford University Press, 1999.

———. "The Birth of Film Out of the Spirit of Modernity." In *Masterpieces of Modernist Cinema*, ed. Ted Perry. Bloomington: Indiana University Press, 2006.

———. "Crazy Machines in the Garden of Forking Paths: Mischief Gags and the Origins of American Film Comedy." In *Classical Hollywood Comedy*, ed. Kristine Brunovska Karnick and Henry Jenkins, 87–105. New York: Routledge, 1995.

———. "Mechanisms of Laughter: The Devices of Slapstick." In *Slapstick Comedy*, ed. Tom Paulus and Rob King, 137–51. New York: Routledge, 2010.

———. "Modernity and Cinema: A Culture of Shocks and Flows." In *Cinema and Modernity*, ed. Murray Pomerance. New Brunswick, NJ: Rutgers University Press, 2006.

———. "The Whole Town's Gawking: Early Cinema and the Visual Experience of Modernity." *Yale Journal of Criticism* 7, no. 2 (1994): 189–201.

Haggins, Bambi. *Laughing Mad: The Black Comic Persona in Post-Soul America.* New Brunswick, NJ: Rutgers University Press, 2007.

Hansen, Miriam. *Babel & Babylon: Spectatorship in American Silent Film.* Cambridge, MA: Harvard University Press, 1991.

Hengen, Shannon, ed. *Performing Gender and Comedy: Theories, Texts and Contexts.* Amsterdam: Gordon and Breach, 1998.

Hennefeld, Maggie. "Death from Laughter, Female Hysteria, and Early Cinema." *differences: A Journal of Feminist Cultural Studies* 27, no. 3 (December 2016): 45–92.

———. "Destructive Metamorphosis: The Comedy of Female Catastrophe and Feminist Film Historiography." *Discourse* 36, no. 2 (Spring 2014): 176–206.

———. "Miniature Women, *Acrobatic Maids*, and Self-Amputating Domestics: Comediennes of the Trick Film." *Early Popular Visual Culture* 13, no. 2 (2015): 134–51.

———. "Slapstick Comediennes in Silent Cinema: Women's Laughter and the Feminist Politics of Gender in Motion." In *The Routledge Companion to Cinema and Gender*, ed. Kristin Lené Hole, Dijana Jelaca, E. Ann Kaplan, and Patrice Petro, 141–53. London: Routledge, 2017.

———. "Slapstick Comediennes in Transitional Cinema: Between Body and Medium." *Camera Obscura* 86, vol. 29, no. 2 (2014): 85–117.

Horak, Laura. *Girls Will Be Boys: Cross-Dressed Women, Lesbians, and American Cinema, 1908–1934*. New Brunswick, NJ: Rutgers University Press, 2016.

Jacobs, Lea. *The Wages of Sin: Censorship and the Fallen Woman Film*. Berkeley: University of California Press, 1995.

Jenkins, Henry. *What Made Pistachio Nuts? Early Sound Comedy and the Vaudeville Aesthetic*. New York: Columbia University Press, 1992.

Karnick, Kristine Brunovska. "Comedy Is Hard: Labor, Beauty, and Louise Fazenda." Unpublished paper presented at the Society for Cinema and Media Studies conference, Montreal, 27 March 2015.

Karnick, Kristine Brunovska, and Henry Jenkins, eds. *Classical Hollywood Comedy*. New York: Routledge, 1995.

Kasson, John F. *Amusing the Million: Coney Island at the Turn of the Century*. New York: Hill and Wang, 1978.

Kerr, Walter. *The Silent Clowns*. New York: Da Capo Press, 1975.

Kibler, M. Alison. "Nothing Succeeds Like Excess: Lillian Shaw's Comedy and Sexuality on the Keith Vaudeville Circuit." In *Performing Gender and Comedy: Theories, Texts and Contexts*, ed. Shannon Hengen, 59–77. Amsterdam: Gordon and Breach, 1998.

———. *Rank Ladies: Gender and Cultural Hierarchy in American Vaudeville*. Chapel Hill: University of North Carolina Press, 1999.

King, Geoff. *Film Comedy*. London: Wallflower Press, 2002.

King, Rob. *The Fun Factory: The Keystone Film Company and the Emergence of Mass Culture*. Berkeley: University of California Press, 2009.

Kitch, Carolyn. *The Girl on the Magazine Cover: The Origins of Visual Stereotypes in American Mass Media*. Chapel Hill: University of North Carolina Press, 2001.

Koszarski, Richard. *An Evening's Entertainment: The Age of the Silent Feature Picture, 1915–1928*. Berkeley: University of California Press, 1990.

Krefting, Rebecca. *All Joking Aside: American Humor and Its Discontents*. Baltimore: Johns Hopkins University Press, 2014.

Krutnik, Frank. "The Clown-Prints of Comedy." *Screen* 25, no. 4–5 (July–October 1984): 50–59.

———. "A Spanner in the Works? Genre, Narrative and the Hollywood Comedian." In *Classical Hollywood Comedy*, ed. Kristine Brunovska Karnick and Henry Jenkins. New York: Routledge, 1995.

Laffey, Bruce. *Beatrice Lillie: The Funniest Woman in the World*. New York: Wynwood Press, 1989.

Landay, Lori. *Madcaps, Screwballs, and Con Women: The Female Trickster in American Culture*. Philadelphia: University of Pennsylvania Press, 1998.

Latham, Angela J. *Posing a Threat: Flappers, Chorus Girls, and Other Brazen Performers of the American 1920s*. Hanover, NH: Wesleyan University Press, 2000.
Laurie, Joe, Jr. *Vaudeville: From the Honky-Tonks to the Palace*. New York: Henry Holt, 1953.
Lee, Betty. *Marie Dressler: The Unlikeliest Star*. Lexington: University Press of Kentucky, 1997.
Levine, Lawrence W. *Highbrow/Lowbrow: The Emergence of Cultural Hierarchy in America*. Cambridge, MA: Harvard University Press, 1988.
Lewis, Jon, and Eric Smoodin, eds. *Looking Past the Screen: Case Studies in American Film History and Method*. Durham, NC: Duke University Press, 2007.
Lillie, Beatrice. *Every Other Inch a Lady*. Garden City, NY: Doubleday, 1972.
Loos, Anita. *The Talmadge Girls*. New York: Viking, 1978.
Martin, Linda, and Kerry Segrave. *Women in Comedy*. Secaucus, NJ: Citadel Press, 1986.
Massa, Steve. "Alice Howell and Gale Henry, Queens of Eccentric Comedy." *Griffithiana* 73/74, (2004): 95–139.
McLean, Albert F., Jr. *American Vaudeville as Ritual*. Lexington: University of Kentucky Press, 1965.
McMahan, Alison. *Alice Guy Blaché: Lost Visionary of the Cinema*. New York: Continuum, 2002.
Mizejewski, Linda. *Pretty/Funny: Women Comedians and Body Politics*. Austin: University of Texas Press, 2014.
———. *Ziegfeld Girl: Image and Icon in Culture and Cinema*. Durham, NC: Duke University Press, 1999.
Mizejewski, Linda, and Victoria Sturtevant. *Hysterical! Women in American Comedy*. Austin: University of Texas Press, 2017.
Moore, Colleen. *Silent Star*. Garden City, NY: Doubleday, 1968.
Mullenix, Elizabeth Reitz. *Wearing the Breeches: Gender on the Antebellum Stage*. New York: St. Martin's Press, 2000.
Mulvey, Laura. "Visual Pleasure and Narrative Cinema." In *Film Theory and Criticism*, ed. Gerald Mast, Marshall Cohen, and Leo Braudy, 746–57. 4th ed. New York: Oxford University Press, 1992.
Neale, Steve, and Frank Krutnik. *Popular Film and Television Comedy*. London: Routledge, 1990.
Paulus, Tom, and Rob King, eds. *Slapstick Comedy*. New York: Routledge, 2010.
Peiss, Kathy. *Hope in a Jar: The Making of America's Beauty Culture*. New York: Henry Holt, 1998.
Pizzitola, Louis. *Hearst over Hollywood: Power, Passion and Propaganda in the Movies*. New York: Columbia University Press, 2002.
Rabinovitz, Lauren. *Electric Dreamland: Amusement Parks, Movies, and American Modernity*. New York: Columbia University Press, 2012.
———. *For the Love of Pleasure: Women, Movies, and Culture in Turn-of-the-Century Chicago*. New Brunswick, NJ: Rutgers University Press, 1998.

Rapf, Joanna E. "Queen of the Movies: Marie Dressler and *Politics.*" *Quarterly Review of Film and Video* 19, no. 4 (2002): 309–22.

Rodger, Gillian. "He Isn't a Marrying Man." In *Queer Episodes in Music and Modern Identity*, ed. Sophie Fuller and Lloyd Whitesell. Urbana: University of Illinois Press, 2008.

Rowe, Kathleen. *The Unruly Woman: Gender and the Genres of Laughter.* Austin: University of Texas Press, 1995.

Russo, Mary. *The Female Grotesque: Risk, Excess and Modernity.* New York: Routledge, 1994.

Seidman, Steve. *Comedian Comedy: A Tradition in Hollywood Film.* Ann Arbor, MI: UMI Research Press, 1981.

Sherman, William Thomas. *Mabel Normand: A Source Book to Her Life and Films.* New York: New York Times Company, 2004.

Singer, Ben. *Melodrama and Modernity: Early Sensational Cinema and Its Contexts.* New York: Columbia University Press, 2001.

Slide, Anthony. *Eccentrics of Comedy.* Lanham, MD: Scarecrow, 1998.

———. *The Encyclopedia of Vaudeville.* Westport, CT: Greenwood, 1994.

———. *Inside the Hollywood Fan Magazine: A History of Star Makers, Fabricators, and Gossip Mongers.* Jackson: University Press of Mississippi, 2010.

———. *She Could Be Chaplin! The Comedic Brilliance of Alice Howell.* Jackson: University Press of Mississippi, 2016.

Smith-Rosenberg, Carroll. *Disorderly Conduct: Visions of Gender in Victorian America.* New York: Oxford University Press, 1985.

Snyder, Robert W. *The Voice of the City: Vaudeville and Popular Culture in New York.* Chicago: Ivan R. Dee, 1989.

Staiger, Janet. *Bad Women: Regulating Sexuality in Early American Cinema.* Minneapolis: University of Minnesota Press, 1995.

Stamp, Shelley. *Lois Weber in Early Hollywood.* Berkeley: University of California Press, 2015.

———. *Movie-Struck Girls: Women and Motion Picture Culture after the Nickelodeon.* Princeton: Princeton University Press, 2000.

Staples, Shirley. *Male-Female Comedy Teams in American Vaudeville, 1865–1932.* Ann Arbor, MI: UMI Research Press, 1984.

Stenn, David. *Clara Bow: Runnin' Wild.* New York: Cooper Square Press, 2000.

Straayer, Chris. *Deviant Eyes, Deviant Bodies: Sexual Re-Orientations in Film and Video.* New York: Columbia University Press, 1996.

Sturtevant, Victoria. *A Great Big Girl Like Me: The Films of Marie Dressler.* Chicago: University of Illinois Press, 2009.

Unterbrink, Mary. *Funny Women: American Comediennes, 1860–1985.* Jefferson, NC: McFarland, 1987.

Uricchio, William, and Roberta E. Pearson. *Reframing Culture: The Case of the Vitagraph Quality Films.* Princeton: Princeton University Press, 1993.

Usai, Paolo Cherchi. *Burning Passions: An Introduction to the Study of Silent Cinema.* Trans. Emma Sansone Rittle. London: British Film Institute, 1994.
Walker, Nancy A. "Toward Solidarity: Women's Humor and Group Identity." In *Women's Comic Visions*, ed. June Sochen. Detroit: Wayne State University Press, 1991.
———. *A Very Serious Thing: Women's Humor and American Culture.* Minneapolis: University of Minnesota Press, 1988.
Welter, Barbara. "The Cult of True Womanhood: 1820–1860." *American Quarterly* 18, no. 2, part 1 (Summer 1966): 151–74.
Whissel, Kristen. *Picturing American Modernity: Traffic, Technology, and the Silent Cinema.* Durham, NC: Duke University Press, 2008.
Whitfield, Eileen. *Pickford: The Woman Who Made Hollywood.* New York: Faber and Faber, 1997.
Zeitz, Joshua. *Flapper: A Madcap Story of Sex, Style, Celebrity, and the Women Who Made America Modern.* New York: Three Rivers Press, 2006.

Selected Primary Sources

Albert, Katherine. "Two True Troupers—Louise & Marie." *Photoplay* (March 1930): 34–35.
"Alice Howell, L-Ko Comedienne." *Moving Picture World*, 2 March 1918, 1215.
"Alice Howell without Make-up." *Moving Picture World*, 15 December 1917, 1625.
Biery, Ruth. "The Love Life of Clara Bow." *Motion Picture Magazine* (November 1928): 44–45, 104–6.
Boone, Arabella. "One's Blue and One's Brown." *Photoplay* (February 1919): 50.
Brown, Beth. "Making Movies for Women." *Moving Picture World*, 26 March 1927, 342.
Busby, Marquis. "Three's a Crowd." *Photoplay* (June 1930): 77, 114.
Busby, Marquis. "You Don't Have to Be Beautiful." *Photoplay* (January 1930): 47, 115–16.
Carlisle, Helen. "Enter and Exit, Smiling." *Motion Picture Magazine* (December 1926): 38, 115.
Carr, Harry. "No! They're Not Happy Even with Wealth and Fame." *Motion Picture Magazine* (September 1925): 36–37, 110–11.
———. "Putting the Fizz in Fazenda." *Motion Picture Magazine* (January 1919): 61–62, 109.
Cheatham, Maude. "A Toiling Lily." *Motion Picture Magazine* (March 1921): 54–55, 112.
Chic, Mlle. "Alice Howell—Funniest Woman in Pictures." *Moving Picture Weekly*, 13 May 1916, 31.

"Coiffure Note: Louise Fazenda Still Wears Those Old Pigtails." *Herald-Tribune*, 23 January 1938, n.p. Louise Fazenda clipping file, NYPL.

"Colleen Moore, Triangle-Fine Arts Ingénue." *Moving Picture World*, 20 January 1917, 384.

"Comedienne Sighs for Other Worlds." *Los Angeles Times*, 4 May 1924, 24.

"The Coming Film Comedy of Ideas." *Christian Science Monitor*, 4 November 1919, 16.

Coquelin, Constant. "Have Women a Sense of Humor?" *Harper's Bazaar* 34, no. 2 (12 January 1901): 67–69.

Corliss, Allen. "Fazenda—Comic Venus." *Photoplay* (April 1918): 67–68, 117.

Daney, Margrete. "Here Is Peep into Future When Women Will Wear Mustaches." *Toledo News-Bee*, 11 October 1924. Colleen Moore scrapbook #2, AMPAS.

Darnton, Charles. "'So Long Letty' Almost as Broad as It Is Long." *New York World*, 1916, NYPL.

Denny, Margaret. "How Fay Tincher Regards Her Profession." *Motion Picture Magazine* (August 1916): 77–80.

"Dorothy Gish Gratifies Early Stage Ambition." *Philadelphia Inquirer*, 13 April 1930, n.p. Dorothy Gish clipping file, NYPL.

Fairfield, Lynn. "Why Not Homely Movie Stars?" *Motion Picture Magazine* (December 1927): 54, 93.

"Fay Tincher." *Motion Picture Magazine* (October 1916): 68.

Fazenda, Louise. "How to Get in!" *Motion Picture Magazine* (December 1916): 71–72.

———. "Me by Myself: The Confessions of a Comedienne." *Motion Picture Classic* (May 1919): 34–35, 69.

———. "Plain or Pretty as You Will." *Pantomime*, 5 October 1921, 8.

"Fazenda Would Quit Comedy for Drama." *Brooklyn Daily Eagle*, 10 August 1924, E3.

Fender, Robert. "What Is Beauty?" *Photoplay* (July 1928): 35, 124.

"Gale's Infinite Variety." *Moving Picture Weekly*, 10 March 1917, 15.

Gassaway, Gordon. "Everybody's Little Sister." *Picture-Play Magazine* (January 1920): 78–79.

Gebhart, Myrtle. "La Fazenda Tops the Waves." *Picture Play* (October 1930): 54–56, 110–11.

Goldbeck, Willis. "Stuff of Gold." *Motion Picture Magazine* (November 1921): 52–53, 95.

Hall, Gladys. "Have YOU Got the Makings of a COMEDIAN?" *Movie Classic* (December 1934): 30–31, 68.

———. "In Defense of Clara Bow." *Motion Picture Magazine* (January 1931): 28–30.

———. "Is It Tragic to Be Comic?" *Motion Picture Classic* (May 1931): 48, 91, 93.

Howe, Herbert. "Is Mary Pickford Finished?" *Pre-View*, 25 March 1925, 7, 11.

"'Is Polite Comedy Polite?' Asks Fay Tincher." *Photoplay* (August 1919): 94.

Kingsley, Grace. "The Wild Woman of Babylon—Oh, Yes! She Has Tame Moments." *Photoplay* (May 1917): 80–82, 148.
Kutten, Jane. "The World's Best Friend." *Motion Picture Magazine* (January 1931): 31, 92.
Lee, Carol. "Oddities of Screen Makeup." *Motion Picture Magazine* (May 1917): 33–36.
Lloyd, John. "Let Fay Try It!" *Photoplay* (June 1916): 53–56.
Mack, Grace Lee. "The Girl Who Put Stripes in Comedy." *Photo-Play Journal* (June 1919): 37.
Manners, Dorothy. "It Pays to Be Homely." *Motion Picture Magazine* (November 1928): 31, 87–88.
Meredith, Edith. "The Miracle of Louise Fazenda's Baby." *Photoplay* (August 1933): 33, 96–97.
Moore, Colleen. "The American Girl of Today." Unsourced, ca. January 1925. Colleen Moore scrapbook #2, AMPAS.
"The Next Griffith Wonder Child?" *Photoplay* (July 1917): 112.
Normand, Mabel. "How to Be a Comedienne." *New York Dramatic Mirror*, 19 June 1920, 1244.
"Please May I Bob My Hair?" *Liberty Magazine*, 30 June 1928, 28.
Quirk, James R. "The Girl on the Cover." *Photoplay* (August 1915): 39–42.
Remont, Fritzi. "Featuring Fay." *Motion Picture Magazine* (August 1918): 29–30, 121.
Sennett, Mack. "The Psychology of Film Comedy." *Motion Picture Classic* (November 1918): 20–21, 70.
"She Insisted on Idealizing Her Man." *Motion Picture Magazine* (June 1918): 128.
"Slow Music for Louise at Last." *Toledo Blade*, 1 February 1923. Louise Fazenda clipping file, NYPL.
Smith, Frederick James. "Mabel in a Hurry." *Motion Picture Magazine* (November 1918): 31–33, 119.
"Spectators Seldom Know She Is Pretty." *Cincinnati Star*, 16 January 1918. NYPL.
Squier, Emma Lindsay. "'Pies Is Pizen.'" *Photoplay Art* (September 1918): 4.
St. Johns, Adela Rogers. "Black Sheep Gish." *Photoplay* (January 1919): 37–38.
———. "An Impression of Marion Davies." *Photoplay* (January 1925): 59, 104.
———. "Matrimony and Meringue." *Photoplay* (July 1919): 80–82.
———. "The Most Versatile Girl in Hollywood." *Photoplay* (June 1925): 84, 128–29.
Talmadge, Constance. "Here's How Kid Connie Landed in the Movies." *Toledo Blade*, December 1919, n.p. Constance Talmadge clipping file, NYPL.
———. "The Tragedy of Being Funny." *Motion Picture Magazine* (August 1927): 54–55, 102.
———. "Why Men Fall in Love with Actresses." *Photoplay* (February 1925): 32–33, 117.

"Tanguay's Posters Banned." *Variety*, 10 March 1915, 5.

Thirer, Irene. "Film Beauts Come and Go—Funny Fazenda Lingers." *New York Evening Post*, 29 April 1936, n.p. Louise Fazenda clipping file, NYPL.

Underhill, Harriette. "Constance on Masculinity." *New York Tribune*, 7 October 1917, n.p. NYPL.

Vogdes, Walter. "Twenty Minutes with Constance." *Select Pictures Magazine* 4, no. 11 (ca. 1918): 5. Constance Talmadge clipping file, AMPAS.

Wade, Peter. "The Girl on the Cover." *Motion Picture Magazine* (April 1917): 167.

Webster, Dorothy Faith. "The Bear Facts about Gale Henry." *Picture Play* (January 1920): 48–49.

Willis, Richard. "Dot Farley: Comedienne, Tragedienne and Photoplaywright." *Photoplay* (November 1914): 139–41.

Woodward, Michael. "That Awful 'It'!" *Photoplay* (July 1930): 39, 133.

Index

Ackroyd, Jack, 105
acting: as a profession, 211–12; film vs. stage, 5
action films, 190. *See also* serials
action heroines. *See* serial queens
actors: and audience interaction, 136–37; dramatic, 89, 134; and publicity, 15–16, 19, 47; as stars, 15–18, 78, 81; and studios, 45; transitioning from silent to sound film, 233–34. *See also* acting; actresses
actresses: as frivolous, 138; as gold diggers, 139; as prostitutes, 138, 139–41; salaries, 211. *See also* acting; actors; chorus girls; comediennes; ingénues; vamps
advertisements, 89, 91, 92, 93, 171, 209–10
Alice in Wonderland (1933), 236
Allen, Gracie, 234, 238
Ambrose's Fury (1915), 85, 146, *147*, 166
amusement parks. 6, 20, 22, 135, 142, 147, 165, 166–68, 189, 197, 220
Anna Christie (1930), 236, 237
Anything Once (1927), 191
Arbuckle, Roscoe "Fatty," 1, 14, 175–76
Arnaz, Desi, 238
Art Arches (1917), 103, *104*
Arthur, Bea, 238
Arthur, George K., 112, *113*
Arthur, Jean, 237
athleticism, 79, 100, 143, 169, 173, 183, 184, 195, 198–99, 200–201, 230, 239; diving, 143, 169, 170, 197, 198; swimming, 142, 169–71, 193, 195, 198, 200, 201, 202. *See also* dancing; stunts
audiences, 4, 5, 7, 8, 10, 14, 15, 16, 18, 19, 33, 53, 87, 89, 114, 115, 116, 117, 133, 140–41, 167, 204, 214, 226, 230, 231; as aspiring performers, 80–81, 89, 92–93, 105, 154; and charged humor, 3–4; emulating stars, 209; as fans, 16, 91–92; female, 6, 7, 10, 12, 39–40, 78, 88, 93, 105, 124, 128, 136, 137–38, 154, 180, 184, 221, 222; and interaction with performers, 5, 31, 37, 136, 159–60, 187–88; and modernity, 189, 190, 198; onscreen, 164; and passive spectatorship, 163; and physical reactions to films, 163–65, 198, 274n62; and queer moments, 175, 176, 177, 178, 179, 180, 181, 182; reactions to comedy, 36, 40, 58, 59, 60, 64, 67; and respectability, 20, 39–40, 135–38, 163, 164; and suggestive material, 135, 137, 141, 150, 151–52, 157, 168; unruly, 37, 38, 136, 163, 165. *See also* movie struck girls; stagestruck girls
automobiles, 100, 112, 121, 143, 184, 188, 189, 190, 191, 193, 194, 195, 198, 200, 201, 202, 217, 219; and driving, 112, 195, 200–202; and traffic, 166, 191, 200, 219, 220

Baby Mine (1928), 101–2
Badger, Clarence, 133
Ball, Lucille, 7, 26, 238
Banner, Lois, 9, 75, 92
Bara, Theda, 134, 272n3
Barr, Roseanne, 238
Bathing Beauties, 12, 31–32, 33–34, 77–80, *78*, 86, 92, 105, 123, 137
bathing costumes, 141–42, *142*, 143, 170, 269n27
Bayes, Nora, 137
Bean, Jennifer, 11, 163, 188, 190, 195–96
beauty, 10, 18, 237, 239, 266n111; as artifice, 74, 107, 114, 128, 131; broad standards of, in comedy, 10, 73, 85–86; comediennes calling attention to non-normative, 93–94, 97, 100, 105–07, 118, 120, 122, 127, 128–29, 131; and consumption, 92, 93, 107–8, 122; as an essential element of idealized femininity, 9, 74, 108; film industry standards of, 78–79, 80–82, 89, 93, 94, 100, 103, 105, 107, 117, 122, 124, 127, 128, 131, 239; as incompatible with comedy, 9, 10, 74, 76–78, 118, 126, 127; linked to morality, 9, 74–75, 92; and personality, 10, 89–90, 131; as quantifiable, 79; and race, 79–80; types of comedy linked to, 10, 74, 76–77, 120
beauty contests, 52, 55, 86, 92, 224. *See also* Fame and Fortune Contest
beauty products, 17, 89, 92, 93, 210
Behind the Screen (1916), 180, *181*
Bell, Rex, 140, 150, 160
Bergson, Henri, 2, 29, 30, 32
Big Parade, The (1925), 55
Blache, Alice Guy, 180
Blondie of the Follies (1932), 236
bobbed hair, 11, 86, 157, 161, 184, 201–2, 222–26, 230–31. *See also* flappers

Bossypants (Fey), 28–29
boundary crossing, 11, 75, 90, 135, 146, 156, 178, 202, 204–10
Bow, Clara, 1, 5, 8, 14, 22, 46, 133, *158*, *159*, *160*, *168*, *172*, *173*, 210, 234–35, 237, 280n6; and bobbed hair, 224; and dancing, 174; and flirtation, 143–44; love life of, 91, 140, 150, 160; and modernity, 219–21; performance style of, 22; and sexuality, 133, 134, 140–41, 158–60, 167–68, 171–73; shopgirl characters of, 216, 218–19. *See also Hula*; *It*; *Mantrap*; *Plastic Age, The*
Brice, Fanny, 75, 94, *95*, 203
Broadway, 21, 39, 101, 103, 104, 139, 213, 221, 236
Brook, Clive, 172, *173*
Brooks, Louise, 134
Bunny, John, 1, 105
burlesque, 47, 94, 135, 142, 151, 172, 173, 174, 187
Burnett, Carol, 7, 238
Burns, George, 234, 238
Busch, Mae, 44

Cain and Mabel (1936), 236
Campbell, Eric, 180, 275n94
Cardboard Lover, The (1928), 204
carnivalesque, 12, 189
cars. *See* automobiles
censorship, 5, 151–52, 180
Century Comedies (Alice Howell), 121, 213
Chaplin, Charlie, 1, 14, 42, 44, 45, 47, 97, 100, 103, 180, *187*, 204, 212, 213
Chase, Charley, 103
chase films, 41, 49, 68, 190, 191, 195
Chasing Rainbows (1930), 236
Cho, Margaret, 7, 239
chorus girls, 33–34, 52, 75–76, 94, 103, 137, 138–39, 172, 185, 236. *See also* Ziegfeld Girl

Christie, Al, 71
Christy, Howard Chandler, 185
Cinderella Cinders (1920), 49, 207
Cinderella stories, 2, 55, 87, 89, 139, 215–16, 219, 221
cinema of attractions, 66
cities: and comediennes, 191–95, 218–22; as dangerous, 166, 189–90, 191; modern, 184, 192, 193, 194–95, 202
class, 20, 31, 36, 37, 39, 76, 88, 112, 116, 135, 138, 142, 161, 184, 202, 204, 206–9, 215, 216, 217, 220, 222, 236, 267n120; and audiences, 20, 38, 39, 163, 164–65, 167, 175
Clinging Vine, The (1926), 108–12, *109, 110, 111,* 113
comediennes: alternative model of femininity presented by, 5–6, 7, 8, 22–23, 51, 73, 92, 128–29, 131; ambivalence toward comedy, 8, 9, 25–26, 56–57, 62–63, 64–65, 66, 67, 69; anxieties about, 27, 18, 29, 34; and audience interaction, 5, 31, 136–37, 159–60, 187–88; and beauty standards, 9, 82–86, 89, 93, 94, 105, 107, 122, 127; behind-the-scenes labor of, 45, 210–15; as crazy machines, 7; critiquing social structures, 5, 7, 8, 12, 17, 27–28; and cross-dressing (*see* cross-dressing); cultural impact of, 7–9, 15, 18, 237–40; and debates about women's humor, 9, 14, 25, 26, 27, 42, 44–45, 46, 64, 71; and desire to leave comedy, 9, 26, 45, 63, 64–66, 69; downplaying traditional femininity, 10, 33–34, 51, 126–27; in early cinema, 17; embracing comedy, 26, 55–57, 63, 68–71; erasure from public memory of, 1–2, 13–14; as "female Charlie Chaplin," 47, 61–62; and "feminine humor," 26, 34, 45, 46, 47; and first discoveries that they're funny, 63–64; and flirtation (*see* flirtation); and impersonation, 202–10; and light comedy, 26, 39, 46, 67–68; and marriage (*see* marriage); and modernity, 7, 11, 184, 188, 191, 194–202; as naturally funny, 9, 50–52, 57, 64, 71; and New Humor, 37–38, 188; and the New Woman, 11, 184, 185, 199–202; off-screen lives of, 140, 149–50, 160; on set injuries of, 196; performance styles of, 19–22; and physical comedy, 9, 11, 19–20, 26, 36, 37, 38–39, 47–49, 64, 66–68; and pretty/funny binary, 9, 10, 36, 74–79, 127; and race, 19; and self-deprecating humor, 6, 8, 46, 94, 105; and sensuality, 11, 13, 135, 163, 165–74; sexually charged performances of, 10–11, 134, 137, 140, 150–62; as skilled artists, 57–59, 61, 63; and sound film, 233–37; as tragic, 10, 18, 62–72, 118, 120; and True Womanhood, 8–9; as unattractive, 122–25; as unfeminine, 9, 25, 26, 27, 37, 38, 49, 63, 64, 65, 66, 224–26; as unsuited for drama, 51, 125–26, 127; using appearance as a source of comedy, 10, 93–107, 116–17, 118–22; as working women, 11, 184, 210–16, 221–22. *See also* comedy; feminine humor; flappers; light comediennes; slapstick comediennes; stage comediennes; unruliness; women
comedy: audience reactions to, 40, 59, 60, 64, 67, 163–65, 198, 274n62; and charged humor, 4; comediennes' ambivalence toward, 8, 9, 25–26, 56–57, 62–63, 64–65, 66, 67, 69; comediennes' desire to leave, 9, 26, 45, 63, 64–66, 69; comediennes'

comedy (*continued*)
embrace of, 26, 55–57, 63, 68–71; feminine, 26, 34–42, 44, 45, 46, 47, 76; as incompatible with femininity, 9, 18, 25, 27–29, 30, 31, 33, 34, 35, 36, 37, 38, 45, 46, 49, 50, 63, 65, 66, 67, 69, 74; labor involved in the creation of, 57–59; as a means of challenging traditional gender roles, 4, 5, 6, 8, 11, 12; as a means of critiquing social structures, 2, 4, 5, 6, 7, 8, 11, 27–28, 180; and modernity, 189, 190–91, 196–97; as more difficult than drama, 59–60, 64; and power, 2, 4, 7; and refinement, 38–39, 40–41, 45, 46, 66, 67; as a safe genre, 4–5, 10, 157, 180. *See also* comediennes; gags; light comedy; New Humor; slapstick comedy

comedy-drama. *See* light comedy

Compson, Betty, 224

Coney Island. *See* amusement parks

Conklin, Chester, 119

consumerism, 92, 107–08, 135, 162, 181–82, 188, 275n78; conflated with sexual desire, 155, 161–62

Cooper, Gary, 140, 233

Coquelin, Constant, 34–36

Coquette (1929), 235

Cosmopolitan Pictures, 235

costumes, makeup and hair, 21, 85, 97, 105, 151, 153, 155, 156, 176, 204; comediennes designing their own, 58–59, 97, 118, 213; comediennes' discomfort with, 18, 69, 119–20; used to cover beauty, 10, 77, 82, 114, 118; and makeover comedies, 107, 109–10, 112–13, 114, 116; as a rejection of beauty standards, 74, 93, 94, 100, 118, 120–22, 128–29, 238; and slapstick, 10, 20, 77, 97, 121. *See also* bathing costumes; cross-dressing

Court House Crooks (1915), 191

Crawford, Joan, 134, 149–50, 160, 174, 233

cross-dressing, 11, 135, 174–81, 204, 230; female impersonation, 175–76; male impersonation, 135, 174–75, 176, 180; and temporary transvestite films, 175, 176, 178, 230

Crowd, The (1928), 55, 164

cult of domesticity, 29

Cult of True Womanhood. *See* True Woman

Dame aux camélias, La (Dumas), 134

Dana, Viola, 44

dancing, 22, 88, 94, 101, 134, 135, 149, 150, 170, 173–74, 192, 193, 195, 200–202, 217, 226; dancers, 31, 34, 206, 207, 236, 237

Daniels, Bebe, 1, 44, 45–46, 65, 200, 277n55

dating, 135, 136 141, 146, 156, 166, 167, 185, 200, 220. *See also* flirtation; marriage

Davies, Marion, 9, 19, 52, 53–55, 61, 107, *108* 154–55, *156*, *157*, 235–36, 237; and beauty, 113–14, 115, 117, 120, 125–26; and flirtation, 134; and impersonation, 203–4, *205*; and light comedy, 78; performance style of, 21. See also *Cardboard Lover, The*; *Patsy, The*; *Red Mill, The*; *Show People*

department stores, 159, 190, 204, 206, 217, 218

Depression-era comedy, 235, 238

Devil's Daughter, The (1915), 134

Devore, Dorothy, 26, 234; ambivalence toward comedy, 65, 67; and beauty, 85, 86, *87*; and cross-dressing, 176; as head of production company, 212; and modernity, 191, 192, 194, 197;

performance style of, 21. *See also Hold Your Breath*; *Know Thy Wife*
Diller, Phyllis, 26, 238
Dinner at Eight (1933), 237
Down on the Farm (1938), 236
drama, 10, 51, 52–55, 57, 69, 124, 233, 235, 236, 237; and beauty, 86, 89, 92, 93, 118, 125, 126; comediennes' attempts at, 63, 125–27, 128; comediennes' preference for, 26, 63, 64, 65–66, 68; comedy more difficult than, 59–60, 64; as a suitable genre for women, 60–61, 64–65, 70; and sexuality, 133–34, 154, 182. *See also* melodrama
Dream Lady, The (1918), 177
Dressler, Marie, 1, 5, 6, 12, 22, 33, 61, *101*, 113, 146, *148*, 167, *169*, 203, 236–37, 265n72, 273n35; and beauty, 10, 73, 75, 78, *83*, 85, 91, 103, 127; embracing comedy, 71; excessive body of, 6, 93, 100, 103–4, 105, 106; and the New Woman, 185, *187*; performance of as authorship, 213; and physical comedy, 33, 40, 100, 197; rivalry with Mabel Normand, 200; and sexuality, 167; and working women, 221–22. *See also Patsy, The*; *Tillie Wakes Up*; *Tillie's Punctured Romance*; *Tillie's Tomato Surprise*
Duchess of Buffalo, The (1926), 145–46
Dulcy (1923), 236

Edwards, Snitz, 113
Ella Cinders (1926), 9, 42, 44, 52, 55, *56*, 61, 62, 64, 115, 216
Ellis, Havelock, 173, 175
Exit Smiling (1926), 204
Extra Girl, The (1923), 9, 52–53, *53*, 64

Faber Sisters, 137
Fairbanks, Douglas, 41, 61, 204
Fairbanks, Douglas Jr., 149
Fallon, Jimmy, 28
Fame and Fortune Contest, 16, 209
fan magazines, 10, 15–17, 18–19, 46–47, 49–50, 59, 62, 68, 71, 74, 89, 92, 105, 118, 126, 128, 140, 201, 203, 204, 209, 210, 212, 213
Farley, Dot, 212, 213
Fatty's Faithful Fido (1915), 191
Fay Tincher Productions, 212
Fazenda, Louise, 2, 7, 10, 14, 22, 42, 52, *99*, 107, 146, *147*, 176, 184, 236, 237, 266n105, 269n27, 277n34; ambivalence toward comedy, 62, 63–64, 66, 119–20, 122, 125–26; and beauty, 77, 82–85, *83*, 89, 91, 103, 105, 106–7, 123–24, 127, 128; behind-the-scenes labor of, 59, 213–15; and comedy as hard work, 60; and costumes, 97–100, 117, 119–20; as naturally funny, 50, 51, 57; and the New Woman, 199, 200; and on-set injuries, 196; performance style of, 20; and physical comedy, 19, 20, 33, 44, 47–50, *48*. *See also Ambrose's Fury*; *Hearts and Flowers*; *Lighthouse by the Sea, The*; *Red Mill, The*; *Willful Ambrose*
feminine humor, 26, 34–42, 44, 45, 46, 47, 76
femininity: beauty essential to, 9, 74, 108; changing in late nineteenth and early twentieth century, 8, 135, 239–40; comediennes challenging dominant notions of, 6, 7, 8–9, 12, 22, 33, 34, 47, 49, 50, 66, 72, 73, 93, 107, 120, 122, 126, 127, 238, 239; comediennes positing alternative models of, 8, 10, 12, 22, 33–34, 78, 105–7, 128, 131, 152, 238, 239; idealized, 6, 31, 35, 38, 64, 72, 74, 77, 78, 79, 107, 117, 126, 180, 238,

femininity (*continued*)
239; as incompatible with comedy, 9, 18, 25, 26, 27–29, 30, 31, 32–33, 34, 35, 36, 37, 38, 45, 46, 49, 50, 63, 65, 66, 67, 68, 69, 74; and modern life, 11, 184, 185, 224, 231; and the New Woman, 184; as performative, 10, 34, 74, 108, 114, 128
feminists, 40, 75, 111, 151, 152, 211
Fey, Tina, 28, 239
Fields, Totie, 238
Fields, W. C., 233
Finch, Flora, 17, 75, 105, 265n72
Fitzgerald, F. Scott, 222, 261n44
Flaming Youth (1923), 222, 223–24, 261n44
flapper films, 22, 134, 143, 145–46, 158, 161, 224. *See also* comedy; light comedy; slapstick comedy
flappers, 2, 10, 11, 22, 112, 115, 149, 203, 234, 235, 237; and bobbed hair, 223, 224, 230; and dancing, 173–74; and modernity, 198; and sexuality, 134, 139, 140, 141, 150, 154, 158, 161, 162, 173, 174. *See also* comediennes; light comediennes; slapstick comediennes
Fleming, Victor, 140
Flesh and the Devil (1926), 134
flirtation, 20, 21, 22, 85, 134, 141, 150, 152, 154, 155, 167, 181, 195, 210, 219, 227, 235; as alternative to marriage, 146–49; as control, 141, 143–46; in cross-dressing comedies, 176, 179; and stage comediennes, 136–37. *See also* dating; marriage
Floradora (1900), 103
Floradora Girl, The (1930), 236
Florida Enchantment, A (1914), 179
Franklin, Irene, 137
Freud, Sigmund, 2, 32, 172
Friganza, Trixie, 33, 46, 94

gags, 5; as crazy machines, 6–7; development of, 58, 59, 60–61, 213–14, 234; and gender, 11, 31, 36, 45; and light comedy, 21, 41, 42, 66, 68; and modernity, 195, 197–98; and narrative, 66–67; and slapstick, 20, 47, 49, 100; and sound film, 233–34
Garbo, Greta, 86, *87*, 88, 93, 134, 204, 233, 236–37
Garon, Pauline, 44, 45
gender inversion, 11, 12, 37, 93, 226–31
Gentlemen Prefer Blondes (Loos), 139
Gibson, Charles Dana, 185
Gibson Girl, 52, *186*
Gilman, Charlotte Perkins, 226
Gish, Dorothy, 19, 60, 85, 134, 169, 192, 198–99, 234
Gish, Lillian, 125, 198, 203–4
Glenn, Susan, 34, 75, 128, 139, 187, 202, 208
Gold Diggers (Hopwood), 139
Goldberg, Whoopi, 26, 238, 280n9
Gorman, Margaret, 79. *See also* Miss America
Goudal, Jetta, 86, *87*, 88, 93, 204
Grant, Sydney, 104–5, *106*
Greenwood, Charlotte, *106*, 113; ambivalence toward comedy, 63–64, 119, 122–23; and beauty, 75, 85, 91, 103, 104–5, 106–7, 124, 125, 126, 127; and comedy as hard work, 59, 60; embracing comedy, 71; and lowbrow comedy, 39, 40; as naturally funny, 50, 57; and the New Woman, 199, 201; physicality of, 93, 100–*102*, 104–5. *See also Baby Mine*; *Jane*; *So Long Letty*
Griffin, Kathy, 28
Griffith, D. W., 41, 70
Gunning, Tom, 6–7, 66–67

Hardy, Oliver, 14, 233
Harlow, Jean, 237

Harper's Bazaar, 25, 32, 34
Haver, Phyllis, 176
Hazards of Helen, The (1914–17), 163
Hearts and Flowers (1919), 176, *177*, 179–80
"Heaven Will Protect the Working Girl" (song), 221
Heidegger, Martin, 13, 197
Hennefeld, Maggie, 2, 12, 31, 184, 189
Henry, Gale, 5, 7–8, 10, 12, 14, 65, *98*, 226, 227, 230; and beauty, 85, 102–3, *104*, 106–7, 126, *130*; behind-the-scenes labor of, 213, 230; and costumes, 97, 100; and dangerous stunts, 196; embracing comedy, 26, 70, 125; as head of production company, 212; performance style of, 20; and slapstick, 68. See also *Art Arches*; *Her First Flame*; *Mighty Like a Moose*
Hepburn, Katharine, 237
Her First Flame (1920), 226–27, 228, *228*, 230, 231
Her Night of Romance (1924), 115, *115*
Her Painted Hero (1915), 85, 153–54
Her Torpedoed Love (1917), 48
Her Wild Oat (1927), 13, 42, *43*, 207–9, *208*, *209*, 216
Hines, Johnny, 44, 147, *148*
History of the Joke (2008), 28
Hitchens, Christopher, 27, 28, 29–30
Hold Your Breath (1924), 191, 194–95
Holmes, Helen, 183
homosexuality, 135, 174, 175, 176–78, 179–80, 204. See also cross-dressing
Horak, Laura, 175, 177, 179, 180
How Bridget Made the Fire (1900), 17
Howell, Alice, 10, 12, 14, 19, 20, 49, 61–62, 185, 201, 207, 280n4; and beauty, 103, *129*; and comedy as hard work, 58, 59; and costumes, 100, 117; embracing comedy, 26, 120–22; as head of production company, 212;

as naturally funny, 50; performance style of, 20–21; and physical comedy, 49; and stunt work, 196; and working women, 221. See also *Cinderella Cinders*
Hula (1927), 171–73, *172*, *173*, 174

immigration, 7, 37, 38, 79–80, 188, 191
intertitles, 6, 21, 41–42, *43*, 66, 109, 141, 146–47, 161, 166, 176, 179, 180, 206, 218, 226–27, 275n94
Irene (1926), 112–13, *113*, *114*
Irwin, May, 17, 33, 46, 94, 138
It (1927), 133, 158–60, *159*, *160*, 161, 167–68, 216, 218, 219, 220

Jane (1915), 40, 101, 104
Janis, Elsie, 46, 202–3
Jazz Singer, The (1927), 233, 280n1
Jenkins, Henry, 4, 27, 33, 66
Joy, Leatrice, 108, *109*, *110*, *111*

Keaton, Buster, 1, 14, 42, 191, 213
Keith, B. F., 151
Kellerman, Annette, 141, 171. See also bathing costumes
Keystone, 14, 20, 21, 31–32, 48, 67, 79, 82–85, 97, 146, 164, 175–76, 189, 191, 195, 196, 212, 214, 234, 267n120, 275n78. See also Bathing Beauties; Keystone Kops; Sennett, Mack; *Tillie's Punctured Romance*
Keystone Kops, 191
Kibler, M. Alison, 12, 40, 135, 136
King, Rob, 2, 7, 12, 20, 31, 38, 75, 92, 135, 142, 163, 164–65, 167, 188–89, 202, 267n120, 275n78
Kiss, The (1896), 17
Kitchen Maid's Dream, The (1907), 17
Know Thy Wife (1918), 176, *178*, 179
Krafft-Ebing, Richard von, 174–75
Krefting, Rebecca, 2, 3–4, 12, 74

Langdon, Harry, 1, 44, 47, 61
Laughing Gas (1907), 19
laughter, 2, 4, 6, 7, 10, 19, 21, 22, 27, 42, 52–54, 55, 58, 59, 60, 62, 65, 66, 67, 68, 70, 71, 94, 119, 120, 122, 123, 125, 129, 146, 147, 154, 167, 187, 219; as dangerous, 31, 164, 189; derisive, 6, 53; and femininity, 27, 29–30, 32, 34, 36, 38, 77; and modernity, 189, 198, 199, 200; physicality of, 31, 163–65, 198; and power, 3, 5, 7, 13; as social corrective, 2
Laurel, Stan, 14, 233
leading men, 5, 154; comediennes larger than, 93, 103–5, 113
LeRoy, Mervyn, 60
Let Us Be Gay (1930), 237
Lewis, Jerry, 26–27, 28, 30
light comediennes, 64, 169, 237, 240; and athleticism, 195; and beauty, 85, 118, 120, 125; and New Women, 185; and sexuality, 10, 22, 134, 139, 140, 150, 154, 157, 158, 272n22. *See also* comediennes; flappers; slapstick comediennes
light comedy, 10, 21, 22, 36, 39, 41–42, 44, 45, 47, 51, 60, 76, 224, 235–36, 237, 267n123; as alternative to slapstick, 21, 66, 68, 70; and comediennes' appearance, 74, 76, 82, 85, 118; as a comedy of ideas, 41, 68; and comedy-drama, 19, 39, 41, 67–68; and refinement, 26, 38, 39, 40, 46, 65, 67, 72, 76; and sexuality, 134, 143, 145, 148, 155, 158, 162; as situational, 21–22, 41–42, 45, 58, 66–68, 267n123; and working women, 161. *See also* comedy; flapper films; intertitles; slapstick comedy
Lighthouse by the Sea, The (1924), 126
Lillie, Beatrice, 34, 57, 61, 122, 203, 204
Lively Affair, A (ca. 1912), 228

Lloyd, Harold, 1, 14, 44, 45, 47, 61, 97, 191
Loftus, Cecilia, 202–3
Lombard, Carole, 233
Loos, Anita: and the comedy of ideas, 41, 68; and Constance Talmadge, 21, 234; and *Gentlemen Prefer Blondes*, 139; and intertitles, 21, 41–42; and *A Virtuous Vamp*, 144, 272–3n22
Love, Loot and Crash (1915), 191
Love Will Conquer (1916), 85
Loy, Myrna, 237

Mabel's Dramatic Career (1913), 195
Mabley, Jackie "Moms," 238
makeover comedies, 107–17, 210
Manhandled (1924), 190–91, 216–17, 219, *220*, 221
Mantrap (1926), 143–44, 145, 148–49, 155, *158*, 174
marriage, 52, 110, 112, 146, 154, 158, 166, 176, 181–82, 194, 204, 219, 226, 234; comic critiques of, 5, 166; companionate, 141; as containment, 134, 145–46, 148, 150, 158; and flirtation, 146, 148, 149; as happy ending, 215; as joyless, 6, 146; and material desires, 161–62, 181–82; real-life, of comediennes, 140, 149–50, 160; sex outside of, 135, 138, 158; and slapstick, 148, 179, 190. *See also* dating; flirtation
Marx Brothers, 234
Mayflowers (1925), 103
Mayhew, Stella, 94
McVey, Lucille, 117
melodrama, 20, 52, 54, 55, 86, 103, 125, 133–34, 165, 174, 175, 182, 236. *See also* drama
Mickey (1918), 169–71, *170, 171*, 172, 275n73
Mighty Like a Moose (1926), 103

Min and Bill (1930), 237
minstrel shows, 174
Miss America, 79, 80, 86
Miss Fatty's Seaside Lovers (1915), 175
Mizejewski, Linda, 2, 12, 74, 77–78, 79, 80
modernity, 11, 37, 135, 166, 191, 192, 193, 195, 202, 219, 220, 221; anxieties about, 166, 167, 188–90, 196, 199; changing gender roles linked to, 184–85; and lostness of the present moment, 197–98; and technology, 165, 167, 188, 189, 190, 194, 200; as thrilling, 184, 185, 189, 190, 192, 193
Moore, Colleen, 2, 9, 10, 13, 15, 44, 45, 52, 55, *56*, 61, 112, *113*, *114*, *162*, 207, *208*, 221, 234–35, 237, 261n44; and beauty, 86–90, *87*, 114, 115–*16*; and bobbed hair, 222, 223–24, 226; and Cinderella stories, 215–16; embracing comedy, 69–71; and feminine humor, 35; and comedy as hard work, 60, 214; and impersonation, 204; and light comedy, 42, *43*, 44, 46; and modernity, 192, *193*; as naturally funny, 57; and the New Woman, 185, 201; performance style of, 22; and sexuality, 134, 161. See also *Ella Cinders*; *Flaming Youth*; *Her Wild Oat*; *Irene*; *Orchids and Ermine*; *Wall Flower, The*
Moore, Mary Tyler, 238
Moore, Owen, 154, *156*
Moran, Polly, 14, 20, 61, 66, *84*, 183–84, 236–37, 240; and aggressive sexuality, 153, 154, 155; ambivalence toward comedy, 62, 120; and beauty, 75, 82, 85, 103, 105, 106, 118; and costumes, 100; embracing comedy, 26, 71; as naturally funny, 50, 51, 52; and on-set injuries, 196; performance style of, 21; and physical comedy, 49; and stunts, 183, 198. See also *Her Painted Hero*; *Love Will Conquer*; *Sheriff Nell's Tussle*
Motion Picture Classic, 51, 62, 71, 123, 143, 170, 209
Motion Picture Magazine, 57, 59, 65, 68, 91, 123, 125, 140, 153
Motion Picture News, 40
Motion Picture Story Magazine, 18
Movie Classic, 62
movie-struck girls, 154. See also audiences; stagestruck girls
Moving Picture Weekly, 58, 103
Moving Picture World, 36, 47, 104, 121, 198, 212, 213
Murray, Mae, 203, 204, 224
My Best Girl (1927), 204–5, 215, 216, 218–19, *221*, *222*

Nathan, George Jean, 34
Negri, Pola, 86, *87*, 88, 134, 203, 204, 210
New Humor, 37–39, 185–88
New Woman, 11, 135, 142, 163, 184–85, *186*, *187*, 192–93, 198–202, 208
Normand, Mabel, 1, 9, 14, 19, 33, 44, 52, 53, *53*, 61, 85, 104, *142*, 144, 155, 195, 216, 269n27, 275n78, 280n4; and beauty, 76, 81–82, 85, 92; on beauty and intellect, 90; behind-the-scenes labor of, 212–13, 214; and comedy as hard work, 59; and comedy as undignified, 67; and flirtation, 141; as head of production company, 212, 265n72; and impersonation, 206, 207; and lowbrow comedy, 39; and modernity, 191, 192, 197; and the New Woman, 185, *187*; and on-set injuries, 196; performance style of, 20; and physical comedy, 41, 44, 49; and rivalry with Marie Dressler, 200; salary of, 211; and sexuality, 169–71, *170*, *171*, 172; shopgirl characters of,

Normand, Mabel (*continued*)
216–17, *218*. See also *Anything Once!*; *Extra Girl, The*; *Mabel's Dramatic Career*; *Mickey*; *Should Men Walk Home?*; *Strong Revenge, A*; *That Ragtime Band*; *Tillie's Punctured Romance*; *Water Nymph, The*; *What Happened to Rosa?*
Not So Dumb (1930), 236

O'Neil, Sally, 46
Orchids and Ermine (1927), 161–62, 216

Page Miss Glory (1935), 235–36
Pastor, Tony, 37, 151
Patsy, The (1928), 203–4, 210
Perils of Pauline, The (1914), 163
personality, 10, 17–18, 89–93, 131, 184, 202–4, 208–10
Photoplay, 18, 22, 47, 49, 54, 64, 70, 71, 73, 139, 196, 214, 224
phrenology, 188
physical comedy. *See* slapstick comedy
Pickford, Mary, 14, 19, 79, 116, *117*, 160, 204, *221*, *222*, 235; behind-the-scenes labor of, 212; and bobbed hair, 201–2, 222–23; as head of production company, 212, 265n72; performance style of, 21; salary of, 211; and sexuality, 155; shopgirl characters of, 215, 216. See also *My Best Girl*; *Suds*
Pickpocket, The (1913), 75
pies, custard, 2, 7, 9, 20, 22, 23, 26, 32, 33, 36–37, 47, 49, 50, 67, 68, 121, 195, 197
Plastic Age, The (1925), 174
Poehler, Amy, 7, 28
Powell, William, 233
Power and the Glory, The (1933), 235
Prevost, Marie, 200
Price, Kate, 17

production companies: run by comediennes, 45, 211–12, 265n72
Purviance, Edna, 180

Rabinovitz, Lauren, 163–64, 165, 167–68, 188, 189
race, 7, 19, 78, 75–76, 79–80, 86, 88–89, 206, 238; anti-Semitism, 80; and eugenics, 80
Red Mill, The (1927), 107, *108*, 113–14, 117, 154–55, *156*, *157*, 161
Ragged Earl, The (1914), 177
Regustus, Bertha, 19
respectability: and female audiences, 38, 39–40; and motion pictures, 20, 38, 39, 41, 45, 46, 66, 68, 136, 175; and light comedy, 21, 66, 76, 145; and the theater, 37, 38, 39–40, 46, 51, 136–37
Richman, Harry, 140
Rivers, Joan, 238
Rogers, Charles "Buddy," *221*, *222*
Roping Her Romeo (1917), 198
Rowe, Kathleen, 4, 5, 12–13, 131, 154, 165

Safety Last (1923), 191
Sandow, Eugene, 136
Saturday Night Live, 28
Scarlet Letter, The (1934), 235
screwball comedy, 237
Sedaris, Amy, 238–39
self-deprecating humor, 6, 8, 46, 94, 105
Sennett, Mack, 12, 13, 20, 32, 36, 47, 50, 59, 77, 79, 80, 97, 105, 119, 123, 137, 214, 215; as an actor, 141, 191, 195. *See also* Bathing Beauties; Keystone
serial queens, 11, 183, 185, 195–96
serials, 11, 40, 66, 163, 190
servants, 155, 209, 215, 217; maids, 146, 179; servant and maid roles, 20, 21, 101, 204, 206, 221, 236, 237
sexism, 5, 181

Shaw, Lillian, 137, 151
Shearer, Norma, 233
Sheriff Nell's Tussle (1918), 85
shopgirls, 22, 133, 159, 161, 184, 190, 204, 206–7, 215, 216–21, 236, 237. *See also* working women
Short, Martin, 26
Should Men Walk Home? (1927), 207–8
Show People (1928), 9, 52, 53–55, 62, 64
Silverman, Sarah, 238
Singer, Ben, 11, 166, 184, 188, 189
situational comedy. *See* light comedy
slapstick comediennes, 20, 33, 66, 68, 213, 236–37; and ambivalence toward comedy, 45; athleticism of, 195; and beauty, 74, 77, 82, 85, 97, 100, 105, 116–17, 118, 119, 120, 122, 129; and femininity, 45, 49–50, 64, 66–68, 120; and physical comedy, 47; and sexuality, 10–11, 134, 145, 150, 154. *See also* comediennes; flappers; light comediennes
slapstick comedy, 9, 10, 11–12, 19–20, 31, 33, 35, 36, 41, 44–45, 51, 54, 55, 59, 66, 164, 187, 196, 267n120; and appearance, 74, 76, 77, 82, 94, 97, 100, 105, 116, 118, 121, 122, 129; comediennes' ambivalence toward, 21, 26, 39, 47, 63, 66, 67, 120; and embodied spectatorship, 163–65; labor involved in, 60; and light comedy, 21–22, 38, 66, 68, 70, 76; as lowbrow, 20, 38, 39, 40, 41, 46, 63, 66, 67, 72, 76; and modernity, 166, 167, 189, 190; and physicality, 47–48; and sexuality, 134, 141, 143, 145, 148, 150, 152–53, 154, 181; as unsuitable for women, 26, 36, 37, 45, 49–50, 64, 67, 72. *See also* comedy; flapper films; light comedy
slapstick-ingénues, 20, 21, 84–85, 153, 185

So Long Letty (1916–17), 39, 101
sound films, 14, 17, 280n1; silent comediennes' transition to, 233–37, 280n4
Speed Girl, The (1921), 277n55
St. Johns, Adela Rodgers, 124, 128
stage comediennes, 34, 46, 47, 71, 211, 234; and audience interaction, 137, 159; challenging gender norms 5; and comedy based on appearance, 75, 94, 97, 131; as a counterpoint to stage beauties, 75; and imitative comedy, 202–3; and modernity, 191–92; and New Humor, 37–38; and race 19; and sexuality, 151–53, 158, 174; and unruly performances, 33. *See also* vaudeville
stagestruck girls, 85, 154. *See also* audiences; *Her Painted Hero*; movie struck girls
stand-up comedy, 12, 238
Sterling, Ford, 49, 141, 191
Strong Arm Squad of the Future, The (ca. 1912), 75
Strong Revenge, A (1913), 191
studios, 13, 14, 17, 19, 89, 124, 180, 195, 214, 223, 235; and publicity, 10, 15–17, 18, 69, 74, 88, 92, 117, 120, 125, 126, 127, 128, 183, 196, 200, 211; treatment of comediennes, 45, 79, 82, 85, 118, 122, 128. *See also* production companies
stunts, 5, 21, 42, 45–46, 66, 196–97; dangers of, 195–96, 211; and modernity, 184, 195, 197–98; stuntwomen, 239. *See also* athleticism; gags
Suds (1920), 116, *117*, 155, 156, 157
suffrage, 5, 131, 135, 138, 185, 226, 228, 231; suffragists, 75, *76*, 185, *186*, 228, 239
Swain, Mack, 85, 119, 146, *147*

Swanson, Gloria, 44, 160–61, 190, 204, 216–17, *220*
Swing Your Lady (1938), 236

talking pictures. *See* sound films
Talmadge, Constance, 10, 14, 26, 44, 91, 169, 234, 236, 237, 240, 272n22; on actresses as prostitutes, 139–40; and beauty, 78, *87*, 114–*15*, 117, 120, 124; and bobbed hair, 224, *225*; and comedy as hard work, 59, 60; and difficulties faced by comediennes, 65–66; embracing comedy, 70, 71; and flirting, 144; as head of production company, 212, 265n72; and light comedy, 41, 68; and modernity, 193; as naturally funny, 50, 51; and the New Woman, 192, 193, 198, 200–201; performance style of, 21; and sexuality, 134, 145. See also *Her Night of Romance*; *Duchess of Buffalo, The*; *Virtuous Vamp, A*
Talmadge, Natalie, *225*
Talmadge, Norma, 124, 272n3
Tanguay, Eva, 7, 33, 75, 94, *96*, 137, 151–52, 188, 192
technology: and modernity, 7, 11, 167, 184–85, 188–89, 190, 194, 200; and slapstick comedy, 190, 195
television, 14, 234, 238
Temptress, The (1926), 134
That Ragtime Band (1913), 164
Three Ages, The (1923), 191
Tillie Wakes Up (1917), 6, 40, 146–*48*, *149*, 166, 167, 168, *169*, 197, 273n35
Tillie's Nightmare (1910), 221
Tillie's Punctured Romance (1914), 100, *101*, 103–4, 164, *187*, 273n35
Tillie's Tomato Surprise (1915), 40, 273n35
Tin Type Romance, A (1910), 17
Tincher, Fay, 12, 26, 68–69, 71, 197, 234; and beauty, 90; behind-the-scenes labor of, 212; and comedy as hard work, 214; and comedy-drama, 68; as head of production company, 212, 265n72; and lowbrow comedy, 39; rejection of comedy, 64, 65, 67
True Woman, 9, 25, 163, 174, 184–85; Cult of True Womanhood, 185. See also New Woman
Tucker, Sophie, 38, 75, 94, 137, 151, 152
Turner, Florence, 17
Turpin, Ben, *78*, 85, 105
Two Wise Maids (1937), 236

Unholy Night, The (1929), 236
unruliness, 6, 9, 12, 33, 37, 51, 72, 105, 131, 137, 154, 165, 185, 235, 238, 239; and aggressive sexuality, 153, 154, 173–74; and appearance, 33, 94, 100, 131; and audiences, 38, 39, 165; and slapstick, 33, 49; and makeover comedies, 107, 113, 117; and modernity, 191, 195. *See also* Rowe, Kathleen

vamps, 9, 85, 86, 88–89, 134, 135, 139, 145, 153, 157, 203, 204–6, 208; vamping, 141, 143; "virtuous vamps," 21, 134, 140, 145. *See also* Bara, Theda; Negri, Pola; Talmadge, Constance; *Virtuous Vamp, A*
vaudeville, 5, 20, 25, 33, 46, 47, 94, 100, 104, 124–25, 139, 164, 165, 192, 199, 202–3, 206, 213, 226; and audience interaction, 5, 31, 187–88; and male impersonation, 135, 174; and refinement, 37–38, 40, 136, 151; salaries, 211; transgressive performances in, 137, 151, 152, 173. *See also* burlesque; cross dressing; Keith, B. F.; minstrel shows; New Humor; Pastor, Tony; stage comediennes; Ziegfeld *Follies*

Victorian era, 7, 10, 31, 135, 137, 145, 165, 166, 167, 223
Vidor, King, 55, 164
Virtuous Vamp, A (1919), 144–45, 155, 272n22

Wall Flower, The (1922), 115–*16*
Water Nymph, The (1912), 141–43, 144, 155, 169, 170, 269n27
Weber, Joe, 103
West, Mae, 151, 213, 234, 237
What Happened to Rosa? (1920), 155–56, 157, 206, 207, 216–17, *218*, 219
What's the World Coming To? (1926), 227–28, *229*, 231
White, Bessie, 19
White, Pearl, 183
Whitman Sisters, 19
Wid's Daily, 40, 41, 171
Wild Party, The (1929), 235
Willful Ambrose (1915), 85
women: aligned with nature, 9; aren't funny stereotype, 3, 8, 9, 14, 25, 27–33, 42, 50, 51, 57, 61, 63, 64, 65, 69, 71; and bobbed hair, 224–26; and dancing, 173; as emotional, 9, 25, 29–30, 34, 51, 60–61, 70; and feminine humor, 34–36; as guardians of morality, 25, 32, 38, 39–40, 75, 136; and independence, 5, 135, 156; and laughter, 31, 164; and lesbianism, 174–75; and the modern world, 112, 199, 200, 201, 202, 203, 209–10; as nags and killjoys, 30, 32; as passive and refined, 5, 9, 25, 31–32, 38, 51, 72, 137, 152; presence in the public sphere of, 8, 135–36, 141, 156, 200; and reproduction, 30–31; and sexuality, 135, 136, 144, 145, 150–51, 152, 156, 157, 159–60; and social and political power, 3, 5, 7, 27–28, 105, 110–11, 131, 226, 228–31, 239; as spectators, 6, 7, 10, 12, 39–40, 78, 88, 93, 105, 124, 128, 136, 137–38, 154, 163, 165, 180, 184, 221, 222; as unruly (*see* unruliness); and voting (*see* suffrage); in the work force, 11, 58, 59, 211, 215, 221–22. *See also* beauty; comediennes; feminine humor; femininity; New Woman; True Woman
Women Aren't Funny (2014), 28
working women, 142, 156; as characters, 161, 183–84, 215–22, 235, 236, 237. *See also* shopgirls

Ziegfeld, Florenz, 79, 80, 94, 105, 123
Ziegfeld *Follies*, 75, 77, 137, 170, 188, 236
Ziegfeld Girl, 79, 80, 86, 151, 152, 172, 185. *See also* chorus girls

www.ingramcontent.com/pod-product-compliance
Lightning Source LLC
Chambersburg PA
CBHW070753230426
43665CB00017B/2340